Year 2

LODGING
MANAGEMENT
PROGRAM

EDUCATIONAL INSTITUTE
American Hotel & Motel Association

Disclaimer

This publication is designed to provide accurate and authoritative information in regard to the subject matter covered. It is sold with the understanding that the publisher is not engaged in rendering legal, accounting, or other professional service. If legal advice or other expert assistance is required, the services of a competent professional person should be sought.

> —*From the Declaration of Principles jointly adopted by the American Bar Association and a Committee of Publishers and Associations*

Nothing contained in this publication shall constitute a standard, an endorsement, or a recommendation of the Educational Institute (the Institute) or American Hotel & Motel Association (AH&MA). The Institute and AH&MA disclaim any liability with respect to the use of any information, procedure, or product, or reliance thereon by any member of the hospitality industry.

The authors are solely responsible for the contents of this publication. All views expressed herein are solely those of the authors and do not necessarily reflect the views of the Educational Institute of the American Hotel & Motel Association (the Institute) or the American Hotel & Motel Association (AH&MA). The contents of this book were taken from the following Institute publications:

Abbey, J.R., *Hospitality sales and marketing* (1998)

Cichy, R.F., Wise, P.E., *Food and beverage service* (1998)

Jefferies, J.P., *Understanding hospitality law, third edition* (1995)

Kavanaugh, R.R. & Ninemeier, J.D. *Hospitality supervision* (1991)

Ninemeier, J.D., *Planning and control* (1998)

Woods, R., & King, J. *Managing for quality in the hospitality industry* (1996)

Project Editor: Bridgette Redman

Editors: Robert Bittner
         Jennifer Smith

Acknowledgements

We would like to thank the following organizations and people for their contributions to helping this program achieve excellence:

American Hotel & Motel Association
William Fisher, PhD, President and Chief Executive Officer

American Hotel Foundation
Doug Viehland, Vice President

National Restaurant Association
Steven Anderson, President and Chief Executive Officer

Educational Foundation of the National Restaurant Association
Stephen J. Caldeira, former President and Chief Operating Officer
Reed Hayes, President and Chief Operating Officer
Jennifer Hulting, Product Development Leader
Bettina Tahsin, Group Product Manager, Professional Development

Hospitality Business Alliance
Michael Bartlett, Executive Director
Suzanne Morrison, Director of State Governing Partnerships
Kathyrn Sullivan, Manager of Program Implementation
Wendi Safstrom, Manager, Hotel Programs

Instructors, Contributors, and Reviewers

Patricia Breeding, Hotel Management Magnet Coordinator, Florida

Leta Durrett, Hospitality Services Coordinator, Skyline Career Center

Milton Ericksen, Director of Public Relations and Education, Arizona Hotel & Motel Association

Jeralyn Forcier, Georgia Hospitality and Travel Association

Faye Gayes, CRDE, Executive Director, Indiana Hospitality & Tourism Foundation

Mary Kreps, former Director of Educational Programs, Texas Hotel & Motel Association

Carol Parker, Education Director, Florida Hotel & Motel Association

Christopher Rott, Sunburst Hospitality Corporation

Jill Staples, CHA, Coordinator, Hotel/Motel Program, Virginia Beach, VA

Heath Trehame, Hospitality Instructor, Wood County Technical Center

Contents

Unit 1—Leadership and Management 1

Chapter 1—Leadership and Management
Profile: Robert Steele
President and CEO, American Hotel & Motel Association 2

Section 1.1—Management Styles 4
Traditional Management Styles 5
Hurdles to Effective Management 6
Managers—and Leaders 7

Section 1.2—Power and Empowerment 9
Where's the Power? 9
Decentralization and Empowerment 11
The Basics of Power and Authority 11

Section 1.3—Quality Service 14
Moments of Truth 14
New Leadership and Management Responsibilities 16

Section 1.4—Diversity 19
The Benefits of Diversity 19
Under the Gavel: The Family and Medical Leave Act 20
Equal Employment 21
Under the Gavel: Discrimination in Employment 22
The Americans with Disabilities Act 23
Under the Gavel: Americans with Disabilities Act 24
Claims of Sexual Harassment 25

Chapter 2—Communication Skills
Profile: Jane Mackie
Vice President/Branch Manager 30

Section 2.1—Stucture of Communication 32
Myths About Communication 32
The Communication Process 33
Communication within an Organization 35
Barriers to Effective Communication 36

Section 2.2—Speaking and Presentations 41
Formal Presentations 41

Controlling the Presentation Environment 44
Presentation Delivery Tips 44

Section 2.3—Listening 46
The Four Stages of Active Listening 46
Active Listening Techniques 47

Section 2.4—Business Writing 50
Business Writing Tips and Examples 50
Use Specific, Active Language 51
Use Plain English and Shorter Sentences 52
Inverted Pyramid 53
Topic Sentence 53
Memos and Business Letters 54
Conclusion 56

Chapter 3—Team Building
Profile: Gina-Lynne Scharoun
Vice President, Franchise Services 60

Section 3.1—Defining Teams 62
Types of Hospitality Teams 63
Characteristics of Successful Teams 63
Team Mission Statement 63
Team Code of Conduct.. 65
Team Leaders 66

Section 3.2—Stages of Team Development 69
Stage 1—Forming 69
Stage 2—Storming 71
Stage 3—Norming 72
Stage 4—Performing 73
Stage 5—Transforming.. 74

Section 3.3—Roles of Individuals 76

Chapter 4—Career Development
Profile: Erika Alexander
Vice President, TownePlace Suites by Marriott 82

Section 4.1—Self-Assessment 84
Strengths 84
Weaknesses 84
Interests 86
Values 86
Researching Organizations and Positions.. 86
Career Fairs.. 88
Corporate Presentations 89
Internships 89

Section 4.2—Self-Marketing and Personal Promotion 91
    Networking 91
    Cover Letters 94

Section 4.3—Interviewing 97
    Prepare for an Interview 97
    Anticipating Interview Questions 97
    Preparing for Behavior-Based Interviews 98
    Illegal Interview Questions 101
    Questioning the Interviewer 101
    Thank-You Letters 102
    Preparing for Second Interviews 103

Section 4.4—Responding to Job Offers 105
    Handling Rejection 105
    Responding to Job Offers 106
    Evaluating Job Offers 106
    Choosing the Best Offer 108
    Parameters of Negotiation 109

Section 4.5—Lifelong Learning 111
    What Is a Portfolio? 111
    How Are Portfolios Created? 111
    A Blueprint for Success: Covey's Seven Habits 113
    Career Planning Beyond Your First Job 116

Unit 2—Marketing and Sales 123

Chapter 5—Hospitality Marketing and Sales
    Profile: Kelly Moyers-Ham
    MBA, CHE, Hospitality Lodging Program Instructor 124

Section 5.1—Marketing and Sales 126
    Marketing vs. Sales 126
    Product and Service Marketing 127

Section 5.2—The Marketing and Sales Division 129
    The Marketing and Sales Division 129

Section 5.3—The Four *P*s of Marketing 137
    Product: What Do You Sell? 137
    Place: Where Do You Sell It? 138
    Price: What Do You Sell It For? 138
    Promotion: How Do You Spread the Word? 139

Section 5.4—Lodging Market Segments 141
    Individual Business Travelers 141
    Corporate Groups 142
    Convention and Association Groups 142
    Leisure Travelers 142
    Long-Term Stay/Relocation Guests 142

Airline-Related Guests 143
Government and Military Travelers 143
Regional Getaway Guests 143
Guest Mix 143

Chapter 6—The Marketing Plan
Profile: Feliz Peñaloza Jarvis
Vice President of Sales & Marketing Bristol Hotels & Resorts 148

Section 6.1—Putting the Plan Together 150
The Marketing Plan 150
The Marketing Team 151
Steps of a Marketing Plan 151

Section 6.2—Conducting a Marketing Audit 154
Property Analysis 154
Competition Analysis 155
Situation Analysis 157

Section 6.3—Target Markets and Positioning 160
Selecting Target Markets 160
Positioning the Property 162

Section 6.4—Marketing Objectives, Action Plans, and Evaluation 165
Determining Marketing Objectives 165
Developing and Implemention Action Plans 166
Budgeting 167
Monitoring and Evaluating the Marketing Plan 168

Chapter 7—The Sales Office
Profile: Mike Cheatham
Director of Sales Recruitment, Hyatt Hotels 172

Section 7.1—Communication Systems 174
Sales Meetings 174
Sales Records 175

Section 7.2—Filing Systems 180
Filing Systems 180

Section 7.3—Automation 184
The Automated Sales Office 184
Computerized Client Information 184
Yield Management 188

Chapter 8—Banquet and Meeting Room Sales
Profile: Traci Ehrhardt-Mead
Assistant Director of Catering, Arizona Biltmore 192

Section 8.1—The Banquet Department 194
The Banquet Department 194

Section 8.2—Banquet Sales 199
    Banquet Promotions 199
    Developing Leads 199

Section 8.3—Special Types of Food and Beverage Sales 204
    Refreshment Breaks 204
    Hospitality Suites 205
    Receptions 205
    Special Functions 205
    Off-Premises Catering 206

Section 8.4—Meeting Room Sales 208
    Meeting Room Sales 208
    Meeting Room Furniture 209
    Booking Meeting Rooms 211
    Managing Meetings 212

Chapter 9—Selling Is Everyone's Job

Scott Ringer
General Manager, Aruba Marriott Resort and Stellaris Casino,
and Aruba Ocean Club 216

Section 9.1—Everyone's Sales Role 218
    The Role of the General Manager 218

Section 9.2—Relationship Selling 220
    Building Relationships 220
    The Role of Training 221

Section 9.3—Upgrading 225
    Upgrading 225

Section 9.4—Suggestive Selling and Cross-Selling 227
    Suggestive Selling 227
    Cross-Selling 229

Section 9.5—Departmental Selling 231
    Switchboard 231
    Reservations 232
    Front Desk 232
    Food and Beverage 233
    Service Personnel 235
    Employee Incentive Programs 236

Chapter 10—Telephone Sales

Profile: Patricia Tam
General Manager, Halekulani Resort 240

Section 10.1—Basics of Telephone Communications 242
    Basics of Telephone Communication 243

Section 10.2—Outgoing Calls 247
    Prospecting and Qualifying Calls 247

Appointment Calls 250
Sales Calls 253
Other Outgoing Calls 254

Section 10.3—Incoming Calls 256
First Impressions Are Forever 256
Incoming Calls 257

Section 10.4—Telephone Sales Operations 260
Telephone Sales Blitzes 260
Telemarketing Operations 260

Unit 3—Food and Beverage Service 267

Chapter 11—Hotels and the Food Service Industry
Ian D. N. Fetigan, CCM
General Manager, The Country Club of Darien, Inc., Darien, Connecticut 268

Section 11.1—Food Service Industry 270
Composition and Size of the Food Service Industry 270
Eating and Drinking Places 271
Hotel Operations 272
Food Services for the Transportation Market 272
Food Services for the Leisure Market 273
Retail Food Services 273
Business/Industrial Food Services 274
Student Food Services 275
Health Care Food Services 275
Club Food Services 275

Section 11.2—Food and Beverage Organization 277
History of Hotel Food and Beverage Divisions 277
Food and Beverage Departments 279
The Role of the Hotel Food and Beverage Division 279

Section 11.3—People in Food Service 281
People in Food Service 281
Managers 281
Production Personnel 282
Service Personnel 285

Section 11.4—Sanitation 288
Food Safety Starts with You 288
Professionals Prevent Contamination 289
Store Smart 291
Under the Gavel: Cracking the Code 292
Tend to Time and Temperature 292
Wash Clean, Rinse Clear, Sanitize Safely 292
Watch Out for Warnings 293

Chapter 12—The Menu
   Profile: Tim Pugh
   Partner/Regional Manager, Damon's 298

   Section 12.1—Menu Styles and Schedules 300
      Menu Pricing Styles 301
      Menu Schedules 302

   Section 12.2—Menu Types 305
      Speciality Menus 306

   Section 12.3—Menu Planning 310
      Knowing Your Guests 310
      Knowing Your Property 310
      Selecting Menu Items 311
      Menu Balance 313

   Section 12.4—Menu Design 315
      Copy 315
      Layout 318
      Cover 322
      Common Menu-Design Mistakes 322

   Section 12.5—Menu Pricing 324
      Subjective Pricing Methods 324
      Simple Mark-Up Pricing Methods 325
      Contribution Margin Pricing Method 326
      Simple Prime Costs Pricing Method 327

Chapter 13—Dining and Beverage Service
   Profile: Dixie Eng
   General Manager, Hilton Washington Embassy Row 334

   Section 13.1—Dining Service Staff Positions 336
      Server 336
      Busperson 337
      Host 338
      Cashier 338
      Dining Room Manager 338

   Section 13.2—Dining Service Styles and Procedures 341
      Plate Service 341
      Cart Service 342
      Platter Service 346
      Family-Style Service 347
      Buffet Service 347

   Section 13.3—Providing Superior Service 350
      Preshift Meetings 351
      Suggestive Selling 351
      Service Guarantees 353
      Resolving Guest Complaints 354

The Team Approach to Service 357
Serving Guests Who Have Disabilities 357

Section 13.4—Responsible Beverage Service 360
Liability Laws 360
Under the Gavel: Dram Shop Liability Acts 361
Verifying Legal Drinking Age 361
Monitoring Alcohol Intake 362
Cutting Off Alcohol Service 364

Chapter 14—Casual/Theme Restaurants
Amy Isom
Vice President of Development and Operations, Carlson Vacation Ownership 370

Section 14.1—Marketing Perspective 372
Casual/Theme Markets 372
Guest Feedback 373
Menu Considerations 374
Value 374
The Dining Environment, Supplies, and Equipment 376

Section 14.2—Getting Ready for Service 378
Training 378

Section 14.3—Delivering Service 382
Taking Reservations 382
Managing Waiting Guests 384
Greeting and Seating Guests 385
Presenting the Menu and Taking Beverage Orders 386
Placing Beverage Orders 386
Serving Beverages 386
Taking Food Orders 386
Placing and Picking Up Orders in the Kitchen 387
Serving the Orders 387
Presenting the Guest Check 388
Serving Special Guests 388
After Service 389

Chapter 15—Banquets and Catered Events
Chef Richard "Pete" Bowden, CEC
Executive Chef, Country Club of Fairfax 394

Section 15.1—Booking and Planning Events 396
The Function Book 396
Contracts or Letters of Agreement 397
Function Sheets 400

Section 15.2—Getting Ready for Service 403
Setting Up Function Rooms 403

Scheduling Staff Members 404
Preparing, Plating, and Storing Food 405

Section 15.3—Delivering Service 408
Beverage Service 408
Protocol for Special Banquets and Catered Events 410

Section 15.4—After Service 412
Controls 412
Guest Comments 414
Using Feedback in Planning 415

Chapter 16—Room Service

David A. Stout

Vice President of Operations, Grand Hotel, Mackinac Island, Michigan 420

Section 16.1—Getting Ready for Room Service 421
Room Service Issues 422
Getting Ready for Room Service 423
Staffing Requirements 424
Forecasting and Staff Member Scheduling 426
Preparations for Service Shifts 426

Section 16.2—Delivering Room Service 421
Taking the Order 429
Routing the Order 431
Preparing the Order 433
Delivering the Order 433
Clean-Up and Follow-Up 435
Providing Special Services and Amenities 435

Section 16.3—After Room Service 437
Income Control Procedures 437
Guest Comments 437
Using Feedback in Planning 438

Unit

Leadership and Management

CHAPTER 1   LEADERSHIP AND MANAGEMENT

CHAPTER 2   COMMUNICATION SKILLS

CHAPTER 3   TEAM BUILDING

CHAPTER 4   CAREER DEVELOPMENT

Profile

Robert L. Steele III
General Manager, Hyatt Regency Baltimore

Robert Steele's first hospitality job was as a dietary assistant in a hospital when he was 16. He made the shift from hospital to hospitality in college, waiting tables while working on his bachelor's degree at Tennessee State University.

When a Hyatt hotel opened in Nashville, Steele applied for a job as a waiter. Within three months, he was promoted to dining room captain, then dining room manager. That was the beginning of a 25-year career with the Hyatt chain. Steele's career path has taken him from waiter to general manager—with steps along the way as beverage manager, banquet manager, catering manager, assistant director of food and beverage, food and beverage director, and hotel manager.

You might think that a career spent entirely with one brand and in one functional area would be boring. Not according to Steele.

"What I love most about this field is the fact that it is always changing—there are new trends, best practices. The ability to learn and grow daily has always motivated me," says Steele.

Lots of careers say that you need to be a "people person," but in hospitality, that's really true.

"You have to possess a genuine love of people," says Steele. "You are on stage constantly and you have the ability to affect people instantaneously."

Steele promotes the hospitality industry in his role as chairman of the Maryland Hotel & Motel Association. He is also active in his community as a board member of the Boy Scouts of America-Maryland Chapter, the Downtown Partnership of Baltimore, the Maryland Chamber of Commerce, and the Pride of Baltimore II, the city's goodwill sailing ship. He provides direction to future hotel and restaurant leaders as an advisor to hospitality programs at two area colleges and a local high school.

Leadership and Management

Sections

1.1   Management Styles

1.2   Power and Empowerment

1.3   Quality Service

1.4   Diversity

1.1 Management Styles

AFTER STUDYING SECTION 1.1, YOU SHOULD KNOW HOW TO:

♦ Describe some of the changes in the hospitality industry that have redefined management responsibilities

♦ Define an autocratic manager

♦ Explain how bureaucratic managers make decisions

♦ Illustrate the way a democratic manager acts

♦ Apply different management styles to different situations

♦ Identify the factors that limit the use of different management styles

♦ List the challenges managers face in balancing the focus of management with the vision of leadership

More has been written about leadership and management in the last decade than in all of the previous 50 years. Today, we are seeing an explosion of new organizational theories and managerial practices. The cause: the ever-increasing speed of change, largely the result of new technologies. These technologies have actually changed the structure of many companies. And when the structure of a company changes, so does the nature of leadership and management in that organization.

Imagine that you were the general manager in a large, national chain just 10 years ago. If you had discovered a cost-cutting measure that could benefit all other chain GMs, your proposal for the appropriate changes would have to work its way up the chain of command, through multiple layers of managers. It might take corporate headquarters months to receive and review your proposal, collect supporting data,

Ready, Set, Dive!

It's a hotelier's dream: every room in the hotel has an ocean view. Granted, guests arrive slightly soggy at check-in, but the aquanauts who stay at Jules' Undersea Lodge aren't complaining.

This underwater property off the coast of Key Largo, Florida, was originally built as a research lab, but it was converted to a hotel in 1986. Now it can room six guests—but only if they scuba dive 30 feet down. A porthole in each room offers an incomparable view of the underwater world. For those who prefer *Flipper* reruns to the real thing, the lodge even offers television.

make a decision, and then distribute a recommendation. Your suggestions could be outdated before they ever reach other local hotel managers. With today's electronic information management systems, though, information can be distributed throughout an organization—whether regional or global—from any point within the organization at the very moment it is collected.

Today, there are new opportunities for company leaders to rethink and, in some cases, reinvent the way they do business. Many hospitality companies have flattened their organizational structures, redistributed power and responsibility, and given decision-making authority to every employee. These changes have redefined managers' roles, responsibilities, and competencies at every level.

Traditional Management Styles

Management styles are patterns of behavior that managers use to interact with other managers and with their staff. Three traditional styles are those of the autocratic manager, the bureaucratic manager, and the democratic manager.

The Autocratic Manager. Autocratic managers stress immediate, short-term results over concerns about people in a department or organization. They often give orders without explanations and expect those orders to be obeyed without question. They make decisions without staff input and don't usually delegate work. Autocratic managers assume that employees are motivated only by money.

Employees often become extremely dependent on the autocratic manager. Work gets done when the manager is present, but things fall apart when the manager is absent. Since employees are given little, if any, choice about how to perform their jobs, they learn to simply follow orders. In other words, they learn behaviors that match their boss's expectations.

The Bureaucratic Manager. Bureaucratic managers make decisions by enforcing rules, regulations, policies, and procedures that are already in place. Concerns for results and for people take a back seat to doing things the way they have always been done. Bureaucratic managers resist change. They rely on higher levels of management to make decisions about issues not covered "by the book."

Like the employees created by autocratic managers, employees under the thumb of bureaucratic managers quickly learn to suppress their initiative and simply follow the rules. When no rule seems to apply to a situation, employees cease to act and call the bureaucrat.

The Democratic Manager. The democratic manager is almost the reverse of the autocratic manager. Democratic managers tend to focus more on a participative process than on short-term, immediate results. They keep employees informed about matters directly affecting their work and often delegate responsibilities so employees gain greater job satisfaction.

Democratic managers share decision-making and problem-solving responsibilities with their staff. Open to new ideas, democratic managers often champion change within their departments and company. These managers want employees to be less dependent on them, to willingly accept responsibility, and to take the initiative to get things done themselves.

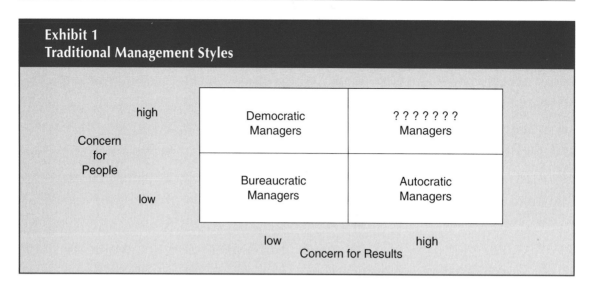

Exhibit 1
Traditional Management Styles

Concern for People		Democratic Managers	? ? ? ? ? ? ? Managers
high		Democratic Managers	? ? ? ? ? ? ? Managers
low		Bureaucratic Managers	Autocratic Managers

low   high
Concern for Results

A Mix of Management Styles. Exhibit 1 shows the three traditional management styles along two dimensions: concern for people and concern for results. Can a single style maximize concern for people and concern for results at the same time? That's the big question suggested by the question marks in the upper-right quadrant.

Many people find the democratic style the most appealing. But even this style—when taken to extremes—can stifle an organization. Some extreme democratic managers experience "paralysis by analysis," waste time in unproductive meetings, and forfeit responsibility while calling it delegation.

While there are negatives to being a bureaucratic manager, every management position has some bureaucratic functions. For example, legal issues related to hiring and firing require managers to strictly adhere to established policies and procedures. Reckless autocratic or democratic decisions could result in expensive lawsuits.

Finally, most people believe the autocratic manager should be a thing of the past. However, when situations call for immedi-

ate action, an autocratic manager is able to take charge. Consider what happens when twice the expected number of guests need to be served at lunch. It isn't possible to consult with staff on every issue. It isn't reasonable to do everything by the book. The manager must act.

The most effective managers don't restrict themselves to one management style that they apply in every situation. Instead, they are flexible enough to adopt different styles for specific circumstances.

Hurdles to Effective Management

Flexibility is not entirely within a manager's control. Even though a manager may be prepared to use different management styles in different situations, there may be hurdles in the way that cannot easily be overcome.

A manager who has been successful with a particular management style may not be willing to adopt a different one. After all, if it works, why change it?

Exhibit 2
Balancing Management and Leadership

The Focus of Management	The Vision of Leadership
Do things right	Do the right things
Direct operations	Monitor guest expectations
Enforce policies and rules	Communicate vision and values
Design procedures and tasks	Manage systems and processes
Control results	Support people
Foster stability	Engage in continuous improvement

In addition, the manager's personal background, employee characteristics, and the culture of the property may also limit flexibility.

Personal background includes personality, knowledge, attitudes, feelings, and experiences. Some managers feel comfortable freely delegating work; they recognize the need to involve employees in a team approach to defining and resolving problems. Other managers prefer to do almost everything themselves.

Employee characteristics often limit the management styles a manager can successfully adopt. Departments with a large number of new and inexperienced employees might benefit from autocratic and bureaucratic styles. A democratic style may work best in departments with knowledgeable, experienced employees who are capable of greater independence and decision-making responsibility. The ability of employees to work well in teams may also affect a manager's success with specific management styles.

The greatest limiting factors in a manager's choice of management styles, though, may be the structure and culture of the organization. Managers invite disaster when they adopt styles that don't fit the traditions and values of their organizations.

For example, the democratic style fits well in corporate cultures that have relatively few levels of management. Being an autocratic or bureaucratic manager in such an environment would most likely lead to failure.

Managers—and Leaders

Modern managers face challenges that the managers of 50 years ago couldn't have imagined. In today's successful hospitality companies, the best managers balance the details of management with the vision of leadership.

Exhibit 2 outlines some of the seemingly contradictory responsibilities that managers need to balance.

- Managers must do things right. But they must also constantly ask themselves whether they are doing the *right things.* For example, they know they need to direct operations, but they learn what to direct and how to direct by knowing what guests expect.

- Managers must enforce policies and rules. But they must help their staff understand "Why these particular policies?" and "Why these rules?" by communicating a vision of the organization and the corporate values that drive that vision.

- Managers must work with their staffs to develop efficient, effective procedures in their departments. But they must also manage the "big picture" systems and processes of the organization and understand how they all fit together.

- Managers are responsible for the results of their operational areas, but they achieve results by supporting the people in their departments.

- Managers are responsible for fostering stability within their areas. Stability does not necessarily mean preserving the status quo—it can mean creating a learning environment by promoting continuous improvement efforts.

Apply Your Learning 1.1

Please write all answers on a separate sheet of paper.

1. Which type of manager emphasizes immediate, short-term results more than concerns about people in the organization?

2. List some of the characteristics of a bureaucratic manager.

3. What type of manager is most likely to share decision-making and problem-solving responsibilities with staff?

4. Why is a flexible management style considered the best?

1.2 Power and Empowerment

AFTER STUDYING SECTION 1.2, YOU SHOULD KNOW HOW TO:

♦ Define empowerment

♦ Distinguish between centralized and decentralized organizations

♦ List the factors that affect the degree of centralization within an organization

♦ Explain the effect an organization's culture has on the distribution of power

♦ Recognize learned helplessness as a symptom of over-centralization

♦ Describe some of the outcomes for an organization that empowers managers and employees

♦ Illustrate why a manager's authority must equal the manager's responsibility

---

When many hospitality companies began restructuring in the 1990s, *empowerment* became one of the great industry buzzwords.

The goal of **empowerment** is to enhance guest service and increase profits for the organization by passing decision-making responsibility, authority, and accountability to every level within the organization.

Where's the Power?

Power is the ability to influence others' behavior. A manager's power is a function of responsibility, authority, and accountability. In **centralized organizations,** most decision-making authority is at top management levels. **Decentralized organizations** distribute decision-making authority throughout the company.

The degree of centralization or decentralization is not determined by how many levels of management there are on an organization chart. What matters is where decisions are made—at corporate headquarters or at an individual hotel. The organization chart of a mid-size hotel may be flat—with very little bureaucracy—yet power may be centralized in the general manager's position, especially if he or she micro-manages every department and functional area.

It is not a matter of one approach being right or wrong. In times of financial crisis, a high degree of centralization may be most appropriate; a financially troubled organization will probably benefit when top managers take control of the situation and work out the crisis. Decentralization may be most appropriate for organizations that face tough competition in fast-changing market or business conditions. Decentralized organizations can usually respond faster and more effectively to change than centralized organizations.

Changing the structure of power in an organization can be difficult. When companies become more centralized, power is taken away from middle and lower management levels and given to top-level managers. When companies become more decentralized, power is taken from higher-level managers and given to middle and lower managers. Managers who lose power may feel threatened, while the newly empowered managers may be intimidated or pressured by their new responsibilities.

Learned Helplessness. At excessively centralized organizations, managers at each level report to the managers above them and closely monitor the actions of the managers below them. Information moves up through the organization, and directives come down. Each manager has a limited, well-defined area of responsibility and a narrow span of control, usually with three to seven managers reporting to him or her from below.

Managers and employees in these hotel companies simply go through the motions of serving guests. Procedures established by upper management start to control the actions and thoughts of staff members, a phenomenon known as **learned helplessness**. Focusing solely on the activities of their own departments, department managers lose the wider perspective needed to identify and solve problems that cut across functional areas; such problems always seem to belong to someone else.

Horst Schulze, president and CEO of The Ritz-Carlton Hotel Company, tells this story:

A large downtown hotel constantly received guest complaints about room service: the food was superb, but service took forever. The general manager told the room service manager to speed up service. Service improved briefly, then declined again.

The GM fired the room service manager, hired another, and issued the same order. The results were the same: Service improved briefly, then declined again. After a third unsuccessful staff change, the GM took matters into his own hands.

He personally assessed the room service process by timing each task, from taking the order to delivery. Nothing seemed unusual until he accompanied a room service attendant delivering an order to a room on the 28th floor. The elevator stopped at the 2nd floor, and a houseperson entered with an armload of sheets. At the 4th floor, the houseperson left the elevator, and another one entered carrying an armload of towels. This houseperson got off on the 6th floor. At the 8th floor, another houseperson entered the elevator burdened with bed linens and towels; he got off at the 12th floor. The parade of housepersons, sheets, and towels continued up to the 28th floor and all the way back down to the lobby. The slowdown in room service was taking place at the elevators.

Linen deliveries were supposed to be made at specific times that would not interfere with the needs of guests or other operations. So the GM asked a houseperson why he was delivering linen at that hour. The houseperson said the standard procedures were being followed, but the housepersons never received enough sheets and towels to service their areas. They were constantly having to raid the linen closets on each others' floors.

The GM finally discovered the real problem: Room service was slow because linen pars were too low. But why didn't the room service manager make the same connection? Why didn't room service attendants ask the housepersons what they were doing? Why didn't the housepersons inform their supervisors of the linen shortages? Why didn't the executive housekeeper request more linen from purchasing? The answer: Because the entire staff was stuck in the mire of learned helplessness. No one looked beyond his or her narrowly defined responsibilities.

Decentralization and Empowerment

In highly decentralized organizations, there are relatively few levels of management. Reporting and monitoring functions are designed to support lower-level managers rather than control their actions. Information flows freely in every direction.

In the late 1980s and early 1990s, Taco Bell flattened and decentralized its organization. A hierarchy of regional, district, and area managers was replaced by a single level of "market managers," each supporting the activities of 30 or more unit managers. Unit managers, previously charged with the day-to-day operations of a single restaurant, were given responsibility for two or three restaurants each. A team approach to unit operations increased the responsibility of line-level employees.

Decision making, troubleshooting, and problem solving became a much faster process. Successful restaurant managers were supported, rather than second-guessed, by upper management. They were encouraged to take risks, try new ideas for promoting local sales, and learn from their mistakes.

At the heart of Taco Bell's decentralization effort was a strategy of empowerment—letting managers and staff perform their jobs more efficiently and effectively in the highly competitive fast-food industry.

Decentralization and empowerment begin with changes in the leadership roles of top managers. The president, the CEO, and other high-level managers spend less time controlling the activities of lower-level managers and more time communicating their shared vision of the company. That vision typically includes where the company is today, where it is going tomorrow, why it's heading in that direction, and how it will get there.

The Basics of Power and Authority

Authority is the formal power granted by an organization to a management position. A manager exercises authority when making decisions, issuing orders, and using resources to achieve departmental and organizational goals.

It's important to note that authority is placed in a *position*, not in the individual who holds it. In addition, authority carries with it responsibility and **accountability**; managers with authority must accept responsibility for their decisions and be able to justify their actions to those above them in the **chain of command**. Managers placed high in the chain of command carry more responsibility and greater authority than managers below them.

A manager's authority should match the responsibility of his or her position within the company. When managers are given responsibility for achieving certain goals but don't have sufficient authority to take the necessary steps toward achieving them, their jobs become more difficult, if not impossible.

Responsibility—but Little Authority. Consider the fictional case of the Scalar Center Plaza, a large convention hotel. Sheronna is a salesperson who reports to Paul, the sales director, who in turn reports to Marguerite, the GM. Sheronna is responsible for booking a specific number of room nights each month, but she does not have much authority to negotiate with meeting planners. Just about every item on each draft of a contract—and all subsequent changes—must be approved by Paul, and he must get Marguerite's blessing on each item before giving his response to Sheronna.

Sheronna feels she is more like a gofer ("go for" this, "go for" that) for Paul than a professional sales associate. Anything she does on her own is interpreted as flouting authority and bypassing her boss. At the same time, Paul feels like a paper-pusher and wonders what sales directors do at other organizations.

Meanwhile, the hotel is losing business. Some meeting planners distrust Sheronna, believing that her constant need to "talk to her boss" is simply a cheap negotiating trick. Other meeting planners wonder if this is the kind of run-around they can expect when their groups stay at the hotel. Bookings decrease, Marguerite dumps on Paul, Paul dumps on Sheronna, Sheronna quits, and Paul starts updating his résumé.

Authority—but Little Responsibility. When managers' authority exceeds their responsibility, departments can become like street gangs plagued by constant in-fighting and turf wars. Consider the fictional case of the Bernstein Convention Center, a competing hotel across town from the Scalar Center Plaza. The general manager, David, orders the sales director, Julia, to increase occupancy—or else. So Julia authorizes the sales representatives to do whatever it takes to exceed their monthly quota of room sales. The sales reps negotiate lower function prices and throw in offers of free coffee breaks and fully stocked complimentary hospitality suites. Tentative bookings increase dramatically.

Meanwhile, David meets with Fritz, the executive chef, and yells at him for exceeding budgeted expenses. He orders Fritz to reduce food costs—or else. Fritz meets with his food and beverage managers and tells them to do whatever it takes to bring food costs in line with the budget.

Neither Julia nor Fritz is aware of each other's meetings with David. When the sales contracts are reviewed at an executive committee meeting, Fritz and Julia jump at each other's throats. If the "sweet deals" Julia authorized are accepted, food costs will skyrocket and Fritz will look like a fool to his staff. However, if the deals are re-negotiated, meeting planners will be upset, room nights will be lost, and Julia will look like a fool to *her* staff.

While there are some bigger issues involved in these scenarios, in both cases the general manager is at fault for not ensuring that the authority of the managers is in line with their responsibility. At the Scalar Center Plaza, Marguerite narrowly defined responsibility and withheld virtually all authority from the director of sales and the sales reps. With so little responsibility, and less authority, how could Paul or Sheronna be held accountable for sales? And at the Bernstein Convention Center, David failed to involve his department heads in collaborative goal setting. Instead, he gave both Julia and Fritz seemingly boundless authority. It's no wonder the staff meeting turned into a battle.

Apply Your Learning 1.2

Please write all answers on a separate sheet of paper.

1. The goal of empowerment is to:

    a. influence others' behavior.
    b. enhance profitability and guest service.
    c. create new management styles.
    d. shield managers from criticism resulting from poor decisions.

2. Hotel companies that place most decision-making authority at top management levels are known as _____ organizations.

    a. bureaucratic
    b. autocratic
    c. empowered
    d. centralized

3. Learned helplessness most likely occurs at _____ organizations.

    a. autocratic
    b. centralized
    c. democratic
    d. empowered

4. What is the difference between power and authority?

5. Describe the relationship between authority and responsibility.

1.3 Quality Service

AFTER STUDYING SECTION 1.3, YOU SHOULD KNOW HOW TO:

♦ Describe how a guest perceives value in the products and services offered by hospitality companies

♦ Define "moments of truth"

♦ Explain how service strategy relates to guests' perceptions of value and critical moments of truth

♦ List the responsibilities managers have in fostering quality service

---

Customers have more options for spending their dollars, more well-defined expectations of quality, and less tolerance for poor service than ever before. They are likely to ignore brand or company loyalty and spend their money for products and services offered by whatever company provides hassle-free, above-average service. In a word, today's customers seek value. They find value when the products and services they receive consistently meet or exceed their expectations and can be purchased at an acceptable price.

Providing the highest possible quality at acceptable prices is a formula for success in any segment of the hospitality industry.

Business *survival* depends on providing value for customers. But truly *successful* companies go one step further. They not only provide value, they also increase customers' perceptions of the value they are providing. They make sure their customers actually know how much value is being offered. As one industry analyst has said, "It's not the quality of service that you give but the quality of service that the customer *perceives* that causes him to buy and come back." How, when, and where can you make your customers aware of the value you provide? By properly handling "moments of truth."

Moments of Truth

For today's hospitality manager, one of the keys to success is understanding how moments of truth affect service strategies and create new management responsibilities.

Some experts define a **moment of truth** as "any episode in which the customer comes into contact with any aspect of the organization and gets an impression of the quality of its service."

A hospitality consultant recalls asking a group of hotel managers to brainstorm all the moments of truth in their hotels. The managers had trouble identifying specific guest experiences. Instead, they listed such things as efficiency, cleanliness, and courtesy. These items may be important guest expectations, but they aren't moments of truth. Moments of truth are specific events, situations, or interactions:

Exhibit 1
Sample Service Strategy—Hospitality Partners

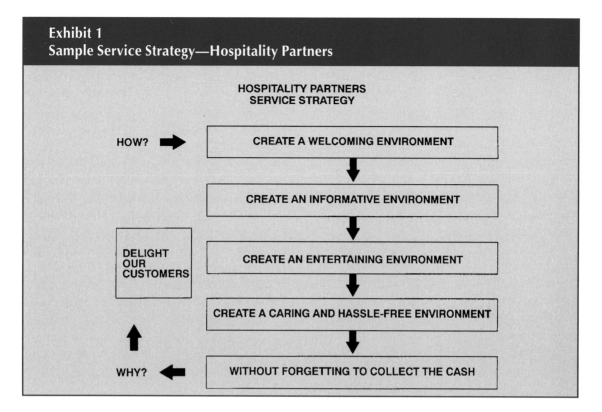

- A guest waiting at the front desk during check-in
- A guest entering a guestroom after check-in
- A guest receiving a morning wake-up call

What the guest experiences in these very specific situations affects his or her perception of the quality of service. The moments of truth throughout a guest's hotel stay form a continuous chain of events that builds a perception of overall value.

A Real-World Example: Hospitality Partners. Hospitality Partners, a hotel management company, has developed a service strategy that illustrates the simplicity and complexity of quality service. Exhibit 1 shows the "why and how" of Hospitality Partners' service strategy and also represents the company's mission statement. The mission of the company is to delight its guests, owners, and employees. That is accomplished by creating a welcoming, informative, entertaining, caring, and hassle-free environment in all of the hotels the company manages. Each hotel develops its own unique way of achieving it.

The staff at one hotel created a welcoming environment for their guests with a "Where Do You Come From?" map. When guests check into that hotel, front desk employees place a pin on a large map on the wall behind the front desk, to indicate the traveler's hometown. This gives each arriving guest an individualized welcome and helps him or her feel like part of the hotel "family."

At another Hospitality Partners property, employees wear miniature flag pins on their uniforms that indicate the foreign languages they speak. This helps international guests feel welcomed, and it tells them which staff members could provide assistance in their native language.

Hospitality Partners has identified 39 critical moments of truth in the company's cycle of hotel service. Each moment of truth is an opportunity for hotel employees to analyze how they can delight guests and create value for them.

For example, consider the following moments of truth, which typically occur many times daily in every lodging operation.

Guest arrives in front of the hotel. Is the area in front of the hotel clean and welcoming? Or is it dirty and menacing?

Guest enters the lobby. Is there a directional sign that informs guests how to get to the front desk or to their meeting? Or is the guest left wondering where to go?

Guest walks up to front desk. Is the guest made to feel welcomed by the front desk staff? Or is the staff too busy with paperwork to look up and greet the guest immediately?

Guest checks in. While the more tedious details of the check-in process are occurring, is the guest being entertained by the lobby environment or by the front desk staff? Or is the guest being treated like an inconvenience and just one more piece of paper to process?

Guest is escorted to room or suite. Is the guest informed as he or she is escorted to the room or suite? Or is the journey a long, silent, boring, and uncomfortable one?

Guest enters room or suite. Does the guest feel welcomed by the sight of a clean room or suite? Or does the guest feel frightened by the giant dust ball that has collected in the bathroom?

Guest turns on television. Does the guest enjoy a hassle-free evening watching a favorite program? Or does the guest get irritated because the remote control's batteries are dead and the front desk staff doesn't seem to care?

Guest calls for wake-up call. Does the guest get a good night's sleep, confident that the wake-up call will come because a staff member cared enough to repeat the time and room number when he made the request? Or does the guest toss and turn, sure that the wake-up call will not come due to the staff's less-than-professional attitudes and actions?

New Leadership and Management Responsibilities

The main challenge for a company's managers is to create a company culture that encourages providing quality service to customers.

Within such a culture, managers serve the hotel's staff, who, in turn, serve guests. As shown in Exhibit 2, this flips the traditional organization chart upside down. Customers now replace managers at the top.

Just as employees sometimes react negatively to being placed at the bottom of a traditional organization chart, managers sometimes react negatively to being placed at the bottom of the inverted chart. So, a third diagram has been created to show the relationships among customers, employees, and managers at the point of customer contact (see Exhibit 3). This diagram shows that customers are at the center of everything a business does.

Exhibit 2
The Traditional Pyramid of Authority and the Inverted Pyramid

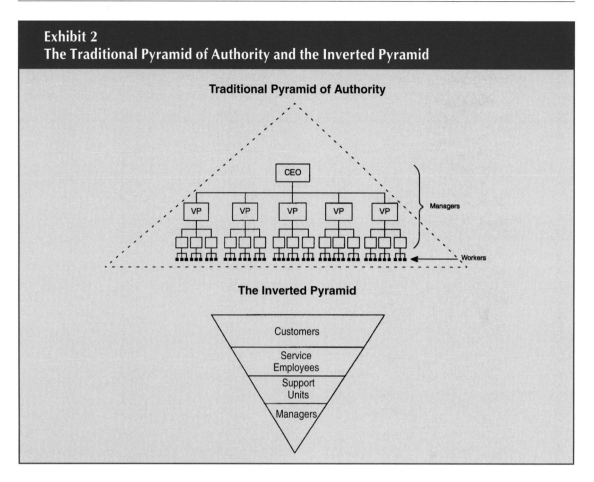

Traditional Pyramid of Authority

The Inverted Pyramid

Exhibit 3
The Point of Customer Contact

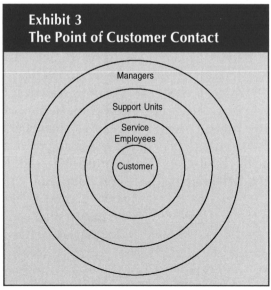

It takes more than a theory and a diagram to create a service culture, however. The traditional management functions of directing, controlling, and commanding must give way to the new management responsibilities of enabling, empowering, and supporting.

- Managers enable their employees by providing the necessary skills training to help them become competent in performing the fundamental tasks of their jobs.

- Managers empower staff members by first enabling them and then supporting their decisions and actions.

- Managers support their employees by encouraging them to accept greater personal responsibility and exercise more control over the way they perform their jobs, assuring them that the hotel values their ideas, has confidence in their judgment, and will stand behind their efforts.

Apply Your Learning 1.3

Please write all answers on a separate sheet of paper.

1. Increasing customers' perceptions of the value you provide is the key to _____.

2. What is a "moment of truth"?

3. Which of the following is typically *not* a moment of truth?

   a. a guest checking in at the front desk
   b. a guest calling a taxi cab from the hotel
   c. a guest watching television in a guestroom
   d. a guest receiving a morning wake-up call

4. A hotel built around a service culture will typically turn the traditional organization chart upside down, placing _____ at the top.

   a. customers
   b. managers
   c. supervisors
   d. employees

5. Managers enable their employees by:

   a. providing skills training.
   b. giving them more decision-making authority.
   c. rewarding their accomplishments.
   d. assuring them that the hotel values their ideas.

1.4 Diversity

AFTER STUDYING SECTION 1.4, YOU SHOULD KNOW HOW TO:

♦ Define diversity

♦ Explain the importance of managing diversity

♦ List the benefits of diversity

♦ Explain the effect of equal opportunity laws on hospitality managers

♦ Summarize the Americans with Disabilities Act

♦ Respond to sexual harassment complaints

There are two major reasons for managers to be concerned with **diversity**, the presence in the workplace of people who differ in gender, culture, race, ethnicity, and other attributes.

The first is demographics. A diverse work force is simply a fact of modern corporate life. If a company is currently not diverse, it soon will be.

The second is productivity. Once you have a diverse work force, simply throwing different people together does not create a productive work environment—or even a genuinely diverse one. Why? Because people tend to cluster with people like themselves. Because cultural misunderstandings and prejudice can cause conflict, bad decisions, and poor results.

Managing diversity means accommodating differences in style and perspective among workers from different backgrounds.

The Benefits of Diversity

Four good reasons for encouraging diversity are to:

• keep and increase market share

• reduce costs

• increase productivity

• improve the quality of management

Keeping and Increasing Market Share. Increased diversity within an organization can result in larger shares of more diverse markets. A customer is more likely to buy from someone he or she can identify with.

A hotel that has no minorities at the front desk or in sales or management may be less attractive to an African-American or Hispanic group than one that does. A hotel gift shop that does not stock ethnic grooming products or diverse periodicals on the shelves risks sending the message that the hotel's management is not sensitive to the needs of different groups.

Reducing Costs. Costs associated with recruiting, training, relocating, and compensating employees are major expenses for organizations. Increased diversity practices

UNDER THE GAVEL

The Family and Medical Leave Act

The Family and Medical Leave Act (FMLA) provides for a period of mandated unpaid employee leave of up to 12 weeks per year for the birth, adoption, or serious illness of a child, or the serious illness of a parent or a spouse, with a return to the same or equivalent job. The FMLA also provides an exception for highly paid, "key" employees.

An employer may require—or an employee may elect—to substitute any accrued vacation leave, personal leave, or family leave for the unpaid leave; however, the FMLA does not authorize the use of paid family leave for medical leave taken because the employee has a serious health condition.

During any leave under the FMLA, the employer must maintain an employee's coverage under the company's group health plan at the existing level and under existing conditions.

---

save money by reducing turnover and providing nonmonetary reasons for employees to stay with a hotel. For example, a hospitality company with no sensitivity to diversity issues may hire women and minorities and invest money in training them, only to have them leave because the company doesn't have a welcoming atmosphere.

Increasing Productivity. People who enjoy coming to work generally produce more. People who believe that their work will be valued or that their work will lead to advancement are also inclined to work harder.

Research has shown that diverse groups of people are generally more creative and innovative than homogeneous groups. At the University of North Texas, ethnically diverse teams of business students were pitted—without their knowledge—against all-white teams for 17 weeks. At first, the all-white teams sprinted ahead, but by the study's end the more diverse groups were viewing situations from a broader range of perspectives and producing more innovative solutions to problems.

Improving the Quality of Management. Including nontraditional employees in competition for managerial positions may open the door to highly qualified individuals who may have been unable to advance due to policies that discriminated against them. Exposure to colleagues from a variety of backgrounds can help managers develop new ways to solve workplace problems.

Additional Benefits. Hospitality companies that increase diversity can also expect to experience a more competitive organization, increased creativity and innovation, enhanced corporate flexibility, and an enhanced understanding of social responsibility.

Exhibit 1
Major EEO Laws and Their Implications

EEO Law	Major Implication
Title VII of the Civil Rights Act (1964)	Bars discrimination on basis of race, sex, religion, color, and national origin.
Age Discrimination in Employment Act (1967)	Bars discrimination against people over 40. Involuntary retirement prohibited.
Vocational Rehabilitation Act (1973)	Bars discrimination against otherwise qualified people with disabilities.
Pregnancy Discrimination Act (1978)	Prohibits discrimination against pregnant women.
Immigration Reform and Control Act (1986)	Prohibits recruiting and hiring of aliens not eligible for U.S. employment.
Americans with Disabilities Act (1990)	Prohibits workplace discrimination against people with disabilities. Reasonable accommodations required to make workplace accessible for all qualified employees.
Family and Medical Leave Act (1993)	Provides opportunity for employees to take up to 12 weeks unpaid leave for birth, adoption, care for elderly or ill parent, spouse or child, or to undergo treatment. Applies to employers with 50 or more employees. Affects 40% of employees and 5% of employers. Executives excluded.

Equal Employment

The Equal Employment Opportunity Commission is the federal body created by the Civil Rights Act of 1964 to establish and monitor employment standards in the United States. All employers are required to follow Equal Employment Opportunity (EEO) laws and regulations. Major EEO laws and their implications are highlighted in Exhibit 1.

Discrimination can occur in any number of ways, including:

- recruitment and selection
- age discrimination
- employee benefits and sex discrimination
- religious discrimination
- seniority
- wrongful discharge

Recruitment and Selection. Hotel managers may be tempted to recruit and hire underqualified candidates simply to fill vacancies quickly. However, such hiring practices can be construed as discriminatory. For instance, if a hotel has posted a job description for a bell attendant that specifically calls for "experience," it must not deviate from this condition for employment. If it does—even just once—the employer can be

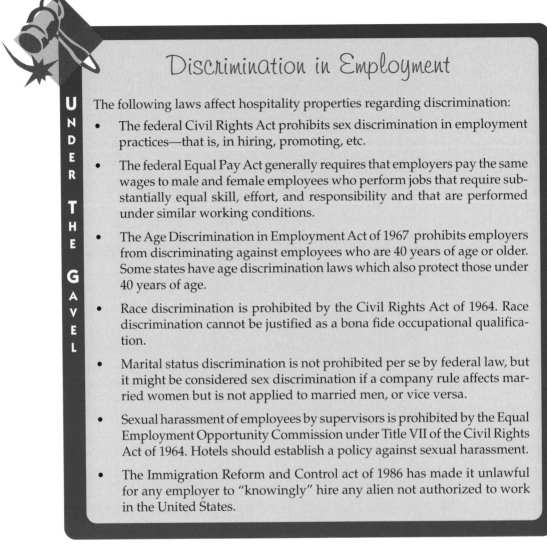

Discrimination in Employment

UNDER THE GAVEL

The following laws affect hospitality properties regarding discrimination:

- The federal Civil Rights Act prohibits sex discrimination in employment practices—that is, in hiring, promoting, etc.

- The federal Equal Pay Act generally requires that employers pay the same wages to male and female employees who perform jobs that require substantially equal skill, effort, and responsibility and that are performed under similar working conditions.

- The Age Discrimination in Employment Act of 1967 prohibits employers from discriminating against employees who are 40 years of age or older. Some states have age discrimination laws which also protect those under 40 years of age.

- Race discrimination is prohibited by the Civil Rights Act of 1964. Race discrimination cannot be justified as a bona fide occupational qualification.

- Marital status discrimination is not prohibited per se by federal law, but it might be considered sex discrimination if a company rule affects married women but is not applied to married men, or vice versa.

- Sexual harassment of employees by supervisors is prohibited by the Equal Employment Opportunity Commission under Title VII of the Civil Rights Act of 1964. Hotels should establish a policy against sexual harassment.

- The Immigration Reform and Control act of 1986 has made it unlawful for any employer to "knowingly" hire any alien not authorized to work in the United States.

viewed as practicing discrimination if an applicant is turned down later on for lacking experience.

A hotel owner's desire to employ only certain age groups or races would not be legally recognized. Other policies that would not be allowable include:

- Refusing to hire women as hotel stewards because they cannot lift heavy objects

- Hiring only pretty or young employees as restaurant greeters because the company likes the impression they make on guests

- Hiring only male servers because management views their image as more "professional"

Age Discrimination. The Age Discrimination in Employment Act prohibits discrimination against employees age 40 and older in all employment conditions (although there are specific exceptions). Refusing to put older workers in training programs, not promoting older employees, and forcing older employees to retire or to move to less desirable positions all represent age discrimination. While many hospitality companies have made great strides in overcoming the perception of hiring only young, attractive employees, others have not.

Employee Benefits and Sex Discrimination. In the past, employers sometimes offered one benefits plan to men and another to women. Such practice is now illegal. Employers cannot discriminate on the medical benefits, hospitalization, accident and life insurance, retirement plans, and so on. In addition, employers cannot discriminate against women because of pregnancy. The Pregnancy Discrimination Act of 1978 protects pregnant women regarding such issues as eligibility for employment and promotion.

Religious Discrimination. Title VII of the Civil Rights Act makes it illegal to refuse to hire someone simply because of his or her religious beliefs. It is illegal to refuse to hire individuals whose religious beliefs might prevent them from working at certain times (for example, on holy days).

Hospitality companies may face other issues involving religious beliefs such as appearance, dress codes, and work schedules. In addition, employers must keep the workplace free from religious bias or intimidation by employees who attempt to impose their religious beliefs on others.

Seniority. Seniority is a frequent source of grievances, which typically involve promotions and other benefits based on seniority

systems. The U.S. Supreme Court has ruled that seniority systems are legal as long as they do not discriminate on the basis of race, color, religion, national origin, or gender. Therefore, employers or unions can legally discriminate on the basis of seniority.

Wrongful Discharge. There are two basic categories of wrongful discharge: contract theory and public policy theory. In **contract theory,** an employee might claim that a personnel manual, for instance, created an employment contract and that she was dismissed in violation of this "contract." In **public policy theory,** an employee might claim that he was dismissed either for refusing to break the law or for insisting on obeying the law.

Most employers can protect themselves from wrongful discharge complaints and lawsuits simply by establishing a discharge policy and sticking to it. Employers can follow one of two main policies: employment at will and dismissal for just cause. **Employment at will** allows an employer to terminate employees with or without notice, at any time, and for any reason. **Dismissal for just cause** assures employees that they will receive fair and equal treatment and progressive discipline, if discipline is necessary. Many hotels incorporate elements of both approaches in their employment policies.

The Americans with Disabilities Act

The Americans with Disabilities Act (ADA), which went into effect in 1992, prohibits discrimination against people with disabilities. The Act includes five parts, or "titles," that specifically address issues related to employment, public services, public acommodations and services operated by private

Americans with Disabilities Act

The Americans with Disabilities Act (ADA) makes it illegal to discriminate against qualified individuals with disabilities. The ADA covers five areas:

- Employment
- Public services
- Public transportation
- Public accommodations
- Telecommunication services

The sections of the ADA that are of most concern to hotel and restaurant operators are Title III, which covers public accommodation, and Title I, which covers employment.

Title III—Public Accommodations. The ADA prohibits discrimination against individuals with disabilities in the full and equal enjoyment of the goods, services, facilities, privileges, advantages, or accommodations of any place of public accommodation, requiring that these be offered in the setting appropriate to the needs of the individual, except where the individual poses a direct threat to the health or safety of others.

This means that hospitality properties must make reasonable modifications to policies, practices, and procedures to give people with disabilities access to the property. Properties must also remove any physical barriers (such as curbs, narrow doorways, etc.).

Title I—Employment. Title I of the ADA prohibits hotel employers from discriminating against a "qualified individual with a disability" in regard to job applications, hiring, advancement, discharge, compensation, and training, or other terms, conditions, or privileges of employment.

An individual with a disability is broadly defined as anyone who (1) has a physical or mental impairment that substantially limits one or more major life activities, (2) has a record of such an impairment, or (3) is regarded as having such an impairment.

entities, telecommunications, and miscellaneous concerns. For managers, Title I "Employment" is the most significant, covering recruiting, hiring, promotion, training, layoffs, pay, termination, job assignments, leave, and benefits.

In the language of the ADA, an individual is considered to have a disability when he or she: (1) has a physical or mental impairment that substantially limits one or more major life activities, (2) has a record of such an impairment, or (3) is regarded as having such an impairment. Major life activities include seeing, hearing, speaking, walking, breathing, performing manual tasks, learning, caring for oneself, and working.

The ADA protects people with disabilities that involve speech, vision, and hearing, as well as disabilities caused by mental retardation, a specific learning impediment, and emotional illness. In addition, people with diseases such as cancer, heart disease, epilepsy, multiple sclerosis, arthritis, asthma, and diabetes are protected, as are people with HIV and AIDS.

Under the ADA, people with disabilities are considered qualified for a job if they can perform the essential functions of the job with or without reasonable accommodation. **Essential functions** are job tasks that are fundamental. For instance, cooking skills would be considered fundamental for a cook. But the ability to hear orders called by servers to a cook might not be considered fundamental. As a result, an operation might be required to make reasonable accommodations so that cooking positions are open to people with auditory disabilities.

Reasonable accommodation refers to what employers must do to make the workplace accessible to people with disabilities. As a general rule, employers are required to accommodate people with disabilities unless doing so imposes an undue hardship on the employer. For example, the following efforts are typically considered reasonable accommodations by the EEOC:

- Making facilities accessible—constructing wheelchair ramps, widening aisles, lowering a cashier station for a person in a wheelchair, etc.

- Restructuring jobs to eliminate non-essential functions

- Reassigning a person to another job if he or she becomes unable to perform in an existing job

- Modifying work schedules to allow for medical and other related appointments

- Modifying or acquiring equipment—which may include special equipment needed by a person with a disability to perform essential job functions

- Providing readers or interpreters for people who cannot read or have visual impairments

Claims of Sexual Harassment

Perhaps it seems odd to discuss sexual harassment in a section on diversity. Yet, claims of sexual harassment may arise when men and women from different cultural backgrounds share the workplace.

More and more managers and supervisors are learning that a wide range of activities can be labeled as sexual harassment. All complaints must be carefully considered and investigated.

Sexual harassment does not necessarily involve sexual contact or overt sexual advances or suggestions. Basically, sexual harassment can occur when:

- Employment decisions are made based on an individual's acceptance or rejection of sexual involvement

- A person's job performance is adversely affected by sexual conduct

- Sexual conduct creates an intimidating, hostile, or offensive work environment for an individual

- An employee is subject to unwanted sexual conduct from nonemployees and the employer fails to exercise control over the work environment to stop the improper behavior

Companies wishing to establish strong policies against sexual harassment should:

- Issue a strong policy statement against sexual harassment

- Make it easy for employees to file harassment charges

- Take every complaint seriously

- Gather facts, and avoid prejudging

- Take remedial action to correct past sexual harassment

Apply Your Learning 1.4

Please write all answers on a separate sheet of paper.

1. What are the two most compelling reasons for managers to be concerned with diversity?

2. How can a diverse work force actually help a hotel increase its market share?

3. What does "employment at will" mean?

4. Which of the following individuals would *not* be considered disabled, according to the Americans with Disabilities Act?

   a. a reservationist who uses a wheelchair
   b. a front desk agent who requires corrective lenses
   c. a housekeeper who has just been diagnosed with diabetes
   d. a security officer who is HIV-positive

Write whether the following statements are True or False.

5. Managers should focus on preventing new claims of sexual harassment and avoid trying to make up for harassment problems in the past.

6. To prove sexual harassment, there must be an eyewitness testimony from an objective third party.

7. Sexual harassment requires actual physical contact between the parties involved.

Quick Hits

Chapter 1

SECTION 1.1—MANAGEMENT STYLES

- New technologies—and the ever-increasing speed of change—have actually altered the structure of many companies. When a company's structure changes, so does the nature of leadership and management in that organization.

- Today, many hospitality companies have flattened their organizational structures, redistributed power and responsibility, and given decision-making authority to every employee. These changes have redefined the roles, responsibilities, and competencies of managers at every level.

- **Autocratic managers** stress immediate, short-term results over concerns about people in a department or organization. **Bureaucratic managers** make decisions by enforcing rules, regulations, policies, and procedures that are already in place. **Democratic managers** tend to focus more on a participative process than on short-term, immediate results.

- The most effective managers today don't restrict themselves to a single management style. They are flexible enough to adopt different styles for specific circumstances. Hospitality managers' flexibility may be affected by three barriers: their personal background, characteristics of the employees they manage, and the culture of their hotel company.

- In today's successful hospitality companies, the best managers balance the details of management with the vision of leadership.

SECTION 1.2—POWER AND EMPOWERMENT

- **Power** is the ability to influence others' behavior. A manager's power is a function of responsibility, authority, and accountability.

- **Empowerment** is the redistribution of power within an organization. The goal of empowerment is to enhance guest service and increase profits for the organization by passing decision-making responsibility, authority, and accountability to every level within the organization.

- In **centralized organizations,** most decision-making authority is at top management levels. **Decentralized organizations** distribute decision-making authority throughout the company.

- A centralized power structure may lead to **learned helplessness,** with employees unwilling or unable to provide guest-pleasing service because "it's not my job."

- In a decentralized hotel, top managers help everyone understand how their work fits into the company's vision and contributes to the company's success. Departments cooperate with other departments. Focusing on the values, mission, and goals of the organization, every employee works together to identify and solve problems.

- **Authority** is the formal power granted by an organization to a management position—not the individual who holds that position. A manager exercise authority when making decisions, issuing orders, and using resources to achieve departmental and organizational goals.

- A manager's authority should match the responsibility of his or her position within the company.

SECTION 1.3—QUALITY SERVICE

- Today's customers seek *value*. They find value when the products and services they receive consistently meet or exceed their expectations and can be purchased at an acceptable price.

- Business success depends on increasing your customers' perceptions of the value you are providing to them.

- **Moments of truth** are the interactions between a customer and a hotel's staff that bring the company to life for a particular customer at a specific moment in time. They are specific events, situations, or interactions—and they occur dozens of times during a typical guest's stay.

- Value for guests and profits for the company depend on managers and employees successfully handling moments of truth.

- Because of their customer focus, some companies have created organizational charts that place the customers at the top, managers at the bottom. Others prefer a chart of three concentric circles that places customers at the center, employees in the next larger ring, and managers on the outer ring.

SECTION 1.4—DIVERSITY

- **Diversity** refers to the presence in the workplace of people who differ in gender, culture, race, ethnicity, and other attributes. Managing diversity means accommodating differences in style and perspective among workers from different backgrounds.

- There are two reasons for managers to be concerned with diversity: demographics (because diversity is a fact of modern business life) and productivity (because cultural misunderstandings and prejudice can cause conflict, bad decisions, and poor results).

- Four good reasons for encouraging diversity are:

  - *Keeping and increasing market share.* Increased diversity within an organization can result in larger shares of more diverse markets.

  - *Reducing costs.* Increased diversity practices save money by reducing turnover and providing nonmonetary reasons for employees to stay with a hotel (for example, a more comfortable workplace).

  - *Increasing productivity.* Research has shown that diverse groups of people are generally more creative and innovative than homogeneous groups.

- *Improving the quality of management.* Exposure to colleagues from a variety of backgrounds can help managers develop new ways to solve workplace problems.

- The Equal Employment Opportunity Commission (EEOC) is the federal body created by the Civil Rights Act of 1964 to establish and monitor employment standards in the United States. All employers are required to follow Equal Employment Opportunity (EEO) laws and regulations.

- Discrimination can occur in any number of ways, including: recruitment and selection, age discrimination, employee benefits and sex discrimination, religious discrimination, seniority, and wrongful discharge.

- There are two basic categories of wrongful discharge: contract theory and public policy theory. In **contract theory**, an employee might claim that a personnel manual, for instance, created an employment contract and that she was dismissed in violation of this "contract." In **public policy theory**, an employee might claim that he was dismissed either for refusing to break the law or for insisting on obeying the law.

- Employers can follow one of two main policies: employment at will and dismissal for just cause. **Employment at will** allows an employer to terminate employees with or without notice, at any time, and for any reason. **Dismissal for just cause** assures employees that they will receive fair and equal treatment and progressive discipline, sary. Many hotels incorporate elements

of both approaches in their employment policies.

- The Americans with Disabilities Act (ADA) prohibits discrimination against people with disabilities. An individual is considered to have a disability when he or she: (1) has a physical or mental impairment that substantially limits one or more major life activities, (2) has a record of such an impairment, or (3) is regarded as having such an impairment.

- Under the ADA, people with disabilities are considered qualified for a job if they can perform the essential functions of the job with or without reasonable accommodation. **Essential functions** are job tasks that are fundamental. **Reasonable accommodation** refers to what employers must do to make the workplace accessible to people with disabilities. As a general rule, employers are required to accommodate people with disabilities unless doing so imposes an undue hardship on the employer.

- Sexual harassment does not necessarily involve sexual contact or overt sexual advances or suggestions. Companies wishing to establish strong policies against sexual harassment should:

  - Issue a strong policy statement against sexual harassment

  - Make it easy for employees to file harassment charges

  - Take every complaint seriously

  - Gather facts, and avoid prejudging

  - Take remedial action to correct past sexual harassment

Profile

Jane Mackie
Vice President/Brand Manager
Four Points Hotels

J ane Mackie is one of those tried-and-true hotel veterans who fell in love with the business and decided not to check out.

The 35-year-old executive was promoted to vice president and brand manager of Starwood's Four Points hotel chain in 1998, and is excited about building Starwood's rapidly expanding mid-market brand.

Mackie started her career at the Sheraton Boston in 1982, when she started a summer job as a trainee while attending college. She spent that summer and subsequent summers working at the front desk and pool. When she was a senior in college, recruiters for major corporations came to campus to woo students to come work for their companies. But nothing measured up to the potential career she saw with ITT Sheraton. After graduation, she went to work for Sheraton and was placed in a year-long training program in Jacksonville, Florida.

She then went to work as manager of guest services at Sheraton's hotel in Stamford, Connecticut. "I knew I loved the hospitality industry and Sheraton had room (to promote) people with specific skills," Mackie said.

Eventually, Mackie was appointed as the director of advertising and marketing programs for the European division of Starwood Hotels & Resorts Worldwide. She moved to Brussels, Belgium, where she was responsible for developing new products and promotions. She also managed the marketing and communications strategies for the division.

"I had five sensational years there," she said of her new job and life in Europe.

Starwood picked Mackie for the key brand manager job soon after it acquired and integrated the Westin and Sheraton hotel brands with the existing Starwood hotels. It wanted people with experience in both marketing and operations to help grow the brands. Mackie's name rose to the top of the list.

Excerpted with permission from Lodging, *June 1999.*

Communication Skills

Sections

2.1 Structure of Communication

2.2 Speaking and Presentations

2.3 Listening

2.4 Business Writing

2.1 Structure of Communication

Managers spend as much as 80 percent of their day communicating with others. Their ability to communicate often determines whether they succeed or fail as managers.

Communication skills are used in every important managerial activity—including recruiting, interviewing, training, motivating, evaluating, coaching, counseling, leading, and interacting with guests. Yet many managers lack ability in this important area. One study shows that while 95 percent of managers believe that they have good interpersonal communication skills, only 30 percent of their employees agree. In this specific study, managers and employees couldn't even agree on whether they had met during the last week!

Communication is a message sent and received. But *successful* communication requires something more: both the sender and the receiver must understand and act on the message. This chapter will help you learn how to communicate more effectively in the hospitality workplace.

Myths About Communication

Before discussing how the communication process works, let's look at seven myths about communication.

1. *We communicate only when we want to communicate.* We communicate all day, often without realizing it, through our words, actions, and body language.

2. *Words mean the same to both the speaker and the listener.* Words hold different meanings for different people, based on their experiences, perceptions, and biases. For example, when you tell an employee that her work is "above average," you may mean that she is doing extremely well and you believe she has great potential. Your employee, however, may have always perceived herself as a high achiever; to her, "above average" means she is just above "merely acceptable." You intended to offer a compliment; she took it as a criticism.

3. *We communicate chiefly with words.* In reality, most communication is nonverbal. We may say one thing but reveal another through our facial expressions, tone of voice, gestures, eye contact, or how we sit or walk.

4. *Nonverbal communication is silent communication.* Some people believe that all nonverbal communication can be seen but not heard. This is not true. We can hear laughter, weeping, or the tone of voice in which something is said. If you hear co-workers whistling as they do their jobs, you naturally assume they are having a good day.

5. *Communication involves an active speaker and a passive listener.* Communication is better when both parties actively participate. There is greater participation when a listener provides feedback to a speaker through verbal and nonverbal cues. Shaking your head or furrowing your brow may be a stronger indication that you do not understand something than what you actually say in response.

6. *The message we communicate is the message the listener receives.* Managers often assume that others receive their messages exactly as they intended them. Suppose that your boss gives you an assignment on Monday and states that she wants it done "soon." You look at your schedule and decide that you can work on it Thursday and get it to your boss first thing Friday morning. On Tuesday, your boss asks you for the completed assignment. "Soon" meant "tomorrow" to your boss, while it meant "sometime this week" to you.

7. *There is no such thing as too much information.* Both too little and too much information can be bad. Few employees need to know every little detail about an assignment. And information overload can result in less information actually being understood. Managers should concentrate on the quality of their communications as much as the quantity of them.

The Communication Process

Here is a story to illustrate the process of interpersonal communications.

Joe is a busperson at the hotel restaurant. He knows the restaurant is short of servers today because two of them called in sick just before the lunch rush began. He approaches Molly, the dining room supervisor, and volunteers to help out.

Molly considers Joe's offer based on her knowledge, experience, feelings, attitudes, emotions, and perceptions. She knows she is short two servers and the noon rush is about to begin. She knows that her staff will be busy with an extra banquet, as well as the usual number of guests. She decides she is lucky that Joe has offered to help. Since he has bused tables for almost three months, she believes he understands the importance of guest service. Molly smiles, breathes a sigh of relief, and says, "We sure can use another pair of hands today. Why don't you take tables 11 and 12 to start with, and we'll see how you do."

Based on his own knowledge, experiences, feelings, attitudes, and emotions, Joe mentally responds to the message. He has never waited tables before, but he has been watching the servers and thinks he can serve as well as they can. He figures that busing tables isn't much different from taking orders and serving food to guests; all you have to do is ask guests what they want and then bring it to them. "No problem," he tells himself. He sends feedback to Molly by saying, "Sure thing, Molly. I'll get on it right away." Then he turns toward the kitchen.

"Thanks," Molly says. "I really appreciate this."

Because Joe seems confident that he can handle the work, Molly thinks he will do a good job. She doesn't have time to think for long, though, because the banquet guests have begun arriving. In addition, the main dining area is filling up quickly. Molly is busy with guests and other servers. When Joe said he'd "get on it right away," Molly turned her attention to other matters.

In the kitchen, Joe joins a heated discussion with the other busers about the basketball championships. He fails to bring his guests the restaurant's signature basket of freshly baked bread. When he finally remembers to take orders, his pen runs out of ink—but Joe thinks he can remember the orders anyway. He fills out the guest checks when he returns to the kitchen, but he gets the orders wrong.

Joe makes other mistakes. He fails to make eye contact with his customers, doesn't bother to learn about the daily specials, and responds to questions by saying only, "I don't know." And he is much too slow—in waiting on the guests, in placing their orders, in bringing their (wrong) meals.

For one table of furious guests, this is the last straw. They angrily get up to leave the restaurant and loudly demand to see the manager. Other guests turn to watch. When Molly arrives, the guests tell her all about Joe's poor service. Molly tries to calm the guests, but they don't want to listen. They speak of horrible service and of never returning, and they stomp out.

Molly angrily steps into the kitchen, where Joe is—once again—talking about basketball.

"Joe, I want to see you in my office. Now."

Molly compares her knowledge of guest service and waiting tables to what she's heard about Joe's performance. She explodes, "That was the worst job of waiting tables that this restaurant's ever seen! I thought you knew about guest service!" Her feelings, attitudes, and emotions are very apparent to Joe. He looks astonished. Molly rips into him for ignoring the guests, for getting their orders wrong, for not being courteous. She tells him that, because of him, some guests will never return. In addition, their reputation as a first-class hotel restaurant is ruined.

Joe looks at her, wide-eyed. He can't understand what the big deal is. He thinks Molly is really out of control. He also thinks that everyone else can hear her, even though the door is shut.

Joe compares his knowledge, experience, feelings, attitudes, and emotions about serving to what he thinks Molly's knowledge, experience, feelings, attitudes, and emotions must be. It's true that he messed up the orders, but he solved that problem by telling the guests it was the kitchen staff's fault. The way Molly's acting, you'd think it was the end of the world. He flushes, then shrugs his shoulders. He decides that he'd rather wash dishes for the rest of his life than volunteer to help Molly again. "OK, Molly," he says bitterly, "it'll never happen again."

She nods and opens her office door, making it clear that Joe is to leave. She slams the door shut as soon as he's gone. After pacing around her office for a minute or so, she begins to calm down. She feels bad about losing her cool with Joe. "He was only trying to help," she tells herself. Molly wonders what she could have been thinking when she allowed Joe to wait tables without any instructions, training, or direct supervision.

At the end of the work shift, Molly asks Joe to return to her office. They talk about how her expectations for the job had differed from his. They also discuss the importance of guest relations and service, of paying attention to guests, of writing down orders, and of actually working instead of talking with friends. Molly realizes that she should have made her expectations clear before Joe started serving. She also thinks that Joe might make a good server if he were given adequate training.

Molly and Joe talk for some time about how to avoid misunderstandings in the future. They decide that the best way to communicate more effectively is to make sure the entire message is received, understood, and acted upon by both the speaker and the listener.

Communication within an Organization

Managers must effectively communicate upward to their boss, downward to their staff, and laterally (or across) with fellow managers. The following tips can help.

Upward Communication. A successful manager knows that communicating with his or her boss is very important. However, **upward communication** takes care and planning.

- Be sure your message is important; your boss's time is limited.

- Be sure the information is accurate and complete.

- Be brief.

- Communicate both good and bad news.

- Communicate regularly.

- When you present a problem, suggest potential solutions.

- Make an agenda. Some bosses appreciate receiving a list of topics you will discuss in advance so that they, too, can be prepared.

- Be sure your timing is right. Trying to present information to your boss at the wrong time can derail the communication process.

- Establish clear objectives. Know in advance what you want to accomplish during your talk.

- Don't go over your boss's head unless it is absolutely necessary.

Downward Communication. Developing effective **downward communication** skills helps managers identify potential problems, gain staff commitment, and gather information for making decisions. However, managers must work hard to establish an effective downward communication style.

- Let employees know they can come to you with problems.

- Listen attentively and objectively to your employees' concerns and contributions.

- Don't react emotionally or critically when someone brings you bad news. Becoming angry with the message bearer will cut off your communication in the future.

- Use active listening skills (discussed later in the chapter).

- Be sure employees know that you care about their opinions and suggestions.

Lateral Communication. Communicating effectively with other managers helps ensure that information will continue to flow your way and enhances your career opportunities. The following tips can help you develop better **lateral communication** skills.

- Get to know as many other managers in the organization as possible.

- Look at peer communication as a chance to establish relationships that work for both parties.

- Be willing to share information.

- Constantly look for overlapping areas of responsibility or interests that might help improve your interaction with other managers.

- Take a "big picture" perspective and communicate about issues that might help the whole organization, not just your part of it.

- Give sincere and positive feedback when asked.

- When appropriate, offer your help.

- Use positive body language when communicating.

Barriers to Effective Communication

Many barriers can interfere with a manager's ability to communicate. For example, some clearly stated and well-intended messages can still come across as insensitive or abrasive. The result is that the message itself is not heard or understood.

Before you read the rest of this section, try taking the Interpersonal Communication Self-Test (Exhibit 1).

Barriers to effective interpersonal communication include:

Misinterpretation. People receiving a message must interpret the message and the intent of the sender. Since many messages could have multiple meanings or are incomplete, it's easy to jump to inaccurate conclusions about what is being said.

Evaluation of Sender. We commonly evaluate those who send us messages, and our evaluations influence how we interpret the messages. When managers see everything someone does as positive—a phenomenon called the **halo effect**—they often interpret that person's messages positively. The opposite is also true: when managers hold a negative opinion of a sender—the **devil's horns effect**—they often interpret that person's messages negatively. Suppose an employee tells his manager that he made a minor error on a guest folio. A manager who sees the employee with a halo will probably dismiss the mistake as no big deal. If the manager sees the employee with devil's horns, she might view this confession as proof that the employee constantly makes mistakes.

Projection. It's natural to assume that others feel or perceive things the same way you do. Yet, **projecting** your own attitudes, assumptions, or beliefs into messages often leads to misunderstandings. The most common example is the simple statement "I know how you feel." In reality, we often don't know how the other person feels; saying so minimizes the importance of the sender's statement.

Exhibit 1
Interpersonal Communication Self-Test

Find out how good your interpersonal communication skills are by completing this self-assessment. Put a number next to each of the following statements, using the scale below:

1—Seldom   2—Sometimes   3—Often   4—Usually

_____ 1. I adjust my vocal and body communication to fit what I'm saying.

_____ 2. I coach my staff to use positive vocal and body communication.

_____ 3. I can tell how people *feel* about what they are saying.

_____ 4. When talking with people of different cultures, I adjust my vocal and body communication to match theirs.

_____ 5. I try to avoid giving negative vocal and body messages to people I don't care for.

_____ 6. I don't let guests' or employees' emotional behavior distract me from the point they're making.

_____ 7. I use simple and clear language when I speak.

_____ 8. People do not ask me to repeat or clarify what I say.

_____ 9. My employees follow my directions.

_____ 10. When I speak, I know when to use examples or repetition.

_____ 11. I emphasize to my staff why it is important to do certain things.

_____ 12. When giving a message to guests or employees, I check to see if they understand it.

_____ 13. I have time to listen to employees and guests.

_____ 14. I wait until a person finishes speaking before I make my point.

_____ 15. When I don't understand a person's message or if I want more information, I ask questions.

_____ 16. I check to see if I understand people's messages by briefly repeating to them what I hear them say.

_____ 17. I avoid giving advice when employees come to me with personal problems.

_____ 18. I use different listening skills according to the type of listening situation I'm in.

_____ 19. I have no problem getting my boss to listen to me.

_____ 20. I know when I should take information to my boss.

_____ 21. I make myself available to my employees so they can talk to me.

_____ 22. My employees hear bad news from me before they hear it from anyone else at the property.

_____ 23. I consult other managers when I need help or advice.

_____ 24. I willingly offer help or advice to other managers when appropriate.

Add the numbers you wrote next to the self-assessment statements, then put a check mark in the box below that corresponds to your total.

❑   72–96:   Congratulations! You manage your interpersonal communication effectively.

❑   48–71:   Careful! Your interpersonal communication skills may be affecting your work performance and your personal relationships.

❑   24–47:   Warning! You need to significantly improve your interpersonal communication skills.

Source: Adapted from *Hospitality Management Skill Builders: Interpersonal Communication* (East Lansing, Mich.: Educational Institute of AH&MA, 1994), pp. 4–7.

Stereotyping. People who hold preconceived opinions about others based on their ethnicity, gender, age, nationality, class, or sexual orientation are guilty of stereotyping. The solution is to view people as individuals and give them an opportunity to show their strengths.

Arrogance and Superiority. Arrogance and superiority lead people to assume that others have little to offer. Constantly interrupting others, refusing to talk to "inferiors," and dominating conversations are examples of how someone with an arrogant and superior attitude inhibits communication.

Defensiveness. People sometimes have insecurities and can become protective of actions they take or projects they complete. A defensive manager who is asked about a report may interpret the question as a challenge and respond accordingly, even though the inquirer may simply have wanted more information.

Inarticulateness. Not all people express themselves clearly at all times. An inability to say what you mean inhibits communication. One of the best ways to avoid this problem is to follow the KISS rule: Keep It Short and Simple.

Hidden Agendas. Senders who are perceived to have **hidden agendas** are generally thought of as deceptive. Receivers with hidden agendas often don't hear the sender's intended message because they interpret everything in relation to their own agendas. A front office manager may believe that gaining more power and prestige for her department will lead to promotions or pay raises, so she works to ensure that the front office is seen in a positive light. As a result, she may not hear correctly what others are saying about the department or may send messages about the department that others distrust.

Status. When a manager talks to an employee, many employees are thinking something like, "This is my manager talking, so I better listen and do what I'm told." Some employees are so eager to do a good job that they hear the first part and immediately start thinking of how they are going to perform that part of the task—and then miss the rest of the message.

Environment. Noisy, frenetic, or otherwise distracting environments make it difficult to communicate. To clearly communicate, meet in a location free of such distractions as telephone calls, e-mail alerts, outside noise, and interruptions from other staff members.

Emotions. Either the sender's or receiver's emotions can create communication barriers. For example, you schedule a performance evaluation meeting with an employee in which you suggest that the employee's job performance must improve. You do this calmly, expecting the employee to receive the message calmly. But the employee might become angry, which might make you angry. What started out as a positive communication experience could deteriorate rapidly.

Differences in Backgrounds. Differences in education, experience, age, knowledge, and other background variables may impede communication. An employee with minimal education may not fully understand a message sent by a manager with more education and a larger vocabulary, for example.

Poor Timing. People sometimes say things in haste or anger that they later regret. Or, communication may not occur because one party is distracted or unwilling to listen. The best communication takes place when both the speaker and the listener are ready.

Exhibit 2
Common Communication Errors

First Impression Errors
Basing communication opinions on your first impressions of a sender or receiver

Similarity Errors
Favoring those who we believe are like us

Contrast Errors
Ranking people by comparing them with others we know

Leniency or Severity Errors
Being overly lenient or severe in our opinions of others

Overweighing Negative Information Errors
Hearing more of the negative than we do the positive

Faulty Listening or Memory Errors
Mishearing or incorrectly remembering what someone says

Recency Errors
Remembering only the most recent behaviors or communication signals

Central Tendency Errors
Viewing everyone as about the same

Nonverbal Cues Errors
"Listening" more to nonverbal cues than to what is actually said

---

Suppose that you call in Sharon, one of your best housekeepers, for a meeting about how to help new housekeepers clean rooms effectively. You want to hear Sharon's ideas. However, Sharon appears distracted and unwilling to help. Her reluctance may not be because she is unwilling. Instead, Sharon's reaction may be because she is preoccupied with a family problem or some other issue. To overcome this obstacle, you will probably have to reschedule the meeting.

Personality Conflicts. Sometimes people do not get along with each other because of personality conflicts, and this can influence how senders and receivers communicate. If Paco, an employee whom you do not like, comes to you for assistance, it is likely that your communication with Paco will be influenced by your dislike of him.

There are certainly many other behaviors that block effective communication. For example, each of the following might influence either the sender, the receiver, or both:

- Interrupting/allowing others to interrupt
- Talking too much/too little
- Arguing
- Over-generalizing
- Blaming others
- Commenting or judging too soon
- Using sarcasm
- Speaking, listening, or writing poorly
- Having no interest in the subject
- Pretending to understand

Other communication problems are listed in Exhibit 2.

Apply Your Learning 2.1

Please write all answers on a separate sheet of paper.

1. What is required for successful communication?

2. What is lateral communication?

3. What two barriers to effective communication are at work when a manager interprets everything an employee does as either positive or negative?

4. What does *KISS* stand for?

For statements 5–8, write whether the answer is True or False.

5. Nonverbal communication is the same as silent communication.

6. Information overload is a myth.

7. We communicate through our words, actions, and body language—often without realizing it.

8. Most communication is verbal.

2.2 Speaking and Presentations

AFTER STUDYING SECTION 2.2, YOU SHOULD KNOW HOW TO:

♦ Outline tips for effective speaking

♦ List and briefly describe the parts of a formal presentation

♦ Use visual aids effectively

♦ Control the presentation environment

♦ Use your voice and body effectively

Most of the communicating managers do is face to face. In this section, we will review tools and techniques that can help you to become a better communicator whether you are delivering a formal presentation to senior management or leading a training session for several dozen front desk agents.

Formal Presentations

Most of your oral communication will consist of three parts: an introduction, the main body, and a conclusion. Some presentation experts describe this as: "Tell them what you are going to tell them, tell them, then tell them what you told them."

Formal presentations require planning and organization. Begin by asking what the presentation should accomplish. Persuasive presentations are used to sell an audience on something (the importance of following new security procedures); informative presentations are used to explain a topic (how to use the new electronic lock system). Determining whether you want to persuade or inform helps you prepare the right material for your presentation.

Next, analyze your audience. Different types of audiences require different presentation approaches. Ask yourself:

• What values are important to my audience?

• Why does the audience need the information I want to present?

• What might keep audience members from doing what I want them to do or understanding what I want them to understand?

• What is the audience's demographic profile—age range, education, level of experience, etc.?

Each of these factors might influence how you should prepare for and deliver your presentation.

The Introduction. Your introduction should get the attention of your listeners, earn their interest, and communicate your purpose. You can begin a presentation in many different ways.

• Show how the information relates to the audience.

• Establish your competency as a speaker on the subject.

Tips for Effective Speaking

The following guidelines can help most speakers present their points more effectively to individuals or groups.

Identify Your Main Point in the Introduction

Most ideas can be communicated in a single sentence. If the message is too complex for one sentence, it should either be put in writing or broken down into steps.

Use Repetition or Examples

Repeating or providing examples that illustrate your main idea is especially useful for complex messages.

Use Concrete Language

"Erudite verbiage obfuscates cognition." That is, big words make a message hard to understand. Keep the language simple, use jargon sparingly or not at all, and explain terms that your audience may not understand.

State Things Positively

When the manager told the employee, "Don't fill out the form with a pen," she thought the message was clear. However, the employee only remembered the words "form" and "pen" and filled out the form with a pen. Whenever possible, state the message positively. The manager would have been better off saying, "Use a pencil to fill out the form."

Tell Why the Message Is Important

The message is not important to everyone just because it's important to you. Tell listeners why the message is important to them and why they should pay attention to it. They will take your message more seriously.

Check for Understanding

The number one reason that employees fail to carry out a manager's message is that they do not understand it. However, it probably won't do any good to ask employees if they understand; they often answer "yes" even when they don't understand. Sometimes they believe that they understand when in fact they don't; other times, they simply do not want to look stupid. Look for nonverbal clues that illustrate understanding. Ask specific questions about the message, and ask listeners to repeat the message in their own words to make sure they understand.

- Use humor, but don't force it if you aren't comfortable being humorous.

- Refer to the unusual to capture the audience's attention.

- Refer to the familiar to establish a bond between you and the audience.

- Reassure the audience about the importance of what you have to say.

- Shock the audience with an unusual statistic or little-known fact related to your topic, to capture their attention immediately.

- Use a quotation from someone else to focus attention on your topic.

You don't have to begin preparing a presentation by writing the introduction first. Instead, an introduction can often be pulled together from materials in the body of the presentation. Try working from the center outward—that is, from the main body to the introduction and conclusion.

The Main Body. This is where you present information in a logical sequence. Each point mentioned in the body should support your purpose for speaking. (Information that does not support your purpose will detract from your presentation.) The main body should also mention any benefits the audience is likely to experience as a result of accepting your presentation. Good speakers summarize information from time to time during the main body. These are called internal summaries.

The Conclusion. The conclusion summarizes the presentation for your audience. It is not the place to introduce new information or material.

Visual Aids. Visual aids can add substantially to a presentation if used properly. Many managers use too many visual aids or make them too complicated. Follow these guidelines when preparing visual aids:

- *Use the KISS system.* Keep visual aids short and simple.

- *Use visual aids sparingly.* The rule of thumb is a maximum of one visual aid for every two minutes of speaking.

- *Use graphics.* Graphs, pictures, flowcharts, and so on make better visual aids than words on a page.

- *Make text and numbers legible.* For most presentations, 18-point is the minimum font size you should use. Before your presentation, go to the back of the room in which you will be presenting and see for yourself whether you can read the visual aids.

- *Use color sparingly.*

- *Use bullets.* If you use a visual aid to present written ideas, set off the important points with bullets, numbers, indents, or some other method.

- *Develop titles for visual aids.* Your audience is more likely to remember a visual aid if it has a title.

- *Use overlays when possible.* Most people dislike the "hide and peek" method of revealing portions of a visual aid as you go. Instead, develop a series of overlays.

One final note: A wide range of business software makes it possible to put together a fast-paced and professional-looking computer-based presentation with relative ease. Such presentations are far more appealing than an overhead projector with black-and-white transparencies. However, it is possible to become so enamored with the software or the technology that your real message gets lost or overshadowed. Sometimes a computer-based presentation is simply overkill; for example, there is no need to add computer setup time and risk last-minute computer glitches for the sake of a one-time 20-minute introduction to your property's new rules regarding fitness center use. Make certain you are using the most appropriate means—whether high-tech or low-tech—to deliver your message.

Controlling the Presentation Environment

Before you begin a presentation, make sure the environment is properly prepared.

- *Equipment:* Test overhead projectors, computers, slide projectors, and other equipment in advance. Have spare bulbs ready. Have a pointer accessible, if necessary (and check the batteries, if using a laser pointer).

- *Flip charts:* Make sure you have ample paper and pens on hand.

- *Handouts:* Make sure handouts are easily accessible.

- *Microphone:* Test the microphone in advance. (Presentations to more than 75–100 people will likely require a microphone.)

- *Lighting:* Determine how to turn lights on or off if needed during your presentation. Leave some light on when using overheads or slides; speaking in a completely dark room may encourage listeners to fall asleep!

- *Seating:* Arrange appropriate seating.

Presentation Delivery Tips

How you deliver your presentation is often the key to success. The following tips can help you deliver your presentations more successfully:

- *Posture:* Stand relaxed and erect. Evenly distribute your weight, and don't shift back and forth from one foot to the other.

- *Movement:* Moving nearer the audience emphasizes main points. If you are using a lectern, move out from behind it occasionally. Avoid staying frozen in one spot or moving too rapidly or too much. Wringing your hands or keeping them in your pockets, "handcuffed" behind your back, or folded in front of you all detract from your presentation.

- *Orientation:* Keep your shoulders turned toward the audience to be considered more engaging.

- *Gestures:* Gestures are an important form of nonverbal communication when used appropriately. However, avoid quick hand movements, nervous tics, and other visual signs of anxiety.

- *Eye contact:* Make eye contact with the audience to reinforce your message. If the group is very large, focus on those immediately in front of you while you speak.

- *Volume, pitch, tone, and pace of speaking:* If your voice is too loud, you may sound pushy or overbearing; speaking too quietly signals sheepishness or nervousness. Strive to speak at a medium volume. The pitch of your voice is most effective when it comes naturally to you. Your voice's tone should change according to the situation; monotones bore audiences. A moderate pace is usually best. A quick pace generally sends the message that you are trying to get through too much material or are nervous. Speaking slowly gives listeners the opportunity to absorb your words, but some listeners may become bored or distracted.

Apply Your Learning 2.2

Please write all answers on a separate sheet of paper.

1. What is the first question to ask when developing a presentation?

2. Typically, which part of a formal presentation should you prepare first?

3. In which part of a presentation is it most appropriate to establish a bond between yourself and your audience?

For statements 4–7, write whether the action is appropriate or inappropriate when giving a presentation.

4. Emphasize main points by talking loudly.

5. If using a lectern, it is best to stand behind it throughout your presentation.

6. Try to make eye contact with the audience, or at least the people immediately in front of you.

7. Speak quietly to encourage people to stop shuffling papers or talking among themselves.

2.3 Listening

AFTER STUDYING SECTION 2.3, YOU SHOULD KNOW HOW TO:

♦ Focus on a speaker

♦ Interpret what a speaker is communicating

♦ Evaluate the message that a speaker is communicating

♦ Respond to a message when the speaker is done

♦ List techniques for active listening

Half of communication is listening. In this section, we'll look at ways you can develop your listening skills to become not only a better listener but a better overall communicator.

The Four Stages of Active Listening

Active listening involves four stages: focusing, interpreting, evaluating, and responding to the message heard.

Focusing. Focusing is the most important stage of active listening. It involves turning all of your attention to the speaker, putting all other matters aside, and concentrating on receiving the message. There are four aspects of this stage.

Decide to listen. Tell yourself that the goal is to concentrate on the speaker's words and message, not on his or her appearance, age, position, or speaking style. Listen without becoming defensive or critical. Be open to new ideas and concepts.

Create the proper atmosphere. Minimize outside distractions as much as possible. If meeting with someone one-on-one, choose a suitable location. Ask someone to take your phone calls and eliminate as many interruptions as possible.

Focus on the speaker. Establish and maintain eye contact with the speaker. Give him or her time to speak before you begin to question or comment. Concentrate. Listen to the content of the message. Avoid thinking about how you will answer when the speaker is finished. If you must take notes, keep them brief.

Show that you are paying attention. Use appropriate nonverbal signs to show you are receiving the message and paying attention. When necessary, ask questions to get more information. Ask the speaker to repeat parts of the message that you do not hear well or understand.

Interpreting. Use this stage to identify why the speaker is communicating. Determine the speaker's meaning, confirm that you understand, and show your understanding.

Keep from judging. Keep your personal biases out of the way. Don't judge the speaker by your personal standards or emotions.

Determine the speaker's meaning. The speaker may be making casual conversation, expressing an idea, wanting to trade information, or hoping to persuade you about something. Try to figure out why the speaker is choosing to discuss this particular subject at this particular time.

Confirm that you understand the meaning. Find out whether the speaker really means what you think he or she means. Do this by asking questions or paraphrasing the speaker's message. Continue questioning until you believe that you agree on what the message means.

Show that you understand. Use suitable words and body language (nodding, leaning forward, facing the speaker) to communicate your understanding.

Evaluating. The goal of this stage is to verify that you have reached a common understanding. You'll try to discover whether the message is based on facts or on the speaker's opinion. To do this, you will gather more information, decide whether it is genuine, make your evaluation, and express your opinion.

Gather more information. Concentrate on the speaker's tone of voice and body language. Concentrate, also, on what the speaker does and doesn't say. Read between the lines. Ask for details when you're given a lot of general information.

Decide whether the information is genuine. Try to separate facts from opinions and assumptions. Again, judge the message, not the messenger.

Evaluate the information. Decide what information you agree and disagree with as you listen. Form your own opinion based on what you have heard.

Communicate your evaluation. As you deliver your evaluation, support your words with body language. For example, if you agree with the speaker, you might lean toward him or her and look enthusiastic.

Responding. A listener responds to the speaker's message both while the speaker talks and after the speaker is finished. Once the speaker is finished, your response depends on learning what the speaker expects, considering your own time and energy, and deciding what to do.

Learn what the speaker expects. Ask questions to find out exactly what the speaker wants from the discussion.

Consider your own time and energy. Decide whether your plans and schedule can or should accommodate the speaker's request. Remember to consider your own objectives, time pressures, and energy level.

Decide what to do. Weigh whether it is possible to meet the speaker's expectations. Determine how to respond. Then, communicate your plan to the speaker. Finally, end the discussion with a positive concluding statement that reviews any actions to be taken.

Active Listening Techniques

Active listeners use a variety of techniques to aid comprehension.

Mirroring. Mirroring involves exactly repeating some of the speaker's key words. This shows the speaker just how a key word or phrase sounds to someone else. It also indicates that you are interested in the speaker's words and want to understand them.

> SPEAKER: This project is the most satisfying one I've ever been assigned.

> LISTENER: This project is the most satisfying one you've ever had? That's great!

Don't overuse mirroring. It can become tedious or sound as if you're talking down to the speaker.

Paraphrasing. When **paraphrasing,** you use your own words to restate what you think the speaker means and feels. It helps you clarify what the speaker is saying. It also helps the speaker, because your paraphrase reveals how his or her message sounds to others.

> SPEAKER: My deadline is next week, which means that I have a lot of overtime to work between now and then. And my baby-sitter just called and said she's sick, so she can't take the kids. I don't know what I'm going to do.

> LISTENER: You're afraid you can't finish the job on time because there's no one to watch the kids.

Avoid trying to put your own words in the speaker's mouth or trying to force your view of things on the speaker.

Summarizing and Self-Disclosure. **Summarizing statements** condense parts of what the speaker said and stress important points. Use them when you want to focus attention on a certain topic, show that you agree on specific points, guide the speaker to another part of the subject, and help reach agreement on specific points. Summarizing statements include:

- "If I hear you correctly, you want—"

- "What we agree on is—"

- "So you believe that what is happening is—"

- "As I understand it, your main idea is—"

Self-disclosure statements show the speaker how you feel about what has been said. When you report experiences or feelings similar to the speaker's, it shows that the speaker is not the only one to think or feel a certain way. This helps the speaker to feel understood and less alone.

- "That reminds me of something that happened to me—"

- "You're feeling the way I feel when—"

- "Other employees have noticed the same thing—"

Self-disclosure can also be used to communicate disagreement with the speaker's point or feelings without giving the speaker the feeling of being attacked.

Clarifying Questions. If you are listening actively, you may notice some statements that seem incomplete or do not tell the whole story. When this happens, ask **clarifying questions.** Sometimes speakers leave out important points because they are caught up in the emotions of the moment. Use questioning or clarifying statements to make the speaker's message clearer. Use either open-ended or specific questions.

Open-ended questions require more than a simple yes-or-no answer. Use open-ended questions when you want to begin a discussion, find out the speaker's ideas, examine a touchy subject, or avoid influencing the reply. For example, instead of asking, "Do you like the changes in the summer vacation schedule?" you might ask, "How do you feel about the changes in the summer vacation schedule?"

Specific questions seek additional information about unclear statements. They ask for details when the speaker has provided only general information. They usually begin with *who, where, when, why, which,* and *how many.* For example, if a speaker tells you, "The guest in 314 has been upset about absolutely everything," you might ask the speaker a specific question, such as, "What do you think caused the guest's dissatisfaction?"

Neutral Words. To encourage the speaker to continue talking, use neutral words that communicate neither agreement nor disagreement. Your purpose is to show that you are interested and want the speaker to continue.

- "That's interesting."
- "I understand."
- "Tell me more."

- "Well, let's talk about that."
- "I see."
- "This seems very important to you."
- "I'd like to hear your point of view."
- "Really."

You can encourage the speaker further by using **empathy**, which is the ability to see circumstances from the other's viewpoint. Your empathy shows the speaker that you are a willing and understanding listener who can personally relate to his or her experiences and feelings. It shows that you are attentive and interested, and it tells the speaker that you want to establish a good relationship.

Apply Your Learning 2.3

Please write all answers on a separate sheet of paper.

1. What are the four stages of active listening?

2. What does it tell a speaker when you mirror her words?

3. Which active listening technique is exemplified by the statement "So, if I understand you correctly, you'd like—"?

4. What is the primary difference between specific questions and open-ended questions?

5. Which of the following steps is *not* part of the focusing stage of active listening: decide to listen, create the proper atmosphere, determine the speaker's meaning, focus on the speaker?

6. What does it mean to have empathy for a speaker?

2.4 Business Writing

AFTER STUDYING SECTION 2.4, YOU SHOULD KNOW HOW TO:

♦ Explain the importance of good writing

♦ Describe the guidelines for better business writing

♦ List basic business writing rules

♦ Write a standard business memo

♦ Write a standard business letter

You may think that there's little point in spending much time on the subject of business writing. After all, everybody can write, right? Well, yes. . . and no. While most of us can easily dash off a grocery list or an e-mail to a friend, business writing is one of the most difficult forms of communication for anyone to master.

Everyone in business—especially in supervisory or management roles—must know how to communicate effectively in writing. In fact, the importance of your writing skills will increase as you gain responsibility. For example, when you are a new hospitality supervisor, you will have to learn to write memos to employees, co-workers, and managers. In addition, your boss may ask you to investigate something and write a report summarizing your findings. And you will need to write clear, concise comments when evaluating an employee's performance or when filling out disciplinary action forms.

The messages or reports you write represent you and, to some extent, your management ability. Organized writing tells readers that your thinking is similarly organized. The opposite is also true. A poorly written and disorganized communication will tell the world that you are a sloppy, disorganized thinker.

In fact, your written words may represent you long after some of your spoken words are forgotten. Your memos in the general manager's files, for instance, can serve as lasting, concrete reminders of you and your abilities. Your strongly written reports may remind upper management that you are a capable supervisor who is worth promoting. It is important, then, to learn to write well and effectively from the beginning.

Business Writing Tips and Examples

Good writing communicates information or ideas as briefly as possible to intended readers. At the same time, it obeys certain rules of grammar, spelling, sentence structure, and punctuation. While it is not easy to write effectively, the task will be less difficult if you plan well. Planning also helps to clarify your thinking.

Write with your intended audience firmly in mind. For example, a memo to your staff about summer vacation schedules would be far more informal than, say, a memo to your boss's boss about next quarter's sales forecast. Know whom you are writing to, and gear your tone, language, and level of writing to your audience.

Know your objective. Know your topic and stick to it. Determining a particular purpose for writing will keep your thoughts and your writing clear.

Decide which essential information to include. This may involve some research. For instance, you may have to consult your files or speak to others in your department. However, you will do much of your writing without having to research. Determining exactly what you want to say will save time and effort developing material that is off-topic.

Decide how to present the information. The best way to do this is to make an **outline**, which is a list of significant points. But don't restrict yourself to the traditional *I., A., 1., a.* format you may use for school assignments. Business writing is more flexible. Think in terms of headings that summarize in three-to-five words the information you want to convey. Once you decide on your key points, feel free to shuffle them around to find the most logical—and, therefore, the most easy to understand—order.

For example, imagine you need to write a memo to room attendants regarding procedures for guestroom cleaning. After thinking about the tasks involved, you might decide to cover the following key points:

- Making the bed
- How final inspections are handled
- Dusting
- Vacuuming
- Replacing guest amenities
- Completing the necessary paperwork
- Common mistakes
- Bathroom cleaning tasks

You wrote down these points as they occurred to you. Once you are certain there are no gaps, you can go back and decide how to logically order them. In the process, you may decide to combine "dusting" and "vacuuming" in the same section. Maybe you will choose to put information about final inspections in a separate document altogether. In your first draft, neatness does not count. Because you are not restricted to a rigid format, you are free to shift information around, add and subtract topics until you have the most appropriate content, and revise as you deem necessary.

Traditional outlines have a reputation for being drudgery. In fact, they require you to plan the structure of your writing before you even commit a word to paper. A more free-form outline can actually make writing easier, allowing for creativity and revision without sacrificing logic or important information.

As your writing skills improve, your outlines may become briefer and easier to develop. You may modify them to your needs as you gain writing expertise, or you may modify them to fit each type of writing task. No matter how skilled you become at business writing, you should continue to prepare some sort of outline every time you start to write.

Use Specific, Active Language

Specific, active language creates strong images in the minds of your readers, helping your message to be understood as quickly as possible.

Specific language begins with concrete nouns. It is livelier and more specific to say, "The general manager met with four supervisors from our new Boise hotel" instead of, "The general manager met with people from Idaho." Note these additional examples:

GENERAL: Last week, the executive housekeeper hired three individuals.

SPECIFIC: Last week, the executive housekeeper hired two new room attendants and a valet.

GENERAL: Chris, the new supervisor, is interested in many things.

SPECIFIC: Chris, the new food supervisor, is interested in fishing, the martial arts, traveling, and camping.

Sentence structure also can help or hurt your message. For example, it is almost always better to use the active voice rather than the passive voice. Yet, writing in the **passive voice** is one of the most difficult habits for many writers to break. In fact, many even fail to notice when they write a passive-voice sentence. In the passive voice, the subject typically appears at the end of the sentence, receiving the action instead of doing the action. Passive voice sentences sound dull and boring. In addition, they often use far too many words, sounding self-important or bureaucratic.

In **active voice** sentences, the subject of the sentence does the acting. Such sentences are tighter, more powerful, using words economically to get to the point. They enliven every sentence and, therefore, your entire piece of writing.

PASSIVE: The decision was made by George to hire four more room attendants.

ACTIVE: George decided to hire four more room attendants.

PASSIVE: The reservation for the Thompsons' stay in the presidential suite was taken by BreeAnn.

ACTIVE: BreeAnn took the reservation for the Thompsons' stay in the presidential suite.

In those rare instances when the receiver of the action is more important than the doer, the passive voice is appropriate:

Lee's managing style was copied by many new supervisors.

The new hotel was opened by the company in May.

Use Plain English and Shorter Sentences

Some writers try to use complicated words to impress others. Generally, it is a good idea to substitute plain words for fancy ones. When writing, use the same types of words you use when you speak. Concentrate on informing your readers, not impressing them. Examples of showy words are listed below, with plain-English suggestions in parentheses.

- ameliorate (help, improve)
- ascertain (find out, learn)
- commence (begin, start)
- component (part)
- endeavor (attempt, try)
- facilitate (help)
- impact on (affect)

- optimal (best, finest)

- peruse (read, study)

- prior to (before)

- utilize (use)

In addition, use short sentences. A piece of writing is easier to read and understand if most of its sentences are short. However, not all sentences should be short, because that could be dull. Alternate long sentences with short ones.

How can you avoid long sentences? Begin by breaking the *and, but* habit. That is, break a single, long sentence into smaller, stronger statements by removing the conjunctions *and* and *but.* Consider the following example:

> Some writers try to use complicated words to impress others, but, generally, it is a good idea to substitute plain words for fancy ones. When writing, use the same types of words you use when you speak, and concentrate on informing your readers, not impressing them.

This is a long-winded version of the opening paragraph of this section. The fairly simple original sentences turned into complicated sentences with the addition of the words *and* and *but* in certain places. Reread this section's opening paragraph. Then reread the long-winded, rewritten version. Do you find the original, simpler paragraph easier to understand?

Inverted Pyramid

You may want to adopt the **inverted pyramid** style of writing. Reporters use this method when writing hard-news stories.

They put their most important information at the beginning and leave less-important details for the final paragraphs. The reason? Newspaper editors who are trying to make a story fit into an allotted amount of space don't have time to go through a story and take out words here and there. Thanks to the inverted pyramid style of writing, they can simply start cutting text from the bottom up until the story fits. They know the key information is safe at the top.

There is an added benefit to this style. Readers who have little time to read your entire memo or report will be able to get the main information they need, in the least amount of time. Get to the point as soon as possible, putting your most important topics and paragraphs at the beginning.

Topic Sentence

Make sure every paragraph deals with a single topic. Begin each paragraph with a **topic sentence**—or main point—that explains what the paragraph is about. A short, simple topic sentence is stronger and easier to remember than a long one. In fact, a lengthy topic sentence may blur the intended message, and effectiveness may be lost.

A short topic sentence helps both the writer and the reader. Using the topic sentence as a guideline, the writer can logically develop the rest of the paragraph. For the reader, a briefly stated topic sentence delivers clear, instant information. It gets immediately to the point.

Once you have written your topic sentence, turn to the rest of the paragraph. The remaining sentences should relate to and support the point in the topic sentence by providing detail or backup material.

Exhibit 1
Sample Memo Format

You may want to use the following sample format for memos that you write.

MEMORANDUM

TO: Your Reader

FROM: You

DATE: Today

RE: Subject

Paragraph 1: Contains a clear, direct topic sentence. This paragraph states why you are writing. It might also explain what you want readers to do when they finish reading.

Paragraph 2: Contains the most important proof or details supporting Paragraph 1. Alternatively, it may be about another subject entirely, presented with its own clear topic sentence.

Paragraph 3: Contains less important evidence or material, supported with less detail. Again, it may address a different subject.

Memos and Business Letters

Generally, memos communicate information within an organization. They may contain information from the general manager to every employee, summarize a supervisor's attendance at a convention, or offer an informal weekly report. Length will vary according to the memo's purpose. It is important, however, to keep the memo as short as possible. Be as clear, concise, and to-the-point as possible. (Exhibit 1 presents a sample format to use for your memos.)

Your tone may be friendly, informal, and casual when you are writing to co-workers. You will probably use a more formal tone when writing a cover memo for an important report or when writing to your manager. (Refer to the checklist in Exhibit 2 to help make your memos and letters the best they can be.)

Consider the following points when attempting to write an effective memo:

- The most important paragraph appears first.

- It gets to the point immediately.

- Its words and sentences are easy to understand.

- It is clear, direct, and compact.

- Its tone is appropriate for the intended readers.

- It uses language its writer probably uses when talking.

Business Letters. Like memos, business letters should be clear and concise. Many of the same rules still apply: use short sentences, begin each paragraph with a topic sentence, use active voice, and so on.

One of the primary differences is format. Business letters are written on company letterhead and contain: today's date, the addressee's name and address, a salutation ("Dear Ms. Pakula:"), the main body, and a closing ("Sincerely,").

Exhibit 2
Checklist: Is Your Memo/Letter Well-Written?

1. Is it organized well?
   - Did I write with my readers in mind?
   - Did I determine my objective before beginning to write?
   - Did I decide which important information to include?
   - Did I make an outline first?
   - Do I sort my ideas in a logical order?
   - Will my reader immediately know what I am writing about?
   - Does each paragraph contain a topic sentence?
   - Do other sentences in each paragraph support the topic sentence?

2. Is it clear?
   - Does it clearly communicate my message?
   - Do I use plain English?
   - Are my words specific? Do they mean what I think they mean?
   - Do I use concrete nouns, rather than abstract nouns?

3. Is it concise?
   - Do I use active verbs?
   - Are my words strong and to the point?
   - Do I use words both my reader and I understand?
   - Do I include only what my reader needs to know?
   - Are my sentences limited to three typed lines?
   - Have I eliminated unnecessary instances of *and* and *but*?
   - Have I used the inverted pyramid style of writing?

4. Is it accurate?
   - Is all the information in the memo/letter correct?
   - Do I use proper grammar, spelling, and punctuation?
   - Do I refer to dictionaries and grammar texts when I am uncertain?

5. Is it courteous and friendly?
   - Do I use positive expressions?
   - Is my writing free of bureaucratic, pretentious, and legalistic language?
   - Do I use words like "please" and "thank you"?
   - Is my tone appropriate?

Most business letters are written in the **full block** style, which means that paragraphs are separated by a single line space and are set flush with the left margin.

Conclusion

You will spend much of your time rewriting your memos, reports, and letters. Keep a dictionary and a grammar book at your desk, and refer to them often. The first draft of any communication will serve as the foundation for your finished product. You may go through a few revisions before you are satisfied with your message. This is normal; the best writers spend much of their time revising. Your time will be well worth it, however. More effective writing skills will help you now and in any position you may have in the future.

Apply Your Learning 2.4

Please write all answers on a separate sheet of paper.

For statements 1–5, write whether the answer is True or False.

1. It is important that all business communication be written in the same style.

2. Creating an outline is the best way to know who your audience is.

3. Once a manager learns the basics of preparing written communications, he or she should stop relying on outlines.

4. Everyone in business must know how to communicate effectively in writing.

5. It is almost always better to use the passive voice rather than the active voice.

6. Why are shorter sentences usually better than longer ones in business memos and letters?

7. What does the "inverted pyramid" style of writing refer to?

Quick Hits

Chapter 2

SECTION 2.1—STRUCTURE OF COMMUNICATION

- Successful communication requires that both the sender and the receiver understand and act on the message being communicated.

- There is no such thing as too much information.

- The best way to communicate more effectively is to ensure that the entire message is received, understood, and acted upon by both the speaker and the listener.

- **Upward communication** is communication with one's boss or other higher-level managers.

- Effective **downward communication** with one's employees helps managers identify potential problems, gain staff commitment, and gather information for making decisions.

- Effective **lateral communication** with other managers helps ensure that information will continue to flow your way and enhances your career opportunities.

- Barriers to effective interpersonal communication include: misinterpreting the message; the way we evaluate the sender; **projecting** our own attitudes and assumptions in the messages we receive; stereotyping; arrogance and superiority; defensiveness; inarticulateness; **hidden agendas**; status; distractions in the environment; the sender's and receiver's emotions; differences in backgrounds between the sender and receiver; poor timing; and personality conflicts.

SECTION 2.2—SPEAKING AND PRESENTATIONS

- Most formal presentations consist of an introduction, the main body, and a conclusion.

- The introduction should get the attention of your listeners, earn their interest, and communicate your purpose. The main body contains the important information, presented in a logical sequence. The conclusion summarizes the presentation.

- The first step in preparing a presentation is to decide what the presentation should accomplish. Persuasive presentations are used to convince an audience of something; informative presentations are used to explain a topic.

- The second step is to analyze the audience: who they are, what is important to them, why they need the presentation information, and so on.

- Visual aids can add substantially to a presentation if used properly. Use the most appropriate means—high-tech or low-tech—to deliver your message.

- Before beginning a presentation, make sure you have the necessary materials, including projectors and other equipment, flip charts, handouts, microphones. Make certain that appropriate lighting and seating is available.

- How a presentation is delivered may be as important as the actual content.

Section 2.3—Listening

- Active listening involves four stages: focusing, interpreting, evaluating, and responding to the message heard.

- Focusing is the most important stage of active listening. It involves turning all of your attention to the speaker and concentrating on receiving the message. There are four aspects: (1) decide to listen, (2) create the proper atmosphere, (3) focus on the speaker, and (4) show that you are paying attention.

- Interpreting is the stage in which listeners determine the speaker's meaning, confirm that they understand, and show their understanding.

- In the evaluating stage, listeners try to verify that they have reached a common understanding with the speaker.

- Responding occurs both while the speaker talks and after the speaker is finished. Once the speaker is finished, the response depends on learning what the speaker expects, considering your own time and energy, and deciding what to do.

- Active listening techniques include mirroring, paraphrasing, making summarizing and self-disclosure statements, asking clarifying questions, and using neutral words.

- **Mirroring** involves exactly repeating some of the speaker's key words. It indicates that you are interested in the speaker's words and are trying to understand them.

- **Paraphrasing** involves using your own words to restate what you think the speaker means and feels. It helps you clarify what the speaker is saying and reveals to the speaker how his or her message sounds to others.

- **Summarizing statements** focus attention on a certain topic, show that you agree on specific points, guide the speaker to another part of the subject, and help you reach agreement on specific points.

- **Self-disclosure statements** report experiences or feelings similar to the speaker's, helping the speaker to feel understood and less alone.

- **Clarifying questions** include **open-ended questions** and **specific questions**. Open-ended questions require more than a yes-or-no answer and are used to begin a discussion or avoid influencing a reply. Specific questions seek additional specific information about unclear statements.

- Neutral words encourage the speaker to continue talking.

- **Empathy** shows that you are an attentive and interested listener, and it tells the speaker that you want to establish a good relationship.

Section 2.4—Business Writing

- The messages or reports you write represent you and your management ability. Clear, organized writing tells readers that your thinking is similarly clear and organized.

- Good writing clearly communicates information or ideas, as briefly as possible, to intended readers.

- A free-form **outline** can make writing easier, allowing for creativity and revision without sacrificing logic or important information.

- Specific, active language will help to convey your message as quickly as possible.

- It is almost always better to use the active voice rather than the passive voice. In the **passive voice**, the subject typically appears at the end of the sentence, receiving the action instead of doing the action. In **active voice** sentences, the subject of the sentence does the acting.

- Substitute plain words for fancy ones. When writing, use the same types of words you use when you speak. Concentrate on informing your readers, not impressing them.

- Writing is easier to read and understand if most sentences are short. However, not all sentences should be short, be-cause that could be dull. Alternate long sentences with short ones.

- With the **inverted pyramid** style of writing, the most important information appears at the beginning of the document, rather than interspersed throughout or saved until the end.

- Begin each paragraph with a **topic sentence**—or main point—that explains what the paragraph is about. A short, simple topic sentence is stronger and easier to remember than a long one.

- Memos communicate information within an organization. Be as clear, concise, and to-the-point as possible.

- Business letters are similar to memos. One primary difference is format. Most business letters are written in the **full block** style.

- The first draft of any communication will serve as the foundation for your finished product. You may go through a few revisions before you are satisfied with your message. This is normal; the best writers spend much of their time revising.

Profile

Gina-Lynne Scharoun

Vice President, Franchise Services
Candlewood Suites

Gina-Lynne Scharoun got her first taste of the business world as a young woman who helped her mother care for several rental properties in their hometown of Stillwater, Oklahoma. "I started out by cleaning apartments and doing the books for my mother," Scharoun says. It was hard work, but Scharoun says, "I know how to work hard and I have a detail orientation."

Those two traits led Scharoun to Oklahoma State University, where she majored in marketing and minored in management. During her time at OSU, Scharoun earned scholarship money by winning the Miss Oklahoma pageant and serving as Miss Oklahoma from 1991 to 1992. She also received an academic scholarship and was named the university's Outstanding Woman Graduate of 1993.

Because so many of the people she met in association with the Miss Oklahoma pageant were bankers, she considered making banking her career. "After a few years, I realized banking wasn't exciting enough or fast-paced enough. I wanted to use my creativity and management skills." That desire eventually led her to the hospitality industry.

"I was interviewing in other industries when a friend recommended I contact Jack DeBoer, who was starting a new hotel company." Even though she had no previous hotel work experience, Scharoun wrote a letter to DeBoer, a hotel entrepreneur who had established a national reputation as the founder of Residence Inn and Summerfield Suites. DeBoer was impressed. Although he didn't have a specific position in mind for her, DeBoer told Scharoun he wanted her to join the team at Candlewood Suites, his new, mid-priced, extended-stay brand.

She began by learning about site selection, market feasibility, and franchising. Soon she was promoted to director of franchise development, overseeing a small staff with responsibility for franchise sales, services, and operations. In addition, she headed Candlewood's quality control and public relations departments.

"I love to be very busy, so I would go to all of the other departments and ask for additional work. I was learning the business by just going in and taking advantage of these opportunities.

"I can't imagine being a part of a more dynamic business than the hospitality industry," Scharoun says with enthusiasm. "It is constantly changing. As travelers' needs and wants change, we have to be able to react very quickly."

60

Team Building

Sections

3.1   Defining Teams

3.2   Stages of Team Development

3.3   Roles of Individuals

3.1 Defining Teams

AFTER STUDYING SECTION 3.1, YOU SHOULD KNOW HOW TO:

♦ Identify why hospitality oranizations have been adopting team building

♦ Explain the function of a team mission statement

♦ Describe how a code of conduct can increase the effectiveness of a team

♦ Identify the basic role of the team leader

♦ List factors to consider when assessing an individual's leadership potential

Business organizations have traditionally been led by top-to-bottom management systems that designed jobs for individuals. Managers and supervisors made all the decisions; employees simply followed orders. Hotel functions began with two divisions: the front of the house and the back of the house. From there, departmental boundaries were drawn, and standard operating procedures were set in stone. Today's team-oriented hospitality organizations have reengineered jobs to fit a new business environment, one marked by increased competition, rapidly changing market demands, and higher productivity and quality goals.

Triumphant Teams

Touched by Angels

Months after the hotel's new telephone system had been installed, few employees had learned how to transfer an incoming call directly to the appropriate person in another department. As a result, some incoming calls were bounced from one extension to another until someone happened to make the correct transfer. This created a poor first impression on prospective guests. In addition, meeting planners who experienced this treatment were left wondering, "How are they going to help me put this function together when they can't even transfer my call properly?"

A newly formed problem-solving team of administration employees, called "The Administration Angels," came to the rescue. The Angels conducted training sessions on all aspects of the new telephone system, coached employees in telephone etiquette, and made sure that all departments received updated lists of telephone extension numbers. The training provided by the Angels enabled employees to transfer incoming calls directly to the appropriate person. Callers now get "one-stop service," and their first impression of the property is one of staff friendliness and efficiency.

The old, top-heavy management system limited a hospitality organization's ability to make decisions fast enough to keep up with changing guest needs and expectations. Many hotels have turned to team-based decision making and problem solving to improve the efficiency and overall effectiveness of their organizations. Those organizations gave the responsibility for addressing critical issues, solving operational problems, and improving productivity to teams involving those employees who are closest to the problems and closest to the guests.

Types of Hospitality Teams

Team-oriented organizations support a variety of teams: departmental work teams, **cross-functional teams** (with members from several different departments), **continuous-improvement teams**, and **task-force teams**. Teams can be made up of members from a single department or from several departments. Teams can be temporary or permanent parts of a department, division, or organization. And team meetings can be formal and routinely scheduled or casual and scheduled only on an as-needed basis.

Characteristics of Successful Teams

The size of a team can greatly affect the quality of a team's efforts. Effective teams range in size from three to seven members. Managers or others attending team meetings as advisers or experts on specific issues related to the team's work are not considered members of the team. It may be helpful to limit the number of visitors for each meeting.

Three important characteristics of successful teams are:

- A team mission statement
- A team code of conduct
- Effective team leaders

The team mission statement and code of conduct encourage productive contributions from team members and foster a cooperative team spirit. A mission statement should guide the team in setting goals, establishing priorities, and connecting with the overall goals of the organization. A team's code of conduct states norms and rules for interacting. High-performance teams also have leaders with flexible leadership styles that meet the team's need for guidance and facilitate the members through the stages of team development.

Team Mission Statement

A team **mission statement** is a brief statement explaining why the team exists and how it contributes to the overall goals of a department or organization. A clear, well-defined mission statement rallies members around a shared vision of what the team stands for and strives to accomplish. The statement clarifies the direction of the team and suggests the type of work that lies ahead. The team mission statement also communicates the importance of the team's efforts. Exhibit 1 presents three levels of mission statements—a property-level mission, a departmental mission, and a team mission within that department—and illustrates how the three relate to one another.

One of the first tasks facing a newly formed team is to develop a mission statement. For task-force teams, the mission is simply a statement of what the team has

Exhibit 1
Three Mission Statement Levels

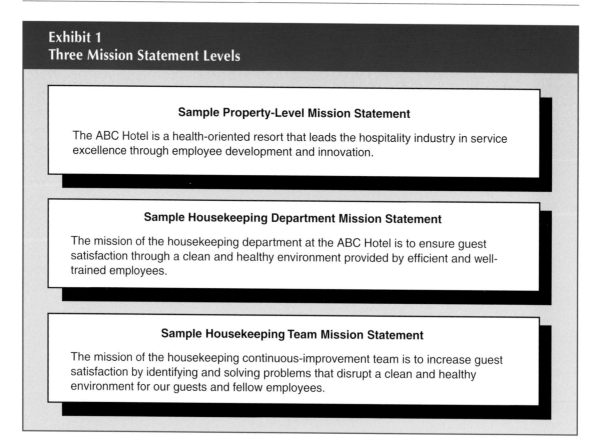

Sample Property-Level Mission Statement

The ABC Hotel is a health-oriented resort that leads the hospitality industry in service excellence through employee development and innovation.

Sample Housekeeping Department Mission Statement

The mission of the housekeeping department at the ABC Hotel is to ensure guest satisfaction through a clean and healthy environment provided by efficient and well-trained employees.

Sample Housekeeping Team Mission Statement

The mission of the housekeeping continuous-improvement team is to increase guest satisfaction by identifying and solving problems that disrupt a clean and healthy environment for our guests and fellow employees.

been formed to achieve. For example, a hotel might assemble a task force to draft procedures that will reduce the time department heads take to analyze and respond to weekly guest comment cards and other forms of guest feedback. The mission of this team is crystal-clear.

Departmental problem-solving teams and cross-functional continuous-improvement teams may find it much more involved and challenging to develop a mission statement. A mission-writing session is conducted either by the team leader or by an outside facilitator. One way to conduct this kind of session is to first **brainstorm** the elements of a mission statement. Generally, a mission statement should answer the following questions:

- What do we do?

- How do we do it?

- For whom do we do it?

The session leader can write each question at the top of a separate flip chart sheet and record the answers brainstormed by the team. With these sheets posted on the wall for all to see, individual team members may then write their own versions of a mission statement on flip chart sheets. These sheets can then be displayed to the group, and the leader or facilitator can help the team come up with a single statement.

Once a draft of the mission is written, the team can test the value of the statement by answering the following questions:

- Does this mission statement foster common goals within our team?

- Can anyone outside our team read this mission statement and understand what we do?

- Can we use this mission statement to evaluate our team's performance?

If the team answers "yes" to all three questions, the mission statement is complete. "No" answers to any of the questions mean the statement needs revising.

Mission writing is an important team-building activity. The interaction required demonstrates how important everyone's participation is to the team's success. In future meetings, if team members become confused or begin to lose their sense of purpose, the team leader can refocus their efforts by reminding them of the team's mission statement.

Team Code of Conduct

Effective teams adopt a **code of conduct** that members are expected to abide by. The conduct code establishes ground rules for behavior on the team and may also include guidelines for team meetings, such as requiring agendas and minutes. The code may include the team's expectations about the quality and type of group interaction. It may also indicate the attendance, level of participation, and preparedness expected of each team member. Exhibit 2 presents a sample team code of conduct. Some organizations may secure the commitment of team members to the ground rules of behavior by presenting the code in the form of a personal pledge or promise.

The code of conduct helps establish the team's norms. These stated norms must be positive and must contribute to the mission

> **Exhibit 2**
> **Sample Team Code of Conduct**
>
> As a member of this team, I agree to:
> - Focus on the mission of the team.
> - Use the team tools presented during training sessions.
> - Contribute to team discussions.
> - Listen to and consider input from other members.
> - Criticize ideas, not individuals.
> - Make decisions by consensus.
> - Confront, not ignore, conflict.
> - Arrive on time for all scheduled team meetings.
> - Keep to the agenda set for each team meeting.
> - Ensure that minutes are taken at each team meeting.
> - Complete assignments on time.
>
> Date _____
> Team Member _____
> Team Leader _____

and goals of the team, the department, and the organization. Norms that promote competition instead of cooperation, or suspicion instead of trust, will hurt the team's overall effectiveness.

The team must monitor itself to ensure that the code is followed. While at times the team leader functions as the disciplinarian, members of effective teams enforce the code themselves. The more actively a team participates in the development of a code of conduct, the more likely its members will be to police behaviors within the team.

Triumphant Teams

Selling Out for Service

Whenever guests who were part of a group stopped at the front desk for information about their group's reservation or room assignments, front desk agents had to retrieve the appropriate paper files from the group reservationist's office. If the group reservationist was not immediately available, they had to sift through the piles of paper on the reservationist's desk or ransack the file cabinets. Meanwhile, bewildered guests waited impatiently for answers to what they thought were simple questions.

A front office team that called itself "The Sellouts" tackled this as one of its first problems. The team discovered that, with the proper training, front desk agents could access the information in group reservation files using the front desk computer terminals. The computer system's operating manuals were finally put to use, and front desk agents were soon answering questions about group reservations without scurrying back to the reservations office. Groups at the property are now likely to be impressed by the staff's competent use of modern technology.

Team Leaders

The primary role of a **team leader** is to function as the servant, not the master, of the team. Team leaders must avoid any temptation to impose their wills on the team's efforts. Team goals should result from the decisions of the team, not from the needs, wants, or desires of the team leader. A team leader should assist the team in reaching the goals that it sets for itself.

Some team-oriented organizations have found that supervisors and department managers are not necessarily the best team leaders within their own work areas. Team members may feel that the presence of their boss inhibits their full participation in team discussions. However, since supervisors and department managers provide team leaders with essential support and necessary guidance, they should be actively involved in selecting individuals who will serve as leaders.

Once individuals are selected for team leader training, completing an initial evaluation of their own leadership skills can be enlightening and create an awareness of a need for further training and development. Exhibit 3 presents a sample team leader self-evaluation form that individuals can use to determine important areas that need their attention during their training sessions.

Exhibit 3
Sample Team Leader Self-Evaluation Form

Think about your leadership experiences and use the following scale to rate yourself on each of the items listed below:

1 point—Weak

3 points—Unsure

5 points—Strong

_____ 1. When speaking before a group, I can project my voice and display enthusiasm.

_____ 2. While listening to a speaker, I am able to observe other people's behavior.

_____ 3. I am able to understand both spoken messages and nonverbal gestures.

_____ 4. I am able to ask open-ended questions that encourage others to share their ideas, feelings, or interests.

_____ 5. I can use effective openers to generate a lively group discussion.

_____ 6. I can focus a group's discussion by discriminating between significant and irrelevant information and comments.

_____ 7. I can restate or clarify another person's ideas.

_____ 8. I can take an unexpected incident or event and use it to teach a concept.

_____ 9. I am able to give constructive pointers to individuals in a nonjudgmental manner.

_____ 10. When working with a group, I can share my own feelings about the topic under discussion.

_____ 11. I am able to elicit participation from most people in a group.

_____ 12. I have a sense of timing for pacing discussions and planning activities.

_____ 13. I can accept anger or criticism from a person or a group without becoming defensive.

_____ 14. I am able to help others comfortably display their emotions or relate their feelings.

_____ 15. I have a sense of humor and can laugh at myself.

Scoring Guide

65–75 points:
   You have solid team-leader skills.

55–64 points:
   You need to work on several areas to become a better team leader.

Less than 55 points:
   You need to enhance your skills before becoming a team leader.

Source: Adapted from Stephen J. Shriver, *Managing Quality Services* (East Lansing, Mich.: Educational Institute of the American Hotel & Motel Association, 1988), p. 218.

Apply Your Learning 3.1

Please write all answers on a separate sheet of paper.

1. Which of the following statements about teams is *false?*

    a. Teams can be made up of members from a single department.
    b. Teams are part of a top-to-bottom management system.
    c. Teams are responsible for solving operational problems.
    d. Teams can be temporary or permanent aspects of a department.

2. Effective teams range in size from _____ members.

    a. one to three
    b. three to seven
    c. eight to ten
    d. ten to twenty

3. One of the first tasks facing a newly formed team is to:

    a. select a team leader.
    b. pick a name for their group.
    c. create a meeting schedule.
    d. develop a mission statement.

4. A code of conduct can increase the effectiveness of a team by establishing:

    a. ground rules for behavior.
    b. when and where the meetings will take place.
    c. who the disciplinarian is.
    d. all of the above.

5. What is brainstorming?

3.2 Stages of Team Development

AFTER STUDYING SECTION 3.2, YOU SHOULD KNOW HOW TO:

♦ Describe the activities that take place during the forming stage of team development

♦ Explain why conflict happens during the storming stage of team development

♦ Identify the changes in attitude that take place during the norming stage of team development

♦ Describe the characteristics of a team at the performing stage

♦ Outline what happens to a team during the transforming stage

Just as there are stages in the development of an individual (infancy, childhood, adolescence, adulthood, maturity, and death), there are identifiable stages in the development of a group or team.

Within team-oriented organizations, team leaders and members are trained to recognize behaviors associated with each developmental stage. This training provides a team with a common vocabulary by which to (1) understand their own developmental process, (2) discuss issues that arise throughout the life of the group, and (3) better prepare the team for resolving conflict, building consensus, and making quality decisions.

While there are probably as many models of group development as there are team-building consultants, a basic model created by B. W. Tuckman has teams going through five stages of development: forming, storming, norming, performing, and transforming (see Exhibit 1).

Stage 1—Forming

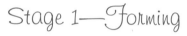

The first stage of team development, **forming**, begins when individuals become members of a group. Team members at this stage are anxious about their roles and responsibilities; they may be concerned about fitting into the group and about their ability to contribute to the team. Some of the questions that individuals may have at this stage include:

• Why am I on this team, and how will I fit in?

• What do the other team members expect from me?

• Can I trust the other team members?

• How will I benefit from working on this team?

• What can I contribute in order to be accepted by the others?

• What is really important to this team?

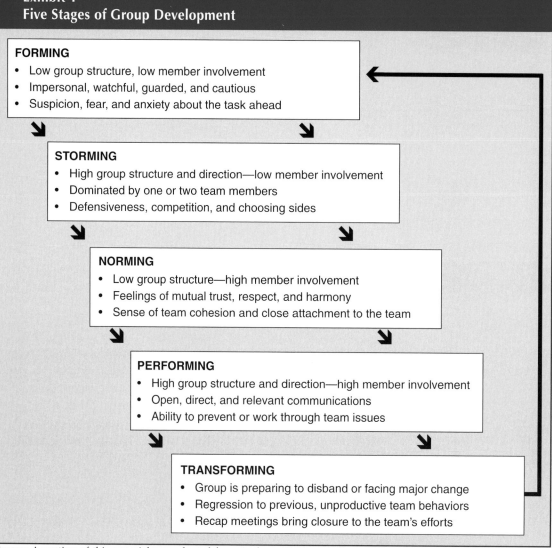

Exhibit 1
Five Stages of Group Development

FORMING
- Low group structure, low member involvement
- Impersonal, watchful, guarded, and cautious
- Suspicion, fear, and anxiety about the task ahead

STORMING
- High group structure and direction—low member involvement
- Dominated by one or two team members
- Defensiveness, competition, and choosing sides

NORMING
- Low group structure—high member involvement
- Feelings of mutual trust, respect, and harmony
- Sense of team cohesion and close attachment to the team

PERFORMING
- High group structure and direction—high member involvement
- Open, direct, and relevant communications
- Ability to prevent or work through team issues

TRANSFORMING
- Group is preparing to disband or facing major change
- Regression to previous, unproductive team behaviors
- Recap meetings bring closure to the team's efforts

Source: A portion of this material was adapted from Anthony R. Montebello and Victor R. Buzzotta, "Work Teams That Work," *Training and Development*, March 1993, p. 63.

- Are the team's goals the same as mine?

- What are the rules?

During this stage, individuals test various behaviors and depend on formal or informal group leaders to guide them into their roles as team members. Individuals enter a group with some tension, anxiety, and even suspicion about this new situation.

They think about how they will fit into the group and to what extent they want to belong. They are generally more concerned with establishing relationships within the group than they are on setting direction for the team or assigning tasks.

At this stage, members may be hesitant to participate in discussions. Communication is often polite and tentative, with

Triumphant Teams

Will the Real Las Vegas Style Please Set Up?

A meeting planner requested a Las Vegas–style banquet setup. The director of catering instructed the setup crew appropriately; however, when the banquet manager inspected the room, he was appalled. "This is not Las Vegas–style seating!" he exclaimed. The setup crew rearranged the room. Once again, when the banquet manager inspected the new setup, he cried, "This is not Las Vegas style!"

As a result of these communication problems, a team was formed comprising the banquet manager, the director of catering, the executive steward, and the supervisor of the setup crew. All agreed that banquet event orders contained information that was often incomplete, vague, and sometimes wrong. The team held brainstorming sessions and eventually produced a list of every type of banquet setup and the proper terms that should be used to describe them. Next, the team diagrammed each type of setup and distributed copies to every department involved in the sale or service of banquet functions. It soon became much easier for these departments to communicate effectively with one another.

Distributing the setup diagrams to prospective banquet customers helped ensure that hotel employees and prospective guests were speaking the same language. This eliminated unwelcome surprises and assured prospective guests that their expectations would be met.

participation limited to one or two of the more vocal members. Often, members seem to wish to avoid the work at hand and instead discuss irrelevant and nonthreatening issues such as the weather, news, or common acquaintances. During this stage, productivity is low and working relationships are cautious and noncommittal.

Members rarely act independently at this point. Many may be confused about what they are supposed to do and how they will accomplish tasks as a group; they therefore tend to depend on the leader for support and direction.

The leader's responsibility during the forming stage of a team's development is to help people move from acting as individuals to working together as team members. The team leader can establish direction for the team and clarify the roles of individual members by setting goals and determining methods for documenting progress toward those goals. The team leader can also present team tools, such as the code of conduct, that will help structure interactions within the group. The more the group participates in creating the code of conduct, the easier it is to manage the conflicts that naturally arise in the next stage of team development.

Stage 2—Storming

The second stage of team development, **storming**, is marked by conflict within the group. Team members push boundaries and challenge authority in an attempt to clarify the team's goals, values, and norms. Some of the questions that individuals may have at this stage include:

- Who has the most power to influence people on this team?

- Who's really in charge of this team?

- Why can't team members criticize ideas instead of each other?

- Do we need to reach a consensus on everything we do?

- How can we keep departmental politics out of the team process?

- How are we going to resolve the conflicts in this team?

At this stage, members may find that their initial expectations of the team are far different from the realities of trying to accomplish something together. Consequently, some may feel frustrated, angry, and disillusioned. Team meetings can become confrontational, with members blaming one another and acting defensively.

The leader's responsibility during the storming stage of a team's development is to manage, not suppress, the conflict. It is important for the leader not to take member rebellion personally. Conflict and tension may be essential in helping the group come together and to clarify the group's structure and goals. Conflict is neutral; how it is handled makes it either positive or negative.

Conflict needs to be managed so that it does not become counterproductive or destructive. The leader must redirect the energies of the team without smothering the initiative, ideas, and talents of individual members. Revisiting the team's mission, code of conduct, and goals can help reinforce the team concept. The leader should

also encourage open communication and interaction among group members. By providing positive feedback for productive behaviors and focusing the group on its task and goals, the leader will be better able to guide the team through the storming stage and further prepare members to work together to accomplish their mission.

Stage 3—Norming

During the third stage of team development, **norming**, team members learn to cooperate and support each other. The team establishes its own patterns of communication and behavior. In this stage, members learn that they can work effectively together as a unit. They are more tolerant of each other and accept the diverse perspectives and personalities that each brings to the group. Conflicts occur less frequently, and the team is better able to cope with differences of opinion.

Questions that blocked productive teamwork in the previous stages are answered. Goals are more clearly defined and a group structure becomes evident. Members recognize how each individual contributes to the group's efforts. Roles within the team are founded on the demonstrated talents and skills of individual members. As mutual trust and acceptance grow among the members, the team becomes much more productive and focused on task-oriented activities rather than on building relationships within the group.

The leader's responsibility during the norming stage of a team's development is to facilitate the group's decision-making and problem-solving activities. The leader blends into the group as an equal participant and, while not forcing direction upon the team, ensures that productive group

Triumphant Teams

Paying the Paid-Outs

In an effort to meet guest needs and expectations, hotel employees had made a practice of purchasing emergency items for guests. However, getting reimbursed for these purchases was like fighting City Hall. First, employees had to track down their department managers for signatures on paid-out slips. Next, employees had to walk the paperwork through the front office, where they were frequently told that the paid-out slip was improperly coded or that more details were needed before the paid-out could be processed.

Employees then had to return to their departments for the correct coding or appropriate details. Understandably frustrated, employees began to shy away from guests' requests that involved emergency paid-outs.

The accounting department's problem-solving team, which called itself "Accountants Have Better Figures," addressed the problem by designating one position in the accounting department to process all paid-out slips. The team made sure that the position was staffed so that employees could be quickly repaid when accommodating guests. Today, employees have no problem getting reimbursed, and they no longer avoid purchasing items to meet guests' needs.

norms and member roles are applied to the tasks at hand.

This stage can also see an increased pressure to conform. The danger at this stage is that the team might sacrifice valuable differences of opinion for the sake of team unity, a phenomenon called **groupthink**. This emphasis on conformity can stifle the team's ability to make good decisions and solve problems effectively. Acting to preserve its newfound harmony by avoiding conflict, the team might become too sure of itself. Members can become complacent and less open to innovative ideas about accomplishing team goals.

To avoid groupthink, the leader keeps the team focused on its tasks and facilitates open communication. Signs of complacency or rigid conformity should be met with prodding questions and suggestions that push the team to explore alternatives. The leader must encourage members to investigate all options before making decisions.

Stage 4—Performing

The fourth stage of team development, **performing**, finds the team functioning at its highest level of productivity. The team's norms become standards for evaluating the performance of individual members and the team's progress toward its goals. The focus of each member shifts completely from individual to group concerns, and members are more likely to phrase their concerns in terms of the full group: the word "we" replaces "I." Questions that team members may have at this stage include:

- What is the ideal way for our group to function most effectively?

- How can we best measure progress toward our goals?

- Are we constantly improving as a team?

- How can we be sure that we are making the best decisions?

At this stage of development, members come to value their differences more than their similarities. The team is eager for conflict of ideas rather than conflict of personalities. Members are able to speak freely and respond to criticism as honest feedback. Members know they can learn from one another, and they take advantage of opportunities to grow personally and professionally.

The leader's role at this stage is to ensure that the organization provides the resources that the team needs to accomplish its goals. The leader serves primarily as the communication channel between the team and the organization, with minimal interaction with the team itself. Many tasks previously performed by the leader are now the responsibility of other team members. The empowered team, with its rules, norms, roles, and goals, applies its full energies to the challenges at hand.

Stage 5—Transforming

The last stage of team development is often called the **transforming** stage because, at this point, the group is either preparing to disband or facing a major change in its mission, membership, or environment. Many teams have predetermined ending points. Even permanent teams have various types of endings, such as the period between completion of one task and initiation of another, or the loss of a team leader or a team member. Questions that team members may have at this stage include:

- What will the new team leader expect from us?

- Will we be as productive a team as we were before?

- How are we going to replace the talents and skills of the member leaving the team?

- How will the new team member fit in with our way of getting things done?

- How fast can we bring the new team member up to speed?

During this stage, members often regress to the unproductive team behaviors characteristic of the forming and storming stages of development. For example, when the composition of the team changes, the carryover members may lose enthusiasm and go back to depending on the leader for direction and motivation. Conflicts may arise again, and members may need to resume active roles in resolving them. Throughout the development of the transforming team, the members should keep in mind that while regressive behaviors will arise, progress back to the performing stage of development will probably be much faster than with the original group.

When a team disbands, it may be appropriate to have a recap meeting at which members can review their work and discuss their development as a team. This can bring closure to the team's efforts, provide members an opportunity to learn from their experiences, and may help motivate individuals to accept future team challenges.

Apply Your Learning 3.2

Please write all answers on a separate sheet of paper.

1. What are the five stages of group development?

Using the five stages listed in your answer to question number 1, fill in the following blanks:

2. At the _____ stage, the focus of each member shifts completely from individual to group concerns.

3. At the _____ stage, individuals test various behaviors and depend on group leaders.

4. At the _____ stage, members often regress to previous, unproductive team behaviors.

5. At the _____ stage, team members may push boundaries and challenge authority.

6. At the _____ stage, members learn that they can work effectively as a cohesive unit.

3.3 Roles of Individuals

AFTER STUDYING SECTION 3.3, YOU SHOULD KNOW HOW TO:

♦ Identify positive roles that individuals play in a group

♦ Identify negative roles that individuals sometimes adopt in group situations

♦ Explain how to manage individuals and specific behaviors to encourage team building

Training programs within team-oriented organizations often address the roles that individuals play in groups. Team leaders and members are trained to recognize behaviors associated with both positive and negative roles. This training enables a team to advance its development as a group, have better discussions at meetings, and resolve conflicts.

Exhibit 1 identifies six positive roles individuals may play in a group. Also identified are three dominant characteristics and some typical comments of individuals in each of these roles. As team members become aware of these roles, they can more easily recognize, appreciate, and encourage the positive roles played by other members of the team.

An awareness of positive roles helps a team to assess the talents of its individual members. It also alerts individuals to specific roles that they can comfortably adopt within the team.

Just as individuals play positive roles, they also play negative ones. Exhibit 2 describes five negative roles that individuals may adopt in group situations. When individuals play negative roles, their behavior decreases the team's productivity and may even prevent the team from reaching its goals. As team members become aware of negative roles, they are better able to recognize and discourage these behaviors.

Being aware of negative roles also helps a team predict potential conflicts within the group. Again, a team leader can ask members to rate themselves on how likely they are to behave in any of the ways outlined in Exhibit 2. Even if some members are not completely honest, the resulting information helps the leader identify the types of conflict likely to emerge in different situations. The exercise may also help individuals become more aware of themselves; some may recognize the roles they need to shed during the norming stage of development and may be more likely to control their own behavior.

When members can recognize negative roles that individuals play in groups, they are able to exert a friendly form of peer pressure to discourage unproductive behavior. For example, a "Dominator" or "Cynic" at a team meeting might represent a potentially explosive situation at any time, especially during the storming stage of group development. But if other team members use some gentle humor to prod the individual toward self-awareness, conflict can be avoided. When individuals persist in negative roles, discussion may be necessary.

Exhibit 1
Positive Roles Individuals Play in Groups

The Inquirer
1. Is concerned with the basics of reasoning.
2. Focuses the group's attention on the facts of a situation.
3. Encourages the group to interpret the facts in different ways.

Typical Comments:
- "Just how many times does this happen?"
- "Does this happen with just certain people or does it apply to everyone in that department?"
- "Does the problem arise because of the worker or because of the work method?"
- "Whose responsibility is this?"

The Contributor
1. Submits factual information.
2. Attempts to build a basis for sound decision making.
3. Offers considered opinions about facts.

Typical Comments:
- "I think our decision should be based on the figures Denise got from the accounting department."
- "Let's see if we can combine that idea with the feedback we received from the dining room manager."
- "I think that we should listen to the facts and discuss what we should do about this later."
- "Let me give you the feedback I got from maintenance and housekeeping."

The Elaborator
1. Translates generalizations into concrete examples.
2. Builds on the ideas of others.
3. Projects a picture of what might happen if a solution is implemented.

Typical Comments:
- "Let's imagine what it would be like if we tried that idea in my department."
- "What do you think other employees would say about that?"
- "How do you think that would work at the front desk?"
- "How would this affect our guests?"

The Reviewer
1. Summarizes the progress of the group.
2. Clarifies relationships among the ideas that are being discussed.
3. Identifies points that the group agrees upon.

Typical Comments:
- "Let's recap what we've done so far."
- "Let me list the points that we seem to agree on."
- "Matt, let me try to rephrase what you just said and combine it with points that Andrew brought up at the last meeting."
- "So far, we have identified five reasons why we need to do this. Let me list them and see if we all agree."

The Evaluator
1. Judges the group's thinking by its own standards.
2. Raises questions about facts and figures.
3. Explores the practical applications of proposed solutions.

Typical Comments:
- "Let's check these figures against the invoices in accounting."
- "Maybe we need a second and third opinion about this problem."
- "There could be another side to this story that we don't know about. We always try to get all of the information."
- "I think that we've tried things like this before and found out that we were on the wrong track."

The Energizer
1. Keeps the group's discussion moving along.
2. Stimulates new ideas that are pertinent to the topic.
3. Prods members to decide on a specific course of action.

Typical Comments:
- "Okay, we get the point, but what about this other idea?"
- "Let's move on to the next idea and come back to this later."
- "Let's wait on this point until we get the feedback we need from other departments. What's next?"
- "We've discussed this enough. Let's make a decision."

Source: Stephen J. Shriver, *Managing Quality Services* (East Lansing, Mich.: Educational Institute of the American Hotel & Motel Association, 1988), pp. 209–210.

Exhibit 2
Negative Roles Individuals Play in Groups

The Dominator
1. Demands attention and tries to run the show.
2. Constantly interrupts other people.
3. Imposes personal opinions on the group.

Typical Comments:
- "Now, I've had a lot more experience at this sort of thing, so let me tell you what to do."
- "The only way we're going to make progress here is by following up on my idea."
- "Hold everything, I know exactly what to do."
- "You're wasting everyone's time discussing these things; let's just do what I suggested earlier."

The Blocker
1. Is a frustrated dominator.
2. Repeats arguments and refuses to listen to anyone else's reasoning.
3. When ignored by the group, the person becomes stubborn and resists everything the group wants to do.

Typical Comments:
- "None of you really understands what I'm trying to say."
- "We went over that idea at the last meeting and I didn't like it then either."
- "Well, that's my opinion and I think it's better than yours, so listen more carefully to me this time."
- "Why are we voting on this issue? There's a lot more I have to say."

The Cynic
1. Scoffs at the group's progress.
2. Tries to start conflicts and arguments among members of the group.
3. Is always negative.

Typical Comments:
- "I don't care what you do."
- "Do what you want; management won't approve it anyway."
- "You're just wasting your time if you're going to do that."
- "This whole thing is stupid; nobody cares what the team wants to do anyway."

The Security Seeker
1. Wants sympathy or personal recognition.
2. Always has it worse than anyone else.
3. His or her personal experiences are always more important than anyone else's.

Typical Comments:
- "I wish somebody would have told me what to do when that happened to me."
- "I never know what to do when that happens in my department."
- "The situation is so bad in my department that even this solution won't work."
- "I always have so many things going on, I'll never have time to do that."

The Lobbyist
1. Always plugs pet theories.
2. Is only concerned with problems that involve his or her own department.
3. Will keep talking about his or her own ideas even though the group has decided to do something entirely different.

Typical Comments:
- "I've been pretty open-minded about this, but don't you think we're being unfair to the people in my department?"
- "That's okay if that's what you guys want to do, but I don't think you really understand my idea."
- "That's a good idea you have, but I think you forgot to consider the things that I said last week."
- "I agree with everything you say, but I just can't buy your conclusion."

Source: Stephen J. Shriver, *Managing Quality Services* (East Lansing, Mich.: Educational Institute of the American Hotel & Motel Association, 1988), pp. 211–212.

Beyond that, the leader and team must recognize when to give up and ask the individual to leave the team.

It is important to note that these roles are not personality types. One person can play several roles during a single team meeting. The topic of discussion, the stage of the group's development, and the influence of the team leader can all affect the roles that members may play at any given time.

Triumphant Teams

Housekeeping and Maintenance Finally Get Together

Housekeeping room attendants were frustrated by the lack of response to work orders that they submitted to the maintenance department. They often had to send two or three requests for each guestroom repair. Room attendants felt that maintenance failed not only to respond to work orders quickly enough, but, more importantly, that they also failed to understand how prompt repair work significantly increased guest satisfaction.

Managers formed a team consisting of room attendants and maintenance employees. The first problem the team tackled was the maintenance department's alleged slow response to repair requests from housekeeping. At team meetings, each department finally got the opportunity to hear the other side of the story. The team agreed on priorities for handling different types of work orders. It also instituted a reply system by which maintenance could keep housekeeping informed about the current status of work orders, including the status of parts or furniture that had to be ordered. In addition, maintenance formed a "Do It Now" Squad that consisted of maintenance workers with moveable carts stocked with parts and tools for most minor repair work. The housekeeping and maintenance departments are no longer at odds with each other because the team opened the communication channels between the two.

Apply Your Learning 3.3

Please write all answers on a separate sheet of paper.

1. Name four of the six positive roles that individuals play in a group.

2. Name three of the five negative roles that individuals play in a group.

3. An awareness of positive roles helps a team to assess the:
   a. influence of the team leader.
   b. talents of its individual members.
   c. reliability of their group decisions.
   d. none of the above.

For statements 4–6, write whether the answer is True or False.

4. One person can play several roles during a single team meeting.

5. Negative and positive roles are considered personality types.

6. When individuals play negative roles, they increase the team's productivity.

Quick Hits

Chapter 3

SECTION 3.1—DEFINING TEAMS

- A team **mission statement** explains why the team exists and how it contributes to the overall goals of a department or organization.

- A **code of conduct** establishes ground rules for team behavior and may also include guidelines for team meetings, the team's expectations about the quality of group interaction, and the attendance, level of participation, and preparedness expected of each member.

- The basic role of a **team leader** is to assist the team in reaching the goals that it sets for itself.

- Some factors to consider when assessing an individual's leadership potential include group speaking ability, listening skills, message comprehension, a sense of humor, and the ability to give constructive pointers and elicit participation from group members.

SECTION 3.2—STAGES OF TEAM DEVELOPMENT

- The five stages of group development are **forming, storming, norming, performing,** and **transforming.**

- **Forming** begins when individuals become members of a group; during this stage, members test various behaviors and depend on group leaders to guide them in their new roles.

- The second stage, **storming,** is marked by conflict within the group; team members push boundaries and challenge authority in an attempt to clarify the team's goals, values, and norms.

- Team members learn to cooperate and support each other during the **norming** stage; they also establish their own pattern of communication and behavior and learn that they can work together effectively as a unit.

- The **performing** stage finds the team functioning at its highest level of productivity; the team's norms become standards for evaluating the performance of individual members and the team's progress toward its goals.

- The last stage is often called the **transforming** stage because at this point, the group is either preparing to disband or facing a major change in its mission, membership, or environment; during this stage, members often regress to the unproductive team behaviors characteristic of the forming and storming stages of development.

SECTION 3.3—ROLES OF INDIVIDUALS

- The six positive roles that individuals may play in a group are The Inquirer, The Contributor, The Elaborator, The Reviewer, The Evaluator, and The Energizer.

- An awareness of positive roles helps a team to assess the talents of its individual members. It also alerts individuals to specific roles they can comfortably adopt within the team.

- The five negative roles that individuals may play in a group are The Dominator, The Blocker, The Cynic, The Security Seeker, and The Lobbyist.

- When individuals play negative roles, their behavior decreases the team's productivity and may even prevent the team from reaching its goals. Being aware of negative roles also helps a team predict potential conflicts.

- When members can recognize negative roles that individuals play in groups, they are able to exert a friendly form of peer pressure to discourage unproductive behavior.

- Positive and negative roles are not personality types; one person can play several roles during a single team meeting.

Profile

Erika Alexander
Vice President
TownePlace Suites by Marriott

I f she had not dragged herself out of bed one Saturday morning to attend a college career forum 10 years ago, Alexander's life might well be quite different. A recruiter's presentation about opportunities with Marriott intrigued her, and she stayed to talk. Today, she is brand vice president for TownePlace Suites.

"I had a great experience going through the interviewing process, learning about the hospitality industry and Residence Inn," she recalls.

Although Alexander's career has revolved around the extended-stay segment, she has yet to lose interest. Instead, her enthusiasm for the segment has intensified. She believes the extended-stay brand complements her own temperament toward serving others, gained from her family. "My parents are generous, loving, good people, and that has helped to spur my interest in the service industry. I always had this deep, personal desire to make my parents proud because I know they value these sorts of things, and it's something that I've carried with me. What is so special about extended stay is our ability to create and to foster relationships with our customers."

Alexander started as an account manager and worked her way up to director of sales and general manager for various Residence Inn properties. By 1995, she had joined the brand's corporate management division, and was part of a four-person team that developed the business case for TownePlace Suites, a moderately priced extended-stay brand. Alexander became the brand's director in 1997, shortly after the first TownePlace Suites opened in Newport News, Virginia. Her work focused on projects, such as creating guest satisfaction systems and pricing studies. Her responsibilities broadened to encompass overall strategic development when she was promoted to brand vice president in August of 1999.

As the brand's champion and leader, Alexander believes her role is to help her people achieve their goals. It's a philosophy she practices in both her personal and professional life. "Friends help friends achieve what they didn't think they had the capacity to do. And as leaders in any business, we ought to inspire people to do what they might not think they have the capacity to do."

This article is excerpted with permission from Lodging magazine.

Career Development

Sections

4.1 Self-Assessment

4.2 Self-Marketing and Personal Promotion

4.3 Interviewing

4.4 Responding to Job Offers

4.5 Lifelong Learning

4.1 Self-Assessment

AFTER STUDYING SECTION 4.1, YOU SHOULD KNOW HOW TO:

♦ Identify your strengths

♦ Examine your weaknesses

♦ Identify your interests

♦ Examine your values

♦ Identify sources of information on organizations and positions

Career planning begins with the question, "What do I know about myself?" While short and simply worded, the answers will provide the foundation for the remainder of the career-planning process. The answers will also reveal your strengths, weaknesses, interests, and values. The time and effort invested in working through self-assessment issues can help you make sense of the answers to the remaining questions.

Strengths

In Year One of this program, you learned how to analyze your strengths by creating a list of things you are proud to have accomplished. In the past year, you have probably gained several new strengths: skills learned during internships, new classes taken, greater accomplishments in extracurricular activities. Set aside time at least twice each year to revisit your list and add items to it. Exhibit 1 presents a form that you used in Year One to help you rate yourself with regard to a number of skills and personal qualities.

After you create your list of accomplishments and rate your skills and personal qualities, match your strengths (those skills and qualities you rated as 4 or 5 in Exhibit 1) with your list of accomplishments. For example, if you gave yourself a 5 in self-management, you might match this to the accomplishment that you have a perfect attendance record at work. With this process, you are in essence documenting your strengths. If someone asks you, "Why do you consider X a strength?" or "In what ways have you used this strength in the past?" you will have a ready list of examples to share.

This documentation should be a source of self-esteem and confidence for you. Later, when you use this documentation in résumés, job search correspondence, and interviews, it also helps potential employers decide whether to extend job offers to you.

Weaknesses

It's also important to review your list of weaknesses. Any skill or quality that earned a 1, 2, or 3 in Exhibit 1 is an area that could use improvement. Pay especially close attention to those weaknesses for which you

Exhibit 1
Self-Rating Tool

Key: 5 = Strongest   1 = Weakest

Basic Skills							Hospitality/Technical/Other					
Reading	1	2	3	4	5		Complaint/Conflict Management	1	2	3	4	5
Writing	1	2	3	4	5		2nd Language (or more)	1	2	3	4	5
Listening	1	2	3	4	5		Hospitality Technical					
Speaking	1	2	3	4	5		(that is, food prep, hotel					
Math	1	2	3	4	5		operations, etc.)	1	2	3	4	5
Computer Literacy	1	2	3	4	5		**Personal Qualities**					
Thinking Skills							Work Ethic	1	2	3	4	5
Creative Thinking	1	2	3	4	5		Self-Esteem	1	2	3	4	5
Critical Thinking	1	2	3	4	5		Sociability	1	2	3	4	5
Visualizing	1	2	3	4	5		Dependability	1	2	3	4	5
Knowing How to Learn	1	2	3	4	5		Initiative	1	2	3	4	5
Reasoning	1	2	3	4	5		Honesty/Integrity	1	2	3	4	5
Analyzing	1	2	3	4	5		Cooperation	1	2	3	4	5
Leadership/Management Skills							Persistence	1	2	3	4	5
Self-Management	1	2	3	4	5		Flexibility	1	2	3	4	5
Communication	1	2	3	4	5		Service Orientation	1	2	3	4	5
Teamwork	1	2	3	4	5		Attention to Detail	1	2	3	4	5
Leadership	1	2	3	4	5		Enthusiasm	1	2	3	4	5
Negotiation	1	2	3	4	5		Optimism	1	2	3	4	5
Problem Solving	1	2	3	4	5		Other _____	1	2	3	4	5
Listening	1	2	3	4	5		_____	1	2	3	4	5
Budget Management	1	2	3	4	5							
Decision Making	1	2	3	4	5							

Source: Adapted from *Life Work Portfolio*, developed by the National Occupational Information Coordinating Committee, Washington, D.C.

identified an action plan and have been working on improving. Compare your scores today with your scores a year ago and evaluate the progress you've made.

Weak skills and abilities are often fairly easy to identify and improve through books, courses, and specific training. Weaknesses in personal qualities may be more complex and difficult to recognize and fix. The services of a professional guidance counselor may be called for. Guidance counselors can help you use written, video-based, or computerized assessment instruments.

Individual counseling sessions in conjunction with these assessments may help you address any perceived deficiencies or weaknesses.

Develop action plans for continuing to improve any weaknesses. For example, if in Exhibit 1 you rated your computer literacy as a 2, your action plan might list the following improvement strategies and time frames:

Strategy	Time Frame
Software tutorial	November
Intermediate computer class	January

Interests

Although knowing your strengths and weaknesses is very important, it is not enough. Because they do not necessarily reflect your current interests, you should also identify the activities and experiences you find interesting. Your proficiency in any given area may be a result of past interests that have little connection to your present ones.

Review your accomplishments and strengths, focusing on those things you like to do the most in your free time. Then think about how they relate to the opportunities and demands of the hospitality industry. Interests that have links to hospitality industry careers include traveling, cooking, acting and performing, organizing events, participating in team activities, and learning and speaking other languages. While you are examining your interests, note areas of strong *dis*interest or *dis*like. Acknowledging an aversion (to, for example, food preparation or travel) is also important and useful in career planning.

Sincere interest and genuine enthusiasm are vital for balanced success in any career. They can provide the motivation for accomplishing great things. Don't worry about the practicality of your interests yet. Starting with what you really enjoy can lead to a variety of career possibilities.

Values

You should also examine your values during the self-assessment process. Carefully consider the relationships, objects, and activities that you value most highly and give special thought to how they do or do not fit into the workplace. Simply pondering the question, "What matters most to me?" can be very thought provoking. As you consider your values, keep in mind that it is usually difficult to find a career that easily and clearly provides everything you desire. There are typically some trade-offs. Exhibit 2 presents an exercise to help you clarify your preferred work environment and work-related values.

Your image of the future should be clearer after you go through the self-assessment step. Having detailed answers to the question, "What do I know about myself?" allows you to compare your strengths, interests, and values with the exciting and challenging careers and occupations of the hospitality industry.

Researching Organizations and Positions

In Year One of the *Lodging Management Program*, you learned how to research companies at the library, through information interviewing, and on the Internet. You will now learn about:

- Company-specific sources
- Career fairs
- Corporate presentations
- Internships and field experiences

Company-Specific Sources. It is inevitable that your search for information will narrow to specific organizations. Researching specific companies will help you determine if your interests, strengths, and values fit those companies. Also, it is common for an interviewer to ask applicants about their knowledge of his or her company. Researching a specific company may also

---

Exhibit 2
Values at Work

Read each pair of characteristics below. If you could have one but not both of these choices as part of your next job, which would you select?

Freedom and autonomy	vs.	Clear direction and close supervision
Managing/delivering service	vs.	Creating a tangible product
Managing a crisis	vs.	Planning a strategy
Success measured by earnings, position, promotions	vs.	Success measured by balance of career, family, friends, and social responsibilities
Owning my own business	vs.	Working in someone else's business
Working individually	vs.	Working with a team
Working in a large group	vs.	Working in a small group
High risk for high reward	vs.	More security with moderate rewards
Managing the details	vs.	Shaping the big picture
Working 10- to 12-hour days	vs.	Time for nonwork activities
Co-workers similar to me	vs.	Co-workers not similar to me
Multicultural diversity	vs.	Homogeneous environment
Stable long-term career with one organization	vs.	Fast-paced career with variety of companies
Consistency of daily work and pace	vs.	Variety of work and changing pace
Living in one area for an extended period	vs.	Frequent relocation, opportunity to move
Adherence to moral/ethical standards	vs.	Achieving financial results at any cost
Working Monday-through-Friday, few weekends, no holidays	vs.	Working when necessary, including weekends and holidays

If you could be certain of having only five of these characteristics in your next job, which would they be?

---

help you identify ways that you can add value to the company and may result in questions about the company that you'll want answers to during the interviewing process.

The quantity of information available on hospitality organizations is almost as varied as the companies themselves. If an organization is large, has been around a while, and is traded on a major stock exchange, there will likely be a great deal of information available in the library's business section or via online services. Publicly

held companies must make public annual reports that contain detailed financial information. Publicly held companies also will be listed in directories and may be written about extensively in books, journals, and magazines. Companies typically receive press coverage for extraordinary performance or events.

Privately held hospitality companies (not traded on stock exchanges) are not required to file annual reports. Information beyond directory listings (which typically contain the company's name, address, number of units, and so forth) is generally tougher to find for privately held companies. Examples of directories that may be useful when researching specific hospitality organizations include the following:

- *Million Dollar Directory*, published annually by Dun & Bradstreet

- *Directory of Hotel and Motel Companies*, published annually by the American Hotel & Motel Association

- *Chain Restaurant Operators Guide*, published annually by CSG Information Services

- *Directory of High-Volume Independent Restaurants*, published annually by CSG Information Services

Give yourself plenty of time to research. Sometimes it is difficult to find information for small or private companies. On the other hand, with large, publicly traded companies, you may face information overload and need extra time to sort through it all. Keep separate files for each organization.

Examples of company information to look for include the following:

- The mission statement, a brief company history, company values, and strategic objectives

- Key people in the company, who owns the company, and how it is owned (publicly or privately)

- What key services and products the company provides, brand names/product lines, and the locations and industry segments in which it does business

- The company's financial history and projections for future performance

- The company's major competition

- The latest news on the company (from trade press, newspapers, online services, and so forth)

Career Fairs

Career fairs present students with excellent opportunities to gather information and make personal contacts with a relatively large number of organizations in a short time. Career fairs are often sponsored by schools. Companies invited to a career fair set up table-top or booth exhibits and distribute information about their organizations while collecting information from students and other participants. To maximize the results you can obtain from participating in a career fair, use the following plan:

- *Before the career fair.* Before the career fair begins, find out which companies will be represented and learn all you can about them. Use the library, online services, and (if possible) visit one of each company's locations before the fair. Based on your self-awareness and what you learn about the companies, create priority lists and assign each company participating in the career fair a rank (for example, A, B, C) based on how attractive it seems. Dress as though you were attending a job interview. If you have a résumé, take copies with you. If you have to register for the fair, do so well in advance of the fair's opening time.

- *During the career fair.* Be sure to arrive early and attend any seminars that may be offered in conjunction with the fair. Start with your "A" list of companies (the companies most attractive to you based on your preliminary research) and begin to conduct abbreviated but enthusiastic information interviews with the representatives of each targeted company. Avoid long lines by shifting to "B" or "C" companies if necessary. You generally won't have much time with each company (usually two to three minutes). Ask each representative you speak with for a business card. It is also a good idea to stay until the end of the fair, as the lines often become shorter and opportunities for longer conversations with recruiters can occur.

• *After the career fair.* If companies are offering employment interviewing opportunities in conjunction with the fair, you may want to sign up and interview. If no interviews are offered, be sure to send thank-you notes to the representatives you spoke with, along with a request for more information and an interview (if appropriate). You should obtain business cards from company recruiters so you'll remember whom to contact.

Corporate Presentations

Corporate presentations are intended to help students learn more about the company—what it is, what it does, and why it would be great to work for. The presentations convey general background information about the company and give students opportunities for one-on-one contact with company representatives.

Corporate presentations are often formal, in which case you should dress as if

for a job interview, but some companies throw informal pizza parties and the like, in which case your dress can be more casual.

Strategies for maximizing results at corporate presentations are similar to those for career fairs, although you have fewer people to deal with: arrive early, dress appropriately, bring résumés, ask great information interview questions, collect business cards, and follow up.

Internships

The *Lodging Management Program* requires students to gain industry experience via internships. These experiences provide many potential benefits to both the student interns and the employing organizations. The employer usually gains an enthusiastic (albeit short-term) employee and the opportunity to evaluate the employee in a realistic work environment. For students, internships are excellent opportunities to learn what it's really like in the work world. Even when a student intern decides that a particular industry segment or employer is not a great career match, he or she is better informed on what direction to head next.

To reap the full benefits of an internship, ask your co-workers questions about the industry, their careers, and so on. A desire to learn and a strong work ethic can lead to a great internship experience. Perhaps the best way to get the most out of an internship is to be the type of employee you would like to manage.

Apply Your Learning 4.1

Please write all answers on a separate sheet of paper.

1. What are the four self-assessment issues to be considered when beginning your career planning?

2. What are some sources you can use when researching organizations and positions?

3. What is the purpose of a career fair?

Using the self-assessment issues listed in question 1, fill in the following blanks for statements 4–6:

4. Asking the question, "What matters most to me?" helps you to examine your _____ during the self-assessment process.

5. Creating a list of things you are proud to have accomplished is an excellent way to begin analyzing your _____.

6. The activities and experiences you prefer to do in your leisure time are good indicators of your _____.

4.2 Self-Marketing and Personal Promotion

AFTER STUDYING SECTION 4.2, YOU SHOULD KNOW HOW TO:

♦ Explain the importance of networking

♦ Begin making networking contacts

♦ Write a cover letter

Getting a job is a sales process. You are selling *yourself*. The "product" is your strengths, interests, values, and accomplishments and your targeted "buyers" are the potential employers. It is time to create a personal sales plan based on all of the marketing research you've already done. The key question is, "How will I get from where I am now to where I want to be?"

Networking

"Networks" are generally defined as interconnected systems. People form networks for sharing social and business information. Employment **networking** has been identified as the primary source by which most jobs are found—and gives you access to the "hidden job market." Approximately 80 percent of available positions are never advertised. Most employers prefer informal and personal methods of identifying employees, and believe personal contacts result in more in-depth, accurate, and up-to-date information. Networking does not eliminate the need to use other job search methods, but it will produce helpful referrals from approximately half of your contacts.

Getting Started. The way to develop your network is by talking to people. The networking process will allow you to tell people about yourself, enlist their support, and help you gather information about available opportunities. The discussion can be formal, such as a meeting at the professional's worksite, or casual, as it might be if you met an acquaintance at a party.

To build confidence and develop your networking skills, start with people you already know: family, friends, parents of friends, teachers, and former employers. People on this list whose work is different from your interests may be able to refer you to others. For example, your family physician or neighbor across the street may be able to provide several helpful referrals.

Be sure you avoid the following self-defeating perspectives and practices:

- *The "I need a job, not a network" perspective.* Networking is not intended to replace interviewing. Instead, networking enhances the selection and interviewing process. Why walk into an interview as a stranger, known only by a résumé and cover letter, when meeting and communicating with the recruiter in advance increases the likelihood of achieving your desired results? Networking is often the best way to reach employment decision makers.

- *Fear of rejection.* The risk of your request being rejected or ignored is a small price to pay for the benefits that may result from making one good contact. Most professionals know that the roles of information "gatherer" and "disseminator" have a tendency to switch back and forth over time. The person you approach for help today may be approaching you for help in the not-too-distant future. Therefore, many of the people you contact will be interested in establishing a business relationship.

- *Aversion to "manipulating" others.* The notion that networking requires you to use others, in a negative sense, is mistaken. Again, successful hospitality professionals recognize the importance of networking, and most like to be "well connected." As service-oriented individuals, most of them enjoy the chance to help others and know they can expect help in return.

- *The "they owe me" perspective.* Just because someone is a family friend does not mean he or she owes you a job or anything else. On the other hand, if approached with respect and courtesy, such people will probably help when possible.

How to Network. Determine the types of referrals you need—are you seeking information about career options or specific employers and positions? Start by compiling a list of initial contacts and the questions you would like to ask them, such as:

- How does one learn about job opportunities in this field? in this organization?

- What skills and experience do you look for when you hire?

- Can you suggest anyone else in the field I might speak with?

- Do you know anyone working in this field? May I use your name when I contact them?

- If you hear of an opening, would you please let me know?

So how do you begin a networking telephone call? If you are calling someone you have kept in touch with throughout the information interviewing stage of your job search, a good way to begin is to let them know you are about to graduate, or—if it's been a while since graduation—give them an update of how your job search is going. If you have developed a relationship with them over the past several months (or even years!), they will be interested in your news and will probably quite naturally begin talking about possible job openings or individuals who may be of help to you.

If you are attending an industry trade show or professional conference, don't let the fact that you're now actively looking for a job lead you into a social faux pas such as the following: "Hi, my name is Ted Johnson. I'm graduating soon, and I really need a job. Can I give you a copy of my résumé?" Even though you are looking for a job, you should

---

Exhibit 1
Additional Ways to Develop a Network

- Do an internship and use that opportunity to interview for information.

- Contact an organization's human resource department directly and ask for the name of someone who works in a department of interest to you.

- Chambers of Commerce, community service centers, and membership rosters of professional associations are sources for career-related information.

- High school and college alumni are an important resource. Meet alumni through on- and off-campus career events and social activities. Identify graduates in news articles and request information interviews.

---

call on the skills you learned when you were asking people for information interviews. Why? People are much more open to a request for advice or a future meeting than to a request for a job or for help in finding a job. See Exhibit 1 for additional ways to develop a network.

When you are at a social function and you want to make networking contacts, introduce yourself to someone—don't wait to be introduced, or for someone to approach you. Extend your hand for a handshake, look the other person in the eye, smile, and say something like the following: "Hello, my name is Joanna Rodriguez. I'm from Syracuse, New York, and I'm just finishing my studies at Brookstone High School." By telling the other person more than just your name, you are volunteering information that can help start the conversation. The other person will probably respond in a similar way.

Learn more about the individual's organization as well as his or her place in it. Stay clear of potentially troublesome topics, such as religion and politics, and don't launch into funny stories about the pranks you pulled during your high school career. In fact, it's a little risky to attempt jokes or humor of any kind during first meetings,

because what may seem funny to you may not be funny to others.

After you've spent enough time (perhaps 10 to 15 minutes) to have a meaningful conversation, you should try to further the relationship before parting. Asking contacts if you can call them in the near future will usually prompt them to give you a business card. This gives you the information you need to send your résumé and a cover letter to them. In the cover letter, remind them of how you met and inform them that you will call within the next few days to see if you can arrange another personal meeting.

Networking takes effort and practice. The good news is that hospitality professionals are sometimes more likely to extend an extra effort on behalf of a student, because they may see a bit of themselves reflected in the student or because they see the student as a potential protégé. Hospitality professionals, by the very nature of the business, enjoy providing service and exceeding expectations. Many of these individuals take great pride and satisfaction in assisting the career development of others. It's good for them and the industry as a whole.

Pay attention to the general media and hospitality trade press to learn who is receiving publicity and awards. If you spot an industry award recipient employed by a targeted employer, why not drop a note of congratulations and a request for advice? By following up on these and other leads, you can learn a great deal and improve your employment prospects.

Modern technology has offered the ultimate in networking via the Internet. Be aware of the international, cost-effective communications capabilities that exist via the World Wide Web. The possibility of reaching anyone almost anywhere is becoming a reality, and access to people and information online creates a previously unheard of potential for employment networking.

Cover Letters

A noted career and job search authority suggests that the purpose of cover letters is "to communicate a specific personalized message to a particular employer, answering the most fundamental employment question of all: 'Why should I hire you?'"

Determining what to write can be intimidating. There are many effective strategies and techniques you can use to apply for employment, express gratitude, and accept or reject job offers. Your written correspondence should communicate why you are writing, how you will add value to an organization, and specify how you plan to follow up.

Professionals suggest five rules for writing effective cover letters:

- *Rule 1: Address it to a particular person by name.* Target each cover letter to a specific person. Call the company to obtain the correct name and title if necessary.

- *Rule 2: Communicate something personal.* One of the most effective strategies is to include the name of the person who referred you; this lets the recipient of your letter know of a common acquaintance. You might also, for example, mention that you noticed that the company recently received positive publicity in the trade or general press, or that you recently learned of a new company unit opening near your home.

- *Rule 3: Answer the question, "Why should I see you?"* A common error is to express *your* needs rather than convey what you will do for the employer. Keep the employer's perspective in mind at all times. The decision to hire you will be based on the value (the skills and ability to produce results) you will add to the organization, not on your need for a job or rent money. The degree of assertiveness you use in pointing out the value you can add must be balanced against the risk of sounding overconfident to the reader. Research and networking should help you decide how far to go in a cover letter.

- *Rule 4: Use their language.* Your knowledge of the industry and the specific company you are writing to should guide your choice of words. If you desire to become an "associate" or "cast member" (because this terminology applies to a targeted organization), then say so.

- *Rule 5: Ask for the interview.* Do not write something like, "Hope to hear from you soon." Request a personal interview. Employers expect you to suggest a time *and* volunteer to confirm the arrangements. Requesting the interview and stating your intention to call and follow up on the request do not guarantee an interview. However, failing to do so substantially increases the likelihood that you will be ignored. Without some sort of follow-up, you can't even be sure your letter reached the intended recipient.

Appropriate print and paper quality and color are just as important for your business correspondence as for your résumé. In fact, ideally the paper and typeface used for your business correspondence should match that used for your résumé. Think twice before using a creative or bold approach.

Be sure to keep a copy of each letter you send, and deliver on any promises you make to follow up. Failure to call when you said you would will not be viewed favorably. Keep this in mind when sending out a quantity of cover letters and résumés. It may be a better strategy to stagger the mailing—and therefore the follow-up phone calls you'll have to make—to ensure that you are able to call everyone as promised.

Beware of copying phrases and formats from other people's cover letters. Consider what an employer might think who receives copies of virtually the same letter from different students at the same school. Use formats and samples (like those in Exhibit 2) as illustrations and guidelines only. Any letter should be a direct and unique reflection of the person signing it. To do otherwise is to risk the positive impact of the letter.

Apply Your Learning 4.2

Please write all answers on a separate sheet of paper.

1. What are the four listed self-defeating perspectives and practices associated with employment networking?
2. What are some questions you might want to ask a networking contact?
3. When you are at a social function and you want to make networking contacts, how should you introduce yourself to someone?
4. What is the purpose of a cover letter?
5. What are the rules for writing a good cover letter?

Exhibit 2
Sample Cover Letter Format/Sample Cover Letter

Your Address	4321 Pine Street Anysuburb, USA 54321 January 10, 20XX
Date	
Employer's Address	Ms. Terry Hogan, Director Voguefoods, Inc. 1234 East Cedar Street Anymetropolis, USA 12345
Dear _____:	Dear Ms. Hogan:
First paragraph: State why you are writing, explain the type of work you are interested in, and indicate how you learned about the employer or the specific job opening.	Recently I spoke with your director of food services, Gordon Burger. He informed me of your intention to implement a more health-conscious food program at Voguefoods, Inc., and suggested that I contact you. My credentials in the food science industry would enable me to successfully promote the growth of such a program.
Second paragraph: Be specific about why you are interested in the position. Briefly summarize some of your strongest qualifications to do the work. Remember to consider this from an employer's point of view. Show what you have to offer the employer, don't merely daydream about what the employer can offer you.	In the spring of next year, I will be graduating from Lincoln High School. In addition to my diploma I will have two years of work experience in the field of food service. This work experience has familiarized me with food costs, menu planning, and food administration.
Closing paragraph(s): Refer the reader to the résumé (or application form) you are enclosing. Declare your interest in an interview and offer to provide more information upon request. Invite a response by asking a question or indicating what follow-up you have in mind.	The Educational Institute of AH&MA recently recognized me for my achievements in hospitality management with the national HBA certificate. I would like the opportunity to meet with you and discuss how I might be able to promote the growth of a nutritional food program at Voguefoods. I will call you on Monday, January 17, to determine your interest and, if appropriate, arrange for a personal meeting.
	I am looking forward to meeting with you.
Sincerely, [signature] Your Name (Typed) Enclosure	Sincerely, [signature] Pat Smith Enclosure

4.3 Interviewing

AFTER STUDYING SECTION 4.3, YOU SHOULD KNOW HOW TO:

♦ Prepare for interviews

♦ Anticipate interview questions

♦ Prepare for behavior-based interviews

♦ Recognize illegal interview questions

♦ Question interviewers

♦ Write a thank-you letter

♦ Prepare for a second interview

Prepare for an Interview

Keep in mind the goals you want to accomplish before and during an interview:

- Find out what the employer is looking for in new hires for the position you've targeted.

- Clearly present what you can add to the company (from their perspective) by being ready to answer questions about your qualifications and experiences.

- Collect more information about the company during the interview to help you evaluate whether this company is right for you.

Exhibit 1 lists a few fundamentals to keep in mind as you prepare to interview.

Before you interview, you should find out as much as you can about the company and the specific job you're interviewing for. Then, you can focus on presenting the ways that your strengths, values, and interests will fit the job.

It is also useful to find out more about the specific interviewer if you can. The correct spelling and pronunciation of the interviewer's name, his or her background with the company or industry, and his or her interviewing style are examples of useful information you should seek. Question classmates who've recently interviewed, teachers at your school, and other contacts to be sure you know all you can before you sit down to interview. Your goal should be to never walk into an interview as a stranger.

Anticipating Interview Questions

Put yourself in the position of the interviewer and think carefully about all you've learned up to now (about yourself; the hospitality industry; and the specific recruiter, company, and job you're interested in), then try to anticipate the questions you will be asked. Some recruiters believe that all interviewing questions flow from three core questions: Why should I hire you? Will you fit in my organization? and Are you

Exhibit 1
Interview Preparation Fundamentals

1. *Be on time.*

   A sure way to upset an interviewer is to show up late for (or, worse yet, cancel) an interview. If you are unfamiliar with the interview location, check it out in advance. Plan for traffic and allow extra travel time. You should arrive at least ten minutes before the interview.

2. *Your appearance matters.*

   A properly fitting, comfortable business suit (this goes for women as well as men) is usually best. Your research on the company should help you figure out its expectations. Jewelry, cologne, hair style, and facial hair should usually be kept conservative. It is suggested that you dress so that you feel successful. As with résumés, being creative with your personal appearance may backfire—the interviewer will probably remember you if you show up with purple hair, but that does not mean you will get a job offer.

3. *A positive attitude may be the most important thing to bring.*

   Leave behind thoughts about bad luck, horrible bosses, crazy teachers, the terrible morning you had, or any other negatives when you head out to interview. Keep your focus on present and future opportunities, not past problems. Strive always to present yourself in the most favorable and positive light possible.

4. *Bring a pen, paper, extra résumés, and your reference list.*

   The pen and paper will be useful for making notes either during or (more likely) right after the interview. You may also be well served by jotting down a few key questions you want to ask the interviewer. The extra résumés and list of references need not be shared unless they are requested.

5. *Practice interviewing with friends, family, and others.*

   Interview with anyone who is willing to help you sharpen your interviewing skills. If possible, have someone videotape your mock interview; this is a great way to analyze yourself in action.

interested in and able to effectively do the job? Armed with this information, you can practice and improve your ability to interview effectively. A list of more specific interview questions is included in Exhibit 2.

Avoid memorizing your answers. Memorized answers usually end up sounding rehearsed and insincere. Also, memorizing can result in total confusion if you lose your place during your answer. Create brief keyword outlines of the points you want to make. Refine these outlines as you practice interviewing. Your confidence level will grow as you practice.

Preparing for Behavior-Based Interviews

Many hospitality employers use an interviewing technique that is intended to determine how you have behaved under specific circumstances in the past. This is known as **behavior-based interviewing.** These employers believe that the best predictor of your future behavior is your past behavior. Having done well under specific conditions in your past is considered a good indicator of your potential for succeeding

Exhibit 2
Sample Interview Questions

- Tell me about yourself.
- What do you really want to do in life?
- Why should I hire you?
- Where do you see yourself in five years? How will you get there?
- How much will you be making in five years? ten years?
- What are your strengths? weaknesses?
- What motivates you?
- Would you work if you were independently wealthy?
- What's the funniest thing that ever happened to you?
- If you could, how would you change your past?
- Describe your perfect job.
- Why have you chosen this career/job?
- Describe your best/worst boss.
- Do you prefer to work alone or on a team?
- Do you have a geographical preference?
- Are you willing to relocate?
- What was the best/worst thing about your last job?
- What did you learn in school that will help you on the job?
- How do you feel about your grades?
- How did you spend your school vacations?
- Describe your best/worst teacher.
- Describe your favorite/least favorite course.
- Tell me about your extracurricular involvement.
- Have you ever quit a job or been fired? Why?
- Who has been the most influential person in your life?
- What makes you angry? How do you express your anger?
- How would your last boss describe you?
- What books and magazines do you read?
- What sort of person annoys you?
- What are your interests outside of work?
- How do you handle stress?
- If you were hiring a person for this job, how would you make your decision?
- How much do you know about our company?
- Why are you interviewing for this position?
- If you joined our company, what is the first thing you'd recommend we change?
- If you joined our company, what is the one thing you'd recommend we never change?
- If you joined our company, what would you plan to accomplish during your first week? day? hour?
- Where else are you interviewing?
- What do you think determines a person's progress in our company?
- How will you decide which company to go to work for?
- Was there anything that you were afraid I was going to ask you today? Why?

in the future (given similar conditions). Exhibit 3 includes sample behavior-based interview questions.

The types of behavior-based interview questions you will be asked are determined by the requirements of the job you are seeking. The employer analyzes the job and determines what qualities and skills are needed for success. During your research, you should also analyze the job. You may then ascertain the skills and qualities necessary for success and, therefore, the sorts of behavior-based questions you will probably be asked. Armed with this knowledge, you can examine your past behaviors to select the examples that best demonstrate the

Exhibit 3
Sample Behavior-Based Interview Questions

- How did you do in school? Which courses were the hardest? the easiest? Why?

- How did you get interested in hospitality? What other areas did you consider? Would you make the same decision if you had to make it over again?

- What are some obstacles you had to overcome to complete high school and get where you are today? How did you handle them?

- Give an example of a time when you had to achieve consensus in a group disagreement. What was your approach? What was the outcome?

- Tell me about a time you saw an opportunity to improve something when no one else thought it needed improving. What did you do?

- What was the toughest decision you had to make in the last year? How did you go about making this decision? What was the result?

- Tell me about a time when you were given a job or assignment where you had no prior training. How did you learn to do it?

- Tell me about a time when you failed at something. What did you learn from it? How did you do it differently next time?

- How flexible and adaptable are you? Can you give me examples?

- Tell me about a time when you worked with others who did not work well together. How did you deal with that?

- Describe a time in which you had to take an unpopular stand on an issue. How did you do it and what was the outcome?

- Describe a situation when you had the responsibility for completing something but you didn't want to. What did you do and what was the result?

- Describe a time when you felt strong in your convictions and the majority of people felt a different way. What was the issue and how was it resolved?

- Describe a situation where you had to motivate a group of people to accomplish a difficult goal. How did you help them set objectives and overcome obstacles?

- Tell me about a time when you had to gain cooperation from an individual or a group in order to accomplish something.

- Give me some examples of people who come to you for advice. How do you help them?

- Have you ever been asked to do something you didn't think was right? What did you do?

- Tell me about a time when you came forward with the truth and put yourself in a difficult position. What did you do?

- How do you go about building trust with others you work with? Give me some examples.

- Do people trust you? How do you know?

- Tell me about a time when you convinced a peer (or a group of peers) to adopt your ideas. What did you do? What was the result?

- When you come up against a roadblock, what do you do?

- Would you describe yourself as a "take charge" person? What does that mean to you? Give me an example of when you took charge and describe the result.

- Tell me about a decision you made in the last year that you're not very proud of.

- Give me an example of when you worked the hardest and felt the greatest sense of achievement.

- Tell me about one or two long-term goals that you have. What have you done to reach them?

- How do you prioritize multiple and conflicting demands? Give me a recent example.

- Tell me about a time when you had to make a decision without having all of the facts.

Courtesy of ARAMARK

qualities and skills you want to share with the interviewer.

To fail to prepare for a behavior-based interview is to practically guarantee rejection. Few people are able to answer behavior-based questions effectively without preparation.

You should expect to be asked to describe times when you were *un*successful. Such behavior-based questions probe for descriptions of times you were unable to resolve a conflict, handle a complaint, make a sale, and so forth. When preparing for these questions, consider why the interviewer would ask them. The interviewer does not expect and probably wouldn't believe an answer like, "I've never been unsuccessful." The interviewer probably wants to check your level of emotional stability and maturity when handling a disappointment.

Illegal Interview Questions

Laws at the federal, state, and even local levels specify that the questions employers may legally ask in interviews must be related to the position under consideration.

The types of information that interviewers cannot legally ask you to provide include the following:

- Your national origin, race, or ethnicity
- Your social and religious affiliations or memberships
- Your age
- Your family and marital status
- Your height and weight
- Whether you are disabled and, if so, the nature of your disability
- Whether you have an arrest record and, if so, what you have been arrested for

Context and word choice are important when it comes to the legality of interview questions. For example, while it is illegal to ask applicants where they were born or whether they are U.S. citizens, it is legal to ask if they are authorized to work in this country. It is illegal for an interviewer to ask you a general question about your arrest record, but the interviewer may be able to legally ask if you have ever been convicted for embezzlement if this crime might affect your performance of the job under consideration (for example, an embezzlement conviction might have a bearing on your fitness for a job in a hotel's accounting department). Exhibit 4 lists possible responses to an employer who asks an illegal question during an interview.

Questioning the Interviewer

Most employers expect you to ask them questions. Asking questions of the interviewer might reinforce your interest in the company and can demonstrate to the employer that you've done your homework before the interview. Questioning the interviewer also provides the opportunity for you to clarify issues and collect useful information.

Avoid asking questions that you could have found answers to before the interview (for example, company mission, size, locations, and so forth). Also, despite the excitement and nervousness you may feel during an interview, try not to ask questions that were answered earlier in the interview. Don't be in a rush to ask too many questions early on, because answers to some of your questions will usually surface during the course of the interview. It is common for the recruiter to wait and ask if you have any questions near the end of the meeting.

**Exhibit 4
How to Handle an Illegal Interview Question**

If you are asked an illegal question in an interview, it is important to recognize your options. The strategy you employ in answering an illegal question will depend in part on your interest in the company and how much you want the job. If asked an illegal question, you can:

- *Simply answer the question.* In most cases, you can assume that the interviewer had no harmful intent when he or she asked the question and was probably just not aware of the law. Answering the question will keep the interview on track and usually will not damage your candidacy. The risk you take in providing any information that is not job related is that the employer may consider it in making a hiring decision and therefore illegally discriminate against you.

- *Point out that the question is illegal and refuse to answer.* This is likely to embarrass or anger the recruiter and could result in a quick termination of the interview. Depending on the strength of your convictions, you may not want to work for a company that breaks the law anyway. However, if the interviewer was well intentioned and simply ignorant of the law, you may have just walked away from an excellent opportunity.

- *Politely ask the interviewer how the particular question relates to your ability to do the job.* In this way, you can better determine why the question was asked. You still must decide whether or not to answer, but you will likely have a better feel for the recruiter's intentions and this may influence your decision.

This allows you to integrate all that you've learned and ask intelligent questions. Exhibit 5 includes examples of questions to ask interviewers.

It is generally wise to avoid asking any questions related to compensation. As part of your company-specific research and networking efforts, you should be able to get a reasonable idea of how a company pays and what benefits it offers. Employers may provide salary ranges and vacation and benefit information in recruitment brochures and literature, for example. During initial interviews, your focus is best placed on answering the employer's "Why should I hire you?" question. There will be a more appropriate time to learn more about (and negotiate) the specific compensation associated with the job.

Employers close interviews in a variety of ways. Some save the "Why should I hire you?" question for last, to give you an opportunity to summarize your job-related skills and potential for success on the job. Others may say, "Any questions?" and then move to an explanation of how the process proceeds. Before you leave, be sure you understand the timetable for the employment decision. Ask questions if the recruiter does not specify this information. Close on a positive note by thanking the interviewer for the opportunity to be considered for the job.

Thank-You Letters

No matter how the process will proceed after the initial interview, it is wise to send a thank-you note to the interviewer. A legible, handwritten note on paper that matches the paper you used for your résumé will generally be well received. It is important to send the letter in a timely fashion, usually within a day or two of the

Exhibit 5
Questions Applicants Might Ask Interviewers

- How would your CEO describe your company's culture? Would a line-level employee give the same answer?

- How would you describe your company's culture?

- How long have you been with this company?

- Why did you join this company?

- What do you wish you had known before you joined the company?

- What do you like most/least about the company?

- What is the turnover history among new hires for the job under consideration?

- What are the biggest challenges/opportunities the company is facing in the next year? five years?

- How often will I be evaluated if hired?

- What types of people seem to do well with your company?

- What would you expect me to accomplish in the first month/year on the job?

- Why is the job I'm applying for open?

- When will the hiring decision be made? What comes next in the process?

- Is there any additional information or anything else you'd recommend I do to enhance my chances of receiving an offer?

- May I have one of your business cards?

---

interview. Follow up after a few days with a phone call to reiterate your interest and ask if there is anything else you can do to maximize the chance of an offer. This demonstration of your initiative and enthusiasm might have a big impact on whether you are offered the job.

Preparing for Second Interviews

From the employer's perspective, only those applicants who show substantial promise are invited to continue the process. For you, a second interview means an additional opportunity to explore the company and sell yourself. Do not assume a job offer is guaranteed simply because you are invited to a second interview.

Second interviews usually differ from initial interviews in a number of ways:

- Their length ranges from half a day to two days

- The number of people you meet and interview with generally ranges from four to eight people (but may be more)

- Meals and other social occasions are likely to be included

When preparing for a second interview, be sure to confirm all of the arrangements in advance (by phone or in writing), including the handling of expenses (expenses are usually covered by the employer) and the names and titles of those with whom you'll be interviewing. Bring extra copies of your résumé—just in case—and remember to treat *every* person you meet the same way you'd treat the interviewer. The interviewer may ask all who come in contact with you for an opinion about you. Assume that virtually everything you do is being evaluated. In turn, carefully consider the environment and people you come in contact with. How does the work environment feel? Do you think you could fit in with the people you meet?

Some organizations may ask you to shadow a manager for a day or two or complete a **job preview**, during which you will actually work in a location for a short period. This allows a more complete opportunity for you and the employer to get to know each other. Show enthusiasm and ask questions.

Dining etiquette. If you have the opportunity to interview over lunch or take any meal with the host company's recruiter and managers, follow their lead. Exhibiting proper table manners is very important, especially when interviewing with a hospitality company.

When you order, be careful to avoid foods that are difficult to eat, such as cherry tomatoes, cornish hens, barbecued ribs, soup, and lobster. Remember that this is, in fact, a business meeting. Unless your hosts comment on the food, you should keep your opinions about the food to yourself. Be sincere and generous in your compliments to the service staff, and do not season food before tasting it. Don't forget to thank your hosts at the end of the meal.

Apply Your Learning 4.3

Please write all answers on a separate sheet of paper.

1. What are the fundamental things you should keep in mind when preparing for an interview?

2. What is behavior-based interviewing?

3. What are the types of information that interviewers cannot legally ask?

4. What are the benefits of questioning the interviewer?

For statements 5–7, write whether the answer is True or False.

5. If the initial interview didn't go well, you don't need to send a thank-you note.

6. For a second interview, you generally meet and interview with four or more people.

7. When interviewing over a meal, you should be generous in your compliments to the service staff.

4.4 Responding to Job Offers

AFTER STUDYING SECTION 4.4, YOU SHOULD KNOW HOW TO:

♦ Handle rejection

♦ Evaluate a job offer

♦ Choose the best job offer

♦ Negotiate a job offer

Handling Rejection

It is important not to take a job rejection to mean you are a failure. A rejection only means that this particular employer at this particular time chose—for whatever reason—not to extend a job offer to you. The best thing you can do is try to objectively assess the situation and determine if your failure to receive an offer resulted from factors you control or factors that were beyond your control. If, for example, you failed to research the company thoroughly, you can control and improve on that aspect of the process. However, it may be that there was a more qualified candidate, a factor over which you have no control.

Did you enthusiastically present clear and compelling examples of how you could do the job under consideration? At the same time, were you careful to avoid coming across as a know-it-all? Consider, too, your feelings and perceptions after the interviewing process. Was there a good fit between you and the company? If you had doubts about working for the company, a rejection may be a blessing in disguise.

In any case, you should follow up a rejection letter by again contacting the interviewer. Send a letter thanking him or her and asking for any feedback he or she may provide to help you strengthen your position for future consideration (if you still think you'd like to work for that

A Golf-Course Gusher

The Industry Hills Sheraton Resort and Conference Center boasts a beautiful property that includes 15 miles of wooded riding trails, two championship golf courses, and a golf library/museum. These features posed quite a challenge to the oil company that was determined to drill for the 22 million barrels of oil that lie 2,000 feet below the surface of the carefully sculpted fairways.

The drilling company built a rig that is hidden behind a pink privacy wall near the 14th fairway. Two drains run from the rig through the nearby reservoir and under the golf course and resort to extract the oil without creating any new surface hazards for golfers.

particular company). Demonstrating professional perseverance and assertiveness in this way has virtually no risk attached. It may, in fact, pay off in some constructive feedback. You might even be considered for future openings! Remember to step back from the anger or disappointment that might be your initial, emotional reaction. Think about your specific career goals and remember that it is the *process,* not a single event, that matters.

Before leaving the topic of rejection, we should discuss what you should do when *you* are doing the rejecting—that is, when you must turn down a job offer. If you determine that it is in your best interest to choose an alternative offer, it is important to notify in writing the interviewer you are turning down. Be conscientious and polite. Keep in mind the strong networks that exist among hospitality professionals. If you turn down a company in a discourteous way, your action might be communicated far and wide along the networks and ultimately come back to haunt you.

Responding to Job Offers

Receiving an offer of employment is an exhilarating experience. The offer feels like the payoff to all your time and effort. Just as with a rejection, however, be careful to keep your initial, emotional responses from getting in the way of an objective perspective. The decision you make may have an effect on your career (and earnings) for a long time.

Job offers may be extended orally, often at the end of a second interview or later over the telephone. Many people are inclined to immediately accept an offer. It is nearly always a better choice to express your appreciation and enthusiasm, but defer on

making a decision until you've taken time to consider the total package. It is wise to ask for a written copy of the offer, along with a deadline for making your decision. You may then objectively (or at least *more* objectively) evaluate the offer and compare it with other options available to you.

Evaluating Job Offers

When evaluating a job offer, according to a professional career counselor, you should start by considering the **FACTS**:

- Fit

- Advancement

- Compensation

- Training

- Site

Fit. Is this job a good match with your strengths, values, and interests? Objectively assess what attracts you to this company. Keep in mind that prestige, reputation, and beautiful work surroundings won't hold much long-term appeal if the work pace and job requirements don't fit your skills and interests. If the company's mission and values aren't congruent with your personal values, there is probably not enough money in the world to keep you feeling satisfied. No matter how impressed your family and friends are with a company, you have to be able to perform the work that will be demanded of you.

Advancement. What are the realistic career paths that lead from this first job? Consider how the company has presented advancement opportunities in its literature and throughout the interviewing process. Try to balance this presentation with what might be a different reality. Ask about promotion from within (including examples), turnover rates, and organizational structures and reporting relationships. Consult your network contacts. A commitment to employee development means more than merely saying "we promote from within."

Compensation. When it comes to compensation, there is usually a great deal more to consider than just the starting base salary. Taking a long-term perspective will help you evaluate the compensation offer. Be aware of the following items that may be included as part of your compensation package:

- *Insurance policies.* Medical, dental, optical, life, and disability insurance may be offered. "Cafeteria-style" plans that allow you to select the type and amounts of coverage and benefit levels you want are becoming more popular.

- *Bonuses or profit sharing.* Financial compensation over and above base salary may be available based on meeting performance goals for your position, property, or unit.

- *Stock options.* Employees may be offered the opportunity to purchase shares of company stock, often at below-market prices. The risk is usually small, the potential payoff great.

- *Paid vacation, emergency, and family leave.* Hospitality organizations may offer one to two weeks of vacation and similar amounts of paid sick/personal leave annually. While current federal law (the Family and Medical Leave Act) requires employers to grant twelve weeks of *unpaid* family or medical leave to employees under certain circumstances, some employers offer paid family leave.

Employee assistance programs, such as help with finding child care or counseling related to drug or alcohol abuse, may also be available through the employer.

- *Retirement programs.* Some organizations offer tax-deferred, fund-matching 401(k) plans, in which the employer matches employee contributions dollar-for-dollar up to a predetermined limit. Be aware of any vesting requirements—you may have to be on the job for a good length of time before you are eligible for the benefit. If a 401(k) or similar retirement plan is available to you, begin investing early.

- *Educational and training assistance.* Beyond the company-specific job training you receive, some organizations may offer reimbursement for college classes or other training opportunities you pursue outside of work.

- *Paid relocation expenses and other benefits.* Your company may also provide assistance and relocation expenses associated with transfers and promotions. Hospitality companies are also known for offering discounted or free hotel stays to employees. Company vehicles, paid parking, laundry services, and paid professional association or club memberships are not usually part of initial job offers.

Training. Some companies require new hires to complete a six- to eighteen-month training program. Others offer more flexible and self-directed programs. Still others may take a "sink or swim" approach with new hires—that is, offer no training at all. A company's commitment to training must be considered in relation to your current skill

---

Exhibit 1
Evaluating Job Offers Using the Multiple Rating System

Issues	Company A Points/Value/Total	Company B Points/Value/Total	Company C Points/Value/Total
Fit	60 × .35 = 21.0	70 × .35 = 24.5	50 × .35 = 17.5
Advancement	50 × .25 = 12.5	60 × .25 = 15.0	40 × .25 = 10.0
Compensation	85 × .20 = 17.0	55 × .20 = 11.0	60 × .20 = 12.0
Training	40 × .15 = 6.0	70 × .15 = 10.5	60 × .15 = 9.0
Site	100 × .05 = 5.0	50 × .05 = 2.5	40 × .05 = 2.0
Total Score	**61.5**	**63.5**	**50.5**

---

and experience levels. You want to make sure you choose a company with a supportive work environment that maximizes your chance at success.

Site. Where you work can have an enormous impact on how you work. Many (but not all) hospitality companies expect you to relocate for promotions and career growth. Newly hired managers sometimes discover that sadness over leaving behind family and friends quickly replaces the initial excitement of a new job in a new location. Some managers develop a good old-fashioned case of homesickness, which may affect their job performance. Having chosen a hospitality career, you need to realize that moving is not usually all fun and excitement; it also involves change and the necessity to build new relationships. Tapping into your network can help ease any transition difficulties you experience when you relocate.

Choosing the Best Offer

A multiple rating system can help you choose among different job offers. A mul-

tiple rating system uses the same criteria to judge each job offer. The criteria consist of those issues that you consider to be of critical importance. After determining the critical issues, you rate each job offer on each issue, using a scale of 1 to 100. The higher the rating, the better you think the job offer handles that issue.

Simply totaling these ratings may not identify the best job offer, because you will undoubtedly feel that some issues are more important than others. Assign to each issue a percentage value that reflects its relative importance to you. Then, multiply the rating for each issue by its percentage value and total the points to yield an overall score for each job offer. The offer receiving the highest overall score identifies the company that you should seriously consider as your future employer.

The following example illustrates how you can use a multiple rating system to evaluate job offers. Assume that Nadine receives three job offers. Also assume that Nadine chooses to evaluate these offers on the following five key issues and that she weights the issues as follows:

Critical Issues	Percentage Value
Fit	35%
Advancement	25%
Compensation	20%
Training	15%
Site	5%
Total	100%

Exhibit 1 shows the results of Nadine's evaluation of the job offers. Nadine will probably not give further consideration to the offer from Company C because it did not score well on any of the key issues. Since the overall scores of Company A and Company B are so close, Nadine may want to further analyze the differences between these companies before making a final decision. For example, the job offer from Company A scored relatively high on compensation and site. On the other hand, Company B had better scores in the areas of fit, advancement, and training. Nadine's final decision may well hinge on the importance she gives short-term career goals (compensation and site) versus long-term considerations (fit, advancement, and training).

Parameters of Negotiation

There may be some room to improve any job offer you receive. This is not to suggest that you should approach negotiations with an adversarial perspective. Rather, your goal is to sell your services at the best rate under conditions you and the company agree are best.

To negotiate effectively, you must know what someone with your education and experience is worth (you can find out through industry and company research) and what you want and need (discovered through self-assessment). You must also understand what the company needs and how much it is willing to pay for it. Specific areas to consider for negotiation include the following:

- Starting salary

- Timing of performance reviews

- Desired geographic location

- Relocation assistance

- Starting time (the date you must report for work)

Be sure you are selling your skills and accomplishments (how you will add value to the company) as the basis for your negotiations. *Your* needs (car payments, rent, loans) will seldom convince an employer to change an offer. Your understanding of the *company's* needs and how you can satisfy them is far more likely to lead to a bump in salary, strong consideration for your preferred geographic location, or whatever you are negotiating for.

You may also consider leveraging your offer with a second offer from a competitor, although you should be cautious about trying to start a bidding war. Remember that your top priority is to start your career under the best conditions. Actions based on short-term thinking may have long-term negative consequences. On the other hand, if you approach negotiating your first offer with maturity and a sense of fairness, you are likely to enhance your employer's impression of you. As businesspeople, recruiters realize that negotiating is a part of life and business. The risk of offending or angering employers by attempting (in a professional manner) to convince them of your worth is minimal.

Though you cannot control the timing of offers, you can ask for extensions on decision dates. This doesn't guarantee an employer will grant an extension, but this is a far better solution than accepting an offer and then later reneging. Even beyond the important ethical considerations, your reneging will be associated with you for a very long time. In the small world of the hospitality industry, you will probably someday cross paths with the individuals you lied to. At the very least, you will probably at some point have to do business with the company you jilted. Why risk so much short- and long-term damage to yourself and others? Use your heart and head as well as your network of advisors (family, friends, industry contacts) to help you work through the stress of managing multiple offers. Compromising your personal integrity to gain a job is a destructive trade-off.

Apply Your Learning 4.4

Please write all answers on a separate sheet of paper.

1. What does *FACTS* stand for, and what is it?
2. Explain what a multiple rating system is and how it is used.

For statements 3–6, write whether the answer is True or False.

3. It is best to immediately accept a job offer to make sure they don't pick someone else.
4. When evaluating compensation, there is a great deal more to consider than base salary.
5. If offered stock options as part of your compensation, you should decline because the risk is great and the payoff is small.
6. Negotiating the terms of and conditions of your first job offer is unacceptable.

4.5 Lifelong Learning

AFTER STUDYING SECTION 4.5, YOU SHOULD KNOW HOW TO:

♦ Create a career portfolio

♦ Follow the seven habits of highly effective people

♦ Plan your career beyond your first job

What Is a Portfolio?

A **portfolio** is a collection of samples that showcases your interests, talents, contributions, and studies, and shows off your finest efforts for others to see. Your portfolio will demonstrate that you have the competencies and skills necessary to be successful in the workplace. A portfolio is used both as a self-evaluation tool and a goal-setting tool. Most importantly, a portfolio is a marketing tool for you to sell yourself to potential employers.

It is important to periodically add to, sort, and reorganize all of the information you gathered during the career-planning process. Exhibit 1 presents categories and materials you might select in creating your **career portfolio**, also known as a career file. The notion of a career portfolio is to arrange examples and documentation of your best work as well as what you have learned dur-ing your life. The materials in your portfolio can help you create the tools (for example, résumés and cover letters) you need to accomplish your career goals.

By maintaining and updating your career portfolio, you stay prepared to adjust to job changes or even to create them when you desire.

How Are Portfolios Created?

Creating a complete and accurate portfolio is an ongoing process. You should be aware of and record any important accomplishments you achieve. It is important to reflect on your experiences in the classroom, at your work sites, and in your life outside of school. You should make a goal of collecting one item every week or at least every other week.

In general, to create your own portfolio, you will:

1. Evaluate your accomplishments and investigate your interests.

2. Identify your goals.

3. Collect and select samples.

4. Analyze your samples.

5. Organize and present your samples.

Step 1: Evaluate your accomplishments and investigate your interests. Looking

---

Exhibit 1
Elements of a Portfolio

The elements of a portfolio can include:

- Lists of accomplished skills and competencies
- Examples of critical thinking and teamwork
- Record of courses completed
- Certificates of recognition and awards
- Samples that show talents or skills that have been mastered
- Attitude and interest test results
- Essays, reports, and papers
- Health and wellness reports
- Letters of recommendation from employers
- Career exploration

- Personal qualities
- Activities outside work or school
- Samples of work
- Résumés
- Work history
- Test scores
- Promotions
- Progress evaluations
- Internships
- Apprenticeships
- Work experience

---

over the past and evaluating it can help you figure out who you are, what you enjoy, and what you do best. The better you know yourself, the better your chances of making a satisfying career choice. Employers appreciate job candidates who know what they enjoy and where their interests lie. People who follow their dreams and do what they love are the ones who enjoy success.

Step 2: Identify your goals. Based on your self-evaluations, you should prepare and determine short- and long-term goals, and put them in writing. Long-term goals can be personal, or they can be related to the your education or career. They can include job types and position titles. Short-term goals are the stepping stones that will get you to your long-term goals. Stepping stones may include additional training and experience, as well as other job skills.

You should aim high and go for what you really want, while at the same time being honest and realistic with yourself. In other words, do your goals reflect what you really want for your future? Are you willing to take the steps and make the effort to achieve these goals? It is important for you to share your goals with potential employers so they can be sure your goals match their business goals.

Step 3: Collect and select samples. You should collect samples based on your audience—your future employers. What would employers want to see in your portfolio? What questions can be answered for them in the portfolio? What are some important things they may want to know about your background?

When searching for quality employees, employers look for characteristics that show students are ready to become a valuable part of their team. They will especially look for examples of leadership and responsibility, such as those listed in Exhibit 2.

Exhibit 2
Examples of Leadership and Responsibility

- Being a camp counselor
- Involvement in a student or youth group
- Involvement in a charity organization
- Making a presentation or speech
- Employee recognition awards
- Suggesting ways to save money
- Making an important decision

- Inspiring and motivating others
- Improving the workplace
- Training or supervising other employees
- Learning more than one job or position
- Balancing a cash drawer
- Planning a special event
- Solving a problem

Step 4: Analyze your samples. Analyze your collection and select those items that show you at your best and also relate to your short- and long-term goals. For each sample, write a short paragraph that:

- Uses action words to describe the sample or activity.

- Tells what you learned from the activity, including things you learned from any mistakes.

- Describes how the sample can be applied to your career goals.

- Explains how the sample helped prepare you for a job.

Of course, there will be items that don't need much explanation (such as letters of recommendation). However, a little explanation goes a long way to help employers see the value in your experiences.

Step 5: Organize and present your samples. Effective presentation is key. A professional look will make the difference between whether future employers look at a portfolio seriously. Exhibit 3 lists some general guidelines for putting together portfolios.

A Blueprint for Success: Covey's Seven Habits

No book could describe every possible challenge you'll face on a new job. Still, there are habits you can develop to help you succeed at your first job and beyond. Perhaps the best recent presentation of these types of habits was developed by Stephen Covey in his book *The Seven Habits of Highly Effective People.*

Covey's position is that our achievements are in great part the results of the habits we learn and live every day. Covey believes there are seven key interrelated and sequential habits that lead to a balanced and successful life. The first three habits move you from dependence on others to personal independence. The next three habits cultivate balanced interdependence with others. The seventh habit renews and maintains the important process of personal growth.

Habit 1: Initiative—Choose Your Course. The first habit is based on acceptance of personal accountability. Each of us controls our response to any set of conditions we will

---

Exhibit 3
General Guidelines for Portfolio Presentation

Portfolios should be complete.

- Samples should cover a variety of skills, talents, and experiences.

- All work should be at least titled and accompanied by a brief, written, proofread explanation.

- Each sample should have a written explanation to offer insight and application.

Portfolios should be neat.

- They should be easy to carry to interviews, fitting easily into a briefcase, backpack, or book bag.

- Make sure samples are firmly attached so nothing will fall out.

- Information should be typewritten whenever possible. It looks professional and shows attention to detail.

- Make clean, clear photocopies of letters, certificates, etc. *Do not risk damaging or losing the originals*.

Portfolios should be organized.

- Three-ring binders, folders, and report covers work well.

- They should be a manageable length, not overwhelming. A good length is no more than ten pages.

- They should be designed to be read quickly. If a long newspaper article is included, you should highlight your name or the important sentences in the article.

- You can use tabs or slip sheets to group similar things together. For example, you can have tabs for letters of recommendation, work experiences, and school activities.

- There should be a cover page that includes:
  - Your full name, address, and phone number.
  - Your career interests and long- and short-term job goals.
  - A brief description of portfolio contents or a table of contents.

Portfolios should be creative.

- Although portfolios should be in basically black and white, color may be used in different ways, but should be tasteful:
  - Use colored borders around photos or articles.
  - Use colored binders, folders, or report covers.

- Use computer graphics or photos to emphasize samples.

- Use creative titles for the different samples.

---

face on the first job. No matter what circumstances befall you, *you* decide what attitude to assume and what response to choose. Exercising this ability to choose is the foundation for success on your first job—and for success in life in general.

Habit 2: Creativity—Begin with the End in Mind. To use your first job to help you achieve long-term career goals, you must know what your long-term career goals are.

With a clear vision of where you want to end up, you are more able to creatively find the way to get there.

It is possible to let other people push you toward an outcome you may not really desire. For example, suppose your friends and family suggest that a career in luxury hotels is more prestigious and therefore better than a career in the segment of the hospitality industry that most interests you. Covey points out that in such a case, if you begin your climb up the corporate ladder with a luxury hotel chain you will likely discover (later) that the ladder is leaning against the wrong wall. Taking time now to clarify your values, interests, and goals pays off in a focused career that will get you where you want to go.

Habit 3: Productivity—Set Priorities, Organize, and Perform. Some new graduates enter full-time work with expectations of fast promotions, impressive titles, and days filled with interesting challenges. Such graduates are usually disappointed. If you don't feel challenged by your first job, it is easy to forget that you still must perform it well if you want to receive new responsibilities or additional rewards. Habit 3 is a reminder to set priorities and organize in order to keep what may feel urgent to you (your desire to be general manager someday) from getting in the way of what is more important to the company and you right now (fulfilling your current responsibilities, learning, and growing). Fulfilling your current responsibilities nearly always depends on your ability to manage or lead a group. That too cannot usually be done effectively without setting priorities, organizing, and performing.

Habit 4: Interdependence—Think Win-Win or No Deal. Approaching the priorities and goals of a group (such as those of your new company) with an independent and highly competitive perspective will likely doom you to failure on your first job. When seeking success on your first job, look for ways to satisfy the guests, your boss, *and* your employees. This sort of thinking requires examining the various options available for solving any given problem and choosing a solution that is balanced in its impact on all involved.

Habit 5: Empathy—Seek First to Understand. To achieve balanced solutions, it is necessary to "seek first to understand, then to be understood." A good way to begin to establish credibility with guests, co-workers, and others you encounter on your first job is for you to try to see the world as they do. To resolve most workplace conflicts, you must understand the various perspectives of the people involved, even if you disagree with those perspectives. If you can begin to see the world through the eyes of your guests and co-workers, you can more easily anticipate and resolve the challenges you'll experience on your first job and beyond.

Habit 6: Synergy—Value the Differences. You are likely to enter a workplace that has staff members from many different racial, ethnic, and socioeconomic backgrounds. You can increase your ability to achieve results through others if you value your co-workers and assist them in treating each other with dignity and respect. Be careful not to mistake "uniformity" for "unity." Just because staff members are wearing the same uniform does not mean they are a unified team with clear, shared goals. It is extremely tough to create and maintain unity and achieve business results without valuing the differences among your co-workers.

Habit 7: Consistency—Sharpen the Saw Regularly. Covey points out that an individual cutting wood cannot achieve maximum, long-term productivity if he or she fails to keep the saw sharp. At some point, a dull blade will slow production and lead to harder work with fewer results. Similarly, balanced success that lasts a lifetime won't happen if you only work hard. Self-renewal is vital and includes your physical health, your mental and emotional well-being, and your moral centering. Burning out on the pace and irregular work hours often associated with hospitality businesses is a real possibility, but an avoidable one. Planning time for physical exercise and social and emotional interaction with family and friends is necessary in order to keep yourself "sharp." As you plan your career, you owe it to yourself to choose and maintain a lifestyle in which you are able to "sharpen the saw regularly."

Keep in mind that all the hard work and good intentions you may bring to your new position are not likely to eliminate the frustrations you experience on your first job. Not every training program is completed exactly as scheduled, initial assignments aren't always as challenging as you'd hoped, and probably not all of your co-workers will welcome you with open arms (especially if some of them feel they were passed over for the position you hold). Ultimately, the work still must be done and you must continue learning—every day for the rest of your life!

Career Planning Beyond Your First Job

Matching your wants and needs with the needs of hospitality organizations is at the heart of any discussion of strategic career planning. The process of finding or creating matches between individuals and organizations is complicated. People are very different from one another in terms of their individual career-related needs. Likewise, hospitality organizations are not all the same, and their needs shift as the global business climate within which they compete changes. Clearly, the matchmaking process is dynamic and complex.

The responsibility for finding and maintaining the best match between you and any organization lies primarily with *you*. Arguably, the responsibility should be shared between the individual and his or her employer. Yet, if you depend on your employer for career advancement, you may be assuming a risk that is best avoided or at least minimized. Who has a greater stake in your career or is more capable of evaluating your career-related needs than you?

In accepting responsibility for managing your career, you owe it to yourself and your employer to share the insights you gain from your ongoing strategic self-assessments. If you are not aware of your interests, values, and needs, you cannot effectively manage your career, nor can your employer be of much help to you.

Communicating career-related interests, values, and needs to your employer may result in your employer sharing in some of the planning and management of your career. In the "old days," organizations accepted the responsibility for their employees' career management, and that mindset hasn't completely disappeared. When researching organizations, remember to learn about their career management policies and programs. Examples of career management policies of progressive organizations include the following:

- Allowing unrestricted career mobility within the organization, including lateral and diagonal moves

- Valuing results (what and how workers contribute) over titles

- Making long-term yet flexible career growth a primary goal for their employees

- Recognizing that expertise is not restricted to upper management

Ideally, a company's culture should support individual career planning and development. In words and actions, organizations should communicate that, although they do not promise jobs for life, they are committed to strong partnerships between company and employee. Examples of specific career resources and programs that some progressive organizations have established for their staff members include the following:

- *On-site career education centers* that include books, magazines, videos, and other resources covering the best and most recent career development ideas and strategies. Some large organizations offer workshops, seminars, and career advising and assessment services.

- *Online job posting* to encourage and facilitate career movement. This computerized job-posting list may include job openings within the company and a database of current employees available for information interviewing.

- *Networking groups,* formal and informal, that meet face-to-face or online to discuss job opportunities, information, leads, and so forth.

Even as an entry-level employee or first-time supervisor/manager, you might have an opportunity to make significant contributions to the organization. Traditionally, anything other than promotions or obvious moves upward in terms of title, pay, and so on has been viewed negatively. As organizations become flatter, the opportunities for exclusively upward career movement are likely to decrease. Organizations can use creative compensation and recognition programs to begin to erase some of the stigma historically attached to any position changes that were not clearly promotions.

Be aware as you plan and manage your career "voyage" that the trip is unlikely to be the shortest distance between where you are now and your ultimate career goal. Straight-line career ladders are going (if they have not already gone) the way of the dinosaurs. A series of continuous promotions within the same organization is not impossible, but the likelihood has diminished significantly. Your career is more likely to be like navigating a trip across an ocean than climbing a corporate ladder. The predictable steps of the old ladder have been replaced by the need to frequently adjust your course. Your ability and willingness to accept, embrace, and create change will be critical to your career success.

Apply Your Learning 4.5

Please write all answers on a separate sheet of paper.

1. What is a portfolio and what is it used for?

2. What are the five general steps used when creating your portfolio?

For statements 3–6, write whether the answer is True or False.

3. When identifying your goals, you should aim high and go for what you really want.

4. It is better just to say, "I participated in a charity fund-raiser" than it is to go into all the time-consuming details.

5. The "Seven Habits of Highly Effective People" are seven key interrelated and sequential habits that will help you create a professional portfolio.

6. Career planning beyond your first job is primarily your responsibility.

Quick Hits

Chapter 4

SECTION 4.1—SELF-ASSESSMENT

- Career planning begins with the question, "What do I know about myself?" The answers will reveal your strengths, weaknesses, interests, and values.

- An excellent way to begin analyzing your strengths is to create a list of things you are proud to have accomplished.

- Weak skills and abilities are often fairly easy to identify and improve through books, courses, and specific training; weaknesses in personal qualities may be more complex and difficult to recognize and fix. Once you have identified weaknesses, develop action plans for improving them.

- To help identify your interests, review your accomplishments and strengths, focusing on how you spend your free time, then think about them as they relate to the opportunities and demands of the hospitality industry.

- Carefully consider the relationships, objects, and activities that you value most highly and give special thought to how they do or do not fit into the workplace. Simply pondering the question, "What matters most to me?" can be very thought provoking.

- The following sources of company information are useful: company-specific sources, alumni mentor programs, career fairs, corporate presentations, and internships and field experiences.

SECTION 4.2—SELF-MARKETING AND PERSONAL PROMOTION

- Getting a job is a sales process. You are selling *yourself*.

- Employment **networking** has been identified as the primary source by which most jobs are found—and gives you access to the "hidden job market."

- Most employers prefer informal and personal methods of identifying employees, and believe personal contacts result in more in-depth, accurate, and up-to-date information.

- The way to develop your network is by talking to people. The networking process will allow you to tell people about yourself, enlist their support, and help you gather information about available opportunities. The discussion can be formal or casual.

- To build confidence and develop your networking skills, start with people you already know: family, friends, parents of friends, teachers, and former employers. Networking takes effort and practice.

- The purpose of cover letters is to communicate a specific personalized message to a particular employer, answering the most fundamental employment question of all: "Why should I hire you?"

- The five rules for writing effective cover letters are: (1) address it to a particular person by name, (2) communicate something personal, (3) answer the question "Why should I see you?" (4) use their language, and (5) ask for the interview.

SECTION 4.3—INTERVIEWING

- When preparing for an interview, keep in mind a straightforward list of goals you want to accomplish before and during your meeting.

- By putting yourself in the position of the interviewer and thinking carefully about all you've learned up to now (about yourself; the hospitality industry; and the specific recruiter, company, and job you're interested in), you can reasonably anticipate nearly every type of question you will be asked.

- Many hospitality employers use **behavior-based interviewing**—an interviewing technique that is intended to determine how you have behaved under specific circumstances in the past. It is rooted in the belief that the best predictor of your future behavior is your past behavior.

- The types of information that interviewers cannot legally ask include: your national origin, race, or ethnicity; your social and religious affiliations or memberships; your age; your family and marital status; your height and weight; whether you are disabled and, if so, the nature of your disability; or whether you have an arrest record and, if so, what you have been arrested for.

- Most interviewers expect you to ask them questions. Asking questions might reinforce your interest in the company and can demonstrate to the employer that you've done your homework before the interview. Questioning also provides the opportunity for you to clarify issues and collect useful information.

- No matter how the process will proceed after the initial interview, it is wise to send a thank-you note to the interviewer.

SECTION 4.4—RESPONDING TO JOB OFFERS

- Being turned down for a job only means that this particular employer at this particular time chose—for whatever reason—not to extend a job offer to you. The best thing you can do is try to objectively assess the situation and determine if your failure to receive an offer resulted from factors you control or factors that were beyond your control.

- When responding to a job offer, it is nearly always a better choice to express your appreciation and enthusiasm, but defer on making a decision until you've taken time to objectively consider the total package. It is wise to ask for a written copy of the offer, along with a deadline for making your decision.

- When evaluating a job offer, you should start by considering the **FACTS**: Fit, Advancement, Compensation, Training, and Site.

- *Fit.* Is this job a good match with your strengths, values, and interests? If the company's mission and values don't fit with your personal values, there is probably not enough money in the world to keep you feeling satisfied.

- *Advancement.* What are the realistic career paths that lead from this first job?

Consider how the company has presented advancement opportunities in its literature and throughout the interviewing process.

- *Compensation.* There is usually a great deal more to consider than just the starting base salary. Be aware of the following items that may be included in a compensation package: insurance policies; bonuses or profit sharing; stock options; paid vacation, emergency, and family leave; retirement programs; educational training and assistance; paid relocation expenses; and other benefits.

- *Training.* A company's commitment to training must be considered in relation to your current skill and experience levels. You want to make sure you choose a company with a supportive work environment that maximizes your chance at success.

- *Site.* Where you work can have an enormous impact on how you work. Many (but not all) hospitality companies expect you to relocate for promotions and career growth.

- A multiple rating system uses the same criteria to judge each job offer and to help you choose the best one.

- To negotiate a job offer effectively, you must know what someone with your education and experience is worth and what you want and need. You must also understand what the company needs and how much it is willing to pay for it.

- Specific areas to consider for negotiation include starting salary, timing of performance reviews, desired geographic location, relocation assistance, and starting time (the date you must report for work).

SECTION 4.5—LIFELONG LEARNING

- A **portfolio** is a collection of samples that showcases your interests, talents, contributions, and studies. Your portfolio will demonstrate that you have the competencies and skills necessary to be successful in the workplace.

- The general steps used when creating a portfolio include: (1) evaluating your accomplishments and investigating your interests, (2) identifying your goals, (3) collecting and selecting samples, (4) analyzing your samples, and (5) organizing and presenting your samples.

- Evaluating your accomplishments and investigating your interests can help you figure out who you are, what you enjoy, and what you do best. The better you know yourself, the better your chances of making a satisfying career choice.

- Identify your short- and long-term goals, and put them in writing. Short-term goals are the stepping stones that will get you to your long-term goals. Long-term goals can be personal or related to your education or career.

- Collect and select samples for your portfolio based on what your future employers would want to see. What are some important things they may want to know about your background?

- Analyze your samples and select those items that show you at your best and also relate to your short- and long-term goals. For each sample, you should write a short paragraph that uses action words, tells what you learned from the activity, describes how it can be applied to your career goals, and explains how it helped prepare you for a job.

- Organize and present your samples in an effective manner. A professional look will make the difference in whether future employers look at a portfolio seriously.

- There are habits you can develop to help you succeed at your first job and beyond. The best recent presentation of these types of habits was developed by Stephen Covey in his book *The Seven Habits of Highly Effective People.* Covey's position is that our achievements are in great part the results of the habits we learn and live every day.

- Career planning beyond your first job is primarily your responsibility, although certain organizations have established career resources for their employees such as on-site career education centers, online job posting, and networking groups.

Unit 2

Marketing and Sales

CHAPTER 5   HOSPITALITY MARKETING AND SALES

CHAPTER 6   THE MARKETING PLAN

CHAPTER 7   THE SALES OFFICE

CHAPTER 8   BANQUET AND MEETING ROOM SALES

CHAPTER 9   SELLING IS EVERYONE'S JOB

CHAPTER 10   TELEPHONE SALES

Profile

Kelly Moyers-Ham, MBA, CHE

Hospitality Lodging Program Instructor
Metro Tech Vocational-Technical School

I t took Kelly Moyers-Ham five years in the lodging industry before she realized that her "job" was a career. Once she made that realization, her career skyrocketed, and she was a general manager for Choice hotels at age 23—before she even completed her undergraduate degree.

"The hospitality industry offers the unlimited potential to advance your career," Moyers-Ham said. "With the proper training and education, you can go into the industry and in just a few years reach your goal of general manager or regional manager. It's a non-stop career with never-ending possibilities on the career ladder. There is rapid advancement for the people who are willing to do the work."

Moyers-Ham began her lodging career at 17 when she and a friend decided to leave their South Carolina town and move to Washington D.C. To support her adventure, she worked for a Residence Inn by Marriott as a reservationist. She enjoyed the job enough that when she returned to South Carolina, she began working for a Red Roof Inn as a front desk person.

Moyers-Ham credits her mentor, Don Landry, with changing her vision of hospitality from a job to a career. He gave her a job as director of sales and later general manager while encouraging her to grow and take on new challenges.

Moyers-Ham began working as a general manager in 1995 for Hampton Inn. She was working 75 hours a week and had a 45-minute commute when her husband suggested she explore her first love: education. "Teaching was always my dream," she said. Metrotech Vocational Technical School was starting a hospitality lodging program and needed someone to put it together. Moyers-Ham was hired and was able to help design the curriculum.

Having left the fast-track of executive management at age 26, Moyers-Ham is able to give students an accurate and experienced eye into the industry. She tells them that she wasn't a prodigy. "I just knew what I wanted to do and was in the right place at the right time. I took the opportunities given to me. You have to work hard and let people know what your goals are so they can help you achieve them."

What does she tell her students are the major factors in a person's success? "Determination and perseverance. It doesn't matter where you come from, it only matters where you want to go."

Hospitality Marketing and Sales

Sections

5.1 Marketing and Sales

5.2 The Marketing and Sales Division

5.3 The Four *P*s of Marketing

5.4 Lodging Market Segments

5.1 Marketing and Sales

AFTER STUDYING SECTION 5.1, YOU SHOULD KNOW HOW TO:

♦ Define marketing

♦ Define sales

♦ Explain the difference between marketing and sales

Today, competition among hotels is fierce. Filling guestrooms is no longer a matter of placing a few ads, sending a few salespeople out on personal calls, and relying on good word-of-mouth advertising. Success depends on well-planned marketing and sales strategies implemented by trained sales and marketing professionals.

That may sound complicated and overwhelming. But the goal of hospitality marketing is actually very simple: to make every guest a repeat guest. It means taking the time to develop relationships with guests and working to meet their expectations.

For some people, the idea of building relationships with guests is surprising. When they think of sales and marketing, they picture the stereotype of a fast-talking, anything-for-a-buck swindler—in a suit that was probably *never* in style. To them, "sales" means pushing substandard products on people who just aren't interested.

Nothing could be further from the truth. Today's hospitality sales and marketing leaders thrive by building cooperative relationships with customers, not by pressuring or deceiving them. There is too much riding on a long-term relationship to ruin it with fast talking or half-truths. Putting business on the books is critical to every property's economic health and growth.

Marketing vs. Sales

Understanding and managing guest relationships—the key to selling guestrooms today—involves equal measures of marketing and sales.

Marketing includes research, product development, advertising, publicity, and sales promotions, as well as the means to monitor the marketing program's effectiveness (surveys, guest comment cards).

Sales consists of direct efforts to sell products and services by personal contact, telecommunication, and mailings. Thanks to marketing's growing influence, sales now focuses primarily on delivering what consumers want rather than on what the property wants to sell.

Some people see marketing and sales as adversaries. In reality, they are most effective only when they work hand in hand. Marketing focuses on trend research, which leads to a better understanding of what guests want and need. That understanding, in turn, leads to the development of sales techniques that directly address guest wants and needs.

The Difference between Marketing and Sales

Marketing focuses on:	Sales focuses on:
Market analysis, planning, and control	Field work and desk work to sell to consumers
Long-term trends, and how to translate problems and opportunities into new products, markets, and strategies for long-term growth	Short-term considerations, such as today's products, markets, consumers, and strategies
Profit planning, such as determining the appropriate mix of business and individual market segments	Volumes and quotas, current sales, bonuses, and commissions

Product and Service Marketing

A hotel or restaurant sells both products (rooms, food, beverages) and services (hospitality). There are significant differences between marketing services and marketing products.

A product can be demonstrated or shown. Open the door to a guestroom or include a picture of the hotel's swimming pool in a brochure, and guests can easily judge its value. Services are less tangible. They often involve an emotional response; they are more "felt" than seen or held. Staff who call guests by name, a hotel restaurant that offers to make a sandwich after the kitchen has closed, a front desk agent who recommends a particularly enjoyable local attraction—it can be a challenge for guests to put a value on such "service products."

Imagine a couple staying at an economy hotel. They might think it ridiculous if such a property offered nightly turn-down service, in which a room attendant visits each room to turn down the bedspread, tidy the room, and leave a small treat (often chocolate or a cookie). They would place little or no value on such service. But guests at a luxury hotel might feel cheated if turn-down service weren't offered. For them, such service is highly valued.

Every service provided must meet the expectations of the guests the property hopes to attract and satisfy. When a property is marketed well, its image and position in the marketplace are so clear that guests know exactly what to expect.

Hospitality is not just something a property presents to a guest on a plate or behind a guestroom door. It includes every aspect of the guest's stay, and it must meet or exceed the guest's expectations if that guest is going to become a repeat visitor.

How does the marketing and sales division tackle the difficult job of selling hospitality to potential guests? It begins with proper planning and it continues through the delivery of products and services to guests. In the following section, we will take a closer look at many of the staff positions involved in these and many more vital tasks.

Apply Your Learning 5.1

Please write all answers on a separate sheet of paper.

1. Define marketing.

2. Define sales.

3. Which of the following is an example of an intangible service?

    a. a dinner prepared exactly as you requested it
    b. a front desk agent who makes you feel welcome
    c. an ocean view that allows you to watch the sunset
    d. a concierge who provides information about the movies at a local theater

4. Why is it generally easier to market products rather than services?

5.2 The Marketing and Sales Division

AFTER STUDYING SECTION 5.2, YOU SHOULD KNOW HOW TO:

♦ Describe the duties of the vice president or director of marketing and sales

♦ Describe the duties of the director of convention service or convention service manager

♦ List the duties of the director of advertising and public relations

♦ Identify the responsibilities of the telemarketing coordinator

♦ Explain the director of sales position

♦ Describe the duties of the sales manager

♦ List the responsibilities of the assistant director of sales

♦ Describe the duties of salespeople or sales representatives

♦ List the tasks that are performed by a clerical sales staff

The Marketing and Sales Division

Marketing and sales divisions or departments vary with the size, type, and budget of the property. Exhibit 1 shows typical organization charts for the sales personnel at a small and a midsize property. Exhibit 2 shows a sample organization chart for the marketing and sales division of a large hotel.

A marketing-oriented general manager is the key to a hotel's sales efforts. In small to midsize properties, the GM may take on

Mouse Unmasked!

Disney's "imagineers" often hide a Mickey Mouse silhouette in plain sight on theme park attractions, Disney-owned hotels, and Walt Disney movies. Although it originally started as an inside joke among the employees, word leaked out and it soon became a tradition among many Disney fans to search for the "hidden Mickeys." (To see them for yourself, go to www.hiddenmickeys.org.)

Exhibit 1
Sample Organization Chart for the Sales Personnel at Small and Midsize Properties

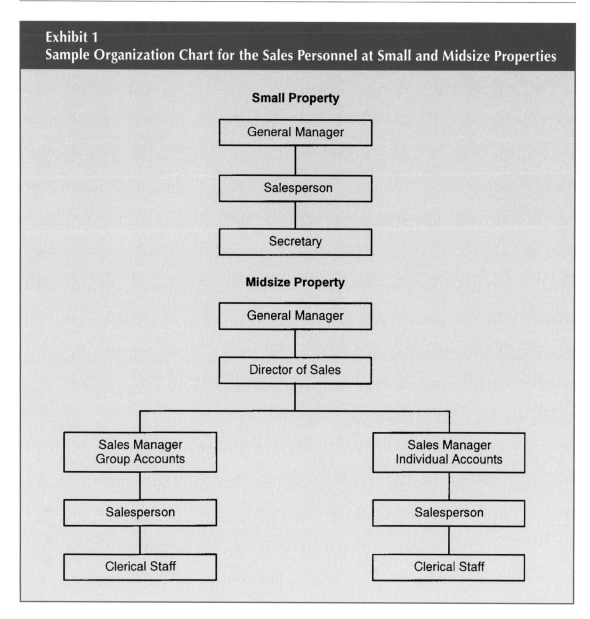

---

the responsibilities of advertising and public relations to give the sales manager time to sell. The GM may also make personal sales calls and spend time talking with guests at the front desk.

The extent of the GM's involvement depends on the size of the property and its sales staff. While specific duties will vary,

there are five primary areas of concern: directing the sales effort, developing the sales staff, participating in the sales effort (including assisting with difficult or key accounts), supporting the sales staff, and evaluating the sales effort.

Typical titles and responsibilities of division members include:

Exhibit 2
Sample Organization Chart for a Marketing and Sales Division of a Large Hotel

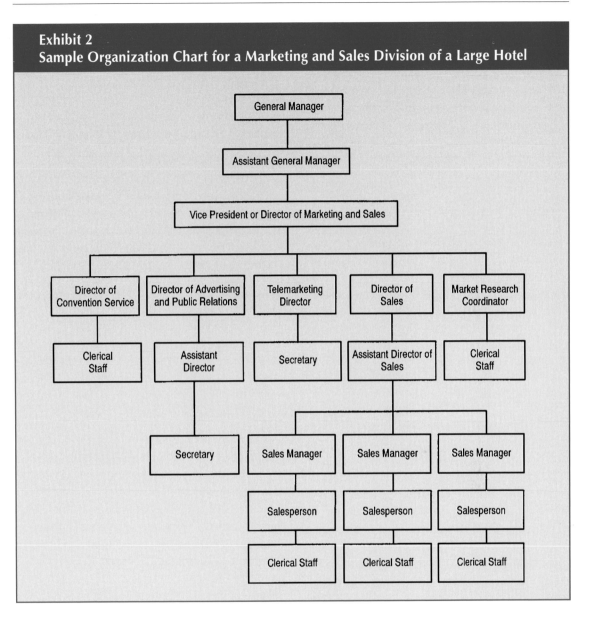

Vice President (or Director) of Marketing and Sales. Considered the head of the sales effort at large properties, the vice president of marketing and sales usually serves on the executive committee of the property. Some people in this position are actively involved in sales; others are administrators overseeing the division.

Director of Convention Service/Convention Service Manager. Hotels with substantial convention and group meeting business will likely employ a director of convention service/convention service manager who oversees the servicing of group business once it has been sold. This person works closely with all departments, coordinating the efforts of the food and beverage department, the front office, and the banquet setup crew.

Telemarketing Director. The telemarketing director supervises and manages the telephone sales staff, which is responsible for developing leads, making prospecting calls, and following up on leads and previous clients.

Market Research Coordinator. Many large properties employ a marketing professional who oversees the development of information regarding the history and past performance of each account being solicited. The coordinator may also research current market trends, the strategies used by competing properties, and general consumer trends.

The following positions represent the heart of the marketing and sales division.

The Director of Marketing. Since marketing is largely a management function, it is important that the director of marketing be capable of performing a variety of management tasks, such as setting objectives and policies, planning, organizing, staffing, directing, and controlling. Planning is probably the most important. It involves determining what needs to be done and deciding how to meet the goals and objectives set. Without proper planning, the other functions are meaningless.

Director of Advertising and Public Relations. The director of advertising and public relations oversees creative staff (writers, designers), coordinates all promotional materials, establishes a good public image for the property, and helps select advertising media.

Director of Sales. The director of sales is usually in charge of the sales office. In addition to supervising office staff and handling administrative duties, he or she may also handle key accounts, assist salespeople when necessary, and prepare sales reports for top management (see Exhibit 3).

Sales Manager. Sales managers usually assign territory or accounts to salespeople, monitor the progress of salespeople, and handle their own accounts. In small properties, this position might be the same as director of sales; in larger properties, the sales manager would report to the director of sales.

Assistant Director of Sales. The assistant director of sales serves as the chief aide to the director of sales, and may manage the sales office, supervise sales staff, and handle his or her own accounts. If the sales office is headed by a sales manager, this position would be called the assistant sales manager.

Account Managers. In many hotels, *account manager* is the title given to all salespeople. (Senior salespeople are sometimes given the title of *sales executive* or *account executive*.) Salespeople are the backbone of any sales organization. They are responsible for contacting, soliciting, and providing follow-up service to clients (see Exhibit 4).

At small properties, a salesperson usually handles all types of business. He or she may call on meeting planners, travel agents, and other sources of potential business. At medium, large, and convention properties, each salesperson may be given a specific assignment: individual sales; group sales; international sales; group or individual sales to tour brokers, tour operators, and travel agents; or food and beverage sales (banquets, functions, and so on).

Exhibit 3
The Role of a Director of Sales

A director of sales is responsible for several important aspects of the sales function:

1. **Coordinating with top management.** A good director of sales works closely with the general manager and other department heads, often on a weekly basis, to ensure that all the sales needs of the property are being met.

2. **Administering a sales support system.** A good sales office needs an efficient filing system, written policies and procedures, and an effective paper flow for correspondence. It is up to the director of sales to ensure that all sales systems are operating smoothly or that needed corrections are made.

3. **Training the sales staff.** The director of sales is often responsible for initial training, but must also continue to coach and counsel the sales staff. It is up to the director of sales to identify weak areas and see that the sales staff corrects them.

4. **Setting sales targets.** A good director of sales determines specific target clients in each market segment and ensures that sales calls are tailored to meet the needs of potential clients. The director of sales also evaluates business potential and steers the sales staff to lucrative areas.

5. **Evaluating sales progress.** It is up to the director of sales to have a written sales plan with definite goals in order to measure progress.

6. **Evaluating sales procedures.** The primary job of a sales office is to sell, and all non-selling functions (sales meetings, travel time, etc.) should be analyzed to be certain they are kept to a minimum. For example, the director of sales might decide to eliminate a few non-productive sales meetings to make more time for selling.

Clerical Staff. The clerical staff is responsible for maintaining sales paperwork, which frees salespeople to solicit clients. But it is a mistake to think of clerical staff as mere file clerks. In many cases, they know as much about the property as the salespeople, and they can often generate leads or even sell a client.

No matter what positions exist in the sales department, every effort should be made to motivate the entire staff and foster teamwork. This means instilling a sense of community and ensuring that everyone involved shares a common direction and a willingness to fill whatever role is necessary to achieve the property's goals.

Exhibit 4
Sample Job Description—Group Salesperson

Job Title:	Group Salesperson
Department:	Marketing and Sales
Reports To:	Director of Sales

Basic Functions: Review the marketing strategy that will obtain maximum occupancy levels and average rate with the director of sales. Responsible for all group business within the western territory.

Consult daily with the director of sales concerning the western territory and how it relates to the sales success of the hotel. Effective merchandising, prospecting, solicitation, and booking of business are among the areas that will be discussed.

Scope: The group salesperson will be the primary person responsible for booking long-term group business (long-term being more than six months out).

Work Performed: Initiate prospecting and solicitation of new accounts in the western territory; manage current accounts to maximize guestroom nights; responsible for administrative efforts necessary to perform these tasks.

Quotas for this position are:

Room nights per month:	1,200
Soft spot percentage:	20%
Phone calls per week:	
Trace/Follow-up	20
Prospecting	25
Personal calls per week:	10
New accounts per month:	10
Referrals per month:	5

The group salesperson must supply weekly, monthly, and annual reports supporting productivity standards.

Probe for client needs: rooms, suites, desired dates, day-of-week pattern, program agenda, food and beverage requirements, and degree of flexibility in each of these areas.

When available, obtain information on a group's past history; i.e., previous rooms picked up, arrival/departure pattern, and double occupancy percentage.

Review availability of clients' required dates and research any alternative dates which should be offered. The dates presented to clients should satisfy their needs while allowing the hotel to maximize occupancy and average rate.

Negotiate with clients the day or days of the week that rooms will be needed (and held), the number of rooms that will be blocked for each day of the function, and group rates (within guidelines as set by the director of sales regarding comps and function space).

Tentatively block rooms and function space in accordance with office policy.

Confirm in writing, according to office standards (via short-term contract or long-term contract and function room outline), all aspects of the meetings. Track to ensure groups receive signed contracts.

Alert all necessary departments (i.e., front office and credit) of pending tentative bookings.

Exhibit 4   *(continued)*
Sample Job Description—Group Salesperson

Upon receiving a signed contract, process definite booking ticket, definite function room outline, and credit application.

Oversee, manage, and track the way in which reservations are made, the pick-up of group blocks, adherence to cut-off dates, and any subsequent adjustment to room blocks (positive or negative).

Periodically contact clients while in-house to be certain all is in order and going well; handle any last-minute needs as they arise.

Conduct an exit interview with clients to determine level of satisfaction and ask for additional business.

Send letter of appreciation to clients. Letter should include actual room night consumption and should be tailored to previous exit-interview discussions.

Attend extra-curricular activities and meetings, and accept any responsibilities or projects as directed by the director of sales.

Supervision Exercised: Supervise one secretary.

Supervision Received: Primary supervision from the director of sales. Initial training, and retraining as needed, also received from the director of sales. Receive direction from the director of sales in regard to room merchandising.

Responsibility & Authority: Upon satisfactory completion of rooms merchandising and operational training, the group salesperson will have the authority to confirm dates, room blocks, and rates directly with clients.

Minimum Requirements: Bachelor's degree, preferably in business, hotel, or restaurant administration. Individual must also be professional in appearance and approach.

Experience: Minimum of two years experience in hotel sales.

Sales Competencies:
1. Ability to negotiate.
2. Ability to prioritize and manage accounts.
3. Ability to prospect.
4. Ability to judge the profitability of new business.
5. Knowledge of product.
6. Knowledge of competition.
7. Ability to make sales presentations.
8. Ability to organize and plan.
9. Ability to utilize selling skills.
10. Ability to overcome objections.
11. Ability to solve problems and make decisions.
12. Ability to write effectively.

Apply Your Learning 5.2

Please write all answers on a separate sheet of paper.

1. What are the typical responsibilities of a director of advertising and public relations.

2. Which position is most likely to provide research information used in developing sales strategies?

   a. field data supplier
   b. sales and marketing associate
   c. assistant director of sales
   d. market research coordinator

3. Which position is primarily responsible for contacting, soliciting, and providing follow-up service to clients?

   a. catering services manager
   b. salesperson
   c. clerical staff
   d. assistant director of telemarketing

4. A marketing-oriented _____ is the key to a hotel's sales efforts.

   a. general manager
   b. customer-service plan
   c. sales team
   d. mission statement

5. List two specific assignments that a hotel salesperson at a medium, large, or convention property might receive.

5.3 The Four Ps of Marketing

AFTER STUDYING SECTION 5.3, YOU SHOULD KNOW HOW TO:

♦ Identify the product of the hotel

♦ Determine where the product is sold

♦ Calculate the price for the product

♦ Explain how to promote the product

Many tactics are used to get and keep customers. For example, a hotel relies on location, size and type of facilities, quality and decor of guestrooms, type of service, and prices to entice guests to stay there. All of these are marketing decisions—choices made to help the hotel stand out from the competition and to appeal to the hotel's prospective customers.

To make these marketing decisions, a hotel's managers must determine (1) what current and potential customers need or want, (2) how to provide it, and (3) how to persuade current and potential customers to patronize the hotel. These activities break down into four basic responsibilities known as the **Four Ps of Marketing**: product, place, price, and promotion. The way these four marketing efforts are combined to meet the objectives of each business is the **marketing mix**.

Product: What Do You Sell?

In the hospitality industry, *product* can mean many things. A product can be a meal or some other tangible item that a hotel or restaurant provides to guests. It can also be an intangible service, such as a food server presenting a meal. *Product* can also refer to a hotel or restaurant's concept—as in, "A La Quinta motel is an economy product developed for traveling businesspeople." In this case, *product* refers to all the things that make the experience of staying at a La Quinta what it is—its philosophy, facilities, amenities, and level of service.

A hotel's concept should be a marketing decision based on providing a better solution to a customer's problem. Some properties sell luxury and superlative service, while others sell cleanliness and economy. Some highlight business services, while others promote superior facilities for families with young children.

A successful concept for a hospitality business requires a clear understanding of what people are looking for and what competitors already offer. To succeed, a business must understand what problems consumers are hoping to solve—then offer better solutions than the competition.

Place: Where Do You Sell It?

Place also has several meanings in hospitality marketing.

First, it refers to the physical location of the business—off the interstate, on the beach, on a lush mountaintop—which can be crucial to its success.

Location can have a profound effect on marketing methods. For instance, the fact that a large number of Holiday Inns are located all over the United States means that people are reminded of the Holiday Inn name wherever they go. Plus, because Holiday Inn is everywhere, the company can advertise on national television or in national magazines, which would be too costly and inefficient for many of its local competitors.

Place also refers to the site where the reservation for the hotel is made. This can be via a central reservation system office, a travel agency, or the Internet. Each place represents a unique opportunity for a sale. Obviously, the more places you can sell a hotel room, the easier it is to fill that hotel.

Price: What Do You Sell It For?

There are a number of approaches to setting prices. We'll look at two here: cost-plus pricing and customer-based pricing.

With **cost-plus pricing**, a hotel determines its actual costs, then adds on a reasonable percentage to arrive at the final retail price. The basic flaw with this approach is that guests don't care what the property's costs are. Cost-plus pricing ignores how guests feel about what they are getting and what they are willing to pay for it. Also, it doesn't take into account **loss-leaders**—items that are sold at prices so low that they are not profitable in themselves but which attract customers who may buy other items that *are* profitable. Bars and lounges that offer a free buffet during happy hour are purposely sacrificing the low profit margin on their food in order to gain higher profits from beverage sales.

Customer-based pricing is a much more realistic method of setting prices: Companies determine what customers want and what they're willing to pay—and then figure out a way to deliver it. Hotels and restaurants that use this system try to give customers what they expect (or more than they expect) for the price being charged.

Businesses that set prices with the customer in mind recognize that consumers may perceive a larger difference between $9.95 and $10 than there actually is, and so try to keep their prices at the lower figure. They also recognize another psychological factor at work—the assumption that quality costs money, and that paying more means receiving better quality.

The price that a hotel charges for a guestroom is not set in stone. It changes constantly, based on availability, discount programs, sales promotions, and other variables. Managing such pricing is a complex job, but it can be made easier with yield management software. **Yield management** software helps to optimize the revenue a hotel receives in any given period by adjusting the rates offered to different market segments, based on the projected room supply and demand. These numbers change constantly as reservations come in and the forecasts are adjusted accordingly.

The cost of making a sale may influence pricing, as well. It may be cheaper to sell a block of 100 rooms to one meeting planner rather than process 100 individual reservations; so room prices can be set lower for the meeting planner. The amount of money a guest is likely to spend in the hotel is also important. Guests attending meetings tend to have all of their meals at the hotel; 100 meeting attendees may be more profitable than 100 individual guests, even if the meeting attendees are charged less for their guestrooms.

Promotion: How Do You Spread the Word?

The fourth *P* in marketing stands for *promotion*. It is last because promotional decisions ideally should be made after product, place, and price decisions.

Every promotional activity falls into one of six categories:

- Personal selling
- Advertising
- Public relations
- Sales promotion
- Direct marketing
- Point-of-purchase communications

Traditionally, hotels have separated these functions. It is not uncommon for a hotel to have its advertising designed and placed by an outside advertising agency that works with the general manager. Meanwhile, direct response programs are being initiated by the marketing department, and point-of-purchase materials are being delivered to the food and beverage department by a local graphic designer or printer.

A new school of thinking, however, says that all of these tasks should be integrated to be effectively managed. **Integrated marketing communications** has become the new model that many firms use in organizing their marketing activities. This ensures that the messages sent to employees, customers, the media, and others are consistent and that they are developed to achieve the overall mission of the organization.

Although these various forms of marketing communications should be integrated, remember that each has unique strengths and weaknesses. Personal selling is the primary way to attract corporate and group business. Advertising is often used to reach leisure travelers (who cannot be reached by direct sales) or to build an image for a brand name. Public relations often attempts to influence a much wider audience—employees, community opinion leaders, the media, financial institutions, unions, and others. Sales promotion is used to quickly boost sales. Direct marketing and point-of-purchase communications are useful for reaching current guests and highly targeted prospects.

To succeed, a hotel or restaurant must know how to use promotional activities and how to organize and combine them so they work together to deliver a result greater than the sum of its parts.

Apply Your Learning 5.3

Please write all answers on a separate sheet of paper.

1. What are the four *P*s of marketing?

2. Which of the four *P*s is concerned with determining a hotel's concept?

3. What does "cost-plus pricing" mean?

4. What are "loss leaders"?

5.4 Lodging Market Segments

AFTER STUDYING SECTION 5.4, YOU SHOULD KNOW HOW TO:

♦ List important types of lodging guests

♦ Identify the lodging needs of individual business travelers

♦ Describe corporate groups that stay at lodging properties

♦ Describe convention and association groups

♦ Identify the needs of leisure travelers

♦ Explain the needs of long-term stay/relocation guests

♦ Describe how airline-related guests use lodging properties

♦ Identify the government and military travelers market

♦ Define regional getaway guests

♦ Define guest mix and its effect on lodging properties

When it comes to satisfying individual tastes, wants, and needs, a one-size-fits-all approach to marketing is not good enough. Rather than attempting to be "all

things to all people," the solution is for hotels to narrow their scope and focus on guest segments.

Eight main guest segments have been identified in the hotel industry:

• Individual business travelers

• Corporate groups

• Convention and association groups

• Leisure travelers

• Long-term stay/relocation guests

• Airline-related guests

• Government and military travelers

• Regional getaway guests

Individual Business Travelers

Individual business travelers usually stay one or two nights, and they account for 60 percent of the hotel industry's business. According to a study by Lodging Hospitality magazine, business travelers choose a hotel based on:

1. Location

2. Room rate

3. Reputation

4. Employer preference

5. On-site amenities

Forty percent of these travelers make their reservations through a travel agency, 29 percent call a hotel company's toll-free phone number, and 28 percent call a hotel directly. Use of the Internet to make hotel reservations is steadily increasing.

Business travelers use a hotel's restaurants, lounges, and room service. They also take advantage of exercise facilities, concierge floors, and business centers. In the guestroom, a working desk is their highest priority, followed by access to a fax machine and copier, proper lighting, a desk phone, and a comfortable desk chair. Travelers who use laptop computers also need easily accessible data ports.

Business travelers care about recognition and special treatment. Frequent-stay programs and airline frequent-flyer programs are appreciated. These travelers may choose hotels and rental car companies tied in with such programs when they have a choice.

Corporate Groups

Corporate groups travel purely for business purposes, and their rooms are booked in blocks by their company or a travel agency. These travelers usually stay two to four days. While top managers are typically assigned single rooms, middle- and lower-level managers often share rooms.

Corporate group travelers favor hotels that offer intimate meeting rooms and private dining facilities. Several conference centers with these features have been built in suburban locations near major cities and airports. The idea is to do away with big-city distractions and give participants a chance to interact not only during meetings but between them as well.

Convention and Association Groups

The number of hotel guests from **convention and association groups** can run into the thousands. Delegates tend to stay in large hotels where a negotiated package price covers rooms, meals, and functions. Convention delegates usually share rooms and stay three to four days.

Large convention groups choose their venues several years in advance, so a hotel's selling efforts are often prolonged and may involve cooperation from airlines and local convention and visitors bureaus. Hotels that have fewer rooms and limited function space often compete for group business by offering extremely competitive rates.

Leisure Travelers

Leisure travelers often travel with their families on sightseeing trips, or on trips to visit friends or relatives. They typically spend only one night at the same hotel (except at resorts), and a room may be occupied by a couple as well as one or more children. Because they travel during peak season, they usually pay full rack rates unless they are members of such organizations as the American Automobile Association (AAA) or the American Association of Retired Persons (AARP), which negotiate discounts with many hotels.

Long-Term Stay/ Relocation Guests

Long-term stay/relocation guests are primarily individuals or families moving to an area and requiring lodging until permanent housing can be found. Their needs include limited cooking facilities and more living space than is available in a typical hotel room. They often are less dependent on room attendant staff and may arrange for once-weekly, rather than daily, room cleaning. All-suite and extended-stay hotels such as Embassy Suites and Residence Inns by Marriott are examples of products designed specifically for the needs of long-term guests. A Residence Inn unit is about twice the size of an average hotel room and typically contains a living area, a bedroom, extra closet space, and a small kitchen.

Airline-Related Guests

Airlines negotiate rates with hotels for **airline-related guests**—airplane crews and passengers who need accommodations because they are bumped from a flight or stranded due to mechanical or weather problems. Rooms are usually booked in blocks at rock-bottom prices.

Government and Military Travelers

Government and military travelers are reimbursed on fixed per diem allowances, which means they only receive a certain amount for lodging expenses, no matter what they actually have to pay for a room. These guests typically choose properties that offer very low rates or have negotiated acceptable rates with their organizations.

Regional Getaway Guests

Regional getaway guests are important to hotels that normally cater to business travelers and convention groups on weekdays. Hotels promote special weekend packages designed to entice nearby residents to check into a hotel for Friday or Saturday night. Often, heavily discounted room, meal, and entertainment packages are available for couples and families.

Guest Mix

Guest mix refers to the variety, or mixture, of guests who stay at a hotel. A hotel's guest mix might consist of 60 percent individual business travelers, 20 percent conventioneers, and 20 percent leisure travelers, for example.

Guest mix depends on a hotel's location, size, facilities, and operating philosophy.

With few exceptions, every hotel strives to reach multiple market segments. At any one time, a large hotel such as the 2,000-room Hilton New York & Towers in Manhattan will lodge several groups, individual business travelers, families on vacation, airline crews, and government employees. By diversifying their guest base, hotels hope to minimize the effects of seasonality, economic recessions, and changing market dynamics.

There are dangers to this strategy, however. Sometimes different kinds of guests just don't mix well together. Business executives may be annoyed to find a large tour group blocking their way to the coffee shop in the morning. Honeymoon couples may be annoyed by noisy children running through the hallways. As a result, some hotels control their mix very carefully, to achieve the best environment possible for all concerned.

Apply Your Learning 5.4

Please write all answers on a separate sheet of paper.

1. What five main concerns most influence an individual business traveler's choice of hotel?

2. Why are more corporate groups booking rooms in suburban conference centers?

3. List one national organization recognized for negotiating special discounted hotel rates.

For 4–10, match each description with its correct guest segment.

convention and association groups   leisure travelers

corporate groups   long-term stay/relocation guests

government and military travelers   regional getaway guests

individual business travelers

4. Business travelers who usually stay one or two nights in a hotel.

5. Business travelers who favor large hotels, usually share rooms, and stay three to four days.

6. People moving to an area and requiring lodging until they can find permanent housing.

7. Guests who are likely to be on a fixed per diem expense account and are interested in very low rates for lodging.

8. Business travelers who usually stay two to four days, need private meeting and dining rooms, and book their stay through their own company or a travel agency.

9. Couples or families who are looking for a quick and economical way to add variety to their weekend routine.

10. Guests who typically pay full rack rate and often travel with their families or on trips to visit friends or relatives.

Quick Hits

Section 5.1—Marketing and Sales

- The goal of hospitality marketing is to make certain every guest is a repeat guest. That means developing relationships with guests and working to make sure their expectations are met.

- **Marketing** includes research, product development, advertising, publicity, and sales promotions, as well as the means to monitor the effectiveness of the marketing program.

- **Sales** consists of direct efforts to sell products and services by personal contact, telecommunication, and mailings. It focuses primarily on delivering what consumers want rather than on what the property wants to sell.

- To be most effective, marketing and sales must work hand in hand. Marketing focuses on trend research and the development of successful sales techniques and efforts. Successful sales depends on effective marketing strategies.

Section 5.2—The Marketing and Sales Division

- A marketing-oriented general manager is the key to a hotel's sales efforts. In small to medium-sized properties, the GM may take on the responsibilities of advertising and public relations to give the sales manager time to sell. The GM

may also make personal sales calls and spend time talking with guests at the front desk.

- The vice president (or director) of marketing and sales usually serves on the executive committee of the property. Some people in this position are actively involved in sales; others are administrators.

- The director of convention service/convention service manager oversees the servicing of group business once it has been sold. This person works closely with all departments, coordinating the efforts of the food and beverage department, the front office, and the banquet setup crew.

- The telemarketing director supervises and manages the telephone sales staff, which is responsible for developing leads, making prospecting calls, and following up on leads and previous clients.

- The market research coordinator oversees the development of information regarding the history and past performance of each account being solicited; and may also research current market trends, the strategies used by competing properties, and general consumer trends.

- The director of marketing performs a variety of management tasks: setting objectives and policies; making decisions; and organizing, selecting, and supervising the sales and marketing staffs.

- The director of advertising and public relations oversees creative staff, coordinates all promotional materials, establishes a good public image for the property, and helps select advertising media.

- The director of sales supervises office staff, handles administrative duties, and may also manage key accounts, assist salespeople when necessary, and prepare sales reports for top management.

- In small properties, the sales manager might be the same as director of sales; in larger properties, the sales manager would report to the director of sales. Sales managers usually assign territory or accounts to salespeople, monitor the progress of salespeople, and handle their own accounts.

- The assistant director of sales is the chief aide to the director of sales and may also manage the sales office, supervise sales staff, and handle his or her own accounts. If the sales office is headed by a sales manager, this position would be called the assistant sales manager.

- Salespeople are responsible for contacting, soliciting, and providing follow-up service to clients. They may be called *account managers*, while senior salespeople are sometimes called *sales executives* or *account executives*.

- The clerical staff maintains sales paperwork. In many cases, the clerical staff knows as much about the property as the salespeople and may be actively involved in handling accounts.

SECTION 5.3—THE FOUR *P*S OF MARKETING

- The **Four *P*s of Marketing** are product, place, price, and promotion. The way these marketing efforts are combined is the **marketing mix**

- *Product* refers to all of the things that make the experience of staying at a hotel what it is—including the operating philosophy, facilities, amenities, and level of service.

- *Place* refers to the physical location of a hotel as well as all of the sites where reservations are made.

- *Price* is a complex part of the marketing mix. One approach is **cost-plus pricing**, in which actual costs are determined, then a reasonable percentage is added on to arrive at the final price. A better model is **customer-based pricing**, in which companies determine what customers want, what they're willing to pay for it, and how the hotel can deliver it.

- *Promotion* includes personal selling, advertising, public relations, sales promotion, direct-marketing, and point-of-purchase communications.

SECTION 5.4—LODGING MARKET SEGMENTS

- There are eight main ways of segmenting guests: individual business travelers, corporate groups, convention and association groups, leisure travelers, long-term stay/relocation guests, airline-related guests, government and military travelers, and regional getaway guests.

- **Individual business travelers** choose a hotel based on location, room rate, reputation, employer preference, and on-site amenities.

- **Corporate groups** travel purely for business purposes, and their rooms are booked in blocks by their company or a travel agency.

- **Convention and association groups** tend to stay in large hotels where a negotiated package price covers rooms, meals, and functions.

- **Leisure travelers** often travel with their families on sightseeing trips, or on trips to visit friends or relatives. Because they travel during peak season, they usually pay full rack rates.

- **Long-term stay/relocation guests** are primarily individuals or families moving to an area and requiring lodging until permanent housing can be found. Their needs include limited cooking facilities and more living space than is available in a typical hotel room.

- **Airline-related guests** include airplane crews and passengers delayed due to mechanical or weather problems. Rooms are usually booked in blocks at rock-bottom prices.

- Because **government and military travelers** are on fixed daily allowances, they typically choose properties that offer very low rates or have negotiated low rates with their organizations.

- **Regional getaway guests** are nearby residents who may be offered heavily discounted room, meal, and entertainment packages to encourage weekend use of a hotel typically frequented by business groups and conventioneers.

- **Guest mix** refers to the variety of guests who stay at a hotel. It might consist of 60 percent individual business travelers, 20 percent conventioneers, and 20 percent leisure travelers, for example. Guest mix depends on a hotel's location, size, facilities, and operating philosophy.

Profile

Feliz Peñaloza Jarvis
Vice President of Sales & Marketing
Bristol Hotels & Resorts

Since high school, Feliz Jarvis has wanted her own hotel. "Hotels were always fun for me…luxury, a new place, special service and treatment, an adventure."

After earning her bachelor of science degree in hotel and restaurant management from the University of Houston, Jarvis became manager of Laventhol & Horwath's hospitality consulting division in Dallas, Texas.

In 1987, she joined Bristol Hotels & Resorts as director of sales for Bristol Suites. Jarvis said, "I love the sales side, because you really see the results of your efforts: the room is occupied or not. The real fun is getting people to say, 'Yes, let's book at your hotel.'"

Jarvis moved to The Harvey Hotel and Harvey Sweets at DFW Airport as director of sales and marketing , then to the Harvey Hotel/Dallas and Bristol Suites with responsibility for the combined sales efforts of two properties.

"I also love the diversity of people you interact with and the challenge of convincing them you have something better, different, unique," said Jarvis.

In 1994, Jarvis was named general manager of the adjacent properties. In 1995, she became vice president of marketing for Bristol. In 1996, she accepted the newly created position of vice president of strategic planning.

Jarvis became vice president of sales and marketing in 1998, leading Bristol's high-profile direct sales effort and overseeing the 650-member sales force.

"Feliz is an excellent choice for this position because of her unique understanding of the Bristol sales culture as well as our strategic marketing focus," said John Beckert, Bristol president and COO. "She is passionate in her drive to ensure that Bristol's sales effort is one of our greatest strengths."

Jarvis cautions that sales is not for everybody. "It's not as glamorous as it seems. You need to be able to take rejection, be a great negotiator and always be on the lookout for a new or potential client."

Does she still want a hotel of her own? "Yes. I just don't want to run it!"

The Marketing Plan

Sections

6.1 Putting the Plan Together

6.2 Conducting a Marketing Audit

6.3 Target Markets and Positioning

6.4 Marketing Objectives, Action Plans, and Evaluation

6.1 Putting the Plan Together

AFTER STUDYING SECTION 6.1, YOU SHOULD KNOW HOW TO:

♦ Explain the benefits of a long-range marketing plan

♦ Identify the components of a marketing plan

♦ Describe the makeup and function of a marketing team

♦ List the steps of a marketing plan

In today's competitive hospitality market, it's important for hotels to increase their market share and profits. No business can afford to just coast. Having great ideas is not enough; sales, advertising, promotions, and public relations strategies must be developed into a structured **marketing plan** that can be communicated throughout the organization.

The Marketing Plan

The marketing plan is a guide for selling hospitality. There are many benefits to creating a long-range marketing plan. A marketing plan can:

• Force managers to think ahead and make better use of the property's resources

• Provide a means for evaluating the results of marketing and sales efforts

• Create an awareness of problems and obstacles

• Identify opportunities to increase market share in some market segments and open new opportunities in other areas

• Provide a source of information for present and future reference

• Ensure that sales promotions and advertising are not wasted due to misdirected efforts

The marketing plan is a property's road map. It tells hotel managers who they are, where they are going, and how they're going to get there. It spells out the steps they'll need to take to gain and retain customers, increase repeat business, and encourage higher guest spending. It typically includes programs to attract business to each of the hotel's revenue centers, making sure that individual programs complement rather than conflict with one another. The plan is then regularly reviewed and updated.

A typical marketing plan may include the following information (discussed throughout this chapter):

• Details about the property, including market share, fair share, and REVPAR

• Guest profiles, target markets, and analysis of the hotel's position in the marketplace

- Analysis of the hotel's competition

- Key objectives that will fulfill the mission statement (for example, how the property will respond during periods of low occupancy or what the specific plans are for group sales)

- Strategies or action steps needed to achieve the key objectives

- Budget details for the action plan

The marketing plan is a guide; it is not etched in stone. Not every activity will be completed as scheduled. Some action plans may be delayed or deleted due to changes in the economy, the marketplace, or personnel. Managers will regularly compare the plan with their hotel's current business climate to know where to increase sales and marketing efforts—and when to shift direction in order to achieve the best overall results.

The plan is usually developed for at least a three-year period. New—and, often, more profitable—market segments might take two or three years to develop. A shorter planning cycle may actually restrict growth and long-term profits.

The Marketing Team

The head of the marketing and sales department is responsible for the marketing plan, but he or she may seek input from other staff to make sure all areas of the property are represented. At some properties, a formal, property-wide marketing team (sometimes called a *sales committee*) is established to create and implement marketing strategies for the entire property.

The team may include at least one representative from each revenue center—banquets, rooms, gift shop, etc. Support centers of the property can be represented on the marketing team as well: the director of sales may be responsible for providing input and plans relating to group business; the GM may be asked to gather information about specific market segments; and the public relations director may be responsible for documenting successful advertising strategies used by competitors. The marketing team can also include employees who are directly involved in day-to-day operations—front desk agents, room attendants, kitchen personnel, and so on.

This approach helps create a sense of ownership when it comes to making decisions about what is profitable and what is not. A salesperson may know basic facts about the property's restaurant, but input from the food and beverage director—perhaps she mentions that the pastry chef has created spectacular cakes for important officials or celebrities—can result in new and creative promotional ideas.

Steps of a Marketing Plan

There are six key steps to a good marketing plan (see Exhibit 1):

1. Conducting a marketing audit

2. Selecting target markets

3. Positioning the property

4. Determining marketing objectives

5. Developing and implementing action plans

6. Monitoring and evaluating the marketing plan

The development of a marketing plan is a never-ending process. After one marketing plan cycle has been completed, the results

**Exhibit 1
The Marketing Plan Cycle**

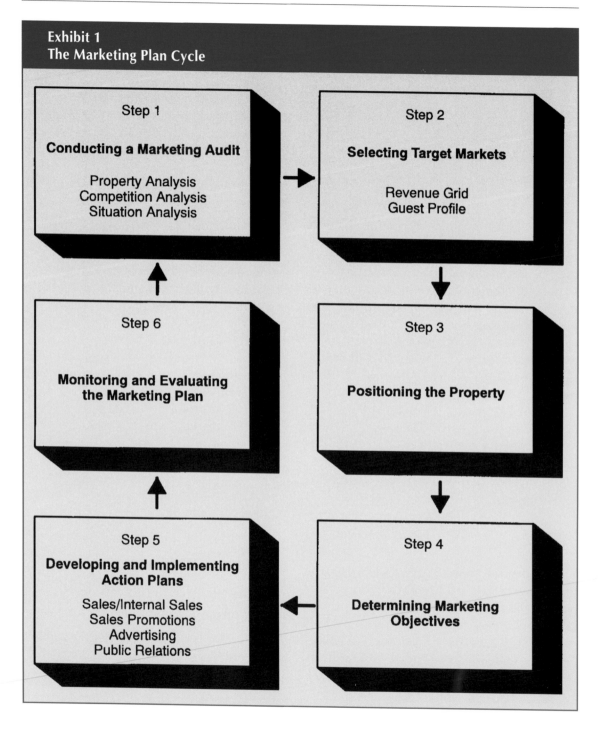

Step 1

Conducting a Marketing Audit

Property Analysis
Competition Analysis
Situation Analysis

Step 2

Selecting Target Markets

Revenue Grid
Guest Profile

Step 6

**Monitoring and Evaluating
the Marketing Plan**

Step 3

Positioning the Property

Step 5

**Developing and Implementing
Action Plans**

Sales/Internal Sales
Sales Promotions
Advertising
Public Relations

Step 4

**Determining Marketing
Objectives**

must be evaluated, and the process returns to the marketing audit portion of the cycle.

In the following sections of this chapter, we'll take a close look at each of these steps.

Apply Your Learning 6.1

Please write all answers on a separate sheet of paper.

1. List two benefits of creating a long-range marketing plan.

2. Why is a one-year planning cycle insufficient?

3. Why is it important that a marketing team developing a marketing plan include representatives from revenue centers and support centers?

4. Marketing plans should be evaluated:

    a. when new managers join the hotel.
    b. twice a year.
    c. when revenues and market share begin to decline.
    d. after each marketing plan cycle.

6.2 Conducting a Marketing Audit

AFTER STUDYING SECTION 6.2, YOU SHOULD KNOW HOW TO:

♦ Define a property analysis

♦ Identify the information needed for a property analysis

♦ Conduct a competition analysis

♦ Define market share and fair share

♦ Calculate REVPAR

♦ Conduct a situation analysis

♦ List resources for preparing a marketplace analysis

The foundation of any marketing plan is the **marketing audit**, the research step in the planning process. A marketing audit is a careful evaluation of the factors relating to sales potential. It gathers, records, and analyzes information about your property, your competition, and the marketplace, and it's of great benefit when it comes to making decisions and selecting appropriate target markets.

A marketing audit consists of three parts:

• Property analysis

• Competition analysis

• Situation or marketplace analysis

Property Analysis

A **property analysis** is a written, unbiased self-appraisal used to assess the strengths and weaknesses of a property (see Exhibit 1). It starts with a detailed room-by-room and facility-by-facility inspection. The person conducting the analysis will:

• Examine building exteriors, landscaping, and the property's sign.

• Evaluate the entire property in terms of traffic flow, accessibility, eye appeal, and compatibility with local surroundings.

Pied Piper Slept Here

The marketing experts may be tearing their hair out, but the Rat Trap Inn in South Wales can't escape its name. The inn is built around an 18th-century house originally meant for coachmen and servants. These accommodations were known as "rat traps."

Over the years, the hotel has called itself "Cottage Inn" and "New Inn," but the name "Rat Trap" stuck—despite the property's modern suites and fine-dining restaurant. (Thankfully, there's *one* meat item that doesn't appear on the menu.)

Exhibit 1
Sample Property Analysis

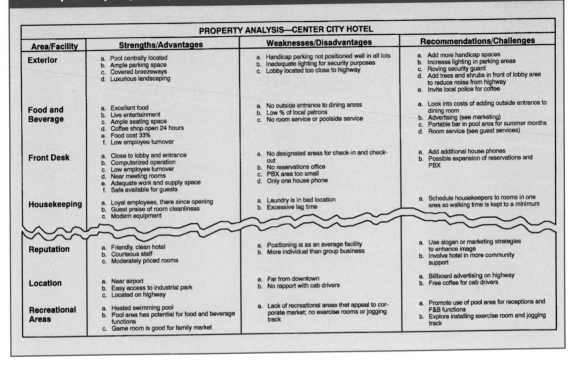

PROPERTY ANALYSIS—CENTER CITY HOTEL			
Area/Facility	**Strengths/Advantages**	**Weaknesses/Disadvantages**	**Recommendations/Challenges**
Exterior	a. Pool centrally located b. Ample parking space c. Covered breezeways d. Luxurious landscaping	a. Handicap parking not positioned well in all lots b. Inadequate lighting for security purposes c. Lobby located too close to highway	a. Add more handicap spaces b. Increase lighting in parking areas c. Roving security guard d. Add trees and shrubs in front of lobby area to reduce noise from highway e. Invite local police for coffee
Food and Beverage	a. Excellent food b. Live entertainment c. Ample seating space d. Coffee shop open 24 hours e. Food cost 33% f. Low employee turnover	a. No outside entrance to dining areas b. Low % of local patrons c. No room service or poolside service	a. Look into costs of adding outside entrance to dining room b. Advertising (see marketing) c. Portable bar in pool area for summer months d. Room service (see guest services)
Front Desk	a. Close to lobby and entrance b. Computerized operation c. Low employee turnover d. Near meeting rooms e. Adequate work and supply space f. Safe available for guests	a. No designated areas for check-in and check-out b. No reservations office c. PBX area too small d. Only one house phone	a. Add additional house phones b. Possible expansion of reservations and PBX
Housekeeping	a. Loyal employees, there since opening b. Guest praise of room cleanliness c. Modern equipment	a. Laundry is in bad location b. Excessive lag time	a. Schedule housekeepers to rooms in one area so walking time is kept to a minimum
Reputation	a. Friendly, clean hotel b. Courteous staff c. Moderately priced rooms	a. Positioning is as an average facility b. More individual than group business	a. Use slogan or marketing strategies to enhance image b. Involve hotel in more community support
Location	a. Near airport b. Easy access to industrial park c. Located on highway	a. Far from downtown b. No rapport with cab drivers	a. Billboard advertising on highway b. Free coffee for cab drivers
Recreational Areas	a. Heated swimming pool b. Pool area has potential for food and beverage functions c. Game room is good for family market	a. Lack of recreational areas that appeal to corporate market; no exercise rooms or jogging track	a. Promote use of pool area for receptions and F&B functions b. Explore installing exercise room and jogging track

- Note areas for change, but suggest changes that are feasible.

The marketing team will try to see the property as guests see it. The introduction of a new menu or a heavily advertised promotion may draw large crowds, but if the staff isn't ready for the increased activity or the restrooms are dirty or the parking lot is full of potholes, new customers attracted by the promotion may never come back (or, worse yet, may tell friends about their bad experience). Sales staff and the property's management may stay overnight at the property to form an impression of the property as a product. An uninvolved outsider may also be invited to spend a night or weekend at the property and then report back to the team to provide additional input.

Competition Analysis

A **competition analysis** helps a property discover:

- Profitable guest groups that are being overlooked by the property—but not by the competition

- Some competitive benefit or advantage the property enjoys that can't be matched by major competitors

- Weaknesses in the marketing strategies of the competition on which the property can capitalize

Competitors are generally other hotels in the immediate area that sell to similar market segments and offer similar products and

---

Exhibit 2
Competitive Fact Sheets

- Number of rooms and their breakdown—double/double, kings, suites, executive floor, etc. Include the condition of the room when it was last renovated, plans for expansion, and so on.
- Location—distance from transportation hubs, key businesses, and area attractions.
- Overall reputation and quality—all areas of the facility.
- Meeting/banquet space and service—number and square footage of each room; banquet menu in terms of items and pricing.
- Restaurants and lounges—outlets, hours of operation, menus and pricing, and nearby restaurants.
- Other amenities and services—gift shops, indoor and outdoor pools, limousine service, valet parking.
- Marketing—size of sales staff and their responsibilities, selling and advertising strategies (direct mail, travel agents, local media).
- Customer mix—present guest mix, likely markets for the future.
- Positioning—current positioning statement, chain affiliation, image, pricing policy, points of difference in the competition.

---

services at similar prices. To get a more accurate picture of your competition, hotels use three key forms:

1. *Competitive Rate Analysis.* Compares all rates and prices of competitors.

2. *Competitive Fact Sheets.* Gauge competitors' activities in such areas as group bookings, guest relations, promotional programs, use of advertising, and market penetration (see Exhibit 2).

3. *Need Fulfillment by Market Segment.* Evaluates how a property or restaurant stacks up against others in specific market areas. Determining how the hotel or restaurant fills the needs and wants of each segment is valuable in finding a competitive advantage.

Once this information is obtained, market share, fair share, and REVPAR can be calculated. The first step in calculating market share and fair share is to set up a table of descriptive data, including each competitive property's number of rooms, available nights for sale (the total rooms multiplied by 365), occupancy percentage, and actual room nights sold over the course of the year (see Exhibit 3).

The **market share** is determined by dividing the number of property room nights sold by the total market room nights sold. Using this formula and the information in Exhibit 3, your property would have a market share of 27 percent based on 83,768 room nights sold, the downtown hotel would have a market share of 38 percent based on 115,997 room nights sold, and the airport hotel would have a market share of 35 percent based on sales of 109,500.

But market share alone doesn't provide enough information to accurately assess how well a property is doing in the marketplace. Managers must also determine their property's **fair share**—the number of room nights the property would sell if demand were distributed based on the number of rooms in each property.

Exhibit 3
Table of Descriptive Data

	Number of Rooms	Available Rooms*	Percentage Occupancy	Room Nights Sold
Your Property	300	109,500	76.5	83,768
Downtown Hotel	454	165,710	70.0	115,997
Airport Hotel	400	146,000	75.0	109,500
TOTAL	1,154	421,210	73.8**	309,265

*Number of rooms multiplied by 365 for yearly total

**Average occupancy

Fair share is determined by dividing the number of rooms available at each property by the number of rooms available in the market as a whole. Using the figures in Exhibit 3, your property would have a fair share of 26 percent (109,500 rooms divided by 421,210), the downtown property would have a fair share of 39 percent (165,710 rooms divided by 421,210), and the airport property would have a fair share of 35 percent (146,000 divided by 421,210).

In this example, your property's market share is one percent more than its fair share, the downtown property's market share is one percent less than its fair share, and the airport property's fair share and market share are the same. Your property is enjoying a small measure of success, while the downtown property is at a disadvantage in the market and the airport property is just holding its own.

A more accurate way to determine how a property is doing against the competition is to calculate **REVPAR (revenue per available room)**. By dividing room revenue by the number of rooms available for sale, you can see precisely what a property is earning in relation to its competitors.

A comparison of a property with the competition can reveal strengths, weaknesses, and important characteristics that will assist in positioning and selling the property. Marketing teams also will walk through competitors' properties, talk with their employees and guests, and study their advertising. They'll book an overnight stay. They'll eat in their restaurants, read their rack brochures and internal literature. All of these are excellent ways to determine differences between a property and its competition. Once these differences are determined, it is possible to set goals to "sell the differences" to each targeted market segment.

Situation Analysis

A **situation analysis** researches the property's current position in the marketplace and reveals opportunities to promote the property. There are two parts: the marketplace analysis and the occupancy and activity analysis.

The **marketplace analysis** identifies environmental opportunities and problems that can affect business, including changes in demographics; positive and negative events in the community, region, state, and nation; the cost and availability of energy; government regulations; and travel costs. Useful statistics can be found in census data, information from industrial commissions such as the state or city division of economic development, and industry reports. Other sources of information are listed in Exhibit 4.

The **occupancy and activity analysis** is an analysis of the property's past, present, and potential operating statistics. It is used to track sales history patterns over a three- to five-year period and highlights the "soft spots"—low-business periods—that most hotels and restaurants have in their sales patterns. Most hotels keep guestroom statistics, but fewer track restaurant, lounge, and function space statistics such as total covers (meals served), seat turnover, average guest check, function room bookings, and average size of functions. Room statistics focus on occupancy and average rate, occupancy by day of the week, geographic origin of bookings, group and individual room nights by segment and source, and the status of future group business already booked.

Apply Your Learning 6.2

Please write all answers on a separate sheet of paper.

1. What are the three parts of a marketing audit?

2. The primary goal of a property analysis is to:
   a. evaluate the quality of competing hotels in an area.
   b. assess the strengths and weaknesses of the property.
   c. pinpoint areas at a property in need of repair and maintenance.
   d. place a dollar amount on the value of a property's total assets.

3. Market share is determined by:
   a. comparing a property's market segmentation mix with the mix of at least two other local competitors.
   b. first calculating a property's fair share of the market.
   c. dividing the number of property room nights sold by the total market room nights sold.
   d. completing a Need Fulfillment by Market Segment form.

4. What does REVPAR stand for?

5. What are the two parts of a situation analysis?

Exhibit 4
Marketplace Resources Analysis

POPULATION AND DEMOGRAPHICS

American Demographics
Ithaca, New York

First Data InfoSource/Donnelly Marketing

State Office of Demographics and Economic Analysis (sometimes called the Division of Research and Statistics)
Found in the governmental pages under the state name.

INCOME/EMPLOYMENT

State Commerce and Economic Development Department
Division of Economic Development found (in telephone directory) in governmental pages under state name.

RETAIL STATISTICS

Sales & Marketing Management

State Office of Demographics and Economic Analysis

State Commerce Department
Division of Economic Development

First Data InfoSource/Donnelly Marketing

COMMERCIAL & INDUSTRIAL ACTIVITY

State Banking Department
See governmental pages of telephone directory under state name.

U.S. Treasury
Controller of the Currency, listed in governmental pages under "United States."

Chamber of Commerce (local)

State Department of Commerce

TOURISM

State Highway Department
State Department of Transportation; Traffic and Safety Division; found in government pages under state name.

Local Airport Authorities
State Department of Transportation; Public Transportation Division; found in governmental pages under state name.

Area Attractions

Area Hotels

AREA ATTRACTIONS

Chamber of Commerce (local)

Convention and Visitors Bureaus

SITE ADAPTABILITY

Community Planning Agencies
See above.

MARKET SUPPLY/DEMAND

Local Hotel and Motel Association

Convention and Visitors Bureaus

Interviewing Hotels

DIRECT COMPETITION

On-Site Inspections

Directories (chain, AAA, Mobil)

Interviews with Hotel Managers

POTENTIAL COMPETITION

Building Permits
Local Department of Buildings found in governmental pages under County or State.

Project Status
Local Department of Buildings in conjunction with local banks.

DEMAND

U.S. Department of Commerce Directories

Local Chamber of Commerce Statistics

Hotel Sales Tax Figures (if available)

Monthly and Yearly Lodging Reports

Convention and Visitors Bureaus

Local Hotel Managers

6.3 Target Markets and Positioning

AFTER STUDYING SECTION 6.3, YOU SHOULD KNOW HOW TO:

♦ Select a target market

♦ Define market segmentation

♦ Identify the present guest base using a revenue grid and an occupancy chart

♦ Create a guest profile

♦ Define positioning and market position

♦ Develop a positioning strategy

♦ Write a positioning statement

Selecting Target Markets

A hotel is a series of businesses catering to a number of different markets. Guestrooms may appeal primarily to leisure travelers on the weekends and to business travelers during the week. The restaurant may serve a local business clientele at lunch and hotel guests at dinner. Meeting rooms may be used by out-of-town conventioneers during the week and by local groups on weekends. This is **market segmentation**—viewing a market as a number of smaller market segments with similar product and service preferences.

There are many ways markets can be segmented, including:

• demographics (senior citizens, young marrieds)

• purpose of trip (business, leisure)

• benefits sought (security, business services, a multilingual staff)

• geography (by zip code)

• lifestyle (fitness enthusiasts, golfers, culture seekers)

While most hoteliers would love to serve all segments equally well, that's just not possible. Properties must realistically define their product in terms of the major market segments they can best satisfy.

Before deciding which market segments to target, a hotel looks at the guests it is currently serving. Two forms help to determine the guest base and the decline or growth of a market segment: a revenue grid, which gathers statistics for each market segment and shows which are the most profitable (see Exhibit 1), and an occupancy chart, which provides insight into the growth patterns of each market segment (see Exhibit 2).

Guest profiles can help identify existing market segments. For each revenue-producing center in the hotel—guestrooms, restaurants, banquet facilities, health club, etc.—the hotel staff will compile such information as: the name of the guest, address, and zip code; gender and age of guest; place

Exhibit 1
Sample Revenue Grid

MARKET SEGMENTS	Room Nights	Average Guest per Room	% of Occupancy	Average Room Rate	Room Revenues	% of Room Revenue	F & B Revenue	% of F & B Revenue	Other Revenue	% of Other Revenue	% of Repeat Business	Time of Year to Promote
Individual Traveler												
Business												
Leisure												
Group Traveler												
Tour												
Convention												
Other												
Airline Crews												
Sports Teams												
Government												

or type of employment; place of residence; mode of transportation to property (car, airplane, bus, train); guest status (new, repeat, corporate); date and method of reservation; arrival and departure dates; length of stay; number in party; room rate paid; type of room chosen; type of guest (convention delegate, businessperson, leisure traveler, and so on); total folio charges and method of payment (cash, credit card, company billing); and salesperson making the booking, if the guest is part of a group. This information will reveal the makeup of the present guest base.

When considering new markets to target, a hotel will strive for a balanced guest mix. A full-service hotel, for example, may target business travelers during the week, leisure vacationers on the weekends, and local food functions, convention business, and perhaps group tours during otherwise slow periods. This mix will ensure that the property maintains a fairly steady occupancy rate regardless of changing market trends.

The property's guest mix is reviewed periodically. Unforeseen events, such as economic downturns, strikes, highway reroutings, and weather may alter the guest mix and trigger changes to the mix. In economic recessions, corporations cut back on travel, laid-off workers drop out of the

Exhibit 2
Sample Occupancy Chart

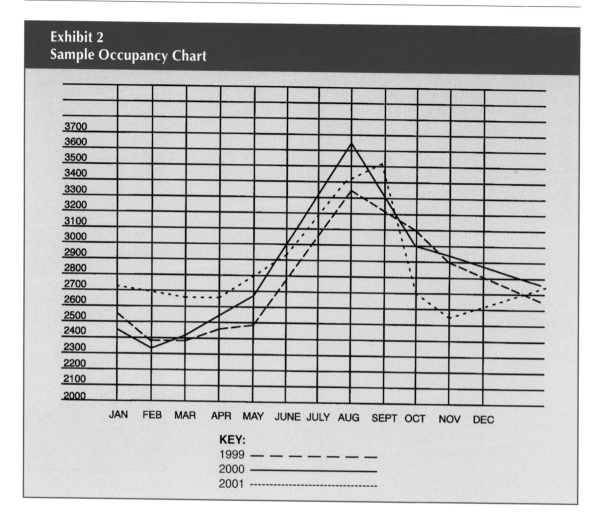

leisure market, and even senior citizens with discretionary income travel less. To fill guestrooms, hotel marketers might decide to go after specialty market segments such as sports teams, family reunion business, and government travelers. Defining and redefining markets is a continual process. Adjustments to the marketing plan are frequently required as conditions change.

Positioning the Property

What do you think of when you think of Motel 6? Chances are, that brand has an identity that you can easily describe and which makes it distinct from the Holiday Inn, Hilton, and Ritz-Carlton brands. This perception of a property by its guests or potential guests is known as the property's **market position**—and every property has one. The process of designing a property's market position is known as **positioning**.

Positioning is not simply about advertising. A property's position consists of the hospitality it offers and the marketer's ability to create unique selling points based on the property's location, internal or external features, and personnel. It creates an image and distinguishes a property from its competition. It helps guests determine what benefits the property has to offer, and it helps managers better understand where the property is going and how it will get there.

Developing a positioning strategy requires identifying the benefits that will be most important to potential guests. Answering these questions will get a property off to a solid start:

- Who are we? What do we stand for? What are our strengths and weaknesses? Does our property have a liability that can be turned into an asset? (The property analysis will help answer these questions.)

- How does our property differ from the competition? Does our property have tangible or intangible advantages over the competition? Are there areas where we can set ourselves apart? (The competitive fact sheets and rate analysis will provide clues.)

- What areas are not producing the desired revenue or response? Are there areas that show a high potential for repeat business? (The occupancy and activity charts will help here.)

- Which target market segments can be most beneficial to us? (Use the revenue grid to evaluate your response.)

- What are the needs and wants of each segment? What benefits do they seek? Does the property offer any features or services that are unique?

- Are there opportunities in the marketplace? How can we go about attracting this business?

Once the property has answers to these questions, it can begin to develop a **positioning statement**, a statement that effectively communicates the property's advantages to its selected target markets. A positioning statement should answer the following questions about customer perceptions:

- Do we really know who our guests are and what they are looking for? How well do our existing services meet the needs of each segment?

- How do our guests perceive our property versus our competition? How do we rate in terms of price, service, facilities, and amenities?

- What do the competition's guests think of our property? Do they know what we have to offer?

The positioning statement should be targeted to market segments of sufficient size to make it financially worthwhile to attract more business from them. And, of course, the property must have the ability to meet the demands of those market segments.

Apply Your Learning 6.3

Please write all answers on a separate sheet of paper.

1. Define market segmentation.

2. What form can help a hotel gather statistics about its current market segments and see which are the most profitable?

    a. REVPAR summary
    b. revenue grid
    c. guest mix report
    d. occupancy chart

3. Which form details the monthly room nights for a particular market segment to help managers assess market trends?

    a. guest profile
    b. revenue grid
    c. guest mix report
    d. occupancy chart

4. Which of the following would most likely *not* lead a property to review its guest mix?

    a. Thunderstorms have been predicted for the next week.
    b. News reports indicate that many corporations are now willing to spend more money on travel and lodging.
    c. Highway repairs will close the off-ramp closest to the hotel for the next two months.
    d. City leaders have announced plans to build a new professional sports stadium.

5. List one benefit of positioning.

6.4 Marketing Objectives, Action Plans, and Evaluation

AFTER STUDYING SECTION 6.4, YOU SHOULD KNOW HOW TO:

♦ Write a marketing objective

♦ List the characteristics of effective marketing objectives

♦ Create an action plan

♦ Identify the components of an action plan

♦ Determine the budget for an action plan

♦ List methods of monitoring an evaluation plan

♦ Describe the importance of evaluating marketing plans

♦ Explain common reasons that hotel sales goals are not met

The marketing audit is done, target market segments identified, and the hotel is positioned. The next step is to establish specific marketing objectives. This step involves establishing goals for each market segment and determining the best ways to reach them.

Determining Marketing Objectives

Monthly goals for the number of room nights, average room rate, and revenue targets typically are established at the beginning of the year. The following questions help set specific marketing objectives:

• Which revenue centers would benefit from additional sales activity? (Would offering two-for-one coupons increase restaurant business? Would a discounted rate for families attract more business? Do such areas as the lounge, banquet facilities, room service, or recreational facilities need additional promotion to increase profits?)

• When are the peak periods? the valleys?

• Which marketing segments can be reached, and what priority should be given to each one?

• What can be done to ensure increased sales in each market segment?

To develop marketing objectives, combine the answers to these questions with marketing team members' own perceptions and research. Objectives should be simple. They should be set for each market segment, revenue center, and revenue-producing service. In addition, they must be:

1. *In writing.* Written objectives ensure that everyone has the same information.

2. *Understandable.* Performance will suffer if objectives cannot be understood by both management and staff.

3. *Realistic but challenging.* Objectives must be attainable, but they must also present some challenge to the staff. For example, an objective to maintain 100 percent occupancy year-round is unrealistic for most properties, but an objective to increase rooms business by 20 percent over the summer months is probably realistic.

4. *Specific and measurable.* For example, rather than having a general objective to "raise room occupancy," you might restate your objective like this: "To increase room nights from the seniors market from 900 to 1,400 during June and July, while maintaining an average room rate of $59." Objectives should be:

   - *Quantity-specific.* Detail expected sales in terms of number of room nights, number of covers, number of banquets, and so on.

   - *Time-specific.* Break objectives down into annual, quarterly, monthly, weekly, or even daily objectives.

   - *Market share–specific.* Target the markets that offer the highest potential. This may mean going after a larger share of an existing market rather than trying to generate business from new (and possibly less profitable) markets.

Developing and Implementing Action Plans

The core of the marketing plan is developing and implementing action plans. Success comes to those hotel marketers who make decisions and take action based on what they've learned about their property, the competition, the marketplace, and their guests.

The marketing plan is actually many small marketing plans—one for each market segment in each of the revenue centers (rooms, banquets, restaurant, lounge, etc.)—combined into one document. There should be detailed action plans for each market segment and revenue center. Responsibility for implementing action plans should be assigned to specific individuals in each of the property's revenue centers.

Action plans can be as simple or as complicated as necessary. They should be very specific, incorporating the following five areas:

A description of the types of business and the market segments to be solicited. A property might wish to increase meeting room business and target local associations to help meet its goal.

A specific definition of the customers who will be solicited. In the case just mentioned, for example, "local associations" is not very specific. Listing the names, addresses, and contact persons for local associations will help implement action plans.

A listing of the rates that will be charged for business within each segment. To attract association business, an incentive package may be developed that includes reduced room rates or complimentary meals for association attendees.

Objectives. It is not enough to say "increase meeting rooms business." A specific goal—"increase meeting rooms business by 20 percent over weekend periods in July"—is much better for establishing action steps and monitoring progress.

The specific action steps that will be taken to achieve objectives. For association business, steps may include a direct mailing to all association meeting planners in the area, an "open house" to introduce meeting planners to the property, and so on.

Each action plan should include the who, what, why, when, and where of each step. If an objective is to increase covers in the restaurant next month by an average of ten per evening, for example, one action plan might be: "The restaurant manager will contact 20 local businesses and invite owners to drop by for a complimentary dessert with dinner." This places the responsibility for implementing this part of the plan—targeting local businesses—on the restaurant manager. Another action plan to meet the same objective might involve a number of employees: front desk agents can suggest to registering guests that they reserve a table in the dining room, or switchboard operators may call guests in the early evening to offer information about the restaurant's dinner special.

This scenario is a good example of involving a number of employees to meet a marketing objective. Cooperation can make it much easier to attain marketing objectives, and employee involvement may result in excellent suggestions for more effective action plans.

Budgeting

In order for action plans to be carried out successfully, money must be budgeted for their implementation. The budget provides funds for producing new business as well as maintaining the property's established business.

There are four common types of marketing budgets.

Percentage-of-sales budget. Based on the previous year's sales or revenue, this budget usually works best for properties that enjoy a significant amount of repeat business. The budget is three to six percent of last year's revenue in most cases, although this may vary depending on the size and needs of the property.

Competitive-parity budget. This type of budget is based on what the competition is doing. A property spends according to what the competition spends, a practice which may or may not result in effective budgeting.

Affordable-funds budget. A portion of the property's profits is used as the basis for marketing expenditures. This is the least desirable method of determining a marketing budget.

Zero-based budget. Monies are budgeted at levels to get the job done, and all expenses must be justified. This is considered the best way to budget for marketing, although a number of variables—room occupancy, the business mix, gross revenues, and so on—must be taken into account when establishing a sound budget.

The principal advantage of zero-based budgeting is that it questions every expenditure. The manager establishes a budget after preparing each detailed action plan and estimating the amount required for each task. This approach takes more time and effort than the other budgeting options, but it ensures that the necessary money is available to reach the marketing objectives for each target market.

Monitoring and Evaluating the Marketing Plan

Monitoring the marketing plan can be fun as well as enlightening, especially if the plan is reviewed periodically so that corrective action can be taken throughout the planning cycle. Monitoring methods include the following:

- Record the number of room nights for each market segment. It may seem tedious to count and code room nights by market segment, but the result will help you compare actual results with marketing goals.

- Chart and compare the number of restaurant covers sold before and after advertising. (Be sure to consider the cost of the promotion compared to the increase in profits.)

- Survey zip codes to determine which media are most effective in local advertising. This type of analysis is especially effective for restaurant promotions and weekend hotel packages.

- Track prospecting results and sales production versus goals by salesperson. If a salesperson started the year with a prospect list of 750 companies, it would be reasonable to expect that one-quarter of these companies had been contacted by the end of the first quarter.

- Record direct mail responses and telephone inquiries in a logbook or in a computer database that indicates the specific salesperson to whom each lead

was assigned. Six months later, measure conversions (the actual bookings realized as a result of the inquiries).

- Use specific response techniques, such as using special telephone numbers or instructing respondents to ask for a specific individual. These techniques can help track the effectiveness of both print and broadcast advertising.

Control is an essential part of the marketing plan cycle, and periodic evaluation is typically designed into the plan from the beginning. Keep records each time an advertising campaign is run; any strategies that don't contribute to the bottom line can be immediately examined and revised.

Managers can't be too quick, though, to abandon a promotion when results aren't exactly everything they hoped for. They need to take a close look at what doesn't seem to be working; sometimes, all that's needed is a little corrective action (such as moving an ad for weekend golf packages from the travel section to the sports pages).

Of course, some strategies just don't work. A failed marketing effort can often be traced to one or more of the following deficiencies:

- *Lack of responsibility.* The marketing team member or team leader for a revenue center has not assumed responsibility for seeing that schedules are met and results evaluated.

- *Lack of communication.* Salespeople or other employees are not aware of their part in the marketing plan.

- *Lack of time.* Insufficient time has been allocated for making outside sales calls or directing advertising efforts in the required markets.

- *Lack of authority.* Salespeople have not been given the authority to commit the budget to specific marketing efforts.
- *Lack of appeal.* Guest benefits are over-rated or pricing is not competitive.
- *Lack of control.* Outside factors (the economy, construction, weather) have made it necessary to lower marketing plan goals.

- *Lack of realistic goals.* Guests have been targeted at a time when they are not planning to buy, or sales goals are simply too high.

Objective evaluations and corrective actions may prevent costly mistakes and can lead to more effective marketing strategies in the future.

Apply Your Learning 6.4

Please write all answers on a separate sheet of paper.

For statements 1–5, write whether the answer is True or False.

1. To be accurately measured, marketing objectives should be realistic.
2. The marketing plan is actually many small marketing plans combined into one document.
3. Marketing objectives should be as detailed and specific as possible.
4. A marketing team's work will likely be completed before marketing objectives are developed.
5. There should be only one action step per marketing objective.

6. What are the four common types of marketing budgets? Which is considered the best approach?
7. List one way to monitor the results of a hospitality marketing effort.

Quick Hits

Chapter 6

SECTION 6.1—PUTTING THE PLAN TOGETHER

- The **marketing plan** is a property's road map. It spells out the steps hotel managers will need to take to gain and retain customers, increase repeat business, and encourage higher guest spending. It usually covers a three-year period.

- There are six steps to a marketing plan: conducting a marketing audit, selecting target markets, positioning the property, determining marketing objectives, developing and implementing action plans, and monitoring and evaluating the marketing plan.

- At some properties, a formal, property-wide marketing team (sometimes called a *sales committee*) is established to create and implement marketing strategies.

SECTION 6.2—CONDUCTING A MARKETING AUDIT

- A **marketing audit** evaluates the factors relating to sales potential. It gathers, records, and analyzes information about a property, the competition, and the marketplace.

- There are three parts of a marketing audit: property analysis, competition analysis, and situation or marketplace analysis.

- A **property analysis** is a written, unbiased self-appraisal used to assess the strengths and weaknesses of a property. It includes a detailed room-by-room and facility-by-facility inspection.

- A **competition analysis** helps a property discover: overlooked guest groups that are being reached by the competition, some competitive advantage of the property that can't be matched by major competitors, and any weaknesses in the marketing strategies of the competition.

- A **situation analysis** researches the property's current position in the marketplace and reveals potential opportunities to promote the property. There are two parts: the marketplace analysis and the occupancy and activity analysis.

SECTION 6.3—TARGET MARKETS AND POSITIONING

- **Market segmentation** involves viewing a market as a number of smaller market segments with similar product and service preferences—for example, by demographics, geography, or lifestyle.

- Guest profiles can help identify existing market segments. For each revenue-producing center in the hotel, hotel staff should compile all relevant guest information. This information will reveal the makeup of the present guest base.

- A hotel should strive for a balanced guest mix. This will ensure that the property maintains a fairly steady occupancy rate regardless of changing market trends.

- The perception of a property by its guests or potential guests is known as the property's **market position**. The process of designing a property's market position is known as **positioning**.

- The goal of a **positioning statement** is to effectively communicate the property's advantages to its selected target markets.

SECTION 6.4—MARKETING OBJECTIVES, ACTION PLANS, AND EVALUATION

- The following questions help set specific marketing objectives: Which revenue centers would benefit from additional sales activity? When are the peak periods? the valleys? Which marketing segments can be reached, and what priority should be given to each one? What can be done to ensure increased sales in each market segment?

- To develop marketing objectives, combine the answers to these questions with marketing team members' own perceptions and research. Objectives should be simple, and they should be set for each market segment, revenue center, and revenue-producing service.

- Detailed action plans should be created for each market segment and revenue center. Responsibility for implementing action plans should be assigned to specific individuals in each of the property's revenue centers. Each action plan should include the who, what, why, when, and where of each step.

- For action plans to be carried out successfully, money must be budgeted for them. There are four common types of marketing budgets: percentage of sales, competitive parity, affordable funds, and zero base.

- Periodic evaluation is typically designed into the marketing plan from the beginning. Any strategies that don't contribute to the bottom line can be immediately examined and revised.

- Failed marketing efforts can often be attributed to lack of responsibility, lack of communication, lack of time, lack of authority, lack of appeal, lack of control, and lack of realistic goals.

Mike Cheatham
Director of Sales Recruitment, Hyatt Hotels Corporation

Mike Cheatham is convinced that, "Nothing but my best can give adequate satisfaction for my efforts."

The director for sales recruitment for the family-owned Hyatt Hotels Corporation, Cheatham said that if he's not giving his best, whether it's shining his shoes, mowing a lawn, or making sales, then it's not worth doing. "If you do your best, it is recognized and rewarded."

Cheatham has been with Hyatt for nearly six years, first as an associate director of sales, then as director of sales, now as director for sales recruitment. Before that, he spent seven years with Marriott Hotels & Resorts in both sales and recruiting.

Cheatham's entry into hospitality was almost accidental. He was the first child of his generation to go to college and started out preparing for med school. Early on, he realized he didn't want to be a doctor. He ended up with a degree in speech communications and began working in retail.

Some friends were working in the hospitality industry and one of them told him how much he loved the industry and how rewarding it was. Cheatham became more intrigued by the prospects hospitality held out. On his friend's advice, he went over to the hotel and realized it was different from his expectations. "It made sense. I knew it fit well with my personality. I saw the clientele, the beauty of the facilities. It was an awakening. My first month on the job, I knew I had made the right choice."

Cheatham soon found out that there were great careers available in the hospitality industry—especially in sales. "For those people that want to be successful and achieve, there is a chance for opportunity and change. We offer chances to work all around the world, to change and to grow."

People who are successful in the industry, Cheatham said, love the industry and are successful, intelligent people. They are also people who give back to their community. Cheatham praised Hyatt for encouraging its employees to get involved as volunteers outside of the workplace. He himself serves on the national board of directors for the Make-A-Wish Foundation, and has volunteered with YMCA, Junior Achievement, Habitat for Humanity, and youth baseball organizations.

Cheatham said that people entering the industry need to have a drive, to be committed, and to realize "that nothing but their best can give adequate satisfaction for their effort."

The Sales Office

Sections

7.1 Communication Systems

7.2 Filing Systems

7.3 Automation

7.1   Communication Systems

AFTER STUDYING SECTION 7.1, YOU SHOULD KNOW HOW TO:

♦ List the types of sales meetings

♦ List types of sales records found in a sales office

♦ Explain the purpose of the function book

♦ Describe the use of a guestroom control book

For a sales office to operate at its peak, clear communication must happen both within the sales office and with other areas of the property. Good communication guarantees that all sales team members have the same information and that potential problems are minimized. A sales office uses a variety of methods to communicate ideas and keep information flowing smoothly.

Sales Meetings

Regularly scheduled sales meetings are an essential part of a successful sales effort. The head of the sales office may rely on brief daily meetings with salespeople to discuss the day's sales calls and the next day's schedule. He or she may also arrange various other meetings, including weekly staff meetings, weekly function meetings, monthly sales meetings, marketing team meetings, and annual or semiannual sales meetings for all employees.

Weekly Staff Meetings. Weekly meetings of the sales staff is usually conducted by the head of the sales effort—the director of marketing and sales, the director of sales, or the sales manager. (The person leading the meeting will vary depending on the size of the property and the structure of the marketing and sales department or sales office.) These meetings often include the general manager and any department heads whose departments will be discussed. Topics may include new business prospects, tentative and confirmed bookings, conventions, promotions, publicity, and lost business. An open discussion and brainstorming period will encourage a mutual exchange of ideas and information.

Weekly Function Meetings. The heads of departments involved in serving groups meet to review each group's meeting agenda (known as the specification sheet or meeting résumé) item by item to make certain everyone understands what's going to happen and to nail down any last-minute details. The convention service manager usually chairs these meetings.

Monthly Sales Meetings. These meetings are usually attended by all sales personnel, who discuss tentative and definite bookings for the next month or quarter, review progress made in achieving sales goals, and discuss new property promotions.

Marketing Team Meetings. Department heads and representatives from each area of the hotel meet to ensure that every area of the property is adequately covered in the property's marketing plan. The frequency and types of meetings held by marketing teams are usually decided by the head of the marketing and sales department or the general manager.

Annual or Semiannual Sales Meetings. These meetings are held to discuss the marketing plan with the property's entire staff. Such meetings provide an opportunity to obtain ideas and suggestions from all employees.

Sales Records

Sales records are a vital part of a sales office's communication system, important for servicing accounts and generating repeat business. Often, sales record information is used to produce a variety of valuable reports and analyses. It's essential, then, that salespeople know how to complete sales forms properly and maintain them according to sales office procedures—whether those forms are kept in paper files or stored on computer.

In most cases, the salesperson's involvement with sales records will begin with a **call report**, a form generated during a cold call on a prospective client (see Exhibit 1). Once it's filled out, the call report is placed in the organization or individual's account file, and a note for follow-up is put in the tickler file. (Account and tickler files will be discussed later in the chapter.) Once a sales presentation is made, a booking form is usually completed—noting whether the reservation is tentative or definite (see Exhibit 2). Once a definite booking has been made,

the salesperson may be required to write and/or sign a contract with the client. If the original booking information changes, a change sheet is required. If the meeting or convention is canceled, a lost business report must be filed with the sales manager (see Exhibit 3).

The Function Book. The key to successful function and banquet space control is the hotel's **function book**. This record shows the occupancies and vacancies of function and banquet rooms, and it's indispensable for effectively planning events.

Function books typically are divided into pages for each day of the year, with sections set aside for each meeting or function room. Information recorded in the function book includes the organization or group scheduling the space; the name, address, and telephone number of the group's contact person; the type of function; the time required for the function; the total time required for preparation, breakdown, and cleanup; the number of people expected; the type of setup(s) required; the rates quoted; the nature of the contract; and any other helpful comments for property personnel staging the function.

There should be only one function book, and it should be maintained by only one person. This is essential. It is not uncommon for the sales office and the catering department to compete for the same function space; if there are two function books or two different staff members booking the space, there is a good chance that two different groups will book overlapping time in the same space. (The likely result? Chaos, angry guests, and lost business.) At some properties, sales office and catering department managers are required to submit reservation request forms to the person in charge of the function book to avoid

Exhibit 1
Sample Sales Call Report

054492

EMBASSY
SUÏTES™

Sales Call Report

Trace Date _____
(Month)   (Year)

Type of Call: _____ Personal
_____ Telephone
_____ Walk-in/Call-in

GENERAL INFORMATION

Account Name _____

Division/Department _____

Address _____

City _____ State _____ Zip _____

Telephone ( ) _____

Individual Called _____

Title _____

Other Contact(s) _____

_____

_____

REMARKS

_____

_____

_____

_____

_____

_____

_____

_____

_____

_____

SAMPLE

ACTION STEP

_____

_____

_____

Potential for other Cities _____

_____

Sales Representative _____

Date of Call _____

File Copy

Welcome to the Suite Life®

(Courtesy of Embassy Suites, Inc.)

double-bookings. In many cases, the senior sales executive controls the function book, but because sales personnel often travel frequently, she or he may designate one clerk to coordinate all entries.

The Guestroom Control Book. Hotels soliciting group business usually have a **guestroom control book** (also known as a hotel diary), which lists the number of guestrooms allotted to each group and

Exhibit 2
Sample Booking Form

METROPOLITAN BUSINESS FORMS - DALLAS, TX

LOEWS ANATOLE DALLAS CONVENTION BOOKING FORM

DATE:_____

Booked By:_____

Assisted By:_____

_____Definite   _____Tentative   _____Option

Decision Date:_____

Group

Contact _____   Phone

Address

City	State	Zip	Assigned To:

Convention Services:_____   Catering_____

Reservations:
____Direct
____Res. Card
____Rooming List
____Housing Bureau
____Cut Off Date

Comp Policy
____1 per 50
____Spec. Staff Rate
No._____Rate_____
Extra Comps_____

Scope
____Nat'l
____State
____Corp.
____Tour/Travel
____Market

Attendance:

Overflow:

Billing:
____I.P.O.
____Rm/Tx To Master
____All to Master
____Catering to Master
____Advance Deposit

Rates: Singles	Doubles	Suites	Concierge	Guest Room Block:

Day/Date _____ Room/Suites

Special Instructions:

Credit References:

Meeting Space ____Yes ____No   TOTAL ROOM NIGHTS

Meeting & Catering Requirements: EXHIBITS____ ____Yes____ ____Number____   Set Up____   Tear Down

DAY	DATE	TIME	FUNCTION	SETUP	ATTENDANCE	ROOM	RENTAL

Book Administrator_____   Date Posted_____

FILE

(Courtesy of Loews Anatole Hotel, Dallas, Texas)

indicates whether the allotment is firm or tentative. This book is kept in the sales office and is usually overseen by the director of sales. In large hotels with a large volume of group sales, however, entries are often coordinated by a diary control clerk.

The guestroom control book specifies the maximum number of guestrooms the

Exhibit 3
Sample Lost Business Report

OPRYLAND HOTEL

Group Booking Status Change or Lost Business Report

Today's Date_____ Salesperson_____ File #_____   ☐ Group Name Change

                      Month   **Day**   **Year**   ☐ Contact Name Change

Current Meeting Dates _____   ☐ Change in # of Rooms

New Meeting Dates _____   ☐ Change in dates

Organization _____

Contact _____   ☐ Tentative Cancellation

Address _____   ☐ Def. Cancellation

_____ Phone # _____

STATUS CHANGE

YEAR	DAY												
	Date												
	Room												

Reason for Cancelling (Tentative or Definite) _____

_____

_____

Where is Business going? _____

_____

Comments_____

_____

_____

_____

_____

(Courtesy of Opryland Hotel, Nashville, Tennessee)

sales office may sell to groups on a given day. The remaining guestrooms (and any rooms allotted to groups that are not sold) are available for individual guests—these are the rooms that can be sold by front desk, reservations, and sales staff. There should be constant communication between these staff to avoid any overlapping room sales.

Confirmations, Options, and Holds

The guestroom control book is used to record all pertinent details regarding group room sales, including confirmations, options, and holds.

A *confirmation* is definite group business for specific dates that have been confirmed in writing.

An *option* is given when a group is unable to make a firm confirmation of room dates. For instance, if a board meeting or approval by a superior is required for confirmation, a *hold* may be placed on the rooms requested and an *option date* (or *release date* or *cutoff*) set. The group must then confirm the requested rooms by the option date or release the rooms to allow the property to sell them to other clients.

Reputable hoteliers will not confirm other orders for the requested rooms during the hold period. If a second group is interested in the same dates, this group may be given an option after being told about the first group's option. This puts the second group in a position to book if the first group releases the rooms on its option date.

Apply Your Learning 7.1

Please write all answers on a separate sheet of paper.

1. What is the purpose of weekly function meetings?

2. Following a cold call on a prospective client, a hotel salesperson is most likely to complete a:

   a. tickler form.
   b. tentative booking report.
   c. function reservation form.
   d. call report.

3. Why is it important that there be only one function book at a property?

4. The guestroom control book is used primarily to monitor the:

   a. rooms committed to group sales.
   b. rates at which sales personnel can sell various guestrooms.
   c. sales activity of front desk staff.
   d. meeting space reservations not covered in the function book.

5. An option is given when:

   a. a group is interested in booking space but cannot yet make a firm confirmation.
   b. two groups have reserved the same meeting space for the same time due to a property's scheduling error.
   c. current group customers wish to book meeting space more than one year in advance.
   d. a hotel is unable to meet a group's needs on the dates requested but is willing to offer a special deal on an alternate date.

7.2 Filing Systems

AFTER STUDYING SECTION 7.2, YOU SHOULD KNOW HOW TO:

♦ Distinguish between the three general methods of filing

♦ Explain the purpose of a master card file

♦ Identify the use of an account file

♦ Define a tickler file and how it works

Filing Systems

Up-to-date information is essential for a successful sales effort, and information must be available quickly. There are several types of filing methods that may be used for storing client data and other sales information. These methods fall into three general categories.

Alphabetical filing. Records are filed in alphabetical order by the name of the client. Many properties also file the names of contact people in alphabetical order. This system seems to be the easiest to implement and use.

Keyword alphabetical filing. Client information is filed alphabetically by a general category keyword that appears in the name of the client's organization. The Association of Petroleum and Oil Products would be filed under "Petroleum," for example.

While this system has its advantages when a firm or organization's exact name is not known, the system may also make multiple entries under several keywords necessary for some accounts. For example, perhaps the hotel serves a police fraternal organization. The account could be filed under "Police," "Fraternal," and "Law Enforcement." Account-management and personal-information management software can usually search multiple keywords that are associated with a single account, making multiple electronic account listings unnecessary.

Never Leave the Loo

The five-star Peninsula New York hotel in New York City has a bathroom that can't be beat.

A television is built into the marble above the tub—as well as a high-tech sound system and a hands-free speakerphone. And just so guests won't be embarrassed by having the sloshing of bath water or the flushing of a toilet being heard by the person on the phone—the unit automatically mutes any television or stereo sound in the room and filters out white noise.

The price tag for such a bathroom bonanza? Room rates start at $535 a night. (Which, come to think of it, isn't all that outrageous for Manhattan.)

Exhibit 1
Sample Master Card

Jan.	Feb.	Mar.	April	May	June	July	Aug.	Sept.	Oct.	Nov.	Dec.	1 to 100	100 to 250	250 to 350	350 to 500	Over 500

Convention Group *NATIONAL LIVESTOCK DEALERS ASSO.   N-02197*

Main Contact   *DAVID PRITCHARD*   Title *ASSO. MANAGER*

Address   Phone
City
Other Contacts

How is Decision Made		When			
Date	City	Hotel	Attend	No. of Hotel Rms.	
				Exhibits	
				Functions	

Numerical filing. Sales files are assigned a number and a corresponding set of files is kept by account number, with the name of the account listed after the number. This system is often used in computerized sales offices.

Once the filing method has been established, the next step is to determine the elements of the filing system. Most hotels use three separate files to record client information: the master card file, the account file, and the tickler file. It's important to realize that these files may vary slightly from property to property—and, depending upon the individual property, they may exist entirely as computer files, entirely as paper files, or as a combination of the two.

The Master Card File. Each **master card** (in a manual system, usually a standard index card) contains a summary of everything needed for an effective sales effort: the organization's name, the names and titles of key executives, addresses, phone numbers, month or months in which the group meets, the size of the group, where the group has met in the past, the group's decision maker, and other pertinent data that can help to win that account's business and hold onto it (see Exhibit 1). In many cases, a trailer card—listing divisions or departments within the account's organization—may be filed behind the master card as a source of additional contacts and business.

The master card file is also a cross-reference. It can be used to see if an account file exists for a particular group without having to go to the file cabinet to look. Master card files are also used to create mailing lists and quickly obtain addresses or phone numbers for additional sales efforts or follow-ups.

Master cards are often color-coded to draw attention to specific areas of consideration: geographic location, months of meetings, follow-ups required, and size of group. Some properties also arrange master cards alphabetically by market segment. For example, IBM and Xerox would be sorted alphabetically under "Corporate Business." Other properties may not separate master cards by market segment, but may use a color-coding system to easily identify specific market segments within the file—an association account may be flagged in blue, a government account in yellow, and so on.

Some properties keep a geographic file of master cards. These cards are organized according to the geographic location of the decision maker. This type of file enables sales personnel to quickly identify accounts in cities to which they are traveling. Salespeople can simply pull the names of the decision makers located in the area they're visiting and call on them during the sales trip.

The Account File. An **account file** is a standard-size file folder holding information needed for serving a client's basic business needs. An account file is started at the time of initial contact with a prospective client and may include programs from previous conventions or meetings the organization has held, convention bureau bulletins, and information relating to the organization from newspapers or trade journals. Sales reports and all correspondence relating to previous efforts to secure business should also be in the file. All information in the account file should be in chronological order. Account files are usually filed alphabetically.

Account files usually exist for potential clients as well as groups currently booked at the property and groups that have booked with the property in the past. Like master cards, they are often color-coded by geographic location or, more commonly, by market segment. When a color-coding system is used, the colors used for the account files should correspond to the colors used for the master cards.

When an account file is removed, a guide card noting the name of the group, its file number, the date of removal, and the initials of the person removing the file should be left in the file drawer in place of the file. This way, the sales staff will always know the whereabouts of the file.

The Tickler File. A **tickler file** (tracer file, bring-up file, follow-up file) is an effective aid for following up on an account. A reminder note or card is placed in the tickler file by month and date; daily dividers are arranged chronologically for the current month. The system is used as a reminder of correspondence, telephone calls, or contacts that must be handled on a particular date.

Suppose a client has reserved space for a training meeting at the property in April. The salesperson will want to contact the client no later than February 15 to finalize meeting plans, so the salesperson would slip a note or an index card (often called a trace card) dated February 15 into the February tickler divider. On February 1, the notes and trace cards for February would be arranged according to date, and the reminder to contact the meeting planner would be placed into the fifteenth slot. This system, as long as it is updated and checked daily, works well, costs very little, and takes very little time to implement. An added bonus is that if a salesperson is transferred or leaves the property, there is a record of clients with pending needs who can be contacted by other members of the sales team.

Apply Your Learning 7.2

Please write all answers on a separate sheet of paper.

1. Which of the following is *not* a general category of filing systems?

    a. chronological
    b. alphabetical
    c. keyword alphabetical
    d. numerical

2. The primary location for a summary of everything needed for an effective sales effort is the:

    a. guide card.
    b. first-contact card.
    c. master card.
    d. trailer card.

3. A secondary document that lists additional contact information within a client's organization is known as a(n) _____ card.

    a. tickler
    b. accompanying
    c. ancillary
    d. trailer

4. A _____ system can provide an effective means for following up with an account.

    a. trace-based
    b. follow-up
    c. tickler
    d. trailer

7.3 Automation

AFTER STUDYING SECTION 7.3, YOU SHOULD KNOW HOW TO:

♦ Identify the benefits of computers in the sales office

♦ Explain how automated systems can provide client information

♦ Describe the lists, reports, and analysis applications that computers can produce

♦ Use yield management techniques

The Automated Sales Office

A typical sales office generates an incredible amount of paperwork, and much of each day is spent managing the information collected through prospecting, selling, booking, and reporting. At most properties today, the majority of this time-consuming and costly effort is handled with one of sales' most effective tools: computer systems.

The benefits of an automated sales office are many. Computers:

• Allow immediate access to sales information.

• Reduce the risk of human error. When specific procedures are implemented, there is less chance of information being lost or misplaced.

• Result in decreased training costs for clerical personnel. Set procedures result in faster training time and less deviation from standard practices.

• Provide the means to easily deliver specific sales promotions or programs to specific targeted guest segments based on zip code, desired time periods, areas of interest, and so on.

• Enhance communication among properties, greatly aiding the sales effort in large hotel chains.

The proliferation of personal computers and the variety of software available from a multitude of vendors have made data processing an increasingly powerful tool in hotel sales offices.

Computerized Client Information

Automated systems can be used in many day-to-day sales office operations. In Exhibit 1, for example, the computer provides an alternative to a master card file. The salesperson can simply call up information needed for an account, whether it be the names of contacts, specifics on follow-up

Exhibit 1
Sample Computerized Master Account File

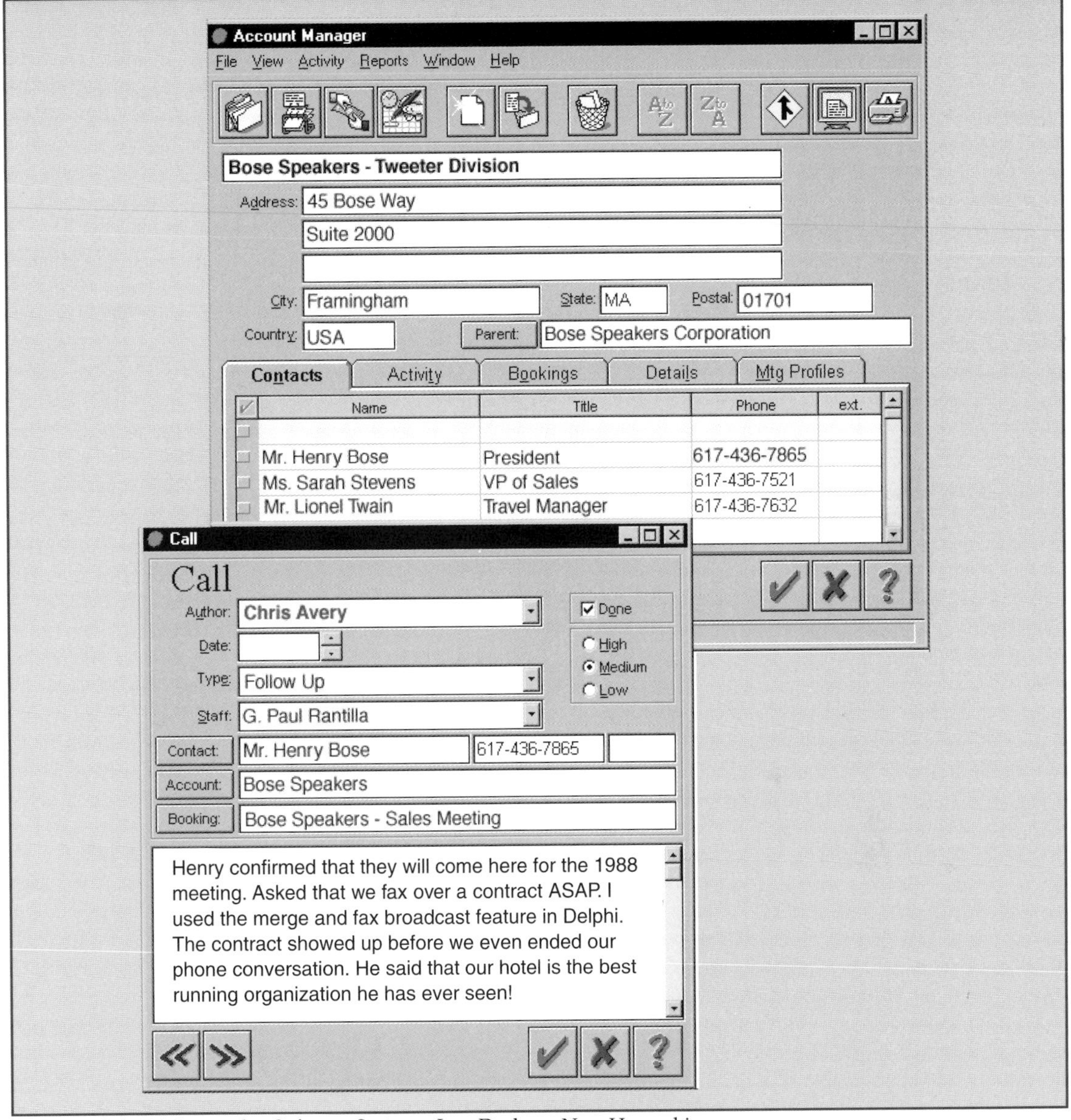

Source: Delphi 7/Newmarket Software Systems, Inc., Durham, New Hampshire.

calls, or helpful remarks from the last phone call. This application is also an excellent management tool: the sales manager can tell at a glance exactly how many calls were made and what the results were.

Automated sales systems can build a function sheet as information is gathered and input by the salesperson into the client's account file (see Exhibit 2). Sample function book reports can be displayed on a

Exhibit 2
Sample Computerized Function Sheet

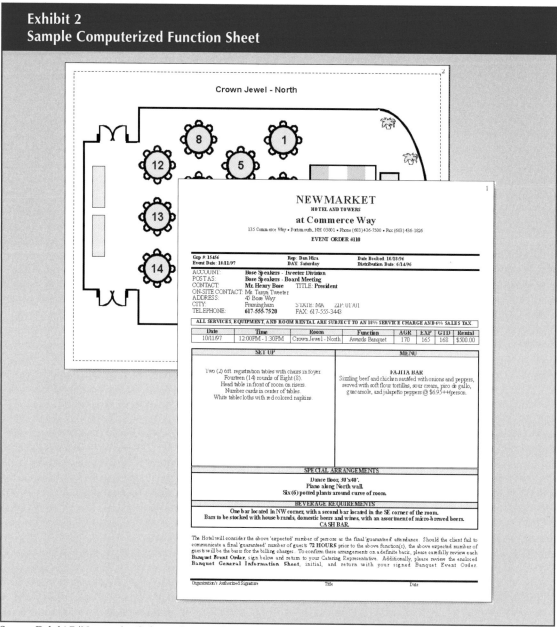

Source: Delphi 7/Newmarket Software Systems, Inc., Durham, New Hampshire.

salesperson's terminal or printed as a report to banquet and convention service departments (see Exhibit 3). These reports list each function room, and give an overall picture of the property's monthly activities to prevent double-booking and to make sure that any available space is obvious to salespeople.

Sales and catering software packages that supplement information on the function sheet are also available. An automated sales system can produce kitchen reports

Exhibit 3
Sample Function Book Report

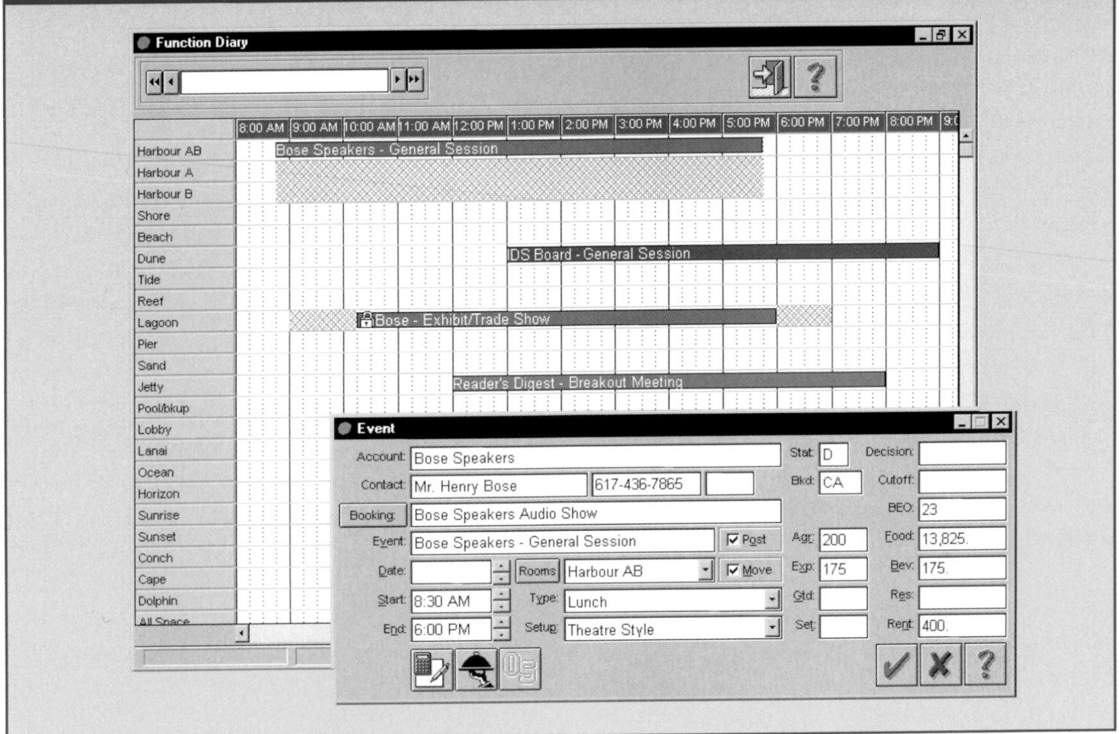

Source: Delphi 7/Newmarket Software Systems, Inc., Durham, New Hampshire.

(menu items needed, listed by preparation area), room setup reports (resources requested for events on function sheets), and revenue forecast reports (anticipated revenue based on function sheets).

This type of application can also be used for the guestroom control book. It is a major challenge for nonautomated sales offices to keep the guestroom control book up-to-date and accurate. For example: a meeting planner calls and requests the best rate the hotel can offer for 50 rooms for three nights in April. The planner also requires a general session meeting room and three breakout rooms. To respond to this request, a salesperson would first have to match availability dates in April in the guestroom control book with open dates for four meeting rooms in the function book. The salesperson might also want to double-check the accuracy of the information in each book with several members of the sales staff—and check with the department manager—before quoting a rate.

The right computer software would make it possible for the salesperson to respond much more quickly. Both the guestroom control book and the function book could be on-screen simultaneously, and the salesperson could perform an easy search to match the meeting planner's needs with the property's available guestrooms and meeting rooms. Accurate rates would typically be in the system already, eliminating the need for checking with the department manager.

Lists and Reports. Computers can store mailing lists of prospective clients, previous guests, and organizations and associations. These lists can be printed out in a variety of configurations—by zip code, by type of guest or prospect, and so on—and can be merged into word-processing functions to provide personalized sales letters. Computerized systems make short work of large mailings.

Data entered into computer systems is often used to generate reports, such as a sales performance by market segment report. This report is valuable to both the salesperson and the director of sales for evaluating performance, and is just one example of the various types of reports that sales offices can generate to provide up-to-date information for a wide variety of uses.

Yield Management

The increasing use of computers in market analysis has led to yet another new application: **yield management**. Yield management is a technique used to maximize room revenue. "Yield" is based on a simple percentage that involves revenue potential and revenue realized: **Revenue potential** is the revenue that would be realized if all of the property's rooms were sold at full rack rates; **revenue realized** is actual sales receipts. Therefore, yield equals the actual revenue divided by the potential revenue.

Yield management requires that room prices be based on demand; rates are raised when demand is high and discounted when the supply exceeds the demand. During a slow period, rooms may be offered at discounted rates rather than allowed to go unsold. When demand is high, it's not good business to offer discounts on rooms that can be sold for higher rates. But until computer technology was available, the most crucial part of yield management—predicting or forecasting demand—was tedious and haphazard at best.

Forecasting demand involves looking at data on previous bookings and projections of guest trends. In addition, forecasting must also include current data, such as weather, the activities of competitors (special packages, contract discounts, etc.), and local events (a highly publicized festival or concert) likely to increase bookings. While these statistics and trends can be analyzed without using computers, the computer has made it far easier to predict demand by generating a number of forecasting reports.

Even so, computerized reports are only as good as the data entered. In some cases, for example, reservations data may show that room revenue was lost, but it doesn't tell why. Was the business lost to a competitor? Was a group trip canceled? Could something have been done to save the reservation?

To better use yield management, many properties have formed forecast committees or yield management teams—consisting of executives from reservations, sales, and the rooms division, as well as marketing and front office personnel—that meet regularly to forecast demand and establish systems and strategies for dealing with changing demand patterns.

Properties also need feedback to assess the application of yield management strategies and offer suggestions for improving performance. For example, marketing's goal may be to fill 80 additional rooms over a typically low-demand weekend, so the hotel quotes a discounted room rate of $65 to potential guests. This rate meets the immediate objective of filling guestrooms. But suppose the guest wants to stay five days, three of which involve days on which room rates are typically $110 per day? The reservations and marketing departments need feedback in this case to develop a yield management strategy that would maximize the property's revenue.

Yield management software can provide a vast amount of information on a number of market factors, such as the property's booking history, market conditions, and bookings by market segment, and can help the manager project the highest revenue-generating guest mix. This software can also be used to monitor and evaluate yield management decisions, and, over time, can be used to create models that show the probable results of marketing decisions. Even the most efficiently organized office and the best computer system that money can buy cannot guarantee that the property's sales efforts will be successful, however. The key to sales success is always the property's *people*.

Apply Your Learning 7.3

Please write all answers on a separate sheet of paper.

1. List three benefits of an automated sales office.

For statements 2–5, write whether the answer is True or False.

2. Computers eliminate the need to keep the guestroom control book up-to-date.

3. Computer-generated reports are only as accurate as the information that is entered into them.

4. Computers typically eliminate the need for meetings among management personnel.

5. Personalized sales letters are not possible when developing computer-based mass mailing.

6. The main goal of yield management is to:
   a. improve the flow of information throughout a property.
   b. maximize room revenue.
   c. assess a property's revenue potential.
   d. eliminate financial losses.

7. What is the difference between revenue potential and revenue realized?

Quick Hits

Chapter 7

SECTION 7.1—COMMUNICATION SYSTEMS

- Communication begins with discussion. In the sales office, this typically involves a variety of meetings, including: daily and weekly staff meetings, weekly function meetings, monthly sales meetings, marketing team meetings, and annual or semiannual sales meetings for all employees.

- Sales records are a vital part of a sales office's communication system, important for servicing accounts and generating repeat business. The salesperson's involvement with sales records will begin with a **call report**, a form generated during a cold call on a prospective client. Once a sales presentation is made, a booking form is usually completed. Once a definite booking has been made, a contract with the client will be required. If the original booking information changes or is canceled, a change sheet/lost business report is required.

- The hotel's **function book** shows the occupancies and vacancies of function and banquet rooms. It is indispensable for effectively planning events.

- A **guestroom control book** (also known as a hotel diary) specifies the maximum number of guestrooms the sales office may sell to groups on a given day.

SECTION 7.2—FILING SYSTEMS

- There are three general categories of filing methods: alphabetical, keyword alphabetical, and numerical.

- A **master card** contains the client organization's name, names and titles of key executives, addresses, phone numbers, and all other pertinent data that can help to win that account's business and hold onto it. A trailer card may contain additional contact information.

- An **account file** holds all of the information needed for serving a client's basic business needs, including correspondence, news and magazine clippings, programs from previous conventions/meetings, and so on.

- A **tickler file** system provides the means for following up on an account at a specific time.

SECTION 7.3—AUTOMATION

- At most properties today, managing information is handled with the help of computer systems.

- Computers can store mailing lists of prospective clients, previous guests, and organizations and associations, and print them out by zip code, by type of guest or prospect, and so on. Sales staff also rely upon computers for a variety of valuable reports.

- **Yield management** maximizes room revenue by raising rates when demand is high and lowering rates when the supply exceeds the demand. It is based on a simple percentage involving revenue potential and revenue realized: **Revenue potential** is the revenue that would be realized if all of the property's rooms were sold at full rack rates; **revenue realized** is actual sales receipts. Yield equals actual revenue divided by potential revenue.

- To better use yield management, many properties have formed forecast committees or yield management teams that meet regularly to forecast demand and establish systems and strategies for dealing with changing demand patterns.

- Despite organizational efficiency and the best computer system that money can buy, the key to sales success is the property's *people*.

Traci Ehrhardt-Mead

Assistant Director of Catering, Arizona Biltmore

Whether she's creating an intimate private wedding reception or organizing a thousand-person luncheon for Tipper Gore, Traci Ehrhardt-Mead is "having a ball" as assistant director of catering for the Arizona Biltmore Resort and Spa.

Mead began her career in food and beverage as a hostess in a local restaurant. She worked there through high school and the beginning of her college years. "I made some of the best friends of my life and had a lot of fun," she recalls. When one of her managers got a job at the Ritz-Carlton Hotel, she recommended her for a job there, too.

"I decided that this was the career path for me," she says. "I loved every facet of the business—the creativity, the great people, the instant gratification of making customers happy." Her jobs at the Ritz-Carlton included assistant room service manager, restaurant manager, department manager for room service, banquet manager, and finally catering sales manager.

When she was 27, Mead left the Ritz-Carlton for the Arizona Biltmore. In less than two years, she was promoted to the newly created position of assistant director of catering. She works with customers to create the perfect event—developing menus, designing a theme, arranging decorations, lighting, set-up—and putting it all together in an exciting package.

"Clients have to feel confident that you can take care of their needs," says Mead. "If you have a passion for what you do, they can see and feel that in you."

One of Mead's most challenging assignments was catering a 900-person dinner for Britain's Princess Anne. "We had to coordinate everything with the British Embassy, the FBI, the Secret Service, the local police, and the protocol experts. It was incredible," she says.

Her favorite events are wedding receptions, because of the personal and professional satisfaction they bring.

"Every wedding is different. The bride and her family put their entire faith in you that you will make their dream come true," she says. "They will live with the memory of that day forever, and you helped to create that memory. That's a powerful feeling."

Banquet and Meeting Room Sales

Sections

8.1 The Banquet Department

8.2 Banquet Sales

8.3 Special Types of Food and Beverage Sales

8.4 Meeting Room Sales

8.1 The Banquet Department

AFTER STUDYING SECTION 8.1, YOU SHOULD KNOW HOW TO:

◆ Identify the basic responsibilities of the banquet department

◆ List the members of the banquet department

◆ Describe the duties of the banquet director

◆ Describe the duties of the banquet manager

◆ Explain the responsibilities of banquet salespeople

◆ List the duties of banquet service personnel

Guestrooms are the primary profit center in a hotel, but at large properties the banquet department runs a close second. Banquets and special events can produce high revenue and generate positive guest relations through well-run banquets and other functions. It also can earn great word-of-mouth advertising for a hotel and lead to repeat bookings.

In this chapter, we'll look at the dynamics of a successful banquet operation—its staffing, responsibilities, and role in relation to overall sales—and learn how banquet and meeting room business contributes to a property's overall image and profitability.

The Banquet Department

Most banquet departments have two main responsibilities: (1) to sell food and beverage functions to businesses and individuals in the local community, and (2) to service in-house convention and group functions sold by the property's sales office. To plan and manage functions, banquet department personnel need extensive knowledge of sales, service, the use of facilities and function space, food production, menu planning, and cost control.

The size and structure of the banquet department (see Exhibit 1) depend on the size of the property and the amount of function space available, the types of banquets provided, the property's business mix, local and regional competition, and departmental budgets.

At most large properties, the banquet department is part of the food and beverage department. At smaller hotels, the sales office oversees the banquet department.

Banquet Department Personnel. At large properties, the banquet department is usually headed by a director of banquets who supervises a banquet or catering manager, banquet salespeople, clerical staff, and service personnel (food servers, buspersons).

The *banquet director's* primary responsibilities are sales and administration. Banquet directors may give a great deal of attention to soliciting or servicing accounts. They are also responsible for the

Exhibit 1
Sample Organization Charts

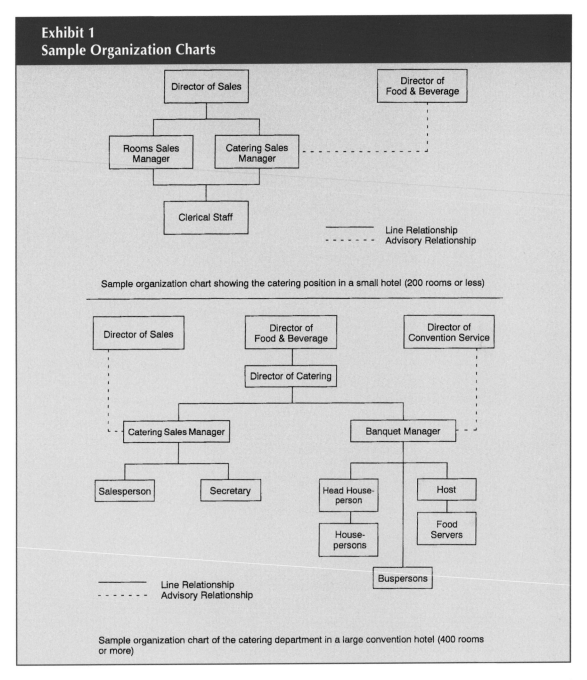

Sample organization chart showing the catering position in a small hotel (200 rooms or less)

Sample organization chart of the catering department in a large convention hotel (400 rooms or more)

cost-effectiveness of the department—meaning they work closely with purchasing agents, chefs, and the marketing and sales department to make certain the banquet operation stays within budget guidelines while still providing good service (see Exhibit 2).

The *banquet* or *catering manager* is responsible for overseeing food and beverage functions, supervising service personnel,

Exhibit 2
Sample Job Description for a Catering Director

Catering Director

Basic Function

To service all phases of group meeting/banquet functions; coordinate these activities on a daily basis; assist clients in program planning and menu selection; solicit local group catering business.

General Responsibility

To maintain the services and reputation of the hotel and act as a management representative to group clients.

Specific Responsibilities

- To maintain the function book. Coordinate the booking of all meeting space with the sales office.

- To solicit local food and beverage functions.

- To coordinate with all group meeting/banquet planners their specific group requirements with the services and facilities offered.

- To confirm all details relative to group functions with meeting/banquet planners.

- To distribute to the necessary hotel departments detailed information relative to group activities.

- To supervise and coordinate all phases of catering, hiring, and training programs.

- To assist the banquet manager in supervising and coordinating meeting/banquet setups and service.

- To assist in menu planning, preparation, and pricing.

- To assist in referrals to the sales department and in booking group activities.

- To set up and maintain catering files.

- To be responsive to group requests/needs while in the hotel.

- To work toward achieving Annual Plan figures relating to the catering department (revenues, labor percentages, average checks, covers, etc.).

- To handle all scheduling and coverage for the servicing of catering functions.

Organizational Relationship and Authority

Is directly responsible and accountable to the food and beverage manager. Responsible for coordination with catering service personnel, the kitchen, and accounting.

Courtesy of Doubletree Hotels

and, occasionally, setting up function rooms. Banquet managers also schedule personnel, prepare payrolls, and work with the banquet director on special functions.

Banquet salespeople are often employed by large properties to actively solicit business not brought in as part of conventions or meetings, such as weddings or Rotary luncheons. These salespeople should also be available to follow up on inquiries. They must know the proper procedures for developing leads, processing paperwork for an account, and following up the account after a function.

The banquet department may employ a *clerical staff* to maintain the paperwork generated by business solicitation, handle routine inquiries, and follow up on accounts. In large properties, a banquet secretary may assist the banquet director with administrative duties or manage the banquet office.

Service personnel serve food and beverages, set up function rooms, and maintain banquet areas and equipment. They include hosts, food servers, buspersons, and maintenance or setup crews.

All banquet employees are involved in sales, whether they are actually selling banquets, servicing existing accounts, or simply projecting a friendly and welcoming attitude as they serve guests.

Apply Your Learning 8.1

Please write all answers on a separate sheet of paper.

1. Which of the following statements is *false?*
   a. Banquets can produce high revenues for a hotel.
   b. Well-run banquets can generate positive word-of-mouth advertising.
   c. Banquet and meeting room business contributes to a property's overall image.
   d. The banquet department is the primary profit center in a hotel.

2. A banquet department's main responsibilities can best be summed up as:
   a. selecting, preparing, and serving food and beverages.
   b. selling and servicing food and beverage functions.
   c. creating and hosting hotel-based parties.
   d. serving food and beverages at special hotel meetings and events.

3. Which of the following banquet positions is primarily responsible for maintaining the cost-effectiveness of the department?
   a. manager
   b. director
   c. clerical staff
   d. salesperson

4. Which of the following banquet department positions is primarily responsible for maintaining paperwork, handling routine inquiries, and following up on accounts?

   a. director
   b. manager
   c. salesperson
   d. clerical staff

5. A banquet _____ supervises service personnel and oversees food and beverage functions.

   a. vice president
   b. salesperson
   c. manager
   d. director

8.2 Banquet Sales

AFTER STUDYING SECTION 8.2, YOU SHOULD KNOW HOW TO:

♦ Explain the types of advertising and promotion that banquet departments use

♦ List ways to develop leads for the banquet department

♦ Solicit business in person or over the telephone

♦ Write sales letters

♦ Respond to banquet inquiries

Banquet Promotions

Advertising and promotion play key roles in the success of a banquet department. They should be targeted to specific audiences and should reflect professionalism and creativity. Each strategy should give potential customers a way to respond—reply coupon, toll-free number, fax number, e-mail address, etc.

Print ads can be effective on billboards and in local newspapers (especially in the lifestyle and business sections), ethnic publications, and specialty newspapers and newsletters, such as those for reunion planners. Banquet departments with larger advertising budgets might also advertise in national magazines that target meeting planners or other users of banquet services.

Direct mail, including sales letters, postcards, and mailings that include brochures, fliers, or menus, can be sent to specifically targeted customers such as meeting planners and reunion planners.

In-house promotions include the use of table tent cards, posters in high-traffic areas (entrances, guest elevators), and advertising on the property's marquee or on closed-circuit televisions. A property may also offer samples of banquet specialties during its restaurant's Sunday brunch or during the lounge's happy hour.

Brochures and fliers can be used both in-house and outside the hotel to attract customers. A property located near a business district, for example, may distribute fliers to businesses in the area. Hotels with a Web presence may benefit by posting photographs, sample menus, endorsements, and, perhaps, basic banquet rates, along with contact information and other property-specific links.

Developing Leads

Salespeople can develop leads through personal selling, telephone sales, letters, and by responding to inquiries.

Personal Selling. Personal selling involves contacting businesses frequented by members of a targeted market segment. The banquet director may call on public relations firms to attract business from cultural organizations, for example. Or a banquet department salesperson may call on the owners of jewelry stores, bridal boutiques, and photography studios for wedding business referrals.

Property tours can be used to promote the property to local civic organizations whose members can provide future business, such as Rotary Club, Kiwanis, and the Chamber of Commerce.

Telephone Sales. Telephone soliciting is another excellent way to develop leads, and it involves far less time than in-person visits. Staff can make most of these calls, freeing the banquet director for other duties.

Successful telephone solicitation begins with a plan that includes targeted prospects, the message to convey, and the results desired. Since there is a limited time to present the hotel's services, most salespeople rely on a script that contains the key points. Callers should rehearse the material until it sounds natural and interesting. For example:

> Good morning, Ms. Alvarez. This is Carlotta Benson from the Midtown Hotel's banquet department. I read the announcement of your daughter's wedding in the *Times* and would like to extend our best wishes to your family. I'd also like to offer our banquet services for the reception. Our goal is to make every event a memorable one, and we specialize in wedding receptions. It would be our pleasure to cater your daughter's reception, and I'd be delighted to meet with you to discuss how we can make your daughter's reception something special.

Ideally, a telephone solicitation will result in a tentative reservation or an appointment to discuss the event. At the very least, the caller should seek permission to send a copy of the banquet department's brochure; this will give the prospect more information and provide the salesperson with an opportunity to follow up.

Sales Letters. Sales letters can be categorized as either form letters or personalized letters. Form letters are most commonly used by the sales office to solicit out-of-town convention and meetings business; the banquet department usually writes personalized letters to solicit local business. But "personalized" doesn't mean every letter has to be written from scratch. Word processors make it easy to personalize a letter by changing names and dates or including various client-specific details.

A sales letter should be written with the client's needs in mind. A meeting planner's needs will be far different from those of a wedding party, and their letters should reflect that. No matter what target market is selected, the letter should follow the *AIDA* formula: attract the prospect's *attention*, create an *interest* in and a *desire* for the product, and give the prospect a means to take *action* (a telephone number, an invitation to visit).

There is sales potential in follow-up letters as well. A written thank-you after an interview or event conveys your commitment to service and can result in additional business.

Inquiry Responses. No matter what type of inquiry you receive, you should obtain important information about the client, the client's organization (if there is one), and function needs *before* trying to make a sale. Inquiries will be made in writing, by fax or e-mail, by telephone, or in person.

Letters of inquiry. A letter from a prospective client should not be answered with a letter. A telephone call is better.

The reason? Letters from prospective clients are rarely specific. Few will include the client's exact specifications—Will the function be formal or informal? What is the budget limit for the function? Does the client expect special services or setups? By talking with the client on the phone, the banquet director or salesperson can determine exact needs, give details about function rooms and banquet menus, and negotiate terms. If a written communication is needed (a letter or proposal to be submitted to a board, for example), it can then be tailored to address specific needs.

Fax and e-mail inquiries. Replying to a fax inquiry with a fax gives you the advantage of responding immediately without interrupting a potential client. Likewise, e-mail inquiries should be answered by e-mail. E-mail provides an immediate reply—and messages can be printed out to help ensure the preservation of the correspondence. E-mail messages can also be forwarded to other people in the department who will be involved in an event, and information can be stored for use on a later date. When using either of these media, responses should be prompt and professional. Fax replies should be typed, not handwritten, and both fax and e-mail responses should be checked for errors. Follow up by mailing any requested information (brochures, banquet menus, etc.).

Telephone inquiries. Telephone inquiries from prospects must be handled quickly and efficiently to ensure that business is not lost. All personnel should try to answer the phone within three rings, project a pleasant and courteous image, and avoid putting callers on hold, if possible. If the employee must put the caller on hold, he or she should ask if the caller minds holding and should periodically tell the caller how much longer

Home to the Stars

Exciting things happen within the walls of a hotel. One of the more legendary hotels (currently slated for destruction), the Ambassador Hotel, has a history that can thrill even the most jaded. The Ambassador opened its doors on January 1, 1921, and closed in 1989. It was a favorite hangout for the Hollywood and international scene.

- Marion Davies rode a horse through the Ambassador's grand lobby to impress her lover, William Randolph Hearst.

- Silent screen star Pola Negri walked her pet leopard on the front grounds.

- Shirley Temple and Bill "Bojangles" Robinson rehearsed their movie dance numbers in one of the ballrooms.

- The Oscar statuette was first introduced inside the hotel's Cocoanut Grove, which hosted the 1930 Academy Awards.

- F. Scott and Zelda Fitzgerald once piled papers and furniture in the middle of their room, set it ablaze, and skipped into the night without paying their bill.

- Albert Einstein called the front desk ("Zend help") to complain about a nearby ruckus, which turned out to be a honeymoon spat between fighter Jack Dempsey and his wife (Dempsey was trying to throw his wife out of the window).

- Artist Josef Segal read the paper in bed next to a slumbering African lion.

- Nikita Khrushchev, the Soviet premier, threw a famous temper tantrum in the Ambassador after hearing that, for security reasons, he could not go to Disneyland. To make reparations, Walt Disney sent Mickey Mouse to cheer him up.

- In 1968, Senator Robert F. Kennedy was assassinated in the pantry of the hotel after winning the Democratic presidential nomination.

the wait will be. A prospect who is put on hold for too long—or is transferred from one department to the next—will usually try another property.

Since one of the banquet director's primary responsibilities is to generate business, he or she must be available at all times. This may include wearing a pager or carrying a cellular phone when away from the property. If this is not always possible, banquet salespeople can handle banquet inquiries. They should take down the basic information (name of caller, type of function, preferred date) and assure the caller that the banquet director will return the call as soon as possible.

The function book and other information related to rates, menu, and availability should be available at all times to those who are "working the phones."

In-person inquiries. Take the following steps when someone drops in unexpectedly and inquires about function space:

1. A staff member (the front desk staff if the person is asked to wait in the lobby, the banquet staff if the person is shown to the banquet department) should welcome the prospective client and offer a seat.

2. The staff person should get the client's name and immediately contact the banquet director or a banquet salesperson. If there will be a wait (which many clients will expect), the client should be told how long it might be.

3. The staff person should offer coffee, tea, or a soft drink and some reading material related to the banquet department—a photo album of previous functions, scrapbooks containing publicity features and photographs, brochures or information sheets, and sample menus are all good choices. This type of material may answer some of the client's more basic questions and set the sales call in motion.

The banquet office itself must make a positive first impression. It should indicate that your operation is well-organized and professional. In addition to the waiting area, the banquet office should have a quiet, private area with seating for four to six people. In such an area, you can meet with your client and provide frequently requested information, such as menus, brochures, price lists, and lists of staging and audiovisual equipment, recommended suppliers, and costs and sources of all rental equipment.

Apply Your Learning 8.2

Please write all answers on a separate sheet of paper.

For statements 1–5, write whether the answer is True or False.

1. Every advertising/promotion should provide a way for potential customers to respond.

2. Offering banquet food samples during the hotel lounge's happy hour does not qualify as an in-house promotion.

3. Direct mail, also called "junk mail," is not an effective way to promote a banquet operation.

4. Table tent cards are a form of direct mail.

5. Property tours are a form of personal selling.

6. What is one main benefit of telephone sales calls?

7. What are the three parts of the sales plan needed at the beginning of a telephone solicitation to help ensure success?

8. When it comes to composing a sales letter, what does the acronym *AIDA* stand for?

9. It is best to respond to all letters of inquiry by:
   a. letter.
   b. e-mail.
   c. telephone.
   d. fax.

10. Which of the following is *not* a recommended step in handling walk-in inquiries?
   a. Get the client's name and contact the banquet director.
   b. Offer the client something to drink, as well as some reading material that will highlight the banquet department's work.
   c. Welcome the prospective client and offer him or her a place to sit down and wait.
   d. Greet the client, but note that it would have been better if he or she had made an appointment.

8.3 Special Types of Food and Beverage Sales

AFTER STUDYING SECTION 8.3, YOU SHOULD KNOW HOW TO:

♦ Describe refreshment breaks

♦ Identify the types of sales associated with hospitality suites

♦ Explain how receptions can increase sales

♦ List special functions that the banquet department might host

♦ Identify the types of off-premises banquets that lodging properties offer

Banquets are important sales, but other food and beverage functions can increase banquet department revenue too. This section looks at a few of the opportunities a creative banquet director has to serve guests, create repeat business, and increase sales.

Refreshment Breaks

Refreshment breaks are usually scheduled at midmorning and midafternoon, last 15 to 30 minutes, and are intended to alleviate boredom and sharpen the attention and enthusiasm of meeting attendees. They typi-

cally include a variety of hot and cold beverages, muffins and other types of bread and pastries, fruits (fresh and dried), cut vegetables, and peanuts. Whatever the choice, speed is often a major consideration for refreshment breaks; menu items should include only those foods that attendees can pick up quickly.

Meeting planners may give up lunch or dinner breaks and choose refreshment breaks instead. The banquet department can build business by offering a selection of creative refreshment break items rather than the usual Danish pastries and coffee.

One alternative to the typical refreshment break is a theme break. Examples include a New York deli break featuring vegetable juice, bagels and lox, cream cheese, jellies, and cream sodas; and a French break with croissants, baguettes, imported cheeses, yogurt, and coffee. Refreshment breaks can also feature unusual house specialties—hot spiced cider or small portions of signature desserts, for example.

Those in charge of setup should plan to have one beverage station per 75 to 100 attendees and should space the stations to avoid traffic bottlenecks. The stations farthest from the main entrance should be opened first, to draw people into the room. Toward the end of the break, coffee stations can be combined (or "married") to speed cleanup.

Hospitality Suites

Hospitality suites are often sold to event sponsors, vendors, or meeting attendees as a place to do business and socialize. In many cases, a hospitality suite is set up in two or more guestrooms with connecting doors.

Most hospitality suites are open only in the evenings, but some may be set up as around-the-clock "open houses" that offer snacks during the day and another menu in the evenings. Hospitality suites are usually serviced by room service personnel.

Receptions

Receptions are an excellent way to generate revenue at a low cost. Most receptions require little in the way of setup time (many receptions require only a few chairs around the room).

Some receptions may take the place of dinner, giving guests a chance to both eat and socialize. If this is the case, a complete balance of food types must be offered to suit all tastes. A good solution is to locate several food buffet stations around the room. At functions where liquor is served, guests may either be served by circulating wait staff or get drinks from a bar. In all cases, there is a need for staff to be available to replenish foods, oversee beverage service, and remove soiled items and trash.

Special Functions

Staging special functions, such as theme parties, family reunions, and wedding receptions, can be the most challenging—and rewarding—aspect of the banquet business. Making these special events truly memorable to clients and their guests shows your willingness to get involved with your clients and to artfully manage even the smallest details.

Weddings. Perhaps the most personal special events are wedding ceremonies and receptions. Such high quality is expected that cost becomes a secondary concern.

The five elements of a wedding reception sold by the banquet department are the *menu and beverages, disposables, equipment, décor,* and *service*. While the program can range from a simple hors d'oeuvres reception to an elegant sit-down dinner, the tastes of the bride and groom should be of paramount concern. The banquet department should be capable of tailoring menus to the couple's desires while keeping the menus within budget guidelines. Disposable items, such as personalized matches, napkins, and favors, should be suggested.

Silver service, champagne fountains, and other equipment can add ambiance to the special day. In some cases, banquet departments have gazebos, trellises, centerpieces, and other decorating items in stock; other departments rent the needed equipment from outside vendors. At the Orlando Peabody, social banquet manager Bonnie Garfield steers couples away from wedding packages, preferring to design events that offer "more individuality, rather than the feeling of a staged, planned event." She says, "We are very flexible and are sensitive to the couple's preferences."

Since there is so much involved in planning a wedding and reception, it is becoming more common for couples to have their ceremony as well as their reception at a hotel in either their home city or their honeymoon destination city. That way, the wedding party and guests do not have to travel to the wedding site and then to the reception; all details are handled by a single person; and the couple can save money. Independent wedding consultants typically charge 15 percent of the gross wedding costs; by servicing all the events, a banquet department can provide added value.

Establishing trust and confidence on the part of potential clients means listening, taking careful notes, and sharing your enthusiasm. Using visual aids, such as photos of decor, table settings, and cake-decorating options, will enhance a sales presentation. The most important aspect of selling to this market, however, is the staff's expertise—being able to deliver a memorable, worry-free event.

Other Functions. Other special functions may include requests for kosher service (see Exhibit 1) or requests for menus that meet special dietary restrictions (for example, vegetarian or vegan). When preparing for these types of functions, the banquet director and kitchen staff must pay close attention to requirements for purchasing and preparing foods.

Off-Premises Catering

Off-premises catering can be divided into two categories. The first, which is offered by many hotels, is a function that is not held in the banquet room but is still on the property—such as a poolside party, a garden wedding, or a function held under tents pitched on the back lawn. This type of catering is popular with many guests. It has the added advantage of being close to the hotel's kitchen and any equipment that may be needed.

The second category of off-premises catering involves servicing functions away from the property. Fewer hotels offer this type of catering. The primary reason is cost:

**Exhibit 1
Kosher Service**

The most special occasions of all are even more special at the Hilton

HILTON INTERNATIONAL
SYDNEY

Kosher perfection

Many hotels offer kosher service when it is requested for weddings, bar and bat mitzvahs, and other special occasions. This brochure promotes kosher services at the property. (Courtesy of the Hilton International Sydney, Sydney, Australia)

high initial startup costs for transportation and equipment to keep foods at appropriate temperatures, and high inventory costs for items such as tables, chairs, and tents. In addition, there are costs for labor (drivers and setup personnel), insurance (both for the vehicles and for liability), and health permits.

Despite these factors, many hotels and restaurants—especially those in areas without much catering competition—have found off-premises catering an extremely lucrative addition to their food and beverage bottom line. The Hyatt Regency Tech Center near Denver teamed up with the Hyatt Regency in downtown Denver to win the catering contract for the gala that opened Denver's international airport. The hotel has also participated in several other high-profile events, including the Denver opening of the musical "Miss Saigon" and catering the Denver Bronco's stadium skyboxes. The Dallas Sheraton catered a society gala at the Dallas Museum of Art and, using those contacts, contracted with the city to cater all events held at the symphony center.

Even small properties can benefit from off-premises catering. The 92-room Little Nell Hotel in Aspen, Colorado, capitalizes on its location by catering functions at the top of Aspen Mountain as well as at off-site weddings and functions in the town's symphony hall. The hotel has an advantage over the other caterers in the area; since it's open year-round, the Little Nell employs a full-time staff, while other area caterers are seasonal and have to rehire every year. The hotel is perceived as a luxury property, and its reputation for quality and style are strong selling points that no other caterer can match.

Apply Your Learning 8.3

Please write all answers on a separate sheet of paper.

1. When planning a refreshment break, how many beverage stations should be set up for a group of 160? Which station should be opened first during the breaks?

2. "Marrying" coffee stations refers to:
   a. assigning specific staff to oversee specific stations.
   b. providing a more extensive selection of food and beverages than is usual, often involving gourmet cheeses, specialty breads, select coffees, and bottled juices.
   c. placing two stations side by side to create a refreshment "island" that helps to establish a more relaxed atmosphere.
   d. combining the food and beverages of two or more stations into one.

3. What are the five elements of a wedding reception catered by a hotel?

4. What are the two categories of off-premises catering? Which is more common for hotels?

8.4 Meeting Room Sales

AFTER STUDYING SECTION 8.4, YOU SHOULD KNOW HOW TO:

♦ Describe the value of meeting room space

♦ List types of meeting rooms

♦ List and define the types of meeting room setups

♦ Describe common meeting room furniture

♦ Book meeting rooms and establish release dates

♦ Manage meetings at a lodging property

Meeting Room Sales

Meeting rooms are usually sold by salespeople in the hotel's sales office who sell group guestroom business to corporations and associations. At some large properties, a separate convention department may solicit meetings and convention business. However meeting room sales are handled, it is important to keep these points in mind:

1. The amount of revenue that can be generated relates directly to the amount of space available. By arranging for the most effective use of meet-

ing room space—for example, meetings following meetings in the same room rather than a banquet following a meeting—costs can be kept down and more space can be sold.

2. If the least desirable space is sold first, it is far easier to sell the desirable space at a later date. If the desirable space doesn't sell, the previously booked meetings can be moved into the prime space.

3. Question "holds" that reserve space for all day or all evening; few meeting planners need rooms for an entire day or evening, and a few hours of "dead" time can be used for another meeting.

4. Salespeople should concentrate on selling space during times when business is usually slow. Meeting rooms will practically sell themselves during peak periods.

At large properties, a convention service manager may set policies on selling meeting rooms; at a smaller property the sales director or manager may deal with sales policies. The current trend, however, is to charge for meeting rooms even if the group uses banquet facilities. This makes it even more important to provide clients with the services they require.

Types of Meeting Rooms. Meeting rooms fall into three basic categories: exhibit halls, ballrooms for large meetings or banquets, and conference meeting rooms. The type of room used will depend on a variety of factors: the type of meeting, the number of attendees expected, the size and layout of the room, and special requirements (audiovisual equipment, modem connections, access to freight elevators, and so on). A meeting planner may also be interested in such room features as ceiling height, the location of electrical outlets, proximity to elevators, the locations of exits, the number of doors and windows, and the presence of pillars or other potential obstructions.

Meeting Room Setups. There are various meeting room setups that can make the best use of space while still meeting the client's needs (see Exhibit 1):

1. *Theater*—Chairs are set up in straight rows (with aisles) parallel to the head table, stage, or speaker's podium.

2. *Senate*—Same as a theater setup, except chairs are placed in a semicircle rather than in rows.

3. *V-shaped*—Same as a theater setup, except that chairs are placed in a V.

4. *U-shaped (or horseshoe)*—Tables are set up in the shape of a block-letter *U*; chairs are placed outside the closed end and on both sides of each leg.

5. *T-shaped*—Tables are set up in the shape of a block-letter *T* and chairs are placed around the outside.

6. *Hollow Square*—A series of tables forms a square with a hollow middle; chairs are placed around the outside.

7. *Schoolroom (or classroom)*—The most common setup. Tables are lined up in rows (one behind the other) on each

side of an aisle. There are usually three to four chairs to a table (depending on table size), and all tables and chairs face the head table, stage, or speaker's podium.

8. *Herringbone*—Similar to a schoolroom setup, with tables and chairs arranged in a *V*.

9. *Board-of-Directors*—This is a popular arrangement for small meetings. It calls for a single column of double tables with seating all the way around.

10. *Banquet*—A meal setup that generally uses round tables.

The type of setup will affect the capacity of a meeting room, so it's essential that salespeople be knowledgeable about room capacities under all possible configurations. Most properties provide detailed scale drawings of all meeting rooms, which include physical characteristics and room capacities (see Exhibit 2).

The equipment required by a group often affects the room size and setup needed. Typical equipment provided by hotels includes audiovisual equipment (microphones, a public-address system, projectors), speakers' equipment (flip chart stands, easels, blackboards), and accessory equipment such as portable stages and podiums.

Meeting Room Furniture

The choice of meeting room furniture is important to most meeting planners, and the types of furniture chosen will affect a room's capacity. Salespeople should familiarize themselves with their property's furniture so they can advise meeting planners regarding room configurations.

Exhibit 1
Meeting Room Setups

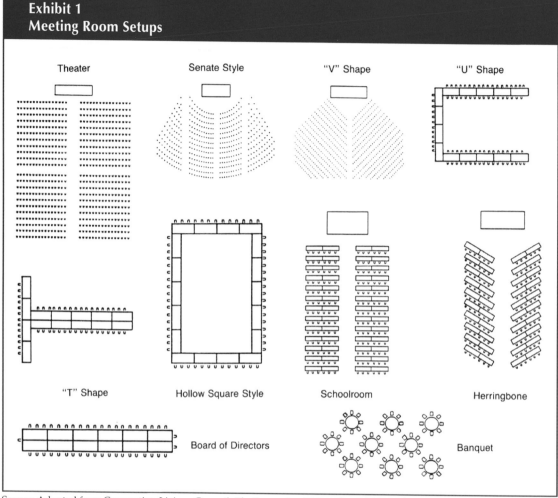

Theater   Senate Style   "V" Shape   "U" Shape

"T" Shape   Hollow Square Style   Schoolroom   Herringbone

Board of Directors   Banquet

Source: Adapted from Convention Liaison Council, *The Convention Liaison Council Manual*, 6th ed. (Washington, D.C., 1994), pp. 81–91.

Chairs. Most chairs used for meetings are 18 inches wide by 18 inches deep by 17 inches high. Most folding chairs are smaller, and not as comfortable as upholstered chairs; folding chairs are generally used for last-minute overflow accommodations.

Tables. A standard table is 30 inches high and either 30 or 18 inches wide. When seating is required on both sides of the table, the 30-inch-wide table is used.

Rounds are used for meeting sessions as well as for food functions, and are most often available in four-, five-, and six-foot diameters. For the most comfortable seating, the four-foot table can accommodate four to six people; a five-foot table, eight to ten people; a six-foot table, ten to twelve people.

Platforms. Folding platforms are often used to elevate the speaker's lectern and the head

Exhibit 2
Sample Meeting Room Plan

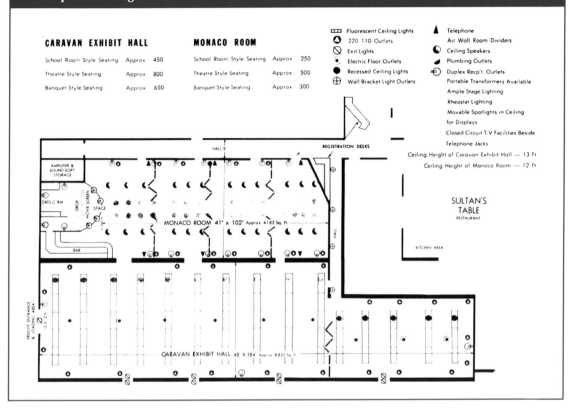

CARAVAN EXHIBIT HALL

School Room Style Seating	Approx	450
Theatre Style Seating	Approx	800
Banquet Style Seating	Approx	650

MONACO ROOM

School Room Style Seating	Approx	250
Theatre Style Seating	Approx	500
Banquet Style Seating	Approx	300

Fluorescent Ceiling Lights — Telephone
220 110 Outlets — Air Wall Room Dividers
Exit Lights — Ceiling Speakers
Electric Floor Outlets — Plumbing Outlets
Recessed Ceiling Lights — Duplex Recp't. Outlets
Wall Bracket Light Outlets — Portable Transformers Available

Ample Stage Lighting
Rheostat Lighting
Movable Spotlights in Ceiling
for Displays
Closed Circuit T-V Facilities Beside
Telephone Jacks
Ceiling Height of Caravan Exhibit Hall — 13 Ft
Ceiling Height of Monaco Room — 12 Ft

MONACO ROOM 41' x 102' Approx. 4182 Sq. Ft.

CARAVAN EXHIBIT HALL 48 X 184 Approx 8832 Sq. Ft

SULTAN'S TABLE RESTAURANT

table at banquets. They are available in a variety of heights, lengths, and widths.

Booking Meeting Rooms

Once arrangements are final, the salesperson can fill out a function book space-request form and detail the client's function room needs.

In some cases, space is placed on hold. A hold period should not extend beyond the time when the space can be sold if the commitment is not firmed up. To avoid this, an appropriate **release date** should be set. If the space is not confirmed by the release date, the reservation is canceled.

Many groups estimate requirements for meeting space a year or more prior to the actual event, based on a rough outline of the convention program. As the convention draws nearer, meeting planners may make extensive program changes. If a specific release date has been set (usually 60 or 90 days prior to the event), meeting rooms that aren't needed can be released, and the hotel can sell this space to other groups.

In many instances, another group can be given a tentative booking if, for example, a group seems to have reserved more space than it will need. If the first group does indeed need all the space it reserved, the second group must be notified immediately and a lost business report should be completed.

Managing Meetings

Policies for managing meetings will vary from property to property, but some requirements are almost universal.

Rooms are set up well in advance, if possible. This allows for any last-minute changes.

Setup teams vary with a property's size. Small properties may use house attendants, medium-sized properties may rely on crews supervised by the banquet manager, and large convention properties may have special setup crews.

Most properties provide general meeting room accessories. These include draped head tables, small bowls of hard candy, and pitchers of ice water and glasses. If the meeting is scheduled to run more than two hours, setup personnel or food servers usually freshen up the room by removing dirty or wet linens, straightening chairs, refilling water pitchers, and replacing glasses. Setup crews may also be involved in setting up exhibit booths or display areas.

Many properties offer partitions that can be used to divide a room into smaller rooms or be opened to provide display or ballroom space. This option offers flexibility and is popular with training directors who wish to divide meeting attendees into small groups after a general training session. Partitions also benefit the property by enabling better space control. Putting 20 people in a room built for 100 wastes space and cuts into profits; with partitions, the room can accommodate several small groups at a time.

After a meeting, follow-up should be prompt—a thank-you letter and an evaluation form should be sent and traced.

Providing hassle-free meeting space and personalized service can help ensure repeat business, great referrals, and on-going profitability of a hotel's meetings business.

Apply Your Learning 8.4

Please write all answers on a separate sheet of paper.

For statements 1–4, write whether the answer is True or False.

1. It is preferable to sell the most desirable meeting space first.

2. Salespeople should especially focus on selling meeting space during peak periods.

3. Salespeople should question meeting planners who ask to hold meeting rooms for an entire day.

4. The trend is to provide meeting rooms free of charge to groups that book banquet facilities.

5. The basic categories of meeting rooms include all of the following *except:*

    a. hospitality suites.
    b. conference rooms.
    c. exhibit halls.
    d. ballrooms.

6. A theater setup in which chairs are in a semicircle instead of rows is known as a:

    a. senate setup.
    b. theater-plus setup.
    c. schoolroom setup.
    d. board-of-directors setup.

7. Which of the following setups includes tables for the attendees?

    a. theater
    b. T-shape
    c. V-shape
    d. senate

Quick Hits

Chapter 8

SECTION 8.1—THE BANQUET DEPARTMENT

- Most banquet departments have two main responsibilities: (1) to sell food and beverage functions to businesses and individuals in the local community, and (2) to service in-house convention and group functions sold by the property's sales office.

- At most large properties, the banquet department is an arm of the food and beverage department. At smaller hotels, banquet is often handled by a salesperson in the sales office.

- The *banquet director's* primary responsibilities are sales and administration. The *banquet manager* oversees food and beverage functions, supervises service personnel, and, occasionally, sets up function rooms. *Banquet salespeople* are often employed by large properties to actively solicit business not brought in as part of conventions or meetings. *Clerical staff* maintain the paperwork generated by business solicitation, handle routine inquiries, and follow up on accounts. *Service personnel* serve food and beverages, set up function rooms, and maintain banquet areas and equipment.

SECTION 8.2—BANQUET SALES

- Advertising and promotion should be targeted to specific audiences and should reflect the professionalism and creativity of the banquet services being offered. They include print ads, direct mail, and in-house promotions.

- Salespeople can develop leads through personal selling, telephone sales, letters, or by responding to inquiries.

- Personal selling involves contacting businesses frequented by members of a targeted market segment.

- Successful telephone solicitation begins with a plan that includes targeted prospects, the information that should be conveyed, and the desired results.

- Form letters are most commonly used by the sales office to solicit out-of-town convention and meetings business. Personalized letters are most often used by the banquet department to solicit local business.

- Sales letters should follow the *AIDA* formula: attract the prospect's *attention*, create an *interest* in and a *desire* for the product, and give the prospect a means to take *action*.

- Telephone inquiries from prospects must be handled quickly and efficiently to ensure that business is not lost. Fax and e-mail responses should be prompt and professional. Walk-in clients should be welcomed appropriately and given reading material that highlights the department's banquet work.

SECTION 8.3—SPECIAL TYPES OF FOOD AND BEVERAGE SALES

- Refreshment breaks are usually scheduled at midmorning and midafternoon, last 15 to 30 minutes, and are intended to alleviate boredom and sharpen the attention and enthusiasm of meeting attendees.

- Hospitality suites are sold to event sponsors, vendors, or meeting attendees as a place to do business and socialize. They often are set up in two or more guestrooms with connecting doors.

- The five elements of a wedding reception sold by the banquet department are menu and beverages, disposables, equipment, decor, and service.

- Other special functions may include requests for kosher service or requests for menus that meet special dietary restrictions.

- Off-premises catering can be divided into two categories: outside of the banquet room but still on-premises, and completely off-premises.

SECTION 8.4—MEETING ROOM SALES

- Meeting rooms are usually sold by salespeople in the hotel's sales office who sell group guestroom business to corporations and associations. At some large properties, a separate convention department may solicit meetings and convention business.

- Meeting rooms fall into three basic categories: exhibit halls, ballrooms for large meetings or banquets, and conference meeting rooms.

- The various meeting room setups include theater, senate, V-shaped, U-shaped, T-shaped, hollow square, schoolroom, herringbone, board of directors, and banquet.

- The choice of meeting room furniture is important to most meeting planners. The types of furniture chosen will affect a room's capacity.

- An appropriate **release date** should be set for all meeting rooms placed on hold.

- Providing hassle-free meeting space and personalized service can help ensure repeat business, great referrals, and ongoing profitability of a hotel's meetings business.

Profile

Scott Ringer
General Manager, Aruba Marriott Resort and Stellaris Casino, and Aruba Ocean Club

S cott Ringer grew up in the hotel industry and can't imagine working anywhere else. His childhood summers were spent working at his family's hotel.

"I was a bellman when I was 6 years old," he says.

Ringer learned the hotel business from his dad, who worked at the Statler Hilton in Boston for 24 years. When the general manager went on vacation, Ringer's father brought the whole family to live in one of the hotel's suites. Ringer picked up odd jobs around the hotel. "It was always fun. I was a jack of all trades."

In college, he pursued hotel management and Ringer was one of the first graduates of the hotel school at Florida International University. After graduating, Ringer accepted a job in the accounting department at the Marriott hotel in Atlanta. Accounting came naturally to Ringer, and he quickly rose in the Marriott ranks. He held several property-level controller positions and then was promoted to international director of finance for Europe, the Middle East, and Africa. Living in London, he oversaw financial affairs for Marriott's properties in Jordan, Saudi Arabia, Egypt, Greece, France, Holland, Austria, Germany, and England. In the fall of 1989, he helped open the first Western-managed hotel in Eastern Europe—a Marriott in Warsaw, Poland.

But when it came right down to it, Ringer loved working in hotels more than corporate management.

In 1994, Ringer accepted his current job as the general manager of the Aruba Marriott Resort and Stellaris Casino and the Marriott Aruba Ocean Club.

Ringer tells employees that the three qualities that make people successful in the lodging industry are a love for people, a love of serving people, and common sense.

"If you love to be around people and you're naturally a social person, then what better job is there?" he says. "The hospitality business can be a blast if you remember that being hospitable is what it's all about."

He names the position of bellman as his favorite hotel job, and notes that there are some days when he wishes he was still a bellman.

"The bellman is the grassroots of what we do in hospitality," he says. "Greeting people at the door, being their first sign of welcome, helping them to have a pleasant stay, that's what we're all about in this industry."

Portions of this article were excerpted from Lodging *magazine.*

Selling Is Everyone's Job

Sections

9.1 Everyone's Sales Role

9.2 Relationship Selling

9.3 Upgrading

9.4 Suggestive Selling and Cross-Selling

9.5 Departmental Selling

9.1 Everyone's Sales Roles

AFTER STUDYING SECTION 9.1, YOU SHOULD KNOW HOW TO:

♦ Identify how managers can promote effective guest-employee relationships

♦ Describe the manager's role in hiring sales-oriented employees

♦ Explain the importance of training employees in sales techniques

♦ Motivate employees to sell

Regardless of your specific job title, every hotel employee is involved in sales. Every employee can play a role in promoting additional sales to guests and increasing guest satisfaction. The key is to create effective guest-employee relationships. Management can help by doing three things:

1. Provide an environment that encourages good guest-employee relations.

2. Instill pride among employees, both in the property and in the value of their individual positions.

3. Offer training that equips employees to become more helpful to guests.

A property-wide sales attitude must start with top management and filter down to employees. In that way, an enthusiastic management team can produce an entire staff that sells with enthusiasm.

The Role of the General Manager

If the general manager is not sales oriented, it's unlikely the hotel staff will be highly motivated. A good GM recognizes the value of guest satisfaction and sets goals to attain guest goodwill—and repeat business—by using effective internal merchandising and developing sales-oriented employees. Developing a staff that focuses on sales is a three-part process that includes hiring sales-minded employees, training all employees

Faux Foliage

When hoteliers talk about getting rid of plastic, it isn't credit cards that they're cutting up—it's the plants in the lobby.

While plastic plants have long been an important part of hotel decorating, technology is now offering a new option—preserved plant material. The treescaping company harvests a live tree and then replaces the tree's natural fluid with a chemical preservative. The tree then holds its color and hoteliers can put "real" fake trees in their lobby.

in sales techniques, then motivating all employees to sell.

Hiring Sales-Oriented Employees. Employees who view all of their guest interactions and job responsibilities in terms of their impact on sales will benefit any hotel; sales-oriented employees can greatly increase in-house sales. The human resources department at large properties, or the general manager at smaller properties, should develop sales-oriented job descriptions and be able to recognize sales-oriented applicants. When new employees realize that selling is part of their job and sales is the lifeblood of the property, they will be more willing to learn sales techniques.

Sales skills can be taught; personality can't. That's why some hotel managers say that they "hire the smile and train the skill." Employees—especially those who will have direct contact with guests—should be "sparklers," people who are sincerely warm, enthusiastic, and concerned about guests.

One successful restaurant owner always asks the question, "What's the funniest thing that's ever happened to you?" during interviews. He uses the answer to judge his applicants' enthusiasm and ability to interact with guests. If an applicant looks at him and says, "What do you mean, exactly, by 'funny'?" or, "You know, I guess I can't think of anything funny right now," he knows this is the way the applicant will come across to guests. If, on the other hand, the applicant smiles and launches into a story, the owner knows he has a winner.

Training Employees in Sales Techniques. Once an employee has gained a thorough knowledge of the property and the benefits it offers guests, training can help the employee learn the types of selling required for the position (upgrading, suggestive selling, cross-selling, etc.) and learn to recognize sales cues from guests, including tone of voice and body language. Employees should be well versed in how to "read" others.

Motivating Employees to Sell. General managers can motivate employees to sell by convincing them that they can, indeed, become effective salespeople. Confident, and armed with management's encouragement, employees can put their skills to work to earn more money for the property. Many properties also offer incentive programs to employees to encourage sales.

Apply Your Learning 9.1

Please write all answers on a separate sheet of paper.

1. What three things can hotel managers do to promote effective guest-employee relationships?

2. All of the following are recommended methods for developing a sales-oriented staff *except:*

    a. hire sales-oriented employees.
    b. motivate employees to sell.
    c. train employees in how to effectively use proven sales techniques.
    d. rotate employees through a variety of hotel positions.

3. What does it mean to "hire the smile and train the skill"?

9.2 Relationship Selling

AFTER STUDYING SECTION 9.2, YOU SHOULD KNOW HOW TO:

♦ Explain why relationship selling is important

♦ Describe what employees need to know about a property

♦ Summarize what employees need to know about the area

♦ Interact with guests in a positive manner

♦ Learn and use guest names

♦ Handle complaints

From economy and luxury properties to spa resorts and cruise ships, hospitality choices today abound. A well-known brand name may be enough to bring a guest through the door, but it's the service provided by the property's staff that will build guest loyalty and help ensure that guests don't leave for the competition.

Many employees make hundreds, even thousands, of guest contacts every week. If a property wants to keep all of those guests coming back, it's important to involve employees in internal sales—and use their ideas and suggestions.

Building Relationships

It's easier and less expensive to hold onto existing guests than to find new ones. Most managers focus, therefore, on building relationships with their current guests. After all, where would you rather stay—at a hotel where you're simply the guest in room 109 or at the hotel where staff greet you by name, have the in-room refrigerator stocked with your favorite snacks, and remember at the restaurant that you are allergic to peanut oil? Relationship selling (also called *relationship marketing*) means building guest loyalty by creating, enhancing, and maintaining a relationship with guests.

In everyday life, every new relationship starts with learning more about the other person. Whether you're having a conversation about favorite movies, food preferences, or family background, the goal is the same: to gain information.

The situation is similar for properties that want to build relationships with guests. To get off on the right foot, hotels need information. There are several ways for properties to learn more about their guests.

Guest profiles can be developed by obtaining information from registration forms or conducting guest surveys. To be effective, guest profiles must contain information that will enable property personnel to determine individual guest needs.

Another, more personal way to gain guest knowledge involves asking for employee input. Almost every employee, no matter how limited his or her actual guest contact, can contribute guest information. Room attendants, for example, will know about special requests (extra towels, decaf for the in-room coffeemaker, a foreign newspaper). Food servers can glean invaluable information—special diets, food allergies, and so on—in casual, friendly conversations. This type of input makes it easy to provide favorite items for the guest's next stay—a thoughtful gesture that can build priceless goodwill.

The Role of Training

Employee training should include a number of areas that will enable employees to assist guests and build rapport. These areas include:

- Knowing the property
- Knowing the area
- Interacting with guests

Knowing the property. If employees don't know what the property has to offer, they can't very well promote it. As part of the orientation process, every new employee should be given a complete property tour. All employees should learn an abbreviated form of the property fact book. They should also be informed of special promotional packages, special events, and other property happenings.

To sell effectively, hotel employees must sample the product. Food servers should taste every item on the menu so they can make specific, personal, and honest recommendations if asked by a guest. Front desk agents will do a much better job of relating to customer needs if they have actually slept in the property's suites. It costs little to have

employees stay at the hotel (employees can become "guests" on a slow Sunday night, for example), but the benefits of such stays can be great.

Knowing the area. Employee knowledge of the area surrounding the property can help employees suggest local attractions to visit, recommend a variety of sightseeing or entertainment alternatives, and give accurate directions.

Employees should do more than just provide a brochure on an area attraction or quote from a fact sheet (especially if the employee is as unfamiliar with the attraction as the guest). Properties can ensure that their staff is well informed and helpful by (1) encouraging employees to keep abreast of area events and attractions (including hours, prices, and services); (2) holding training sessions that provide local area information and fact sheets that stress guest benefits; and (3) encouraging the staff to personally experience local attractions (most guests will ask the employee if he or she has been there).

Because of the high potential for word-of-mouth referrals, many attractions offer complimentary tickets to hotel staff. Even if free tickets are not available, management should still encourage employees—especially those in the sales and marketing departments and in guest-contact positions—to visit nearby places of interest so they can tell guests or potential clients about them.

Interacting with guests. Positive interaction with guests is crucial to making a good impression and generating repeat business. Front desk employees are in a prime position. They are very often the first contact that a person has with a property, and a guest's entire perception of a property may be shaped by the way he or she is treated by front desk personnel.

Most properties recognize the value of retaining a friendly and competent front desk staff. Not only are operations smoother, but it is far easier for guests to build relationships when they are greeted by familiar faces. Many properties offer incentives to encourage employees to make a career of front desk operations; through empowerment programs, some front desk agents are given increased authority to make service decisions and otherwise resolve guest problems.

Every employee makes an impression, of course, and should be trained in the areas of proper appearance, courtesy, and personal habits. Every employee should be reminded that each guest is valuable, and a friendly smile and a willingness to help are vital for building rapport. It's especially important to make guests feel welcome.

Using names. In today's automated world, people appreciate recognition more than ever before, and there are a number of ways employees can learn and use names:

1. Many computerized telephone systems automatically display the room number and guest's name on a monitor whenever a guest calls the switchboard from a guestroom. The operator can greet the guest by name: "Good afternoon, Mr. Herndon. How may I help you?"

2. Before a guest registers with the hotel, the bellperson or porter can look for names on luggage tags.

3. The front desk agent gets guests' names upon receiving the completed registration forms. He or she can begin calling guests by name and may

ask the bellperson to "Show Mr. and Mrs. Lewis to their room, please." The bellperson can then begin calling guests by name also.

4. If the guest has restaurant reservations, the host can greet the guest by name and pass the guest's name along to the food server.

5. Switchboard operators can use names when making wake-up calls. A cheery "Good morning, Ms. Ricker. It's seven o'clock. Would you like room service to bring you a fresh pot of coffee and a Danish?" is much more hospitable than "Hello, it's seven o'clock."

6. Anytime guests use credit cards, there is an opportunity to learn and use names.

Name recognition works both ways. Not only do most guests appreciate the recognition accorded them by the property's staff, they also like to see familiar faces and greet staff members by name. Many properties, especially those in busy tourist areas, use name badges displaying the employee's name and home state. These can be excellent conversation starters: "You're from New York? I went to school there!"

Handling complaints. Despite everyone's best efforts, there are times when it's impossible to please a guest. In some cases, a guest's unhappiness is justified—service may be slow, there may be an error in reservations or payment arrangements, or a guestroom may not be ready on time. Sometimes guests may simply be taking out their frustrations with other circumstances on the nearest available person. Regardless, employees must respond to complaints in such a way that goodwill is restored. In many cases, guest complaints have led to the improvement of problem areas at a property—resulting in better service and increased guest satisfaction.

An angry guest can be transformed into a loyal one if his or her complaint is handled efficiently and patiently. To do this, remain calm and determine the exact nature of the complaint. Ask questions to determine the specific reason for the dissatisfaction.

Once you have identified the guest's complaint, take action. If you can't handle the situation personally, immediately contact a supervisor or other person in authority. Promise the guest that you'll follow up.

Since complaints can serve a useful purpose, guests should be given an opportunity to voice them. Some unhappy guests want to be heard, and have no qualms about writing a complaint letter, making a telephone call, or asking to speak to the man-

ager. Resolving problems for them is far easier than dealing with the more typical unhappy guest who never expresses dissatisfaction; he or she just leaves the property to tell hotel "horror stories" to friends and business associates.

To avoid losing this kind of guest, property personnel should try to read guest reactions or simply ask, "How was everything?" when guests check out—and be sincerely interested in the response. In many cases, guests will volunteer information when asked directly. Or, to make it easy to complain without having a face-to-face confrontation, properties can offer a complaint hotline or toll-free number. These steps will help guests feel that what they think is important to your property and that you're willing to not only listen but to do something about the points they raise.

Apply Your Learning 9.2

Please write all answers on a separate sheet of paper.

For statements 1–5, write whether the answer is True or False.

1. Building better guest relationships begins with gaining information about guests.

2. It is typically easier to draw new guests to a hotel than to hold on to current customers.

3. Relationship selling means getting to know someone so you can coerce them into buying a hotel product or service.

4. Almost every hotel employee can provide useful information about guest preferences and needs.

5. Most returning guests are suspicious when hotel staff provide favorite items on their next visit.

6. What are the three areas of training that can help hotel employees build stronger relationships with guests?

7. Which of the following is *not* a recommended means for helping staff become familiar with the area surrounding the hotel?

   a. Encourage staff to personally experience local attractions.
   b. Suggest that staff occasionally accompany guests to local attractions.
   c. Hold training sessions on local attractions.
   d. Encourage employees to stay up-to-date on area events and attractions.

8. Once you have identified a guest's complaint, what should your next step be?

   a. Try to discover why the problem occurred.
   b. Help the guest to see the humor in the situation.
   c. Complete the appropriate paperwork.
   d. Take immediate action.

9.3 Upgrading

AFTER STUDYING SECTION 9.3, YOU SHOULD KNOW HOW TO:

♦ Use the top-down method to increase sales

♦ Use the rate-category-alternatives method of upgrading room sales

♦ Use the bottom-up method of upgrading room sales

Many properties have such amenities as swimming pools, cable television, and 24-hour room service—so what makes your property different? Selling involves pinpointing those differences and presenting them in a convincing manner. For example, a guest usually needs help understanding a tangible benefit. A benefits-oriented employee will not simply mention the property's lounge; he or she also will mention a benefit: "Many of our business guests really enjoy the relaxing atmosphere after a long day of meetings."

Once employees understand the benefits-oriented sales approach, there are several sales techniques they can use. Three of the most effective are upgrading or upselling, suggestive selling, and cross-selling.

Upgrading

Upgrading or upselling reservations is an effective way to increase revenues, but very few front desk or reservations staffs are trained in how to do it. Most hotels have several room types and prices, but there is often no set formula for selling rooms. Employees simply quote a price and make no attempt to sell additional services or amenities.

Maybe managers are afraid guests will be offended or feel pressured. However, a caller may be unaware of varying rates and amenities, and may appreciate the property's efforts to place him or her in a room that meets specific needs. Meeting specific needs is an important part of upgrading, and employees must be trained to listen to the caller and make suggestions for an appropriate accommodation.

Front desk and reservations agents should be trained to recognize when and how to upgrade a guest's request. Upgrading can be accomplished without pressuring a guest by using one of three methods:

• Top-down

• Rate-category alternatives

• Bottom-up

The **top-down method** is used to encourage guests to reserve middle- or high-rate rooms. It begins with the front desk or reservations agent enthusiastically recommending the guestroom sold at the highest rate. The guest may either accept or reject the recommendation. If the guest says no, the agent moves down to the next price level and enthusiastically discusses the merits of this accommodation. The guest may perceive the lower rate as a compromise on the part of the agent and be more open to accepting this recommendation. If the rate quoted is still unacceptable, the agent drops to the next-highest rate, continuing this process until the guest is satisfied with the price quoted.

The **rate-category-alternatives method** is an easy and effective way to sell middle-rate rooms to guests who might otherwise choose a lower rate. The front desk or reservations agent provides the guest with a choice of three or more rate-category alternatives and puts no pressure on the guest. In most cases, people will attempt to avoid extremes: choosing the lowest rate could cause the guest to feel cheap, while choosing the highest rate might make the guest feel unnecessarily extravagant. Under these circumstances the logical decision would be to choose the middle rate.

The **bottom-up method** is used when a guest has already made a reservation or has requested a low-priced room. During the registration process, the front desk or reservations agent can suggest extra amenities or point out the merits of a more expensive room: "For only $10 more, you can enjoy a room with a view of the ocean," or, "For an additional $25, you can have a deluxe room and two complimentary continental breakfasts." The higher rate must appear to be an attempt by the agent to enhance the guest's stay at only a small increase over charges anticipated by the guest.

No matter what method is used to upgrade a reservation, guests should *never* feel they are being pressured; sales pressure has no place in the hospitality industry. Rather, internal sales should be aimed at giving guests the opportunity to purchase additional products and services or to "trade up" from those already purchased. Help guests to realize that they are not just buying a room but a "home away from home," and their needs are important to the property. By combining upselling techniques with a knowledge of guest needs, front desk employees can sell a pleasurable experience to guests while increasing revenues.

Apply Your Learning 9.3

Please write all answers on a separate sheet of paper.

1. Upgrading or upselling is an example of a _____ approach to sales.
   a. suggestive-selling
   b. team-driven
   c. high-pressure
   d. benefits-oriented

2. What are the three primary methods of upgrading?

3. Providing guests with three or more choices based on a range of prices is an example of which upgrading method?

4. What role does sales pressure play in upgrading guests?

9.4 Suggestive Selling and Cross-Selling

AFTER STUDYING SECTION 9.4, YOU SHOULD KNOW HOW TO:

♦ List guidelines for suggestive selling

♦ Describe how various departments use suggestive selling

♦ Describe forms of cross-selling found in lodging properties

♦ Explain the importance of having knowledgeable employees

Suggestive Selling

Suggestive selling means influencing a guest's purchase decision by highlighting available choices. Almost any employee can use this sales technique in most areas of the property. For example, a restaurant host may inform guests of the special of the day after greeting them; a food server may suggest a cocktail before dinner, an appetizer, the special of the day, or a dessert; a bartender may suggest a specialty drink at a discount price. The power of suggestion is also a good way to introduce new menu items, promote low-overhead food items, and increase the server's tip base.

There are two important keys to using suggestive selling successfully.

First, *avoid asking questions that can be answered yes or no.* Give the guest a choice. For example, ask: "Which dessert would you like from our dessert cart?" rather than "Would you like dessert?" Guests to the hotel's spa might be asked, "What facial treatment would you like to try after your massage?"

Second, *suggest in specific terms.* In the hotel's restaurant, don't just suggest an appetizer—suggest a specific item such as fried zucchini, shrimp cocktail, or bruschetta. Even better, paint a word picture for guests. It's more effective to say: "Our catch of the day is rainbow trout stuffed with shrimp and fresh crabmeat, lightly floured and sautéed in butter, and garnished with fresh lemon and parsley," than to say, "Our catch of the day is stuffed trout."

Suggestive selling is only as effective as the verbal communication between the employee and the guest. Employees must know the hotel's products and services and learn the art of making a sales approach. For a sales approach to work, you must be enthusiastic, considerate, and aware of how the sale will benefit the guest (see Exhibit 1).

Suggestive selling can also be used in every revenue center at the property. The health club attendant may suggest a relaxing massage after a workout. The golf pro can suggest a new set of clubs from the pro

Exhibit 1
Sample Sales Phrases

Front Desk	Suggested Sales Phrases
Early morning check-ins	"Our valet service can have your suit pressed and returned to your room within an hour while you freshen up."
Early evening check-ins	"Do you enjoy Spanish music? We are featuring Carlos, one of the finest Spanish pianists in the country, in our La Mancha lounge."
	"Have you seen the exciting Hawaiian revue in our main showroom? It's almost like being on the Islands!"
	"If you'd like to unwind, our Baron's Pub is located in the east wing near the coffee shop. Besides offering the best drinks in town, the Pub features continuous entertainment from 7:00 P.M. to midnight."
Late evening check-ins	"Our excellent room service is still available. Here's the phone number, sir."
Checking out	"Would you like me to make your return reservation for you now?"
	"Your next stop is Orlando, and our chain has another hotel there. Would you like me to confirm a reservation for you?"
Room Service	
After delivering a meal	"Have you tried our Captain's Table restaurant yet? Tomorrow night they'll be featuring a special seafood buffet that I'm sure you'd enjoy."
When coming to clear	"Don't forget that we're available 24 hours a day. If there's anything else you'll need, you can reach us at extension XX."
Valet Parking	
Before parking the car	"Welcome to Complete Resorts. If you like Hawaiian cuisine, you'll love our Lanai Buffet. It's on the second floor above the pool area."
When delivering the car	"I hope you enjoyed your stay. Don't forget that we'll be having a special Western Barbecue next week. I'm looking forward to seeing you then."

shop after a private lesson. The front desk agent can suggest a return visit during a special promotional period.

Of course, suggestive selling also belongs in the sales department. If Tuesday is a typical sellout or high occupancy night, for example, a salesperson might suggest another night of the week to clients. Monitoring competitors' bookings may also point to suggestive selling strategies; if the property is likely to sell out during a particular week due to overflow from a competitor's booking of a large convention, salespeople can suggest dates in the weeks before or after to maximize revenue potential.

Cross-Selling

Cross-selling means using media in one area of the property to promote a different area of the property. For example, a tent card on a hallway table may advertise an upcoming weekend package, a poster at the front desk can promote the hotel's gift and specialty shops, and the matchbooks in the lounge may advertise the property's fine-dining restaurant.

Registration and reservation confirmation forms also offer opportunities to cross-sell. A hotel might use its registration forms to tell guests about on-site restaurants, lounges, and other revenue centers. Reservation confirmations mailed to guests can remind them to bring workout clothes so they can use the hotel's health club.

Employees can also cross-sell. It can begin at the front desk when the front desk agent recommends the property's restaurant. To help front desk employees promote the restaurant, a special display might be posted within sight of the front desk, and menus could be available for guests to browse. A sincere invitation to visit the property's facilities—along with display advertising or other aids to enhance the employees' presentation—can greatly increase revenues and make guests feel welcome.

For cross-selling to be fully effective, every employee must be thoroughly knowledgeable about all aspects of the property's operations. All employees should know the hours of operation for the property's restaurants, shops, pool, and other guest amenities and services. They should be aware of special promotions, live entertainment offered, and special services such as valet, laundry, child-care or baby-sitting services, secretarial assistance, and complimentary transportation.

But the best cross-sellers won't stop there. A bellperson who recommends the property's seafood restaurant can go beyond mentioning the restaurant's name and hours of operation to highlight the restaurant's features that would make it worth this specific guest's visit—focusing perhaps on the food, the atmosphere, or the low prices. It is one thing to make guest's aware of a hotel's features; it is something else to actually link those features with specific guest needs and interests.

Apply Your Learning 9.4

Please write all answers on a separate sheet of paper.

For statements 1–5, write whether the answers are True or False.

1. Suggestive selling is typically effective only for hotel sales and food and beverage staff.

2. "Would you like dessert this evening?" is a good example of suggestive selling.

3. When suggestive selling, it is best to suggest specific items that create mental pictures.

4. Suggestive selling can increase a hotel employee's tips.

5. Using suggestive selling techniques eliminates the need to know details of the hotel's products and services.

6. What is cross-selling?

9.5 Departmental Selling

AFTER STUDYING SECTION 9.5, YOU SHOULD KNOW HOW TO:

◆ Explain how the switchboard operator contributes to sales

◆ Describe the role the reservations department plays in sales

◆ Summarize the role of the front desk in sales

◆ Illustrate the role of the food and beverage department in sales

◆ List the roles lodging property service personnel play in sales

◆ Identify ways employee incentive programs can motivate employees to sell

---

Most guest-employee contacts are potential sales situations, but few staff members strive to make the most of these encounters. Whether checking in a guest, serving a room service meal, or managing the details of booking a large conference, many employees tend to focus entirely on the immediate task at hand, missing numerous opportunities to go beyond merely fulfilling a guest request to deliver truly outstanding service.

Believe it or not, "sales" and "outstanding service" can go hand in hand. Most guests are pleased to think that a hotel employee is concerned enough about their needs and interests to suggest a larger, more luxurious room or a delicious special dessert. And guests remember such actions when booking their next stay, meeting, or restaurant reservation.

To make sure employees learn about all the property's revenue centers and develop successful sales approaches, managers can use a variety of helpful tools. They might have employees participate in role-playing and take periodic quizzes that mix fun with important hotel information. Employee sales skills can be evaluated and changed as necessary during these training sessions (and information kept current) to ensure that each guest-employee encounter will be as productive as it can possibly be.

The following property areas and positions are particularly important to internal sales.

Switchboard

The switchboard operator is often the first contact that a prospective guest has with a property, so switchboard operators should answer calls pleasantly and convey a sincere sense of welcome. Since the switchboard serves as an indicator of the property's efficiency as well as hospitality, all calls should be answered within three rings and transferred to the proper department without delay.

The switchboard operator can also direct guests to the property's revenue centers. A call from the operator in the late afternoon can recommend the hotel's dining room or room service. Since guests have to eat somewhere, this is often all it takes to keep them at the property. Operators can also make suggestions for restaurants or room service when they make wake-up calls.

Reservations

Since the basic function of the reservations department is to turn a prospect into a guest, the reservations staff should be trained to be "order-makers" instead of "order-takers"; that is, they should be well-trained in sales and public relations, as these are the people who can help a property generate additional revenue through securing and upgrading bookings and handling after-hours sales leads. A pleasant, informed reservations agent who is aware of upgrading and suggestive selling techniques can increase the number of room nights sold at higher-than-standard rates.

While it's important that the reservations staff have a guest-oriented approach, it's just as important that they know about room types, prices, special rates, and hotel packages. Staff members should have a complete knowledge of the property and an understanding of what determines the differences in price among the hotel's guestrooms. An ocean-view room, for example, may cost more than a comparable room on the other side of the hotel that overlooks the property's "lovely" three-acre parking lot. By following a policy of selling

from the top down if the inquiry is from a new guest, or using the rate-category-alternatives or bottom-up approach if a reservation has already been made, reservations agents can increase revenues while providing service to guests.

When potential guests telephone for a room after the hotel is full, reservations agents should offer alternatives in an attempt to keep business. For example, the reservations department might use a waiting list system. The reservations agent can tell the caller, "I'm sorry, Mr. Patel, we currently have no rooms available, but we often have last-minute cancellations. If you'll give me your telephone number, I'll call you immediately when a room opens up." If the reservations department is too busy to make callbacks, the agent might assign the guest a reference number and suggest that he or she call again after the 6:00 P.M. cutoff for holding reservations.

A little-used but potentially valuable selling technique is to suggest that the caller change his or her arrival date. Of course, this won't work with everyone, but many business and leisure travelers will change their plans to stay in their "first choice" hotel. The reservations agent can make this option attractive by saying something like, "Ms. Stewart, we are presently booked to capacity and have several names on a waiting list for Wednesday, November 30. But if you could change your travel plans, we do have several attractive suites available on Thursday, December 1."

Front Desk

Front desk personnel play a pivotal role in hotel sales. They can generate additional revenue for a property by capturing walk-in business, upgrading reservations during check-in, marketing in-house facilities through suggestive selling and cross-selling, and securing return reservations during check-out. Therefore, they should also be trained in sales techniques. (At many properties, front desk personnel report to the sales department instead of to the rooms division.)

Meeting front desk employees is often the guest's first *personal* impression of the property. This is where hospitality begins. Each guest should be greeted with a warm smile and a sincere, friendly welcome, *not* a curt "Do you have a reservation?" A repeat guest should be greeted by name and with a warm "Welcome back." From this point on, guests have *names*, not just room numbers.

The check-in function should be handled with a minimum of delay. To encourage guest loyalty, guests should be made to feel far more important than a computer screen or a few sheets of paper. Put aside paperwork that's unrelated to registering the guest until registration is completed. Request additional help if a long line forms.

Front desk personnel often have the opportunity to upgrade existing reservations. A low-key approach is best: "Since you made your reservation, two better rooms have opened up: one with a mountain view for $58, the other with a Jacuzzi for $62. Would you be interested in moving to one of these rooms?" This approach may increase room revenues and guest goodwill. The guest is being sold a better experience, not just a more expensive room.

Check-in is also a good time to mention special coupons or discount offers and suggest hotel facilities and services. The front desk agent can ask if the guest would like a wake-up call and then use this opportunity to make sales suggestions: "Fine, Ms.

Zimmerman. We'll call you at 7:00 A.M. Would you like room service to deliver our breakfast special of hot coffee, a cheese omelet, and freshly squeezed orange juice at 7:30?"

Too often, hotel guests simply don't know what the property has to offer. Suggesting valet service, a light snack in the coffee shop, a relaxing swim or whirlpool in the health club, or room service—even if the guest declines—increases guest awareness, which may generate additional sales at a later time.

Food and Beverage

Good service, which includes a friendly attitude and prompt delivery of the food or drink ordered, is the key to guest satisfaction and sales success in the food and beverage department. In addition to increasing sales, quality service ensures that the guest has a good experience and will want to return.

Food servers who can share their knowledge of the food, its ingredients, and preparation time (as well as the specialties of other property restaurants) add to guest appreciation of the property, which can increase profits. A good sales approach by the server also results in spending less time answering questions, thus avoiding guest irritation.

Food and beverage service offers practically unlimited opportunities to make use of suggestive selling techniques. It is important that food servers offer enticing suggestions that describe a delicious item: "We have an award-winning cheesecake that comes topped with your choice of fresh strawberries or cherries and a dollop of whipped cream" is much more interesting and effective than "Would you care for

Everybody Sells: Building An Effective Front Office Sales Force

All front office agents are salespeople, whether they realize it or not. From the moment they make eye contact with a guest walking into the lobby until their final farewell at check-out, your front desk staff creates an impression that "sells" guests on your property—for better or worse.

In addition to creating a positive guest-service environment that attracts and retains business, front office employees can also impact the bottom line by using suggestive selling techniques to interest a guest in a more expensive room than the one originally requested.

If your employees are reluctant to try selling, point out that suggestive selling is a form of guest service: you are showing that you want guests to have a pleasant stay by offering them accommodations that will meet their needs and enhance their comfort.

The first step in training front desk employees in the art of suggestive selling is to make sure that all agents know the kinds of guestrooms, facilities, and services available at your property. As incredible as it sounds, at many hotels it is not unusual to find front desk agents trying to sell rooms they have never seen. Conducting a property tour for your front desk staff can increase their confidence and enable them to accurately describe your property's rooms to guests.

Next, teach employees to translate your property's features into benefits. A *feature* is a characteristic or amenity; a *benefit* is how the feature addresses a guest's needs. For instance, a suite with a separate sitting area is a feature. For business travelers, the benefit of a room like this may be the ability to meet with clients in the room. For a vacationing family, the benefit of a suite may be having an area for the children to play or for parents to relax after the kids are in bed.

As a training exercise, have front desk employees write down the features of each type of guestroom at your property and explain how those features benefit guests. Or have agents engage in role plays. One agent can play the role of guest, and another the front desk associate, in order to practice their selling techniques. Instructional videos can also demonstrate how to match guests with features and benefits.

In order to match guests with the features that will benefit them, front desk agents must know how to correctly "read" guests. Train employees to listen with their ears *and* their eyes.

* Is the business traveler carrying a laptop computer and a briefcase? Suggest a room with a dataport and large table for spreading out papers.

* Does the family approaching the desk have rambunctious kids who've been cooped up in the car all day? Suggest a room near the pool and tell them about your deluxe guestroom with more space for the children to play.

* Did that young couple mention that they are celebrating an anniversary? Make sure they know about your rooms with king-size beds and Jacuzzis.

In every case, having room layout diagrams, property maps, or pictures can help your front desk employees explain the features they are promoting and help guide their decision. Front office agents should also be aware of any promotions your property or chain is offering and suggest special programs that may meet guests' needs. Guests like to feel that they are getting a special deal and will appreciate being informed about your promotions.

Key steps to effective front office sales include:

* Establish rapport with the guest by making eye contact, using the guest's name, and speaking confidently and enthusiastically.

* Read the guest's body language and tone of voice to discern his or her needs.

> ### Everybody Sells: Building An Effective Front Office Sales Force *(continued)*
>
> - Ask questions to confirm their needs.
>
> - Offer suggestions for a guestroom that will address their needs, using pictures, layouts, or maps to reinforce the suggestion.
>
> - Sell the features by explaining the benefits to the guest. Know what you have to offer and believe that the guest will enjoy the benefits you are offering.
>
> - Ask for the sale, but don't push. Not all guests will want to upgrade their room reservation.
>
>   Finally, encourage front desk employees to promote your property's services—exercise rooms, business centers, complimentary breakfast—even if they don't add any extra money to the bottom line. Giving guests the information they need to have a pleasant stay enhances the value of your property to guests and is another way of providing great guest service that will keep them coming back again and again.

Source: Elizabeth Johnson, *AAHOA Hospitality Buyer's Guide*, September 1999.

anything else?" A food server can give the guest a choice of two or more items and state why the guest should choose one of them. For example, "Would you like a shrimp cocktail to start or would you prefer our freshly made onion soup? The shrimp arrived just this morning and are absolutely fresh, and the onion soup is excellent—the chef prides himself on making the best in the city." Suggestive selling benefits guests, food servers, and the property alike, as it can lead to increased guest satisfaction, increased tips for servers, and increased revenues.

Food servers also can cross-sell. Room service personnel can suggest the dinner special in the main dining room or a special breakfast buffet for busy business travelers. A food server in the gourmet restaurant can ask guests if they have tried the "traveler's lunch" in the coffee shop. These soft-sell techniques are excellent methods of raising revenues and introducing guests to facilities they might not have tried (and might later recommend to friends).

Service Personnel

Service personnel fall into two categories: guest-contact employees and back-of-the-house employees. Valet parking staff, door attendants, bell staff, and housekeepers will likely have a lot of guest contact, while guest contact is not as common for maintenance crews and back-office personnel.

Service employees with a great deal of guest contact have excellent opportunities for suggestive selling. If the hotel is near an airport, the hotel's courtesy van drivers can sell the hotel's facilities and the local area as they drive guests from the airport to the property. A valet parker can welcome guests and mention a particular property restaurant. A bellperson can promote the property's restaurants, lounges, laundry and valet services, and other amenities as guests are shown to their rooms. As guests leave, the door attendant or valet parker can suggest they return for a promotional event or special hotel package. Of course, in all of these situations, it's important that the service staff be sincerely friendly without being pushy.

While employees who have less guest contact may be limited in their selling capacities, they "sell" the hotel by their appearance, attitude, and attention to small details. A friendly greeting from a pool attendant and the cheerful attitude of the maintenance crew can help make a guest's stay memorable.

Employee Incentive Programs

Employee incentive programs should motivate employees to sell and provide a means for tracking sales results. In the hospitality industry, most reward programs have traditionally been based on achieving certain labor or food costs or meeting sales objectives. Management may establish an incentive program for front desk or reservations agents who upgrade reservations, or may provide a bonus to split among the front desk staff for every night on which occupancy reaches a predetermined target. In the property's restaurants, management may promote contests to reward suggestive selling and give bonuses to the servers who sell the most desserts. Other incentive programs may include a cross-selling contest with prizes to employees or departments sending the most guests to a specific restaurant. The bellperson who sells more laundry or dry cleaning services than average and the telephone operator who makes breakfast sales with morning wake-up calls can also be rewarded.

Sales-oriented rewards are important to both the hotel and the employee, but it's also important to launch incentive programs that reward employees for achieving customer satisfaction goals. Such rewards help to develop customer-oriented employees—and often lead to increased repeat business.

The key to an effective incentive program is a method of tracking results. Without it, managers won't have a clue whether increased business is a direct result of employee actions, advertising programs, a shift in the marketplace, or the way the wind happens to be blowing. A discount coupon that bears the name of the food server who has recommended the lounge, a business card or coupon from the bartender that the guest can give to the host of the specialty dining room, a special two-for-one invitation to the lounge show from the bellperson—all provide a means of tracking the effectiveness of both the promotion and the employee.

When developing any incentive program, management should realize that while incentives in the form of cash, merchandise, or trips are often used to motivate employees, recognition is as important as the reward for many workers. Certainly one of the best forms of praise and commendation is public recognition. Honoring top-producing employees with photographs and plaques that are prominently displayed, writing up success stories in the property's newsletter, creating a special "Outstanding Employee of the Month" parking space, and even recognizing exceptional employees at a special ceremony or awards dinner can mean more to some employees than monetary rewards.

Apply Your Learning 9.5

Please write all answers on a separate sheet of paper.

1. Employee knowledge and sales skills can be enhanced by all of the following *except:*

    a. participating in role-playing.
    b. taking occasional quizzes.
    c. attending training sessions.
    d. responding to guest requests.

2. A hotel's switchboard should be answered within _____ ring(s).

    a. 1
    b. 3
    c. 5
    d. It doesn't matter.

3. Which of the following statements is *false?*

    a. Service employees who have less guest contact "sell" the hotel by their appearance, attitude, and attention to small details.
    b. Food and beverage servers are most successful when they limit the use of suggestive selling techniques to dessert items and specialty drinks.
    c. Check-in is a good time for front desk agents to mention any special coupons or discounts the hotel is offering for hotel facilities and services.
    d. If a hotel is booked for the dates a caller requests, reservations agents should suggest that the caller change his or her arrival date.

4. What two things should all successful employee incentive programs do?

Quick Hits

Chapter 9

SECTION 9.1— EVERYONE'S SALES ROLE

• Every employee can play a role in promoting additional sales to guests and increasing guest satisfaction. The key is to create effective guest-employee relationships.

• A good GM recognizes the value of guest satisfaction and sets goals to attain guest goodwill—and repeat business—by using effective internal merchandising and developing sales-oriented employees.

• Developing a sales-oriented staff is a three-part process that includes hiring sales-minded employees, training all employees in sales techniques, then motivating all employees to sell.

SECTION 9.2—RELATIONSHIP SELLING

• It's easier and less expensive to hold onto existing guests than to find new ones. So most managers focus on building relationships with their current guests.

• Building relationships starts with learning more about guests. Hotels use a variety of approaches, including registration forms, guest surveys, and employee input.

• Employee training should include a number of areas that will enable employees to assist guests and build rapport. These areas include knowing the property, knowing the area, and interacting with guests.

• One important facet of interacting with guests involves responding to complaints in such a way that goodwill is restored. In many cases, guest complaints have led to the improvement of problem areas at a property—resulting in better service and increased guest satisfaction.

SECTION 9.3—UPGRADING

• Selling involves pinpointing the unique qualities of a particular property and presenting them in a convincing manner.

• Upgrading can be accomplished by using one of three methods: top-down, rate-category alternatives, and bottom-up. No matter what method is used to upgrade a reservation, guests should *never* feel they are being pressured.

• The **top-down method** is used to encourage guests to reserve middle- or high-rate rooms. It begins with the employee recommending the guestroom sold at the highest rate. The guest accepts or rejects the recommendation. If the guest says no, the agent moves down to the next price level and discusses the merits of this accommodation.

- The **rate-category-alternatives method** is an easy and effective way to sell middle-rate rooms to guests who might otherwise choose a lower rate. The front desk or reservations agent provides the guest with a choice of three or more rate-category alternatives and puts no pressure on the guest.

- The **bottom-up method** is used when a guest has already made a reservation or has requested a low-priced room. During the registration process, the front desk or reservations agent can suggest extra amenities or point out the merits of a more expensive room.

Section 9.4—Suggestive Selling and Cross-Selling

- **Suggestive selling** means influencing a guest's purchase decision by highlighting available choices. Almost any employee can use this sales technique in most areas of the property.

- There are two important keys to using suggestive selling successfully. First, avoid asking questions that can be answered yes or no; give guests a choice. Second, suggest in specific terms.

- **Cross-selling** means using media in one area of the property to promote a different area of the property.

- For cross-selling to be fully effective, every employee must be thoroughly knowledgeable about all aspects of the property's operations.

Section 9.5—Departmental Selling

- The switchboard operator is often the first contact that a prospective guest has with a property. All calls should be answered within three rings and transferred to the proper department without delay. Switchboard operators can also direct guests to the property's revenue centers.

- A pleasant, informed reservations agent who is aware of upgrading and suggestive selling techniques can increase the number of room nights sold at higher-than-standard rates.

- Front desk personnel can generate additional revenue for a property by capturing walk-in business, upgrading reservations during check-in, marketing in-house facilities through suggestive selling and cross-selling, and securing return reservations during check-out.

- Food and beverage service offers practically unlimited opportunities to make use of suggestive selling techniques. Food servers can also cross-sell.

- Service employees with a great deal of guest contact have excellent opportunities for suggestive selling. Employees who have less guest contact can "sell" the hotel by their appearance, attitude, and attention to small details.

Profile

Patricia Tam
General Manager, Halekulani Resort, Waikiki, Hawaii

If Patricia Tam had pursued her childhood ambition, she probably would have been an English teacher. Had she kept her first job out of college, she might still be the proprietor of a bakery. But today she leads the life few academics or bread makers would imagine, as the general manager of Halekulani, Waikiki's premier 5-diamond resort, which was voted the best hotel in the world by Gourmet magazine. Tam was named the 1999 Independent Hotelier of the World by the readers of Hotels magazine.

Tam views her job as an ongoing, mutually beneficial relationship between herself and the owner, Halekulani Corp.

"I always look at it as a kind of management proposition where you can always learn every day," she says. "not only about how to maintain a luxury property, but how to develop it and take it to the next level, because that's what creating experiences is all about."

Earlier in her life, Tam did not seem particularly destined for a career in hospitality. Tam does not even recall staying at a hotel until she was a young adult. She was running her own bakery at age 23 when she was recruited by Amfac Hotels to open the bakeshop at its Royal Lahaina hotel on Maui in 1975.

"When I opened the bake shop there, I liked the whole aura about resort life and hospitality, not just because of the guest experience, but because of the staff, too," she recalls. From there, Tam moved into the resort's management training program.

In 1983, Tam began working at the Halekulani, working in a succession of positions, as a hotel assistant manager, rooms division director, acting GM, and also, just prior to her current assignment, as GM of Halekulani's adjacent sister property, the 4-diamond Waikiki Parc hotel. She has been GM at the Halekulani since 1993.

"She has come up through the ranks, which gains the respect of the employees, as they know she is appreciative of what goes on in the back of the house," says Shuhei Okuda, chairman of Halekulani Corp. "She is an excellent role model for the employees, as well as for young people aspiring to a career in the hospitality field. Her being a local woman, chosen the top hotelier in the world clearly shows that locally trained people can successfully compete with hoteliers educated in the top schools of Europe and the Orient."

This article is excerpted with permission from HOTELS magazine.

Telephone Sales

Sections

10.1 Basics of Telephone Communications

10.2 Outgoing Calls

10.3 Incoming Calls

10.4 Telephone Sales Operations

10.1 Basics of Telephone Communications

AFTER STUDYING SECTION 10.1, YOU SHOULD KNOW HOW TO:

◆ Explain the importance of telephone etiquette

◆ List guidelines for creating a good impression on the phone

◆ Use effective telephone communication skills

◆ Practice listening skills during a sales call

The telephone, if used properly, can be one of the most economical ways to find—and sell to—prospective guests and clients. The phone can be used to:

• Search for sales leads

• Qualify potential customers

• Make sales appointments

• Blitz a market to reach prospects and clients

• Service local accounts quickly and economically

• Service geographically isolated accounts

• Help guests make reservations and plan return visits

• Sell additional services to registered guests

• Receive responses from direct-mail campaigns

Bring Your Umbrella!

One of the world's largest log structures is The Old Faithful Inn—a 104-room lodge built in 1904 near the Old Faithful Geyser in Wyoming's Yellowstone National Park.

The designer wanted a property that would embody the natural surroundings. The inn's foundation was made with rock from one of the volcanic upheavals that created the Yellowstone caldera behind Old Faithful. The first story was built with long pines. Three-foot long California redwood shingles protect the roof from the nearby geyser's punctual eruptions.

The lobby of the Inn is 76.5 feet high and features three sets of balconies, a widow's walk, and a crow's nest. The fireplace is made with lava stones and weighs 500 tons and stands 40 feet high.

To be honest, though, umbrellas are optional. This official historical landmark property is within walking—not watering—distance of its famous spouting cousin.

- Convert inquiries generated by ads (especially ads with toll-free numbers) into sales

- Gather market research data

- Penetrate new markets

- Reactivate former accounts

- Increase the profitability of marginal accounts

- Announce promotional news to clients and generate business for special promotions

- Follow up bids, proposals, direct-mail campaigns, and leads developed at trade shows

Since the telephone is used in so many different ways, telephone sales may be delegated to several different groups of employees. For example, incoming calls for individual guest reservations may go through a front desk or reservations staff; calls promoting room service or the property's restaurant may be made by switchboard operators; sales calls may be handled by salespeople or top management.

No matter how calls are delegated, they play an important role in a property's overall sales effort.

Basics of Telephone Communication

Telephone selling is more difficult than face-to-face sales because you can't read the prospect's body language. You can't make a personal connection by commenting on the photographs on the desk or the plaques on the wall.

Since you can't share a firm handshake over the phone, the words you use and your pronunciation, tone of voice, and delivery take on greater importance. Etiquette, communication skills, and listening skills all play heightened roles in making a good impression and selling the property over the telephone.

Etiquette. The lodging industry offers more than just rooms and guest services. It offers hospitality—and friendliness and courtesy are important parts of any interaction between a property employee and a potential guest. When using the telephone, property employees must communicate warmth and a willingness to serve.

Get an "edge" from the beginning by simply asking the prospect if it's a convenient time to talk. By respecting the prospect's time, you greatly increase the chances of a successful future contact. If the prospect suggests calling at another time, follow through. Many salespeople fail to do so, perhaps losing the opportunity to make a sale.

Telephone etiquette begins by letting the potential guest know that he or she is important to the property. Use phrases that put the guest at ease and show the property's concern (see Exhibit 1). Be polite and understanding.

There are a number of other ways salespeople can make a good impression:

1. *Adequate preparation.* Always have the information you need at hand before calling a client. By being prepared, you can organize your thoughts, readily answer questions, and avoid wasting the client's time.

2. *Adequate time.* Take steps to make sure you will not be interrupted while calling clients. They deserve your undivided attention.

Exhibit 1
Telephone Etiquette

THIS IS BETTER	THAN THIS
Answering the Call	
"Days Inn Reservations, Mr. Eaton speaking. How may I help you?"	"Days Inn Reservations."
"Days Inn Reservations, Ms. Wood speaking. How may I help you?"	"Days Inn, can I help you?"
Making Sure	
"Would you repeat your name for me, please?	"What name did you say? I can't hear hear you."
"Would you spell that for me, please?"	"What did you say? Talk a little louder."
"I'm sorry. I didn't get the name of the person."	"I can't understand what you're trying to say."
Acknowledging	
"Yes, Mr. Martinez. I'll be happy to request that for you."	"OK, I'll do what I can."
"Yes, Ms. Jones, I'd be glad to check that for you."	"All right. Let me see."
Leaving the Line	
"Would you mind waiting while I check, please?"	"Just a minute."
	"I'll try to find out."
Returning to the Line	
"Mr. Glazer, thank you for waiting. I have that information."	"The date on that reservation was June 18."
"Ms. Muzzall, I'm sorry to have kept you waiting."	"Are you still waiting?"
Completing the Call	
"Thank you for calling Days Inn, Ms. Yang."	"Bye-bye." "OK." "So long." "That's OK." "All right, bye."

Courtesy of Days Inns of America, Inc.

3. *Courtesy and respect.* Treat intermediaries (secretaries, receptionists, clerks, assistants, etc.) with as much respect and courtesy as clients themselves.

4. *Brevity.* Keep calls short and to the point unless the client wants to chat. When the call is finished, let the client hang up first.

5. *Timing.* Avoid calling during the late-afternoon or early-morning hours. Be aware of the client's time zone.

Telephone Communication Skills. It is a good practice for employees who use the telephone a lot to listen to their voices on a tape recorder. Check yourself on these important communication skills:

1. *Tone of voice.* Your voice should reflect sincerity, pleasantness, confidence, and interest. It is especially important to smile as you speak. Speak into the receiver as if the client were sitting across the desk.

2. *Pitch.* Low-pitched voices carry better and are more pleasant to the listener.

3. *Inflection.* Generate interest by the way you raise or lower your voice.

4. *Enunciation.* Avoid talking with anything in your mouth. Be careful not to talk too fast; your message may be misunderstood or lost.

Every employee should work to develop a pleasant telephone voice free of slang, jargon, and irritating habits. An enthusiastic, well-modulated voice is half of a successful telephone call.

Listening Skills. The other half of a successful telephone call is listening closely to what the prospective client or guest has to say. A salesperson should be aware of several keys to good listening:

1. *Limit talking.* No one can talk and listen at the same time. The prospect should get a chance to air his or her views, and these views should be given careful attention. If the prospect does most of the talking during a telephone sales call, it's much easier to

make a sale because you'll know the prospect's needs and concerns.

2. *Get involved.* It is usually much easier to be enthusiastic and alert when sitting erect; leaning back and relaxing often interferes with listening. Listen for clues to what is important to the prospect. You can learn a great deal about the prospect's needs by the way things are said.

Successful salespeople also empathize with the caller. A phrase such as, "I hear what you're saying" is an excellent way to show the prospect that what he or she is saying is important to you.

3. *Ask questions.* Asking questions generates prospect involvement and shows that you're interested. Questions are an effective way to keep the prospect talking and gather additional information. Ask, "Why is that important to you?" or, "What else can you tell me about that?" and take notes as the prospect shares opinions and needs. These responses can be used later to build support for the sales message.

Apply Your Learning 10.1

Please write all answers on a separate sheet of paper.

1. What opening question can give salespeople an "edge" when calling a prospective guest?
   a. "Did you know that my hotel can provide quality services at affordable prices?"
   b. "Is this a good time to talk?"
   c. "Can you tell me a little bit about your company's hotel needs?"
   d. "How are you doing?"

2. Which of the following is *not* a recommended way to make a good impression on the telephone?

    a. Assure the client at the outset that you are fully aware of her or his needs.
    b. Avoid calling during the late afternoon and early in the morning.
    c. Speak to clients' assistants as courteously as you'd speak to the clients themselves.
    d. Have the information you need at hand.

3. What are the two halves of a successful telephone sales call over which a salesperson has complete control?

4. Why is it important to ask prospective clients questions?

10.2 *Outgoing Calls*

AFTER STUDYING SECTION 10.2, YOU SHOULD KNOW HOW TO:

♦ Define prospect calls and qualifying calls

♦ List the types of questions that might be asked in a prospect call

♦ Describe the information needed about sales prospects

♦ Reach a decision maker for an appointment call

♦ Prepare an opening statement

♦ Develop respect and rapport

♦ Present information about a lodging property

♦ Overcome objections to an appointment call

♦ Set an appointment

♦ Make a sales call

♦ Make a promotional call

♦ Make a service call

♦ Make a public relations call

Outgoing calls range from prospecting calls, qualifying calls, appointment calls, and sales calls to promotional calls, service calls, and public relations calls.

Prospecting and Qualifying Calls

Prospecting calls are made to gather information and learn the names of decision makers. Many calls that start out as prospect calls end up as qualifying calls. **Qualifying calls** determine whether prospects need and can afford the products and services offered by the property (see Exhibit 1). Qualifying calls are not sales calls, but they're used to find out if an individual or company warrants an in-person sales call. This can be determined by asking several questions:

• Does your company have a need for hotel accommodations, meeting rooms, or banquet facilities?

• How many people travel for your company? What is the destination of most company travel?

• Who decides where your traveling staff stays? What hotels are you currently using?

• Who usually makes the reservations for your traveling staff?

If a prospect seems a likely candidate for an in-person sales call, further information may be gathered by asking:

• How many meetings does your company hold during the year? What times

Exhibit 1
Sample Prospect Qualification Form

Prospect Qualification Form

COMPANY NAME: _____

ADDRESS: _____

CITY/STATE/ZIP: _____

PHONE:_____CONTACT:_____

1. *Introduction*: "My name is _____, and I'm calling you on behalf of L'Ermitage Hotels located in West Hollywood/Beverly Hills. Can you tell me who handles the travel and meeting arrangements for your company?"

   _____

   _____

2. After locating the right contact, state the purpose of your call and ask if any of the company's business travelers stay overnight in the Los Angeles area. If so, ask "Are you familiar with our hotels?"

   _____

   _____

3. "Do you use an outside travel agency?"

   _____

4. If so, "What is the name of the agency involved?"

   _____

OR

   "Do you use an outside travel agency? If so, may I ask which one you work with?"

   _____

5. "Can you estimate how many room nights annually you reserve in the Los Angeles area?"

   _____

6. "Aside from individual travel, do you hold meetings in the Los Angeles area?" "How often?"

   _____

7. "Would you be interested in speaking with one of our sales managers regarding our corporate rate program for your upcoming meetings?" _____

8. Thank the individual for his or her time, and state that you will follow up in an appropriate manner (via telephone or by sending brochures and a general information letter).

Courtesy of L'Ermitage Hotels, Beverly Hills, California

Exhibit 2
Sample Format for Prospecting Calls

Fact-Finding Question	Follow-Up Information Generated
Who?	Future account data—name, address, etc.—as well as description of prospect's business
What?	Prospect's needs for guestrooms, meeting space, catered events, and other facilities/services
When?	Months, weeks, or specific dates for which hotel facilities or services are needed
Where?	Properties with whom the prospect is currently dealing

---

of the year are meetings normally held? How long do they last?

- What types of meetings do you typically hold? What types of facilities do you need?

- How do you decide where to hold a meeting? What criteria do you use to decide on a location?

- When are location decisions made? Who makes them?

When researching information on national corporations, it is necessary to probe deeper and get the answers to these questions:

- Does the corporation have a travel department or a corporate travel directory that advises the corporation's business travelers of properties where they're allowed to stay? Who heads the department for corporate travel?

- Who decides which properties are used? Who makes guestroom and meeting room reservations? Why are certain locations chosen?

- Is there a written contract or any kind of obligation to the property currently

being used? If so, when does this obligation expire?

- How many people travel for the corporation? How many guestroom nights are reserved? What department has the most travelers? Do business travelers carry corporate identification?

- Do business travelers pay their own bills or are accommodations billed to the corporation? Do travelers pay on a per diem (daily) basis?

- From which company properties do most business travelers originate? What's the destination of the majority of the corporation's business travelers?

A good approach to take when making prospect calls is to follow a simple "who, what, when, and where" format (see Exhibit 2).

The answers to these questions will give you the information needed to prepare a sales presentation. You are now in a position to answer exactly how your property can meet the prospect's needs. When appropriate, you can end the prospecting call with a request for an appointment.

Exhibit 3
Sample Appointment Call Conversation

Reaching the Decision Maker

"Hello, my name is Dan Stern. Could you help me by giving me the name of the person who makes the convention planning decisions for your firm?"

Opening the Call

"Good morning, Ms. Merrill. My name is Dan Stern. I'm with Complete Resorts International. I'm calling to explain one of the most innovative programs in convention planning available today!"

The Presentation

"Our unique services will help you save time and money on all of your convention meeting room and banquet needs. We have recently developed a program that includes three exciting features to help you stage successful meetings: your own private operations-headquarters room adjacent to the meeting area; the use of our hotel's limousine to pick up your VIPs; and your own personal meeting aide—a fully qualified staff assistant, supplied by our hotel—to handle any last-minute problems for you."

Setting the Appointment

"I know you will be as excited as we are about our new services that will help you stage successful meetings. When can we meet for just 30 minutes to discuss your upcoming convention for your independent distributors?"

"Which day of the week would be best for you, Tuesday or Wednesday?"

"What time is most convenient for you on that day, 10:00 A.M. or 2:00 P.M.?"

"Great! I'll see you on Tuesday at 2:00 P.M. in your office at 1234 Goodsale Road just west of the Interstate. Thank you for your time, Ms. Merrill. I'm looking forward to meeting you in person. Have a good day!"

Note that in setting the appointment, the salesperson did not set up the possibility of a "no" answer, but asked a forced-choice question that gave the prospect a choice of two alternatives: Tuesday or Wednesday. Other typical forced-choice questions include: "Would you prefer to meet in the morning or afternoon?" and "Is the beginning or the latter part of the week best for you?"

Appointment Calls

Appointment calls are used to briefly introduce a prospective client to the features and services offered by the property and ask for a face-to-face meeting (see Exhibit 3). Appointment calls save time for the salesperson and the prospect because they allow time for both to prepare for a future in-person sales presentation.

Before making an appointment call, you should have all necessary information available—prospect sheets, account records (if any), prices, firm and tentative booking dates (if applicable), and general property information. You should also develop an outlined presentation to help you remember key questions and sales points.

The appointment call is made up of several steps:

1. Reaching the decision maker

2. Opening the call

3. Making the presentation

Exhibit 4
Reaching the Decision Maker

Intermediary:	"Why do you want to know [the name of the decision maker]?"
Salesperson:	"I'm putting together a list of people who would like to be kept abreast of some of the ways other local businesses are reducing their costs through the use of training meetings. I'm sure your manager would be interested in receiving this information."
Intermediary:	"What is the purpose of this call?"
Salesperson:	"I'm sorry, but I can only discuss that with your manager. Can you put me through to her, please?"
Intermediary:	"Is this a sales call?"
Salesperson:	"No, I'm not trying to sell anything on the phone. I'm just doing research on how area businesses are meeting their training needs. I was hoping that your manager could give me some ideas."

---

4. Overcoming objections

5. Setting the appointment

Reaching the Decision Maker. If a prospect call has not been made, you can learn the name of the decision maker through an assistant at the firm or corporation. While intermediaries can be helpful, they can also be obstacles (see Exhibit 4). Appealing to the assistant's sense of responsibility—presenting ideas that might help the decision maker, for example—often helps you avoid the objections they can present.

Prepare an opening statement. Since the intermediary is paid to protect the time of the decision maker, an introductory statement such as "This is Donna Scott from the Concorde Hotel. May I speak with Bob Cross?" is not likely to be successful.

Instead, appeal to a need—of either the decision maker or the company—and to the intermediary's sense of responsibility: "Our hotel has recently developed an incentive tour package that other top incentive companies have said is the best hotel value in years. I'd like to ask Mr. Cross a few ques-

tions to determine if this would be of any value to him."

Develop respect and rapport. Learn the names of secretaries and receptionists and list these names in your diary of clients' telephone numbers. Calling them by name is highly effective, as is timing the call so it will not interrupt a busy schedule. (Avoid making calls on Monday mornings and Friday afternoons.)

Don't leave a message. There may be times when a decision maker cannot be reached. In most cases, when you are told that the decision maker is out of town, out on a business call, or on the telephone, you're being told the truth. You should be concerned, though, if you're repeatedly told, "He isn't available," "She's in a meeting," or, "He's in conference." In these cases, ask the assistant to suggest a time when it is more convenient to call.

Opening the Call. Once you've reached the prospect, a good opening is essential. As with a face-to-face sales call, you should introduce yourself, give the name of your property, and immediately state the purpose of the call. Saying "The reason for my call is that most companies want to house their relocating executives in hotels convenient to company headquarters. Our hotel is located just three blocks from your offices, and we are now offering a special corporate program" is far more effective than opening with "I just called to say hello" or the equally awful "I'm calling because my general manager suggested you might be a good account, and you're on my list of prospects to call today."

Presenting a benefit—and showing sincere interest in meeting a prospect's needs—is a vital step at this point in the conversation. It's important to develop rapport early on, and there are several techniques that can be used to make the prospect more receptive to the presentation to follow.

The prospect's name is important. In most cases, the more you use it (without overdoing it), the better the prospect will feel toward you.

Use a third-party endorsement. You might say: "Mr. Pritchard, a friend of yours—Jane Steward of Woodcraft, Incorporated—suggested that I call because she felt you would be interested in our banquet facilities." The use of third-party endorsements gives credibility to the sales message and provides a common meeting ground between you and the prospect.

An appointment call should be kept short, unless the prospect wants to chat or ask questions. If it is obvious that the prospect is busy or in a totally unreceptive mood, try to get a brief message across and offer to call back at a more convenient time. If the prospect seems interested or at least willing to listen, you can move on to the presentation.

Making the Presentation. The purpose of the presentation is to get the prospect interested enough to agree to an in-person meeting. During the presentation, remember to sell the benefits of the property rather than the features.

Benefit statements must be specific. When talking to a meeting planner, for example, it's a lot better to give a descriptive benefit ("When you book your meeting with us, your group is assigned to one person who has the authority to ensure that everything is handled to your satisfaction; this person will have all the answers for you at every stage to make sure your meeting is successful") than a vague benefit ("We have a great convention service department").

The use of power words such as "excellent," "guaranteed," "quality," and "successful" greatly enhances a presentation and can generate interest. Power words are dynamic, expressive, and highly descriptive, helping clients to "see" the hotel's services over the phone.

Overcoming Objections. Be prepared to overcome objections to specific points of the presentation. It is much easier to handle objections if you have planned some answers to common objections and have backup material available that will support your claims (see Exhibit 5). Public relations pieces and complimentary letters from satisfied customers are important sales aids. Such material also can be read before a sales call to give you the enthusiasm you need to sell the benefits of the property.

Listen carefully to objections and avoid arguing with the prospect. The prospect's objections will often provide clues that will enable you to revise the presentation to meet the prospect's needs or concerns.

Setting the Appointment. Since most appointments are made or lost during the first few minutes of the telephone call, ask for

Exhibit 5
Overcoming Common Prospect Objections

Prospect:	"I'm not interested."
Salesperson:	"I can understand that you might not realize the values offered by our resort from just a brief explanation over the phone, Ms. Kingsbury. But didn't you tell me that you were considering an incentive package for your top salespeople? I'd like to show you in person how our resort can give you just the package you need—at a good value."
Prospect:	"I don't have time to see you now."
Salesperson:	"Mr. Portigo, I realize you have a busy schedule. That's why I want to invite you to visit our hotel for a complimentary lunch or dinner. We can discuss your convention needs over a delicious meal, without taking a lot of time from your business day."
Prospect:	"Just send me a brochure."
Salesperson:	"I'd be happy to send our brochure, but I'd prefer to deliver it personally so I can answer any concerns you might have and explain how groups similar to yours have benefited from our facilities and services. Would 1:30 on Wednesday or Thursday be a good time to visit with you?"
Prospect:	"We can't afford to hold outside training seminars."
Salesperson:	"I understand. But, actually, our low rates make it possible for firms like yours to hold sales training seminars at a price you *can* afford."

the appointment early. By offering choices of a day—"Would Wednesday or Thursday be more convenient?"—you can lead the prospect into a commitment to a face-to-face sales call.

Sometimes the prospect may be unwilling to set an appointment or may request that you send additional information or a brochure for review. If you are unable to get an appointment during the conversation, make arrangements to call back on another day:

Salesperson: "I'd be happy to send a brochure on our sports program. If you receive it by Tuesday, would you have a chance to review it before the end of the week?"

Prospect: "Oh, certainly."

Salesperson: "That sounds great. I'll give you a call next Friday morning to see if you have any questions."

If an appointment is made, end the call by confirming the date, time, and location of the appointment, express thanks, and promise to follow up by sending any additional information (property brochures, menus, etc.) and a letter, fax, or e-mail confirming the meeting date. Ideally, this meeting should be held at your property so you can show the prospect the property's features and facilities.

Sales Calls

Sales calls may be made by a salesperson or by a telemarketer working with a sales script. Hotel chains and many independent hotels work with specially trained telemarketing teams that call on prospects and concentrate on getting bookings or commitments by phone. Unlike an appointment call, the objective of a sales call is to make an immediate sale, and the caller must either close the sale during the conversation or make arrangements to call back on another day.

Closing Techniques. Several techniques can be used to close a telephone sale.

Asking for a sale can be as simple as saying, "Shall I reserve a meeting room for your district managers on Monday, July 12?" However, this technique limits the prospect to a yes or no response, and limits you to one specific area.

A more effective technique is to *assume a sale*. Assuming a sale assumes a yes answer on the part of the prospect: "All right, Mrs. Grauberger, I'll confirm your group at our Lakeview Downtown Inn on November 30. As I said, the rates are $42. Now let me read back the booking requirements."

Forced-choice questions limit the prospect to the answers presented by the salesperson and provide more control than asking for or assuming a sale. Examples include: "Shall I book your tour group for Friday night or Saturday morning?" and "Would your distributors like to try our buffet when they arrive or will they be dining in our Red Lion restaurant?" Forced-choice questions make an effective close because they create a choice between positive alternatives; the salesperson is asking not *whether*, but *which*.

The *pause close* is effective because silence on the telephone is hard for most people to tolerate. Consider this pause close: "Okay, Mr. Fritz. Can I go ahead and book you at the Bayside Inn in Bayport at $65?"

(Pause.) Some salespeople assume that silence means disagreement, and so they start talking, perhaps offering something to sweeten the deal. This is a mistake. The salesperson should be patient and let the prospect voice a decision.

Closing on an objection acknowledges the prospect's objection, but counters the objection with a benefit (or benefits) and asks for the sale: "I agree, Mr. Morton, that our property is away from the city, but many meeting planners have told us they consider that a benefit: our distraction-free location actually enhances attendees' productivity. How many rooms will you be needing?"

A *series-of-agreements close* summarizes the positive statements made by the prospect: "You told me that you thought our rooms were comfortable and attractive. And you agreed that our location was suitable. And didn't you say that our 'Budget Meeting Plan' is just what you're looking for? Then, may I set up your annual sales meeting for the 20th to the 25th?"

Even though many telemarketing operations use a standard telephone sales script, telemarketers and other salespeople should feel comfortable using these closes.

Other Outgoing Calls

Promotional calls are made by salespeople, telemarketers, or top management to introduce special promotions. A banquet sales manager, for example, may call couples who have recently announced their engagements in the local newspaper and describe the hotel's special wedding-reception package.

Client satisfaction and loyalty can be developed through **service calls**, whether the calls are made just to keep in touch or to follow up after a sale. Clients need to know they are important, and service calls are essential to maintaining and building business for the property. If changes are anticipated before a function, or if problems occur during an event, a service call shows concern and can help to smooth over the situation.

Public relations calls are made to generate goodwill. In one case, a restaurant manager made low-key telephone calls to past regulars who had not visited the restaurant for some time. The impact was immediate—the restaurant had 25 additional covers per day. Such person-to-person contact can generate additional rooms business as well. If a general manager picks up the telephone to respond to a guest's complimentary letter, it can have a great impact; the guest is more likely to feel that the property values his or her business and will want to return.

Apply Your Learning 10.2

Please write all answers on a separate sheet of paper.

1. What is the difference between prospecting calls and qualifying calls?

2. What are the five steps of a typical appointment call?

3. Which of the following is the *best* way to open an appointment call?

    a. "Hello, I'm calling to find out if my hotel can help with any upcoming meetings."
    b. "Good morning, Mr. Davis. I'm calling because my boss mentioned that you and he play golf together—he said you were pretty good, actually—and he thought you might be interested in hearing from me."
    c. "Hi, this is Jake Delmar from the Gryphon Grand Hotel. How are you doing today?"
    d. "Mr. Fernandez, I'm calling to let you know of some recent changes at Bay Suites that we launched for companies like yours that are searching for high-quality meeting space."

4. Which of the following is the *best* way to respond to objections?

    a. Assume that objections mean no.
    b. Ignore them.
    c. Expect objections and plan your responses.
    d. Offer to reduce the quoted rates.

5. "Do you think meeting attendees would prefer a classical pianist or a string quartet at the opening reception?" is what type of a close?

6. What type of call would most likely be made if a hotel learned two weeks before a wedding banquet that the requested table decorations would not be available?

10.3 Incoming Calls

AFTER STUDYING SECTION 10.3, YOU SHOULD KNOW HOW TO:

♦ Make a good first impression

♦ Accept reservations over the phone

♦ Respond to calls about print ads

♦ Respond to inquiry calls

First Impressions Are Forever

When a call is answered at the hotel, the spotlight is on the person representing the property. The caller expects a positive first impression. An unprofessional response, such as carrying on a conversation with a co-worker while the caller is on the line, may result in thousands of dollars in lost business.

It's polite and it's good business to answer the telephone promptly. When a call is not answered right away, the caller may become impatient and hang up; waiting time always seems longer than it is. Nancy Austin, co-author of *A Passion for Excellence,* explained in a speech how many callers may feel:

During the first ring, we can hardly wait to speak to someone on the other end!

But by the third ring your patient customer has already decided, "This is it. If they don't answer the phone I'm calling the next hotel." And by six rings, forget it! They are so thoroughly disgusted that if they are asked for a recommendation, the research shows they will *go out of their way* to "disrecommend" that place that didn't bother to pick up the phone. And you know why? They say, "They didn't care."

Once the receiver is picked up, the hotel's representative must be ready to talk. Whether the call is to the switchboard, the reservations department, or a sales office extension, the call should begin with a greeting, the name of the property, the employee's name, and a courteous phrase: "Good morning! This is the New York Hilton; Tom Baker speaking. How may I help you?"

During a conversation, it may be necessary to put a caller on hold. "Hold" is not synonymous with "ignore." If a call cannot be routed or a question answered without leaving the line, the caller should be given an explanation for the delay. Instead of just saying, "Please hold," the employee should say to the caller, "May I put you on hold for a minute while I find that information for you?" If the caller is kept waiting for more than a minute, he or she should be given progress reports ("Mr. McClendon, I'm still checking on your reservation. Do you mind

Navigating the Voice-Mail Maze

Keep the following points in mind when working with a phone system equipped with voice mail.

Keep your greeting current. Record a new personal greeting every day, and include the day or date. This lets callers know whether you are in or out of the office and that you regularly check your voice mail.

Be friendly. The tone you use in your personal greeting is as important as what it says. Callers will be more inclined to leave a message if your greeting sounds friendly.

Speak naturally and smile. Smiling has a profound impact on the sound of your message. People will be more likely to return your call if you sound happy and upbeat.

Speak clearly. Whether recording a greeting or leaving a message, it's important to speak in clear, concise sentences. You'll be more easily understood, and appear professional and organized.

Ask for the information you need. In your greeting, ask callers to provide their name, telephone number, the reason for calling, and the best time to return their call.

Offer an alternative out of voice mail. If voice mail has a bad reputation with some callers, it's likely because they have been "stuck" in a voice-mail maze at some point, unable to get out of the system and speak with a real person. If your voice-mail system allows for it, tell callers to dial "0" to speak to a live person. If you carry a pager, include your number in your greeting.

Check messages regularly and return calls promptly. Don't wait to receive a "Your voice mailbox is full" message before listening to your calls. Return calls as soon as possible, even if it is to say that you are working on gathering the requested information.

Adapted from "Active Voice Guide to Voice Mail Etiquette," Accurate Telecom, Inc., 16108 Covello Street, Van Nuys, California 91406 (www.accuratetelecom.com).

waiting a little longer?"). When the employee returns to the line, it helps get the caller's attention to begin with his or her name. This shows courtesy to the caller and may prevent having to repeat all or part of the information.

Sometimes the caller must be transferred. Far too often, the caller is transferred throughout the hotel before reaching the proper party. To avoid this situation, every attempt should be made to determine the purpose of the call and the person who can help. Then the call can be transferred to the right party with a statement such as, "The catering manager, Mr. Philip Rodriguez, would be glad to take care of that for you. Shall I transfer you to Philip, or would you prefer to leave your name and number so he can call you?"

Incoming Calls

Incoming calls that can lead to sales fall into three categories: reservations, responses to advertising, and inquiries.

Reservations. At small properties, reservations may be handled by a small reservations staff or the front desk agents; at larger properties, reservations may be handled by an extensive in-house staff.

Since reservationists (or front desk agents) are often the public's first contact with the property, more and more emphasis is being put on their training. Because of the sales-oriented nature of the position, reservationists must be trained in the importance of professionalism, product knowledge, and basic selling techniques.

Responses to Advertising. One of the most effective advertising methods for hotels today is a toll-free number listed in print ads or on the hotel's Web site. This method of advertising is an excellent source of immediate reservations and business leads and can generate a large number of calls.

Toll-free calls are often handled by a telemarketing staff that tries to get either a firm commitment for a reservation or information to pass along to a hotel salesperson.

Inquiries. Inquiries from people who call the property on the recommendation of friends, acquaintances, or business associates who are familiar with the property provide excellent leads—as do people responding to ads, mailings, brochures, fliers, and other promotions.

Callers with inquiries usually want a room or seek information about accommodations, and they should be given prompt attention. The salesperson should be courteous and interested. Since no precall research has been done on the prospect, it is especially important to listen and ask open-ended questions to determine the caller's needs. Determine the exact nature of the caller's business before discussing prices or rates.

Handling an inquiry call includes trying to close the sale at that time. But even if the call does not result in immediate business, it is important to follow up. Sending additional information by fax or mail—and keeping a trace card on the prospective account—may lead to business in the future.

Apply Your Learning 10.3

Please write all answers on a separate sheet of paper.

For statements 1–5, write whether the answer is True or False.

1. Many callers will expect an answer within three rings.

2. Saying "Please hold" is the best way to precede placing a caller on hold.

3. Callers on hold should be given progress reports at least every seven minutes.

4. The best way to avoid transferring calls numerous times is to get as much information as possible from the caller.

5. When returning to a caller on hold, you should state your name and the name of the property.

6. What are the three categories of incoming telephone calls?

7. One of the most effective ways to encourage responses to a hotel's print advertising is to include:

    a. full-color photography of the property.
    b. sales copy that describes the hotel's features.
    c. a toll-free telephone number.
    d. the names of the hotel's sales team.

10.4 Telephone Sales Operations

AFTER STUDYING SECTION 10.4, YOU SHOULD KNOW HOW TO:

♦ Explain the function of a telephone sales blitz

♦ Describe the role of telemarketing

♦ Prepare a telemarketing script

♦ Establish a telemarketing program

The telephone can be used in creative ways to boost sales. Two of the most common ways are telephone sales blitzes, which can be extremely effective for small to midsize properties, and telemarketing, which is used primarily by large properties or properties with large sales budgets.

Telephone Sales Blitzes

A **telephone sales blitz**—an intensive sales event when callers contact a large number of new prospects—begins with organization. The property's general manager or sales team usually targets a particular geographic area or market segment and develops a plan for contacting as many people as possible within a short period of time.

One advantage of a telephone blitz is that virtually any staff member can participate, since the prime objective usually is to gather information, not sell. Reservations agents, night auditors, assistants, and other staff members can easily be trained to use a script to ask specific questions and record the answers on a form for follow-up (see Exhibit 1).

Telemarketing Operations

In today's world of skyrocketing personal sales call costs, **telemarketing** is an effective sales tool that provides person-to-person contact, immediate feedback, and the flexibility of a variety of approaches without the costs of an in-person visit.

While telemarketing is often confused with general telephone sales, the two are worlds apart. Telemarketing is characterized by systematic use of the telephone, often by a special staff of trained telemarketers, along with computers and other technology that provides instant access to information. A good telemarketer can reach as many as 50 decision makers a day. Using a carefully scripted message, telemarketers can simply gather information or present a sales message and close the sale.

Telemarketing should not be taken lightly. A trained staff, dedicated exclusively to telemarketing, is the most cost-effective way for a property to use this form of selling.

All potential telemarketers have good communication skills; persistence; the capability to bounce back from rejection;

Exhibit 1
Sample Sales Blitz Form

	Business			Clubs, churches and other non-profit organizations		
THE SALES BLITZ DECISION-MAKER IDENTIFICATION						
Person Contacted	Makes Reservations for Visitors	Makes Reservations for Company Banquets and Meetings	Uses Local Restaurants for Business Lunches	Makes Reservations for Visitors	Makes Reservations for Company Banquets and Meetings	Uses Local Restaurants for Personal Enjoyment
1. Name / Title / Phone						
2. Name / Title / Phone						
3. Name / Title / Phone						
4. Name / Title / Phone						

Source: James C. Makens, *The Hotel Sales and Marketing Plan Book* (Winston-Salem, N.C.: Marion-Clarence Publishing House, 1990), p. 217.

good organizational skills; the ability to adapt to new situations and different types of clients; and, most important, the enthusiasm, friendliness, and flexibility that result in increased sales.

Telemarketing Scripts. Telemarketers use scripts designed to communicate effectively with prospects and either make a sale or gather information necessary to follow up on the call. A telemarketing form can be completed and given to the property's sales representatives for evaluation and possible follow-up (see Exhibit 2).

Most scripts begin with an introduction that explains the purpose of the call: "Good morning. I'm Mary Kelly, representing Best Rest Inns. I'm calling to ask you a few brief questions regarding your company's use of meeting rooms and accommodations for your traveling salespeople. Any information you can provide would be extremely helpful. My first question concerns the number of meetings you hold each year." This type of introduction immediately involves the respondent.

The content of a telemarketing script will, of course, depend on the property's

Exhibit 2
Sample Telemarketing Call Report

TELEPROSPECT CALL REPORT

Date _____

Organization _____

Address _____

_____ Telephone _____

Key Contact _____ Title _____

Additional Contacts _____ Title _____

_____ Title _____

Potential	Yes	No	Frequency
Group			
Individual			
Meeting			
Other			

Hotel(s) Currently Patronized _____

Action _____

Trace _____

Remarks _____

_____

_____

_____

_____

_____
Signature

objectives. Is the script designed to gather information only? Is it designed to generate leads for follow-up by salespeople? Does it offer a benefit or special premium in return for a booking?

No matter what the objective, a telemarketing script is usually:

1. *Short.* Long surveys or presentations may irritate or bore prospects.

2. *Specific.* The script should get to the point. Benefits should be spelled out early.

3. *Simple.* Long words and hotel jargon should be avoided to ensure that the presentation is easily understood.

4. *Structured.* The script should flow from general questions to more specific or

sensitive areas. For example, it's easier to build rapport if the telemarketer begins by asking general questions about the prospect and his or her type of business, instead of immediately starting off with questions about how much the prospect has paid for meeting space or accommodations.

A telemarketing script must keep the prospect on the line long enough to gather information, get a message across, or close a sale. To do this, the script must get the prospect involved and present a benefit of interest to the prospect. Asking for reactions to one program versus another builds interest, as does asking for the prospect's opinions or including stories and analogies that relate to the prospect's background.

Telemarketing Programs. Since telemarketing is so important, it is essential that a telemarketing program—whether established in a large regional or district office for an entire hotel chain, or headquartered at an individual property—be as disciplined as any other form of direct selling. There should be carefully developed production forms, professional training, ongoing supervision, and tracking of results.

If in-house staff are used to fill telemarketing positions, a training program should be implemented and an experienced telemarketing professional hired as either the program director or a consultant.

An example of a successful telemarketing program is the Days Inns Automatic Telemarketing System (ATMS). Days Inns' telemarketing operation focuses on three primary markets (the motorcoach business, group business, the corporate market) and three secondary markets (travel agents, travel agent consortiums, tour operators). The telemarketing program combines experienced telemarketing operators with a computer software package that includes prospect and guest tracking, an inventory of available literature and mailing materials, telemarketing representative productivity tracking, automatic telephone dialing, a program for rapid retrieval of booking information, guest booking histories, a room inventory, a directory of properties, complaint and complaint follow-up records, a program for developing effective telemarketing scripts, and marketing research functions.

In evaluating its program, Days Inns management found that five percent of telemarketing calls resulted in immediate bookings and 20 percent generated appointments with salespeople; 60 percent of the prospects contacted wanted to have further information sent in the mail; only 15 percent had no interest. The program was extremely cost-effective. In its first year, six telemarketing representatives were responsible for over $3 million in bookings.

A successful telemarketing program will provide an efficient means for pinpointing prospects, selling to serious buyers, and keeping in touch with regular clients and guests.

Apply Your Learning 10.4

Please write all answers on a separate sheet of paper.

1. What is the most common objective of a telephone sales blitz?

2. Besides the telephone, what is the most valuable tool of the telemarketer?

3. Which of the following is *not* a necessary trait of an effective telemarketer?

    a. the ability to handle rejection
    b. good organizational skills
    c. persistence
    d. knowledge of the hotel's rates

4. What are the four characteristics of a good telemarketing script?

Quick Hits

SECTION 10.1—BASICS OF TELEPHONE COMMUNICATIONS

- The telephone, if used properly, can be one of the most economical ways to find—and sell to—prospective guests and clients. Both incoming and outgoing calls play an important role in a property's overall sales effort.

- Telephone selling is more difficult than face-to-face sales because you can't read the prospect's body language. Etiquette, communication skills, and listening skills all play heightened roles in making a good impression and selling the property over the telephone.

- When making sales calls, salespeople can make a good impression by being adequately prepared, showing courtesy to the intermediaries who answer the phone, being brief, and scheduling their calls to avoid inconvenient times.

- Effective speaking skills depend on paying appropriate attention to tone of voice, pitch, inflection, and enunciation.

- Tips for effective listening skills include: limit your own talking, become engaged in the conversation, and ask questions.

SECTION 10.2—OUTGOING CALLS

- Outgoing calls range from prospecting calls, qualifying calls, appointment calls, and sales calls to promotional calls, service calls, and public relations calls.

- **Prospecting calls** gather information and learn the names of decision makers. **Qualifying calls** determine if prospects are likely customers for the products and services offered by the property.

- **Appointment calls** are used to briefly introduce a prospective client to the features and services offered by the property and ask for a face-to-face meeting. There are five steps involved: reaching the decision maker, opening the call, making the presentation, overcoming objections, and setting the appointment.

- The objective of a telephone sales call is to make an immediate sale, and the caller must either close the sale during the conversation or make arrangements to call back on another day.

- Closing techniques include asking for a sale, assuming a sale, the pause close, closing on an objection, and the series-of-agreements close.

- **Promotional calls** are made by salespeople, telemarketers, or top management to introduce special promotions.

- **Service calls** are made to enhance client satisfaction and loyalty by maintaining contact or following up after a sale.

- **Public relations calls** are made to generate goodwill.

SECTION 10.3—INCOMING CALLS

- It's polite and it's good business to answer the telephone promptly. When a call is not answered right away (generally within three rings), the caller may become impatient and hang up.

- Calls should begin with a greeting, the name of the property, the employee's name, and a courteous phrase.

- When it is necessary to place callers on hold, they should be asked for their permission to do so.

- To avoid numerous transfers, the hotel representative handling the call should make every attempt to determine the purpose of the call and the person who can help.

- Incoming telephone calls that can lead to sales fall into three categories: reservations, responses to advertising, and inquiries.

SECTION 10.4—TELEPHONE SALES OPERATIONS

- Two of the most common ways to creatively boost sales via the telephone are telephone sales blitzes, which can be extremely effective for small to midsize properties, and telemarketing, which is used primarily by large properties or properties with large sales budgets.

- A **telephone sales blitz** is an intensive sales event when callers contact a large number of new prospects in a short span of time. The primary objective is to gather information, not sell.

- **Telemarketing** provides person-to-person contact, immediate feedback, and the flexibility of a variety of approaches without the costs of an in-person sales call. It is characterized by systematic use of the telephone by trained telemarketers, along with computers and other technology that provides instant access to information.

- Using a carefully scripted message, telemarketers can simply gather information or present a sales message and close the sale.

- The telemarketing script should be short, specific, simple, and structured.

- A successful telemarketing program will provide an efficient means for pinpointing prospects, selling to serious buyers, and keeping in touch with regular clients and guests.

Unit

Food and Beverage Service

CHAPTER 11   HOTELS AND THE FOOD SERVICE INDUSTRY

CHAPTER 12   THE MENU

CHAPTER 13   DINING AND BEVERAGE SERVICE

CHAPTER 14   CASUAL/THEME RESTAURANTS

CHAPTER 15   BANQUETS AND CATERED EVENTS

CHAPTER 16   ROOM SERVICE

Profile

Ian D. N. Fetigan, CCM
General Manager, The Country Club of Darien, Inc. Darien, Connecticut

For a man who didn't want to be a lawyer, the United States was the land of opportunity. Fetigan grew up in a family of lawyers. After going to boarding school in England, he decided he didn't want to follow in the family tradition, but would rather build his career in the incredibly stimulating profession of hospitality and club management.

Growing up in Bermuda—the resort capital of the world—Ian Fetigan began working in the industry at age 10, as a bellhop for a guesthouse. From that position, a decade or so later, he went on to become the youngest general manager of a country club in the Northeast at the age of 24.

"The private club industry is the crème de le crème of the hospitality business," Fetigan said. "It allows you hands-on, face-to-face interaction with the leaders of our society. The opportunities that arise from that are immeasurable."

Fetigan goes on to say that the industry is "an emotional business. It's making people happy. If you make people happy, and show them that you truly care for them and their leisure time, you will be rewarded in both tangible and non-tangible ways. It can be a fun business because you're trying to create fun for your members."

What he calls his first "real job" was working as an apprentice chef in the kitchen at Ariel Sands, a private club and hotel in Bermuda, while studying Hotel and Restaurant Management at Bermuda College. He then transferred to the University of Maryland, Eastern Shore and began work at the Carousel Hotel and the Sheraton-Salisbury. Throughout college, Fetigan worked multiple jobs, typically working an afternoon shift at one hotel, a night shift at another hotel and attending classes during the day.

While Bermuda is filled with resorts and other properties, Fetigan said that advancement there is a little slower. "If you know what you're doing and you are willing to take the necessary risks," Fetigan said, "You can rise to the top very quickly in this country."

Fetigan has spent the past 10 years as the general manager of The Country Club of Darien—outlasting the 2.2-year average tenure of private club managers. While he explains that the nature of the business makes it rare to stay in a single place until retirement, he's happy at Darien. "Your greatest motivator is yourself. You need to constantly be doing things to motivate yourself.

"For those of you seeking an exciting and rewarding career, I would wholeheartedly recommend a career in club management – as of yet, I have never had a dull moment!"

Hotels and the Food Service Industry

Sections

11.1 Food Service Industry

11.2 Food and Beverage Organization

11.3 People in Food Service

11.4 Sanitation

11.1 *Food Service Industry*

AFTER STUDYING SECTION 11.1, YOU SHOULD KNOW HOW TO:

♦ Classify the food service industry by its markets

♦ List the types of businesses classified as "eating and drinking places"

♦ Describe the role of food and beverage sales in hotels

♦ Identify the types of food services offered in the transportation market

♦ Describe food services for the leisure market

♦ Describe retail food services

♦ List the types of business/industrial food services

♦ Describe student food services

♦ Explain how food services are offered in health care facilities

♦ List the types of clubs and the food service they offer

The food service industry is enormous. It includes any type of operation that prepares meals for people away from home—and sometimes even at home, in the case of caterers. This chapter will examine the segments of the food service industry and illustrate that food service operations are not at all limited to fast-food restaurants, conventional restaurants, or hotel dining rooms.

Composition and Size of the Food Service Industry

The food service industry may be classified in many different ways. One way is to categorize it according to various markets. These major categories are shown in Exhibit 1.

Food service operations may also be classified according to the economic objectives of the operation. There are three main categories of food service operations under this type of classification: commercial, institutional, and military. Exhibit 2 lists these main categories and their subcategories.

Commercial, institutional, and military food services each have different economic objectives. Commercial food service operations—such as F&B operations in restaurants and lodging properties—exist primarily to make a profit. The main objective of institutional food service operations—such as schools and health care facilities—is to minimize expenses. The military's main objective is to stay within the budget allotted by Congress.

Whether the food service industry is classified by markets or by economic objectives, a few statistics will detail the size and

Exhibit 1
Major Classifications of Food Service Markets

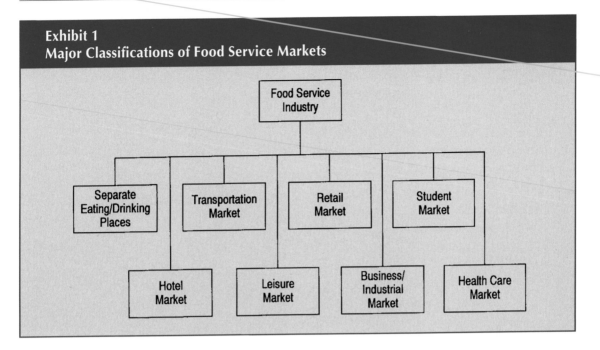

illustrate the importance of this major industry:

- Today, total industry sales are over $320 billion. (Exhibit 3 shows the growth in food service sales, 1970–1997.)

- Eating and drinking places generate about 70 percent of industry sales and about 60 percent of total food and beverage purchases.

- Food and beverage purchases total $116 billion with commercial food service responsible for a little over 76 percent of all purchases.

- The industry has 787,000 units and employs 9.5 million people.

Eating and Drinking Places

This market can be divided into six categories. Each of the categories could include single- or multi-unit companies.

- *Full-menu restaurants and lunchrooms* offer a wide variety of menu items and table service. They may serve only one meal or stay open 24 hours a day. Some offer a menu on which items that are usually served for breakfast, lunch, or dinner are offered at all times. Full-menu restaurants and lunchrooms generally have indoor seating and may serve alcoholic beverages.

- *Limited-menu restaurants and refreshment places* offer only a few items (for example, only or primarily pizza or coffee). Typically, the customer walks to a service counter or drives up to a service window and orders food. Then the customer carries the food to a table, if there is inside seating, or consumes the food off the premises. Some limited-menu properties offer table service.

- *Public cafeterias* are often similar to full-menu restaurants and lunchrooms because they offer a wide variety of menu items, but table service is usually limited. Their markets include families and, as the check average increases, businesspeople and adults without children.

- *Social caterers* prepare meals for large or small banquets and may provide food service in off-site locations.

- *Ice cream, frozen yogurt, and frozen custard stands* offer primarily frozen dairy and related products, sometimes with indoor seating.

- *Bars and taverns* serve alcoholic beverages and offer only limited food service.

Hotel Operations

Food and beverage sales generate about 31 percent of the total sales dollars earned by the U.S. lodging industry. These figures suggest that food and beverage divisions are much more than casual operations offered for the convenience of guests. In fact, many hoteliers and management personnel realize that food and beverage operations usually cannot generate required profits from in-house sales alone; extensive patronage by the community is necessary for food and beverage operations to realize their economic goals.

Food Services for the Transportation Market

Food services offered on planes, trains, in terminals, on interstate highways, and aboard passenger and cargo ships are included in this segment. These services may be provided by a for-profit management

---

Exhibit 2
Food Service Classifications

Group 1 Commercial Food Service
  Eating and Drinking Places
    Restaurants and lunchrooms
    Limited-menu restaurants and refreshment places
    Commercial cafeterias
    Social caterers
    Ice cream, frozen custard, and frozen yogurt stands
    Bars and taverns
  Food Contractors
    Manufacturing and industrial plants
    Commercial and office buildings
    Hospitals and nursing homes
    Colleges and universities
    Primary and secondary schools
    In-transit food service (e.g., airlines)
    Recreation and sports centers
  Lodging Places
    Hotel restaurants
    Motor hotel restaurants
  Other
    Retail host restaurants
    Recreation and sports
    Mobile caterers
    Vending and non-store retailers

Group 2 Institutional Food Service—Business, Educational, and Government Organizations Operating Their Own Food Service
  Employee food service
  Elementary and secondary schools
  Colleges and universities
  Transportation
  Hospitals
  Nursing homes
  Clubs, sporting, and recreational camps
  Community centers

Group 3 Military Food Service
  Officers and non-commissioned officers clubs (open mess)
  Food service—military exchanges

Adapted from *Restaurants USA*, National Restaurant Association, December 1996.

Exhibit 3
Growth of Food Service Sales

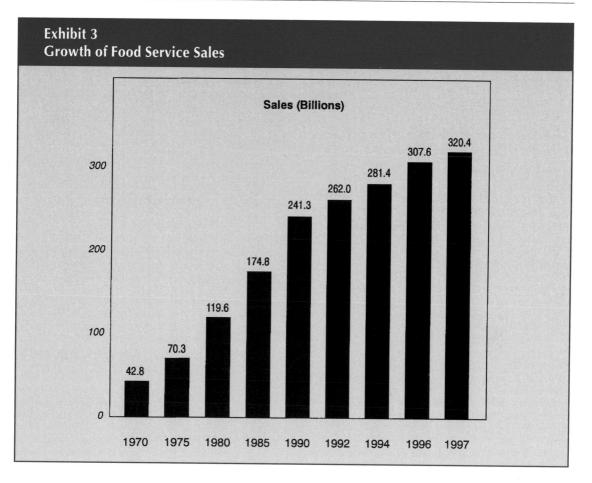

company, or they may be operated by the transportation company itself. Services can range from vending operations to sandwich and short-order preparation to extravagant, expensive food service. As the American public travels more, this market segment will expand.

Food Services for the Leisure Market

This segment comprises food service in theme parks and for sporting events in arenas, stadiums, and racing tracks. Also included are food service operations in drive-in movie theaters, bowling lanes, summer camps, and hunting facilities. These programs may be self-operated or operated by management contract companies. An increase in the public's leisure time will increase sales in this market segment. (Exhibit 4 lists leading food service providers for the leisure market.)

Retail Food Services

Retail food service may range from simple lunch counter or cafeteria service to formal, high-check-average table service. Examples include:

Exhibit 4
Leading Providers for the Leisure Market

The Walt Disney Company

Carnival Cruise Lines

Ogden Entertainment

Club Corporation America

Mirage Resorts

Royal Caribbean Cruise Lines

Delaware North Corporation

Circus Circus Enterprises

Exhibit 5
Major Companies with Self-Operated Food Service

Motorola Company

Aetna Life & Casualty Co.

Ford Motor Company

J.P. Morgan & Company

Procter & Gamble Company

The 3M Company

The EDS Corporation

Hallmark Cards

- *Department stores* that have employee and public dining facilities.

- *Variety and general merchandise stores* that have food service operations for employees—even if only vended services are provided.

- *Drug and proprietary stores* that have public dining outlets and/or vended services for employees.

- *Convenience food stores* that offer sandwiches, snacks, and beverages. Some stores even have booths and tables for in-store consumption.

- *Other specialized retail stores*—grocery stores, gasoline stations, and a variety of other properties—that sell food items for on- or off-premises consumption.

Business/Industrial Food Services

Business and industrial food services include the following categories:

- *Contract food service*—Outside, for-profit companies provide food service in plants and business offices.

- *Internal food service*—Plants and business offices provide self-operated food service. (Exhibit 5 lists some major companies that provide their own food service operations.)

- *Food service to waterborne employees*—This category includes food service to employees on ships, oil rigs, and so forth.

- *Mobile on-street catering*—This category includes programs that visit construction sites and factories, and street vendors who sell a variety of products.

- *Food vending machines*—Foods from snacks to complete meals are offered for customers and/or employees.

- *Food service to military personnel*—Meals consumed by members of the armed forces make up this category.

- *Food furnished to food service employees*—The cost of food purchased merely to feed food service employees runs over $4.7 billion per year, nearly 6 percent of the total purchases for commercial and institutional food services.

Student Food Services

Food service in the student market includes self-operated and management company–operated programs in public and parochial elementary and secondary schools, and in colleges and universities. Elementary and secondary schools may participate in the federally subsidized National School Lunch Program and related Child Nutrition Program. Some programs, such as those in large cities, may serve hundreds of thousands of meals daily. School food service programs may include breakfast, milk, supplemental foods, and senior citizen meals in addition to traditional lunches.

The college and university food service market is tremendous. There are more than 3,000 accredited post-secondary schools in the United States. There are another 3,000 or more trade schools which, while they do not offer extensive food service operations, may have vending machines or snack bars. Perhaps 1,500 of the post-secondary schools arrange for food service through a for-profit management company. Of the remaining schools, an estimated 500 offer only vending machines or buffet food services; 1,000 schools are large enough to have extensive food service programs for boarding students and others attending classes.

Health Care Food Services

Hospitals and nursing homes of all types make up a primary segment of the health care food service market. Some of these facilities are privately owned; others are run by the government. Besides traditional acute-care hospitals and nursing homes that provide permanent residences for patients, there are also homes for orphans and mentally and physically handicapped people.

Club Food Services

Although clubs are not mentioned in Exhibit 1, they form an important segment of the hospitality industry. The service of food and beverages is one of the prime functions of most clubs.

There are many different types of clubs and even subtypes within types. The principal kinds are country, city, yacht, fraternal, military, development, and specialty clubs.

- *Country clubs* have a clubhouse with lounges, food and beverage facilities, and recreational outlets. Country club activities usually center on the golf course(s), but swimming and tennis are also very common. The larger clubs may offer a much wider variety of athletic accommodations. There are about 4,900 private country clubs in the United States.

- *City clubs* serve the needs of individuals working in the city. In addition to the food and beverage function, this type of club may offer athletic facilities, a library or reading room, and overnight accommodations. There are approximately 2,000 city clubs in the United States.

- *Yacht clubs* are similar to country clubs except for location and the fact that activities center on boating rather than golf.

- *Fraternal clubs* are social organizations like the Elks, Knights of Columbus, Eagles, or American Legion. Typically, a restaurant, bar, lounge, billiard room, and card room are found in these clubs.

- *Military clubs* provide recreation areas for the officers and enlisted personnel. These clubs resemble country clubs without golf courses and may provide swimming facilities. Each branch of the armed services operates its own clubs, which are divided into officers clubs, non-commissioned officers clubs, and enlisted clubs.

- *Development clubs* are really country clubs built as integral parts of real estate development projects. The existence of a club is often an incentive for a customer to purchase or rent property in the development.

- *Specialty clubs* center on one particular activity (for example, tennis, swimming, racquetball) and usually do not have a clubhouse but do need a manager. Snack bar food service is often available.

Apply Your Learning 11.1

Please write all answers on a separate sheet of paper.

1. What are the various food service markets?

2. What are the principal kinds of clubs?

For statements 3–8, write whether the answer is True or False.

3. Full-menu restaurant and lunchrooms generally have indoor seating.

4. Public cafeterias generally offer a limited variety of menu items.

5. Limited-menu restaurants may prepare meals for large or small banquets.

6. Food services for the leisure market offer food on planes, trains, and ships.

7. Retail food services may range from simple lunch counter service to formal table service.

8. Less than 500 post-secondary schools are large enough to have extensive food service programs.

11.2 Food and Beverage Organization

AFTER STUDYING SECTION 11.2, YOU SHOULD KNOW HOW TO:

♦ Outline the historic role food and beverage operations played in lodging properties

♦ Describe the current importance of food and beverage to a lodging property

♦ List the primary departments in a large hotel food and beverage division

♦ Describe the mission of the hotel food and beverage division

History of Hotel Food and Beverage Divisions

Through most of the first half of the twentieth century, food and beverage service occupied a position of minor importance in the minds of many hotel operators. In some cases, it was treated as a necessary evil—a service available strictly for the guest's convenience. From an economic standpoint, it was important to break even or to lose as little as possible, a feat made more difficult by the fact that the food and service offered were often of very high quality. Room sales, where the profit was to be made, were expected to make up the difference. As long as one could fill the guestrooms, the profit or loss figures on food and beverages were relatively unimportant.

During the 1950s, this whole concept changed radically. Perhaps the most important factor was the growth and expansion of motels and motor hotels. As motel occupancy rates grew, hotel occupancies declined, and income decreased. At the same time, operating costs increased. Managers could no longer afford to operate the food and beverage division at break-even or loss levels.

Clearly, there were profits to be made in food and beverage sales. After all, restaurants had made money for years. But hotels needed a change of image. The average citizen considered hotel dining too expensive and too formal.

Hotels recognized that the traditional formal hotel dining room was largely obsolete, or at least insufficient in itself. Guests demand a variety of dining alternatives: a rapid-service coffee shop, a snack bar, a cocktail lounge with a distinctive atmosphere, a specialty theme restaurant. Today, the coffee shop is standard in hotels, and specialty restaurants such as steak houses are thriving.

Misconceptions About Food Service

Over the years, some misconceptions about the food and beverage business have evolved. One example is the old saying, "Hire good chefs and leave it to them." This is probably one of the quickest ways to failure. While a good food and beverage operation is almost impossible without a good chef, the entire food service operation must work as a team. The chef is an important member, but there are other equally important players. A complete team is necessary for a successful food and beverage operation. A chef who is capable of running an operation can be promoted to food and beverage manager and coordinate all the division's functions. However, as food and beverage manager, the former chef will still need a good chef to handle food production.

Another misconception: Successful food and beverage managers are "born." This is simply not true. A review of the hospitality industry's past 50 years reveals that all successful operators have one thing in common: the desire to get ahead. There is an old axiom that states, "We do best the things we enjoy." It follows that people who are interested in food and beverage operations and who like to meet people are likely to succeed if they are committed to the job. Perhaps the observations of some successful hoteliers will make the point. Conrad Hilton said many times that he never saw a successful hotelier who did not have much curiosity. Ernest Henderson, founder of the Sheraton Hotels, said that all the successful people that he ever met, regardless of what business they were in, wanted to be the best. Other industry leaders have said that the success of a food and beverage operation corresponds directly to the time and effort the manager gives to it.

One sometimes hears of hotels that "the food and beverage division is a necessary evil," and that "it can't make any money anyhow—so just keep the losses down and forget about it." In fact, however, the leading accounting firms in the country indicate that practically every well-run food and beverage division in a hotel, regardless of size, does make a profit; the better the operation, the greater the profit and contribution to the overall operation.

Some people also believe that a hotel's food and beverage division has to be a loss-leader to attract rooms business. In truth, experience shows that a poorly run food and beverage division actually detracts from overall business. Any manager who would run a food and beverage division at a loss generally does not have the skill to run the rooms division at a profit either.

It is interesting to note that almost every hotel restaurant has a street entrance. In many cases, the guest may not even realize that the restaurant is part of the hotel. The street entrance symbolizes the hotel restaurant's growing importance as a revenue center in its own right. No longer is the food and beverage business simply a necessary evil; it is promoted, merchandised, and sold through creative planning.

Hotels have made tremendous strides in increasing food and beverage sales.

Any manager will acknowledge that making a profit on food is difficult and requires modern operating procedures and experience that is not acquired quickly or easily. Today, there is a tremendous demand for qualified food and beverage managers. Salaries are excellent. In addition, the path to top-level hotel management is wide open for executives with a sound food and beverage background.

Though national figures still show room sales as the number-one source of revenue, many hotels produce more food and beverage revenue than rooms revenue. The importance of the food and beverage division to the overall success of the lodging property is clear.

Food and Beverage Departments

The five primary departments in large hotel food and beverage divisions are:

- Banquet/Catering—responsible for banquets and special functions

- Culinary operations—responsible for food production

- Stewarding—responsible for warewashing, clean-up, and (in some operations) purchasing

- Beverage—responsible for production and service of alcoholic beverages

- Restaurant operations—responsible for food service in all outlets, including room service

The Role of the Hotel Food and Beverage Division

The food and beverage division occupies an important and unique position in the lodging industry. For example, about 31 percent of the revenue in an average hotel comes from food and beverage sales. However, because of the division's complex operation, it contributes only 18 percent to 20 percent of the property's actual profit.

A food and beverage operation in a hotel performs an important threefold mission: (1) to produce an adequate profit; (2) to provide suitable food and beverage service within the hotel; and (3) to help support the role of the hotel in the community.

The importance of the hotel food and beverage operation may be illustrated by the history of two hotels in New York City. For years, the Plaza Hotel has had one of the leading food and beverage divisions in the city. Today, it is considered one of the finest and most profitable hotels in the world. It enjoys a high room rate and a very high occupancy level, and does a very large food and beverage business. As a result, it continues to operate at a substantial profit.

Twenty years after the Plaza Hotel began operating, the Savoy Plaza Hotel was built. Just across from its competitor, the Savoy Plaza was a modern and, in some ways, far better hotel. Unfortunately, over the years, the Savoy Plaza's food and beverage division did not produce its proportionate share of profits. One problem was a very limited catering facility. As a result, the Savoy Plaza was torn down and an office building put in its place.

A good food and beverage operation does more than help establish the quality of the hotel in the eyes of the traveling public. Such an operation may become a very valuable profit maker, may give the hotel a distinct competitive advantage over other operations, may help justify an increase in the average room rates, and may help to keep occupancy levels high.

Apply Your Learning 11.2

Please write all answers on a separate sheet of paper.

1. How was food and beverage service treated through the first half of the twentieth century?

2. What does a street entrance to a hotel restaurant symbolize?

3. What are the five primary departments in large hotel food and beverage divisions?

4. What are the three parts of a food and beverage operation's mission?

11.3 People in Food Service

AFTER STUDYING SECTION 11.3, YOU SHOULD KNOW HOW TO:

♦ Identify three levels of management

♦ Describe typical production positions

♦ Describe typical service positions

Hoteliers consider all objectives of a food service operation as the organization is being developed. For example, if some of a hospital's objectives are to ensure that nutrition requirements are met in all meals, that proper nutrition education is given to all patients and residents, and that community outreach efforts in dietetic services are also provided, it's necessary that the organization create the employee positions to cover these responsibilities. Then people must be hired for these positions and trained.

People in Food Service

The food service industry is labor-intensive: a large number of people are required to do the work necessary to attain food service objectives. The people in food service can be grouped into three general categories: managers, production personnel, and service personnel. For the sake of clarity, we will talk about some production and service managers along with the employees they manage. It should also be noted that the position titles cited in the following sections may vary from operation to operation, and not all of the positions described can be found in every operation.

Managers

In general, there are three levels of managers: top managers, middle managers, and supervisors. How top, middle, and supervisory levels are determined, and the typical duties for each level of management, will vary from property to property. Whether department heads are considered top or middle managers, for example, depends on the size of the organization they work for. Chefs are top managers in some operations, middle managers in others.

Top managers are concerned with long-term plans and goals. They focus more than other managers on the business environment in general. Top managers watch for environmental opportunities and threats such as changes in strategy by competitors, a sluggish economy, and so on.

Middle managers are in the middle of the chain of command. They are in key positions through which communication flows up and down the organization. They are concerned with shorter-term goals, and are typically less concerned with large, environmental issues. They supervise lower-level middle managers or supervisors.

Supervisors are sometimes referred to as "linking pins." They must represent higher levels of management to employees and, at the same time, transfer the wishes and concerns of employees upward. A supervisory position is the first level of management. Supervisors generally use their technical skills more than other managers, and are concerned with such short-term goals as preparing employee schedules and helping employees through the rush times that occur in almost every meal period.

Employees who exhibit superior knowledge and skills and who desire positions with more responsibility often become supervisors. It's a complex job—certainly not for everyone—but an interesting position to which an employee can aspire.

Exhibits 1 and 2 show, respectively, job descriptions for a restaurant manager and a beverage manager. These exhibits describe typical responsibilities of general managers and also list many of their specific job tasks. As the person in charge of operations for the property, the general manager is basically responsible for all aspects of the operation. Much of this work involves setting objectives, creating plans to reach those objectives, and evaluating the extent to which objectives have been attained.

Production Personnel

Production employees are concerned primarily with food production and usually have little contact with guests. There are certain basic production tasks that must be assigned to employees regardless of a food service operation's type or size. Typical production personnel include:

- Chefs
- Cooks
- Assistant cooks
- Pantry-service assistants
- Stewards
- Storeroom and receiving employees
- Bakers

Chefs. Executive chefs are managers in charge of production personnel in the kitchen. In large operations, an executive chef may perform managerial duties only, while other chefs assume production duties. In smaller operations, the executive or head chef (he or she may be the only chef) has both managerial and production duties. Executive chefs may plan menus with the restaurant manager, be responsible for recipe standardization and overall food quality, assist in development of food purchase specifications, prepare daily entrées, plan and oversee special events, develop procedures for food production, and perform miscellaneous production tasks.

Executive chefs may directly supervise a number of different types of chefs, including sous chefs (the principal assistants to the executive chef) and chefs garde-manger (chefs in charge of cold food production).

Cooks. Cooks assist chefs and prepare soups, sauces, and food items to be sautéed, baked, poached, steamed, braised, roasted, grilled, broiled, or fried. They carve and cut meats and prepare cold meat and seafood salad plates, cold sandwiches, hors d'oeuvres, and canapés. Types of cooks include soup cook, sauce cook, fish cook, roast cook, pastry cook, relief cook, and so on.

Assistant Cooks. Assistant cooks help cooks prepare foods for cooking. They trim, peel, clean, grind, shape, mix, or portion foods before cooking and may do simple cooking

Exhibit 1
Job Description—Restaurant Manager

I.   Basic Responsibilities

Responsible for meeting all budget goals; for ensuring that quality standards for food and beverage production and service to guests is constantly maintained; for meeting with clients and booking special catered events; for supervising, scheduling, and training the food and beverage controller and assistant manager; for delegating general management tasks to assistant manager; for verifying through analysis of source documents that all income due is collected from food and beverage sales; for designing/improving existing cash security and recordkeeping/accounting systems; for supervising department heads in absence of Assistant Restaurant Manager.

II. Specific Duties

A.   Develops, with department head assistance, operating budgets.

B.   Monitors budget to control expenses.

C.   Serves as restaurant contact for all advertising/marketing activities.

D.   Supervises, schedules, and trains Food and Beverage Controller and Assistant Restaurant Manager.

E.   Provides required information needed by the controller for payroll, tax, and financial statement purposes.

F.   Reviews all operating reports with department heads; conducts regular and ad hoc meetings to correct operating problems.

G.   Meets with clients; plans and prices special catered events.

H.   Designs and improves restaurant cash security and cash disbursements systems.

I.   Conducts cost reduction/minimization studies.

J.   Audits source documents to ensure that all monies due have been collected.

K.   Delegates miscellaneous administrative tasks to assistant managers.

L.   Serves as restaurant's contact with insurance agent, attorney, banker, and accountant.

M.   Works on special problems as assigned by owner.

N.   Reviews department reports; makes recommendations and follows up to ensure that all problems have been corrected.

O.   Is available to provide assistance as needed during busy periods.

III. Reports to

Owners.

IV. Supervises

Assistant Restaurant Manager, Food and Beverage Controller; department heads in absence of the Assistant Restaurant Manager.

V.   Equipment Used

Must be able to operate all equipment in restaurant.

VI. Working Conditions

Works in all areas of restaurant; long hours, standing, and walking are routine components in the job.

VII. Other

Must know how to operate and do minor maintenance and repair work on all food production and service equipment and building heating, ventilating, air conditioning, plumbing, and electrical systems. Must be tactful and courteous in dealing with the public.

Exhibit 2
Job Description—Beverage Manager

OVERVIEW

The Beverage Manager is responsible to the Director/Manager of Restaurants or the Assistant Director/Manager of Food and Beverage for the successful and profitable management of the lounges and bars to maximize the profitability of the restaurants and of the hotel.

SPECIFIC RESPONSIBILITIES

Responsible for:

1. Maintaining warm, hospitable guest relations in all guest contacts.
2. Meeting or exceeding budgeted goals in sales and profits for the lounges and bars.
3. Developing accurate and aggressive long- and short-range financial objectives relating to liquor sales.
4. Operating within budgeted guidelines.
5. Facilitating highest-quality beverage and service related to the operation of the restaurants.
6. Maintaining the property's housekeeping and sanitation standards in lounges and bars.
7. Implementing corporate sales promotion programs and developing and implementing local sales promotions in the lounges and bars.
8. Knowing the competition and keeping current with industry trends.
9. Maintaining effective controls in the Beverage Department.
10. Implementing and supporting company policies and procedures.
11. Maintaining a high level of professional appearance, demeanor, ethics, and image of self and subordinates.
12. Sustaining professional development of self and subordinates.
13. Communicating effectively between departments and corporate office personnel within area of responsibility.
14. Operating in compliance with all local, state, and federal laws and government regulations.
15. Maintaining fair wage and salary administration in the department in accordance with corporate policy.
16. Assessing and reviewing the job performance of subordinates and maintaining personnel records of assigned employees as described in the Hotel Personnel Policy Manual.
17. Conducting and attending regular department meetings.
18. Directing and coordinating the activities of all assigned personnel and meeting department responsibilities.
19. Hiring, inducting, orienting, and training assigned personnel to meet department responsibilities.
20. Maintaining positive employee relations in a supportive environment.
21. Interfacing department and self with other departments of the hotel to ensure a harmonious working relationship.
22. Ensuring good safety practices of employees and guests throughout the hotel and assisting in the maintenance of proper emergency and security procedures.
23. Performing special projects as requested.

Courtesy of Stouffer Hotel Company

under the instruction or guidance of cooks or chefs.

Pantry-Service Assistants. Pantry-service assistants supply dining room and banquet pantries with necessary items such as utensils, china, glassware, flatware, and other supplies. These employees may also prepare beverages and assist in serving food when required.

Stewards. Chief stewards are managers who typically oversee porters, dishwashing employees, and related personnel. A chief steward may also be in charge of purchasing at some operations.

Chief stewards and their staffs perform cleaning tasks to maintain a high level of cleanliness and sanitation. They may also scrape, wash, and store pots, pans, and other cooking utensils and equipment. Additional duties may include performing janitorial and special cleaning tasks in food and beverage areas, and cleaning and storing china, glass, flatware, and related equipment according to acceptable sanitation procedures.

Storeroom and Receiving Employees. Storeroom employees assist in storing, checking, and dispensing storeroom supplies. Receiving clerks help suppliers unload food and other supplies and verify that the quality, size, and quantity of incoming products meet the property's specifications. They also check to make sure the prices of items ordered are correctly recorded on the suppliers' invoices.

Bakers. Bakers include senior bakers, bakers, and bakers' assistants. Senior bakers are managers who specialize in all phases of bakery preparation and must be able to prepare a wide variety of bakery products following standard recipes. Bakers prepare less complex bakery products such as bread, rolls, pies, and plain cakes, and may assist senior bakers with other tasks. Bakers' assistants help senior bakers and bakers prepare various bakery products.

Service Personnel

Service personnel have a great deal of contact with guests and perform a wide variety of functions and activities. Service personnel include:

- Dining room managers
- Hosts/captains/maître d's
- Food servers
- Buspersons
- Bartenders
- Beverage servers
- Cashiers/checkers

Dining Room Managers. At small properties, the dining room manager not only manages the dining room but often performs the duties of a host as well. At large properties, the dining room manager directly supervises an assistant, whose title may be assistant dining room manager, host, or something similar. The dining room manager helps his or her assistant greet guests and supervise other service employees. The dining room manager has many other duties as well. Typical examples are listed in Exhibit 3.

Hosts/Captains/Maître d's. Hosts, called dining room captains or maître d's at some properties, directly supervise service employees. Hosts check all phases of dining room preparation; complete *mise en place*— a French term meaning "to put everything in place"; and discuss menu specials,

Exhibit 3
Duties of a Dining Room Manager

- Checking the physical condition of the dining room before it opens
- Checking the place settings on tables and the condition of the china, glassware, and flatware (at full-service operations)
- Making sure the menus are in good condition
- Noting the number of reservations that have been made
- If necessary, rearranging tables to accommodate large guest groups
- Checking the schedule to make sure enough service personnel will be on hand
- Observing and, when necessary, recording the job performances of service employees
- Making sure that guests are satisfied and following up on any guest complaints

- Detecting dishonest servers and guests
- Taking appropriate action in case of an emergency or an accident
- Dealing with intoxicated or hard-to-handle guests in a discreet and appropriate manner
- Providing special services (within reason) to guests who request them
- Maintaining a pleasant atmosphere in the dining room
- Performing closing duties, such as turning off lights and adjusting heat or air conditioning levels
- Providing reports and other data requested by upper management

expected regular guests, and anticipated total number of guests with servers and other service employees. During service the host may greet and help seat guests, present menus, and take guest orders. Other tasks can include serving wines, planning for and providing tableside preparation, helping servers when necessary, and preparing flaming desserts. The host may also offer after-dinner drinks and coffee to guests and present the check.

Food Servers. These employees serve food and beverages to guests. The skills food servers need depend on the operation. Guest service at a table service restaurant is different from guest service at a coffee shop. At an elegant restaurant, servers may need to know how to serve wine and flaming desserts; servers in diners may only need basic serving skills. Servers who work at an

operation that uses electronic cash registers, precheck registers, and computer monitors will need to develop different skills than servers who work at an operation that uses a simple hand-written guest check system.

Buspersons. Typical responsibilities for buspersons include setting up tables with proper appointments and removing dirty dishes, linens, and so on from tables. They may also perform *mise en place* before the meal period begins and clean up afterwards.

Bartenders. Bartenders prepare mixed drinks and other alcoholic beverages and serve them directly to guests or to their servers. There are two basic types of bars: public bars and service bars. Bartenders working at public bars serve beverages directly to guests sitting or standing at the bar, or to servers who take the beverages to guests seated in the lounge. Bartenders working at service bars typically do not serve beverages directly to guests; they serve beverages to servers who present them to guests—usually guests in the dining room. Many bars are combination public/service bars. There are age restrictions for serving alcohol that vary by state.

Beverage Servers. Beverage servers provide food and beverage items to guests in lounge areas.

Cashiers/Checkers. These employees may take reservations, total the price of food and beverages on guest checks, and collect guest payments.

Other Service Personnel. Some operations use an expediter during busy periods to help production and service personnel communicate. This person, often a manager, controls the process of turning in orders and picking up food items. The expediter can monitor production times, resolve disputes about when an order came in, and coordinate the interaction among cooks and servers.

Another employee who may assist in the transfer of food from production employees to food servers is the food checker. This employee helps control product quality and costs by examining each tray before it goes into the dining area, checking food for appearance and portion size. Food checkers may also be an important part of the operation's sales income control system. The checker may collect a copy of the guest check and compare items on the check with those on the plate, for example. Today, there is a trend toward eliminating this position.

Apply Your Learning 11.3

Please write all answers on a separate sheet of paper.

1. What are the three levels of management?

2. What positions are included in the production personnel?

3. What positions are included in the service personnel?

4. What is the difference between production personnel and service personnel?

11.4 Sanitation

AFTER STUDYING SECTION 11.4, YOU SHOULD KNOW HOW TO:

♦ List the ways employees contribute to safe food handling and preparation

♦ List the ways employees prevent contamination

♦ Store foods safely and properly

♦ Monitor the temperature of food and the time it spends in danger zones

♦ Wash clean, rinse clear, and sanitize safely

♦ Identify food safety warning signs

Once in a while, you probably hear news reports about people becoming sick or even dying from food poisoning after eating in a restaurant. You may look around the kitchen at the property you work in and say, "That couldn't happen where I work. Everything always looks so clean."

But looking clean isn't the same as being clean. It's up to food service professionals to work as a team to make sure the food served is safe. This section will discuss six food safety principles:

1. Food Safety Starts with You

2. Professionals Prevent Contamination

3. Store Smart

4. Tend to Time and Temperature

5. Wash Clean, Rinse Clear, Sanitize Safely

6. Watch Out for Warnings

Food Safety Starts with You

Safe food is food that is free from danger. Serving safe food is the job of every food service employee.

Foodborne illness occurs when food is contaminated. Contamination means that foreign substances—such as bits of glass, hair, or metal shavings—or microbes are in food. **Microbes** are bacteria, viruses, and parasites that are all around us but are too

Sanitation Standards

Ice for guest consumption should be handled with ice-dispensing scoops or tongs or dispensed by an automatic ice machine. Guests should serve themselves only from automatic dispensers. Utensils for dispensing ice should be stored in a sanitary manner between uses.

small to see. In small numbers, microbes are generally harmless. But in large numbers they cause illness or even death.

Food safety starts at home:

- Stay away from food preparation or service when you are sick.

- Cover infected cuts, burns, or sores with a dry, durable, tight-fitting bandage.

- Shower or bathe daily.

- Wear clean clothes or a clean uniform.

- Keep your fingernails clean and well-trimmed.

- Avoid wearing jewelry.

At work:

- Wash your hands before you start work and whenever you touch something that might carry microbes.

- Properly wash your hands before handling raw or cooked food and after handling raw food or taking out the trash.

- Put on gloves only after you have properly washed your hands. Put on fresh gloves if you do something that would cause you to rewash your hands.

- Wear a head covering.

- Smoke, eat, or drink away from food production and storage, and wash your hands afterward.

- Wash your hands if you cough, sneeze, or handle garbage.

- Change your apron or uniform if it touches raw food, or if you have used it to wipe your hands. Wear street clothes to work, and change into your uniform after you have arrived at work.

- Avoid wearing jewelry, bracelets, and watches that could touch and contaminate food.

Wash hands twice before beginning work, after using the rest room, and before returning to work after a break. See Exhibit 1 for directions on proper handwashing.

Always wash at a hand-washing station, not at a food-prep sink. Wear gloves if your property requires you to.

When you taste food, use the "two-spoon method" shown in Exhibit 2.

Professionals Prevent Contamination

Many sources can contaminate food, including you. Three of the common sources of contamination are:

- Biological sources—bacteria, viruses, parasites, pests, insects

- Chemical sources—cleaning products, pesticides

- Physical sources—metal shavings, broken glass, hair, foreign objects

Sanitation Standards

Staff members should use utensils or gloves when dispensing food to guests. In-use dispensing utensils can be stored in the food with the handles extended. Production staff or servers should never dispense food (biscuits or rolls in a buffet line, for example) with their hands unless wearing single-use gloves; likewise, guests should use utensils and not their hands for serving themselves.

Exhibit 1
Directions on Proper Handwashing

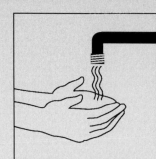

1. Wet your hands with warm water.

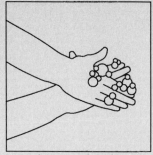

2. Apply soap and wash your hands for at least 20 seconds.

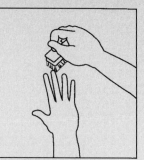

3. Scrub your nails with a nail brush.

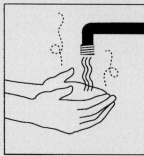

4. Rinse with hot water for at least 20 seconds.

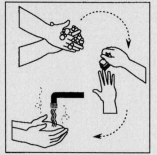

5. Repeat steps 2 through 4.

6. Dry with a single-use paper towel or air dryer.

Exhibit 2
Two-Spoon Method

1. Spoon from the food into a clean spoon.

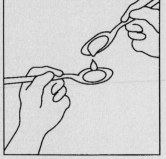

2. Pour the food into a second clean spoon and taste.

3. Never taste over an open container!

Contamination often cannot be seen, tasted, or smelled. **Contaminants** (harmful substances or microbes) can enter through air, water, packaging material, equipment, spoilage, improper handling procedures, or contact with humans.

You can prevent contamination when you:

- Keep raw food separate from cooked or ready-to-eat products.

- Keep food safely stored and covered during preparation.

- Cover food in serving containers.

- Hold food at proper temperatures.

- Stir regularly to keep temperature uniform.

- Do not mix leftovers with fresh food.

- Keep food away from possible contact with chemicals.

- Avoid handling any part of the tableware that will touch guests' mouths.

- Ice is food. Always scoop it with a scoop for that purpose.

- Do not serve food that has fallen off the plate or has been touched by unwashed hands.

- Keep serving carts, trays, transport units, and storage units clean. Be sure to sanitize them daily.

- Wash hands after handling soiled tableware.

- Keep table spray cleaners and sanitizers away from salt, pepper, condiments, and other tabletop food.

Potentially hazardous foods are more easily contaminated than others. **Cross-contamination** occurs when one food contaminates another. Cross-contamination can easily be prevented by properly cleaning and sanitizing surfaces that touch food. Your hands can carry contamination from one food to another, so be sure to wash them often, especially after handling raw food.

Store Smart

Safely store food, equipment, and supplies. Store food safely before, during, and after preparation. An often-used inventory method is FIFO—"first in, first out." This method means you use first the products that came in first. It helps to ensure that you never use products that are too old.

To store food properly after it has been cooked, you should:

- Use the right **food-grade container** (a container specially designed to store food).

- Select the right storage location.

- Label and date the food.

- Move food into storage areas quickly.

Sanitation Standards

Leftover food returned to the kitchen must not be re-served. For example, crocks of cheese or butter should be served only once. The exception to this rule is packaged, non-hazardous food in sound condition. Self-service guests should not reuse tableware when they return to the service area for additional food; however, they may reuse beverage glasses and cups. Unpackaged food on display should be protected from guest contamination by easily cleaned food shields (sneeze guards).

Cracking the Code

The 1993 Food Code, developed by the U.S. Public Health Service of the Food and Drug Administration, suggests that hot leftovers be cooled from temperatures of 140 to 70 degrees Fahrenheit in two hours or less and from 70 degrees to 40 degrees Fahrenheit in an additional two hours of less.

To cool hot leftovers, place the food in shallow pans (no deeper than two inches) or place leftover containers in an ice bath. Cover leftovers loosely and stir often to maintain uniform temperature. Date and label containers before storing.

Store chemicals in their original containers. Follow the storage and handling instructions on Material Safety Data Sheets (MSDSs).

Improperly stored food cannot be made safe again, no matter how carefully it is prepared.

Tend to Time and Temperature

Food service establishments contain many **danger zones**, ranges of temperatures that threaten food safety. Food can be kept safe if you carefully watch both time and temperature. Avoid temperature danger zones by:

- Checking temperatures regularly
- Keeping food out of danger zones whenever possible
- Moving food through danger zones as quickly as possible

Harmful microbes grow best between 41°F (5°C) and 140°F (60°C)—the **temperature danger zone (TDZ)**. Most food that has been in the temperature danger zone for a total of four hours or more should be considered unsafe.

Regularly clean and sanitize your thermometer after each use, and check it for accuracy. Know how to adjust your thermometer and how to use it properly. Place it into the thickest part of the product or between frozen food packages. Wait for the temperature to stabilize. Know how to read and adjust temperature gauges in your area.

Wash Clean, Rinse Clear, Sanitize Safely

Proper cleaning and sanitizing can prevent many food safety problems. **Cleaning** removes visible soil. **Sanitizing** reduces the number of microbes to a safe level. Sanitizing involves three steps:

1. Wash clean by removing visible soil.

2. Rinse clear.

3. Sanitize safely with a sanitizing solution or very hot water.

Many areas, such as floors, walls, and refrigerator doors, need only cleaning. Clean and sanitize food-contact surfaces before and after each changed use or at least once every four hours. **Food-contact surfaces** are any surfaces that touch food. **Changed use** is when you stop working on one type of food and begin working on another.

Hot food-contact surfaces, such as grills, fryers, and ovens, should be cleaned once a day.

To clean and sanitize, you will use special equipment, such as separate wiping cloths for food- and non-food-contact surfaces. Cloths should be stored in a sanitizing solution between use, and the sanitizing solution should be changed at the beginning of every shift. You will also use special cleaning and sanitizing products, and follow cleaning and sanitizing procedures.

Watch Out for Warnings

Not all food contamination comes from microbes. A **food warning sign** is any threat to food safety that you can see. Never ignore food safety warnings. If guests complain to you about food safety, refer them to your manager immediately.

Be aware of and act on the visible warning signs in your area. In the production area, these might include:

- Unusual odor or appearance of meat, fish, or poultry
- Soiled kitchenware
- Unlabeled containers of food or chemicals
- Expired freshness dates
- Leftovers that have changed texture, color, or odor during storage; that have exceeded their expiration dates; or that have been previously reheated
- Food left out of storage
- Signs of insects, rodents, or pests

- Unsanitary activities of other staff
- Problems with equipment

In the warewashing area, these signs might include:

- Broken dishes
- Soil, grease, or dried food
- Spotted, filmy, or streaked glasses
- Coffee, tea, or other stains
- Signs of insects, rodents, or other pests
- Improper lighting

In the service area, these signs might include:

- Broken or chipped tableware
- Flatware that is bent, soiled, spotted, or has dried-on food particles
- Glasses that are spotted, slimy, streaked, or stained
- Melted ice
- Food spills
- Improperly stored or dispensed ice used for drinks

Sanitation Standards

Avoid touching food with your hands. Dishes, cups, glasses, and flatware should only be handled in places that will not come into contact with food or with the guest's mouth. Dishes should be held with four fingers on the bottom and the thumb on the edge, not touching the food. Cups and flatware should be touched only on the handles. A glass should be grasped at the base and placed on the table without touching the rim.

Apply Your Learning 11.4

Please write all answers on a separate sheet of paper.

1. Safe food means that food:

    a. looks safe to eat.
    b. is free from danger.
    c. has spent less than an hour in the temperature danger zone.
    d. is at its expiration date.

2. When washing your hands, apply soap, and wash for at least:

    a. 5 seconds.
    b. 10 seconds.
    c. 20 seconds.
    d. 30 seconds.

3. A potentially hazardous food is one that:

    a. is more easily contaminated than others.
    b. should not be eaten.
    c. is a meat or dairy product.
    d. has been handled with FIFO.

4. Material Safety Data Sheets (MSDSs) must be provided for:

    a. chemicals.
    b. potentially hazardous foods.
    c. all foods.
    d. spices and seasonings.

5. What three steps are involved in sanitizing?

6. What is a food warning sign? Give some examples.

Quick Hits

SECTION 11.1—FOOD SERVICE INDUSTRY

- The food service industry is made up of various markets, including: eating/drinking places, hotel market, transportation market, leisure market, retail market, business/industrial market, student market, and health care market.

- Eating and drinking places include full-menu restaurants and lunchrooms, limited-menu restaurants, public cafeterias, social caterers, ice cream/frozen yogurt/frozen custard stands, and bars and taverns.

- Food and beverage sales generate about 31 percent of the total sales dollars earned by the U.S. lodging industry.

- Food services offered on planes, trains, in terminals, on interstate highways, and aboard passenger and cargo ships are included in the transportation market segment.

- The leisure market segment is comprised of food service in theme parks and at sporting events in arenas, stadiums, and racing tracks; also included are drive-in movie theaters, bowling lanes, summer camps, and hunting facilities.

- Retail food service may range from simple lunch counter or cafeteria service to formal table service, including: department stores with employee and public dining facilities, variety and general merchandise stores with food operations, drug and proprietary stores with public dining outlets, convenience food stores, and other specialized retail stores such as grocery stores or gas stations.

- Business and industrial food services include contract food service, internal food service, food service to waterborne employees, mobile on-street catering, food vending machines, food service to military personnel, and food furnished to food service employees.

- Food service in the student market includes public and parochial elementary and secondary schools, and colleges and universities.

- Hospitals and nursing homes of all types make up a primary segment of the health care food service market.

- Clubs are an important segment of the hospitality industry; food and beverage service is one of the prime functions of most clubs. The principal kinds of clubs are country, city, yacht, fraternal, military, development, and specialty.

SECTION 11.2—FOOD AND BEVERAGE ORGANIZATION

- Through most of the first half of the twentieth century, food and beverage service was treated as a necessary evil—a service available strictly for the guest's convenience. From an economic standpoint, it was important to break even or to lose as little as possible.

- During the 1950s, as motel occupancy rates grew, hotel occupancies declined, and income decreased, managers could no longer afford to operate the food and beverage division at break-even or loss levels.

- Hotels have succeeded in changing the food and beverage format from formal to informal. Alternatives include rapid-service coffee shops, snack bars, cocktail lounges, and specialty theme restaurants.

- The food and beverage business is no longer a necessary evil; it is promoted, merchandised, and sold through creative planning.

- A restaurant's contribution margin is the food and beverage income minus the direct costs of providing the food.

- The five primary departments in large hotel food and beverage divisions are catering, culinary operations, stewarding, beverage, and restaurant operations.

- A food and beverage operation in a hotel performs an important threefold mission: (1) to produce an adequate profit; (2) to provide suitable food and beverage service within the hotel; and (3) to help support the role of the hotel in the community.

SECTION 11.3—PEOPLE IN FOOD SERVICE

- The three levels of management are top managers, middle managers, and supervisors.

- Top managers are concerned with long-term plans and goals. They focus on the business environment in general, watching for opportunities and threats.

- Middle managers are in key positions through which communication flows up and down the organization. They are concerned with shorter-term goals, and are typically less concerned with large issues. They supervise lower-level middle managers or supervisors.

- Supervisors transfer the wishes and concerns of employees upward. A supervisory position is the first level of management. Supervisors are concerned with such short-term goals as preparing employee schedules and helping employees through the meal rush times.

- **Production employees** are concerned primarily with food production and usually have little contact with guests. Included are chefs, cooks, assistant cooks, pantry-service assistants, stewards, storeroom and receiving employees, and bakers.

- **Service personnel** have a great deal of contact with guests and perform a wide variety of functions and activities. Included are dining room managers, hosts/captains/maître d's, food servers, buspersons, bartenders, beverage servers, and cashiers/checkers.

SECTION 11.4—SANITATION

- The six food safety principles are: (1) food safety starts with you, (2) professionals prevent contamination, (3) store smart, (4) tend to time and temperature,

(5) wash clean, rinse clear, sanitize safely, and (6) watch out for warnings.

- Foodborne illness occurs when food is contaminated. Contamination means that foreign substances or microbes are in food. **Microbes** are bacteria, viruses, and parasites that are all around us but are too small to see. In small numbers, microbes are generally harmless. But in large numbers, they cause illness or even death.

- Three common sources of contamination are biological (bacteria, viruses, parasites, pests, insects), chemical (cleaning products, pesticides), and physical (metal shavings, broken glass, hair, foreign objects).

- Contamination often cannot be seen, tasted, or smelled. **Contaminants** (harmful substances or microbes) can enter through air, water, packaging material, equipment, spoilage, improper handling procedures, or contact with humans.

- **Cross-contamination** occurs when one food contaminates another. Cross-contamination can easily be prevented by properly cleaning and sanitizing surfaces that touch food.

- Store food safely before, during, and after preparation. An often-used inventory method is FIFO—"first in, first out." This method means you use first the products that came in first. It helps to ensure that you never use products that are too old.

- Food service establishments contain many **danger zones**, ranges of temperatures that threaten food safety. Food can be kept safe if you carefully watch both time and temperature.

- Harmful microbes grow best between 41°F (5°C) and 140°F (60°C)—the **temperature danger zone (TDZ)**. Most food that has been in the temperature danger zone for a total of four hours or more should be considered unsafe.

- Proper cleaning and sanitizing can prevent many food safety problems. **Cleaning** removes visible soil. **Sanitizing** reduces the number of microbes to a safe level.

- A **food warning sign** is any threat to food safety that you can see. Never ignore food safety warnings. If guests complain to you about food safety, refer them to your manager immediately.

Profile

Tim Pugh
Partner/Regional Manager, Damon's

Starting at the bottom is still a great way to launch a successful hospitality career, and Tim Pugh, part-owner and a regional manager for Damon's (a restaurant specializing in ribs), is proof of that. He began his hospitality career at an A&W when he was 16 years old and went from there to washing dishes in a local restaurant.

But you couldn't have told that teenager that he was laying the foundation for a career. He excelled in sports and public speaking He went to college on a track and cross-country scholarship. He soon discovered that cross-country running wasn't as fun as other sports so he left school and moved to Dallas and took his first job with the Boy's Club.

In Dallas, he began working for hotels as a way to make extra money. He worked as a banquet server for Hyatt Regency in the evenings. When he saw what good money he could make as a banquet server, he became a full-time server for Four Seasons and did banquets in the evening at luxury hotels around the city.

The Four Seasons management team kept making Pugh offers to become a manager, but he wanted to focus on his degree. It was then that he decided there were many more opportunities in hospitality than there were in communications—the degree he had started to pursue. He changed his major and transferred to Michigan State University's hotel and restaurant school.

The next decade was spent in restaurants around the country, before returning to Michigan and working for Damon's owner Steve Montanye. "He gave me my greatest opportunity," Pugh said. "He taught me a lot of life lessons. He's a very good person."

Pugh stresses that it is more important to be a good person than to be a good business-person. "Focus on being a good person and the success will follow. It's hard to be a success if you're not a good person."

For this reason, Pugh believes in giving back to his community and the industry. He spends a lot of time at hospitality schools, working as an honorary professor, helping students with mock interviews, and supporting educational efforts in the industry. He also volunteers in schools and his church.

The dedication to community fits well with a person who characterizes the industry as one that is "all about people. You have to like people in this industry."

Pugh stresses that anyone entering the industry needs "to be energized, have a lot of endurance and stamina, and have a real intensity. You need the ability to work really hard. You also must be honest. If you're not honest, people will know it."

The Menu

Sections

12.1 Menu Styles and Schedules

12.2 Menu Types

12.3 Menu Planning

12.4 Menu Design

12.5 Menu Pricing

12.1 Menu Styles and Schedules

AFTER STUDYING SECTION 12.1, YOU SHOULD KNOW HOW TO:

♦ Explain the importance of the menu

♦ List basic categories of menus

♦ Describe fixed menu schedules

♦ Describe cycle menu schedules

Everything starts with the menu. The menu dictates much about how your property will be organized and managed, the extent to which it will meet its goals, and even how the building itself—certainly the interior— should be designed and constructed.

For guests, the menu is much more than just a list of available foods. The menu also communicates the property's image and contributes to the overall dining experience by helping to set a mood and build interest and excitement.

For production employees, the menu dictates what foods must be prepared. The tasks of service employees are also influenced by what items are offered on the menu.

For managers, the menu is the chief in-house marketing and sales tool. The menu also tells them what foods and beverages must be purchased, the types of equipment

they have to have, the number of workers they must hire, the skill level of those workers—in short, the menu has an impact on almost every aspect of a food service property.

Because almost every guest will look at the menu, managers must be sure it

Lost in the Translation

Many international restaurateurs have left their English-speaking guests scratching their heads as they try to comprehend these menu items:

• In China: Cold shredded children and sea blubber in spicy sauce
• In Vietnam: Pork with fresh garbage
• In Poland: Roasted duck let loose
• In Cairo: French fried ships
• In Europe: Sweat from the trolley
• In Nepal: Fried friendship
• In Japan: Buttered saucepans and fried hormones
• In Cairo: Muscles of Marines/Lobster Thermos
• In Bali: Toes with butter and jam
• In Japan: Teppan Yaki—Before your cooked right eyes

conveys the right message. In an elegant restaurant with a romantic atmosphere, an elaborate menu tied with gold cord and printed on expensive paper can help set the tone for the guests' dining experience. Even the condition of the menu conveys a message. If the property's managers allow torn, dirty menus to be handed out, what other areas of the property are they uncaring about?

Menu Pricing Styles

There is a wide variety of menus, reflecting the wide variety of food service properties. Menus come in all shapes and sizes. Some are printed on parchment, others are written on a blackboard. But all menus can be categorized by how the menu items on them are listed and priced. Three basic categories of menus are:

- Table d'hôte

- À la carte

- Combination table d'hôte/à la carte

Table d'Hôte. A table d'hôte (pronounced "tobble dote") menu offers a complete meal for one price (see Exhibit 1). Sometimes two or more complete meals are offered on the menu, each meal having its own price. Some table d'hôte menus offer guests limited choices within the meal they select—for example, a guest may choose between a soup and a salad, or a choice of desserts may be offered. But for the most part, a meal on a table d'hôte menu is set by the menu planner and guests are given few, if any, choices. Table d'hôte menus are sometimes called prix fixe ("pree feeks") menus. Prix fixe is French for "fixed price."

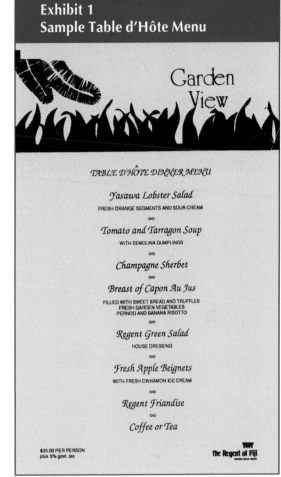

Exhibit 1
Sample Table d'Hôte Menu

Garden View

TABLE D'HÔTE DINNER MENU

Yasawa Lobster Salad
FRESH ORANGE SEGMENTS AND SOUR CREAM
∞
Tomato and Tarragon Soup
WITH SEMOLINA DUMPLINGS
∞
Champagne Sherbet
∞
Breast of Capon Au Jus
FILLED WITH SWEET BREAD AND TRUFFLES
FRESH GARDEN VEGETABLES
PERNOD AND BANANA RISOTTO
∞
Regent Green Salad
HOUSE DRESSING
∞
Fresh Apple Beignets
WITH FRESH CINNAMON ICE CREAM
∞
Regent Friandise
∞
Coffee or Tea

$35.00 PER PERSON
plus 5% govt. tax

the Regent of Fiji

Courtesy of the Regent of Fiji

À la Carte. With an à la carte menu, food and beverage items are listed and priced separately (see Exhibit 2). Guests need not choose a meal that has been planned for them; they can choose from the various appetizers, entrées, side dishes, and desserts listed to make up their own meal. The prices of the menu items they select are added together to determine the cost of the meal.

Combination. Many properties have menus that are a combination of the table d'hôte and à la carte pricing styles. Table d'hôte menus may offer a selection of individually

---

Exhibit 2
Sample à la Carte Menu

Hard Rock CAFE

APPETIZERS

All our soups, chili, guacamole and onion rings are homemade daily with the freshest of ingredients.

HARD ROCK AND ROLL CHILI — HOMEMADE	CUP	2.95
	BOWL	4.95
SOUP OF THE DAY	CUP	1.75
	BOWL	2.25
RUTH'S SPICY CHICKEN WINGS		2.95
HARD ROCK GUACAMOLE WITH CHIPS		3.95
ONION RINGS		2.50

SALADS

All our salads on every plate are made with fresh hearts of romaine.

1. GRILLED CHICKEN BREAST SALAD — 5.95
   marinated sliced chicken served on a mound of tossed California greens with vinaigrette dressing

2. CAFE CHOPPED SALAD — 5.95
   chopped California greens, smoked turkey, bleu cheese, tomatoes, and bacon tossed in a light oil and vinegar dressing

3. HARD ROCK CAESAR SALAD — 5.75
   hearts of romaine lettuce with homemade garlic croutons and our Caesar dressing

4. CHICKEN SALAD — HOMEMADE — 5.95
   an Old Favorite Recipe — Served on crisp greens with tomato, cucumber and pineapple

5. SPINACH SALAD — 5.95
   fresh spinach greens with freshly sliced avocado, crisp bacon, bermuda onions, mushrooms, feta cheese and our House Oil and Vinegar

SPECIALTIES OF THE HOUSE

If you've been to the Hard Rock and haven't had our lime chicken or watermelon ribs, then you haven't been to the Hard Rock!

6. LIME BAR-B-Q CHICKEN — 8.95
   Chicken marinated in our special lime marinade and then grilled and served with fries and a green salad

7. HRC FAMOUS BABY ROCK WATERMELON RIBS — 9.95
   Texas style ribs basted in our special watermelon B-B-Q sauce, grilled and served with fries and a green salad

8. SMOKE HOUSE STEAK — 11.95
   ½ pound grilled, aged New York Steak with fresh garlic butter and served with a baked potato and a green salad

9. FRESH FISH OF THE DAY (Sea Waitress) — Priced Daily
   Truly a Catch! grilled and served with a baked potato and a crisp green salad

10. HRC FRESH GRILLED SWORDFISH — Priced Daily
    served with lime butter, a baked potato and a crisp green salad

HAMBURGERS and SANDWICHES

All the burgers and sandwiches are served with home cut fries, a fresh green salad and your choice of made from scratch creole mustard, 1,000 island, blue cheese or vinaigrette dressings. Sandwiches served on your choice of white or 10 grain whole wheat bread.

11. HRC'S GRILLED BURGERS — 5.75
    ½ pound of the finest hand patted chopped steak

12. ½ pound with melted natural Swiss, Cheddar or Jack cheese — 5.95

13. ½ pound with our Hard Rock and Roll Chili — 5.95

14. ½ pound with crisp bacon, freshly sliced avocado and melted Jack cheese — 6.50

15. ½ pound — any way you want it — 6.75

PIG SANDWICH (Handpulled Hickory Smoked Pork) — 5.95
marinated in our homemade B-B-Q sauce

16. GRILLED CHICKEN BREAST — 6.50
    tender breast of chicken with melted natural Swiss cheese, freshly sliced avocado and tomato on a whole wheat bun.

17. BLUE FIN PACIFIC — 5.75
    White Albacore tuna, lettuce, tomato and water chestnuts.

THE HARD ROCK NATURAL — 4.95
fresh avocado, tomato, carrots, beets, cucumber, red onion, lettuce and daikon sprouts on honey whole wheat bread. Served with our home cut fries.

18. SMOKED TURKEY SANDWICH — 6.50
    Served with lettuce and tomato (Swiss cheese if you like)

19. GRILLED CHEESE SANDWICH — 4.95
    natural Swiss, Cheddar or Jack with tomato

20. THE COUNTRY CLUB SANDWICH — 6.50
    thinly sliced home oven roasted turkey breast, crisp bacon, two kinds of lettuce and tomato

LUNCHEON SPECIALS

SOUP and SANDWICH (served Mon. thru Fri. only) — 4.95
Soup of the day, fresh green salad with your choice of dressing and a half albacore tuna, homemade chicken salad, smoked turkey or grilled cheese sandwich.

LIQUID REFRESHMENTS

WINE — Red, White and Blush	GLASS	2.50
	BOTTLE	8.50
CHAMPAGNE — Domaine Chandon Napa, California	GLASS	4.50
	BOTTLE	19.00
HARD ROCK WINE COOLER		2.50

DOMESTIC BEER — 2.25
BUDWEISER   MILLER LITE
BUD LIGHT   MILLER GENUINE DRAFT

IMPORTED BEER — 2.75
CORONA   BECK'S   HEINEKEN
BASS   BECK'S DARK   FOSTER'S

HARD ROCK HURRICANE (keep the glass) — 6.50

SUNDANCE NATURAL SPARKLERS 1.75 (Cranberry, Apple, Orange or Lemon-lime)		TEA, CAMOMILE OR REGULAR	.95
COFFEE — we fresh grind our own assortment of coffee beans	.95	FRUIT JUICE SQUEEZED FRESH DAILY	1.50
		COKE, DR. PEPPER, SPRITE, ROOT BEER, DIET COKE	.95
CLYDE'S ICE TEA (a real taste treat from inside Of U.S.A.)	.95	PERRIER	1.50
		EVIAN	1.75

BALCONY AVAILABLE FOR PRIVATE PARTIES

Some menus are hand-lettered to give them a more informal personality. (Courtesy of the Hard Rock Cafe, Chicago, Illinois; lettering by B. Perry White)

priced desserts; many à la carte menus include a vegetable and potatoes or rice with the price of the entrée.

A few properties have combination menus that offer an extensive list of complete meal packages and an extensive à la carte section. Chinese and other ethnic-food restaurants are most likely to feature this type of combination menu.

Menu Schedules

Menus can also be categorized by how often they are used. Some properties have a **fixed menu**—a single menu that is used daily. Other properties use a **cycle menu**. A cycle menu is one that changes every day for a certain period of days, then the cycle is repeated.

Fixed Menus. Restaurants such as coffee shops and chain restaurants often use a single menu for several months (or longer) before replacing it with a new fixed menu. Daily specials may be offered to give guests some new menu selections, but there is still a set list of items that forms the basic menu. Fixed menus work best at restaurants and other food service establishments where

Exhibit 3
Sample Cycle Menus

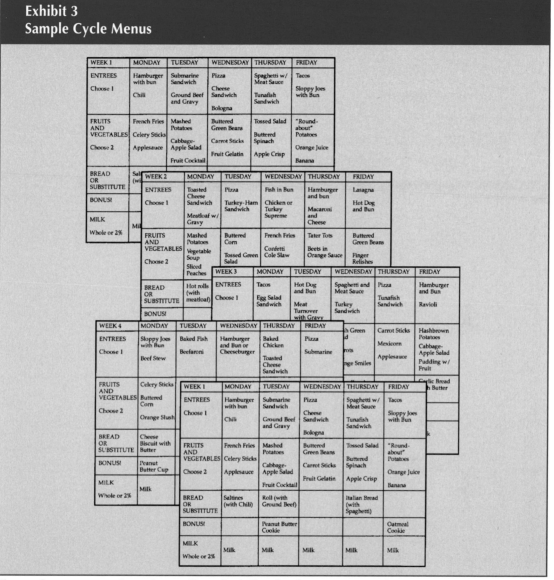

WEEK 1

	MONDAY	TUESDAY	WEDNESDAY	THURSDAY	FRIDAY
ENTREES Choose 1	Hamburger with bun Chili	Submarine Sandwich Ground Beef and Gravy	Pizza Cheese Sandwich Bologna	Spaghetti w/ Meat Sauce Tunafish Sandwich	Tacos Sloppy Joes with Bun
FRUITS AND VEGETABLES Choose 2	French Fries Celery Sticks Applesauce	Mashed Potatoes Cabbage-Apple Salad Fruit Cocktail	Buttered Green Beans Carrot Sticks Fruit Gelatin	Tossed Salad Buttered Spinach Apple Crisp	"Round-about" Potatoes Orange Juice Banana
BREAD OR SUBSTITUTE	Sal... (wi...				
BONUS!					
MILK Whole or 2%	Mil...				

WEEK 2

	MONDAY	TUESDAY	WEDNESDAY	THURSDAY	FRIDAY
ENTREES Choose 1	Toasted Cheese Sandwich Meatloaf w/ Gravy	Pizza Turkey-Ham Sandwich	Fish in Bun Chicken or Turkey Supreme	Hamburger and bun Macaroni and Cheese	Lasagna Hot Dog and Bun
FRUITS AND VEGETABLES Choose 2	Mashed Potatoes Vegetable Soup Sliced Peaches	Buttered Corn Tossed Green Salad	French Fries Confetti Cole Slaw	Tater Tots Beets in Orange Sauce	Buttered Green Beans Finger Relishes
BREAD OR SUBSTITUTE	Hot rolls (with meatloaf)				
BONUS!					

WEEK 3

	MONDAY	TUESDAY	WEDNESDAY	THURSDAY	FRIDAY
ENTREES Choose 1	Tacos Egg Salad Sandwich	Hot Dog and Bun Meat Turnover with Gravy	Spaghetti and Meat Sauce Turkey Sandwich	Pizza Tunafish Sandwich	Hamburger and Bun Ravioli
FRUITS AND VEGETABLES	...h Green ...d ...rots ...nge Smiles	Carrot Sticks Mexicorn Applesauce	Hashbrown Potatoes Cabbage-Apple Salad Pudding w/ Fruit	Garlic Bread ...h Butter	

WEEK 4

	MONDAY	TUESDAY	WEDNESDAY	THURSDAY	FRIDAY
ENTREES Choose 1	Sloppy Joes with Bun Beef Stew	Baked Fish Beefaroni	Hamburger and Bun or Cheeseburger	Baked Chicken Toasted Cheese Sandwich	Pizza Submarine
FRUITS AND VEGETABLES Choose 2	Celery Sticks Buttered Corn Orange Slush				
BREAD OR SUBSTITUTE	Cheese Biscuit with Butter				
BONUS!	Peanut Butter Cup				
MILK Whole or 2%	Milk				

WEEK 1

	MONDAY	TUESDAY	WEDNESDAY	THURSDAY	FRIDAY
ENTREES Choose 1	Hamburger with bun Chili	Submarine Sandwich Ground Beef and Gravy	Pizza Cheese Sandwich Bologna	Spaghetti w/ Meat Sauce Tunafish Sandwich	Tacos Sloppy Joes with Bun
FRUITS AND VEGETABLES Choose 2	French Fries Celery Sticks Applesauce	Mashed Potatoes Cabbage-Apple Salad Fruit Cocktail	Buttered Green Beans Carrot Sticks Fruit Gelatin	Tossed Salad Buttered Spinach Apple Crisp	"Round-about" Potatoes Orange Juice Banana
BREAD OR SUBSTITUTE	Saltines (with Chili)	Roll (with Ground Beef)		Italian Bread (with Spaghetti)	
BONUS!		Peanut Butter Cookie			Oatmeal Cookie
MILK Whole or 2%	Milk	Milk	Milk	Milk	Milk

These cycle menus are used at an intermediate school. Note that the menus are on a four-week cycle and that the menus provide limited choices.

guests are not likely to visit frequently, or where there are enough items listed on the menu to offer an acceptable level of variety.

Cycle Menus. Cycle menus are designed to provide variety for guests who eat at a property frequently—or even daily. Institutional properties such as schools and hospitals frequently use cycle menus (see Exhibit 3). Commercial properties whose guests are likely to visit every day—such as restaurants in isolated resorts, or downtown cafeterias—may use them.

Typical cycles range from a week to four weeks, but some are longer. Establishing the right cycle length is important. With too short a cycle, the menus may repeat too often and guests may become dissatisfied. If the cycle is too long, production and labor costs involved in purchasing, storing, and preparing the greater variety of foods may be excessive. The optimum cycle length varies by type of property and how often its guests are expected to eat there. Some casino hotels in Las Vegas use a seven-day cycle menu because most guests do not stay long enough to notice the repetition. In a resort where the average guest stays two weeks, a two-, three-, or four-week cycle menu may be planned, depending on how concerned the management is with providing variety for guests who stay longer than average. In a nursing home, a cycle menu of six weeks may be appropriate.

Apply Your Learning 12.1

Please write all answers on a separate sheet of paper.

1. Why is the menu so important to a food and beverage property?

2. What are the three types of menu pricing styles?

For statements 3–6, fill in the blanks with the correct answer.

3. A(n) _____ menu is designed to provide variety for guests who eat at a property frequently.

4. A(n) _____ menu lists and prices food and beverages separately.

5. A(n) _____ menu offers a complete meal for one price.

6. A(n) _____ menu uses a single menu for several months before replacing it with a new menu.

12.2 Menu Types

AFTER STUDYING SECTION 12.2, YOU SHOULD KNOW HOW TO:

♦ Describe breakfast menus

♦ Describe lunch menus

♦ Describe dinner menus

♦ List common types of specialty menus

Menus can also be categorized by type. Three basic types of menus are breakfast, lunch, and dinner menus—menus designed around the three traditional meal periods. There are also a large number of specialty menus designed to appeal to a specific guest group or meet a specific marketing need. The types of menus a food service property offers will depend on the number of meals it serves and the type of property it is. Many properties have a separate breakfast menu because they have a cut-off time for serving breakfast. Combining lunch and dinner menus is a common practice. Whether or not to offer specialty menus depends on the property and its clientele. An upscale restaurant may feel that a separate wine or dessert list adds to its image, for example.

Breakfast. Breakfast menus are fairly standard. Most restaurants offer fruits, juices, eggs, cereals, pancakes, waffles, and breakfast meats like bacon and sausage. Some-times regional specialties, like grits in some southern states, are offered.

The watchwords for breakfast menu items are "simple," "fast," and "inexpensive." Guests are more price-conscious at breakfast than at other meals. Guests are also likely to be in a hurry to get to work or make some other appointment, so they want to be served right away. To keep prices down and make quick service possible, most breakfast menus are relatively limited, offering only the essential breakfast menu items.

Lunch. Like breakfast guests, lunch guests are usually in a hurry. Therefore, lunch menus must also feature menu items that are relatively easy and quick to make. Sandwiches, soups, and salads are important in many lunch menus.

Lunch menus must have variety; many guests eat lunch at the same restaurant several times a week because it is located close to where they work. To provide variety, most lunch menus offer specials every day. These specials can be printed on a separate piece of paper and clipped onto the lunch menu. Or a cycle menu can be used to provide variety, in which case the entire menu will change daily for a certain number of days.

Lunch menu items are usually lighter than dinner menu items, because most guests do not want to feel filled up and sleepy during the afternoon. Lunch menus are also less elaborate than dinner menus as a rule. If appetizers are offered at lunch, they are simpler to make and fewer in number. Lunch menus usually include desserts, and some include a list of alcoholic beverages.

Dinner. Dinner is the main meal of the day for most people, and menu items offered at dinner are heavier in character and more elaborate than those offered at breakfast or lunch. Dinner is more likely to be eaten in a leisurely fashion than breakfast or lunch because guests are often seeking a dining experience or celebrating a special occasion at dinner.

Guests are willing to pay more for dinner than for lunch, but they also expect a greater selection of menu items and place a greater premium on service, atmosphere, and decor. Therefore, dinner menus usually offer a wide variety of selections. Wines, cocktails, and exotic desserts are more likely to be on a dinner menu than on a lunch menu.

Specialty Menus

There is a wide range of specialty menus, from poolside menus to menus for afternoon teas. Some of the most common specialty menus are:

- Children's
- Senior citizens'
- Alcoholic beverage
- Dessert
- Room service
- Take-out
- Banquet
- California
- Ethnic

Children's. Children's menus do not necessarily have to blend in with the restaurant's theme or decor; the most important thing is to make sure the menu is entertaining (see Exhibit 1). The goal is to occupy the child long enough for the parents (and other guests) to eat in peace. Children's menus can be shaped like robots, animals, or rocket ships. Many children's menus feature bright colors, cartoons, pop-up designs, or black and white drawings that the child can color. Menus that fold into hats, masks, or other toys are good for small children; puzzles, word games, stories, and mazes can work for older children.

The food offered on children's menus should be simple and nutritious. Portions should be on the small side and prices should be modest.

Tassels, staples, or other potentially dangerous materials that can be removed and swallowed should never be part of a children's menu.

Senior Citizens'. The graying of America means that menus that appeal to the special wants and needs of senior citizens will become more important in the future. Such menus can be separate menus entirely or separate sections of regular menus. More commonly, menu items that meet the needs of seniors are placed throughout the regular menu.

Many seniors have dietary prescriptions or recommendations from their doctors. Most revolve around weight control, diabetes, cardiovascular problems or precautions, and gastrointestinal disorders. Other seniors are just more conscious of the need to eat properly.

Seniors watching their weight and diabetic seniors need simple, non-rich snacks, entrées, and desserts. A piece of fresh fruit served stylishly can allow a diabetic to enjoy dessert with others at the table.

Exhibit 1
Sample Children's Menu

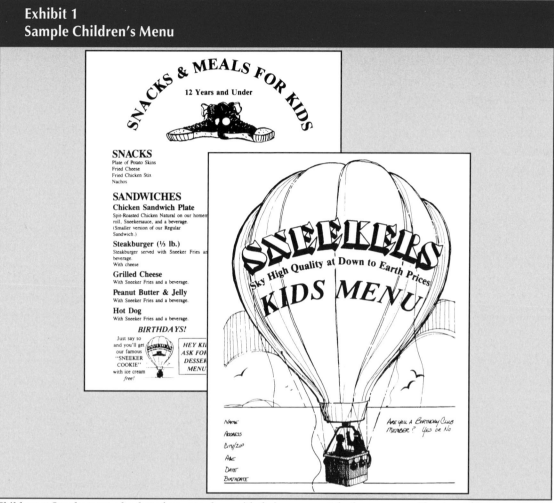

Children at Sneekers get a bucket of crayons along with their one-page take-home menus. (Courtesy of Sneekers Restaurant, Lansing, Michigan)

Many seniors on sodium-restricted diets are on a "no added salt" diet. Many good-tasting menu items can be prepared to meet this diet simply by omitting sodium-rich condiments and avoiding sodium-rich foods. Providing information on the sodium content of menu items can also help seniors on sodium-restricted diets.

Alcoholic Beverage. Cocktails and wines can be listed on a separate menu or included on the regular menu. If included on the regular menu, the drink list should come before the food selections so guests desiring a drink before ordering their meal will have the necessary information. Properties that offer separate alcoholic beverage menus can have separate cocktail menus and wine lists, or can combine cocktails and wines on one menu. Separate beverage menus can be used in the lounge as well as in the dining room.

Food service properties should list alcoholic beverages in large, readable type, with brand names and prices included. Today many beverage menus include no- or low-alcohol drinks creatively named and described to help promote their sale.

Dessert. At the end of the meal, most guests cannot recall the dessert items they saw listed on the main menu. Food servers at some properties use dessert trays to remind guests of desserts. Some properties have a separate dessert menu so that food servers have something they can give to guests at the end of the meal to remind them of the available desserts.

There are many advantages to having a separate dessert menu:

- You can offer more desserts.

- There is more room for bold graphics and descriptive copy.

- You can devote a portion of the menu to dessert specials.

- If dessert prices change, you don't have to go to the trouble and expense of re-printing the main menu.

The types of desserts offered vary with the type of property. Some elegant restaurants feature flaming desserts prepared tableside; many family restaurants offer cake and ice cream; even some fast-food restaurants now offer such simple dessert items as ice cream, pies, and cookies. Upscale restaurants often include after-dinner wines, cordials, brandies, and liqueurs on the dessert menu.

Room Service. Some hotels offer room service to guests. With a few exceptions, such as the room service menus found at luxurious hotels like The Ritz-Carlton, room service menus offer a limited number of menu items. They may offer items from the hotel's regular menu or feature items that are not on the regular menu.

Most room service menus are limited because it is difficult to offer high-quality food that does not deteriorate during transport from the production area to the guestroom, suite, or cabin. This is a problem in every lodging property but especially in high-rise hotels where service staff must contend with elevators, and in resort-type properties where food servers must use a vehicle to transport the food to the guest.

One type of room service menu is the "doorknob" breakfast menu. A doorknob menu lists a limited number of breakfast items and times that the meal can be served. Guests select what they want to eat and the time they want the food delivered, then hang the menu outside the door on the doorknob. The menus are collected and the orders are prepared and sent to the rooms at the indicated times.

Take-out. Some table service restaurants offer take-out menus in an effort to capture consumer dollars that otherwise might be spent at fast-food establishments or on convenience foods in supermarkets.

Like room service menus, take-out menus should be made up of items that can maintain an acceptable level of quality over a long period of time. Guests won't be satisfied unless the food they bought still looks and tastes good when they consume it.

Take-out menus should be inexpensive to produce since guests take them home. Some properties use their take-out menus as direct mail advertising pieces.

Banquet. Hotel food and beverage properties and restaurants that do extensive banquet business often develop pre-set banquet menus in varying price ranges from which guests may choose. They can also plan custom banquet menus when guests request them.

The pricing style for banquet menus is usually table d'hôte—a set meal with few if any choices offered at a set price. The meal tends to be elaborate, with appetizers, soups or salads, and fancy desserts served along with the entrée and its accompaniments.

Managers who plan banquet menus must be careful to select food that can be produced in quantity and still hold its quality.

California. Some restaurants offer breakfast, lunch, and dinner menu items on one menu, with all the items available at any time of the day: if a guest wants spaghetti for breakfast or pancakes for dinner, the guest can order it. This concept originated in California, so this type of menu has come to be called a California menu. Obviously, a property that has no restrictions about when it will serve breakfast, lunch, or dinner items also gives up the production and scheduling convenience such restrictions provide.

Ethnic. Ethnic menus are offered by restaurants that seek to appeal to guests who like a particular cuisine. Restaurants that feature Italian, Chinese, or Mexican food are familiar ethnic restaurants. Other types include those offering Japanese, Polynesian, Scandinavian, Korean, Indian, and Thai cuisines.

An ethnic menu should feature a wide variety of dishes from the particular country or area. The names of the dishes should be in the original language and translated into English. The main ingredients of the dish should also be listed. How authentic should the menu items be? If most of the restaurant's guests are first-generation Americans of the ethnic background the menu seeks to appeal to, then the dishes should closely follow traditional recipes. However, if most of the clientele are second- and third-generation Americans and Americans from other ethnic backgrounds, the recipes can be "Americanized"—i.e., spices can be milder, some ingredients may be eliminated, etc.

Apply Your Learning 12.2

Please write all answers on a separate sheet of paper.

1. What are the three basic menu types?

2. What are some of the most common specialty menus?

For statements 3–6, write whether the answer is True or False.

3. Lunch is the main meal of the day for most people.

4. Dinner menus usually offer a wide variety of selections.

5. Room service menus generally offer all of the items from the hotel's regular menu.

6. The pricing style for banquet menus is usually à la carte.

12.3 Menu Planning

AFTER STUDYING SECTION 12.3, YOU SHOULD KNOW HOW TO:

♦ Identify the types of guests

♦ Classify a property

♦ Select menu items

♦ Provide menu balance

The success of a food service property is to a large extent in the hands of its menu planner. Work will flow more smoothly, guests will be served more effectively, and profits will be greater when the menu has been properly planned. The opposite is also true: a poorly planned menu will cause significant operating problems that will affect guests, employees, and ultimately the financial objectives of the property.

Not all food service managers will be called on to plan or help plan a menu. Managers at fast-food franchise restaurants, for example, may not do any menu planning; their menus will likely be planned at corporate headquarters after extensive market research. In hospitals and schools, menus are often planned by dietitians. At a large independent restaurant, a menu may be planned by a committee that includes the restaurant manager, the head chef, and perhaps the head of purchasing. Menu planning may be done by the owner or the head cook at a small restaurant.

For most menu planners, menu planning consists of selecting new menu items for an existing menu. How does a menu planner go about making these selections? There are two basic rules: know your guests and know your property.

Knowing Your Guests

The quality of all the decisions about the menu depends on knowing your guests well. What kinds of guests eat at your property? What are they willing to pay for a meal? If your most important market is teenagers, your menu should look very different from a restaurant's whose main market is married couples with children.

What do your guests want to eat and drink? Some menu planners think their personal preferences are the same as their guests'. This is not necessarily true. When menu items are selected, the preferences of the guests—not the menu planner—must be considered. Guest preferences are learned by interviewing guests; reading surveys, comment cards, and trade journals; and studying production and sales records.

Knowing Your Property

The type of property helps determine what kinds of menu items are appropriate. At least five components of your property have a direct impact on what kinds of menu items can be offered:

- Theme or cuisine

- Equipment

- Personnel

- Quality standards

- Budget

Theme or Cuisine. The theme or cuisine of the restaurant helps determine what types of menu items are appropriate. A Chinese restaurant has a very different menu than a family-oriented chain restaurant.

Equipment. A menu planner must know types and capacities of equipment in the kitchen. Menu planners can choose a wider variety of menu items if there is equipment on hand for baking, steaming, broiling, frying, etc. In contrast, a property with limited equipment must have a limited menu.

When choosing menu items, planners should spread the workload evenly among the equipment. For example, if most of your entrées and a lot of your appetizers are fried, your fryers may be overloaded while the ovens and broilers are underutilized. For most restaurants, the entrées chosen should reflect a good distribution between frying, baking, broiling, roasting, and other methods of preparation.

Personnel. The number of employees and the skills of those employees will help determine what menu items can be placed on the menu. A menu planner should not put items on the menu that the kitchen staff does not have the skills to prepare.

Just as with equipment, a menu planner wants to avoid overwhelming some kitchen personnel while leaving others with little to do. Careful menu item selection can spread the workload evenly among kitchen personnel.

Quality Standards. Every item on the menu has to meet the property's quality standards. A menu planner should not put items on the menu that can't be prepared and served while maintaining the proper quality.

Budget. Menu planners must recognize financial constraints when planning menus. Commercial properties cannot attain profit objectives and institutional properties cannot minimize expenses unless product costs fall within budgetary limits.

Selecting Menu Items

The items listed on a menu can be categorized as appetizers, salads, entrées, starch items (potatoes, rice, pasta), vegetables, desserts, and beverages. How do menu planners create a pool of possible menu items in each of these categories from which to create or revise menus? There are many possible sources:

- *Old menus.* The property's own previous menus may list menu items that were once popular but were dropped from the current menu for one reason or another. It may be time to consider them for the revised menu.

- *Books.* There are books for the food service industry devoted to recipes and new menu item ideas.

- *Trade magazines.* Trade magazines can be excellent sources of recipes for new menu items.

- *Cookbooks for the home market.* Cookbooks for home use can provide many new ideas for salads, soups, garnishes, entrées, and desserts. Of course, if they are chosen, the recipes have to be modified to yield larger quantities.

Only those menu items that marketing research has indicated that guests may like should be included in the pool. Once the pool has been narrowed down to "items our guests may like," some of these items must be eliminated because of:

- Cost

- Incompatibility with the property's theme or cuisine

- Unavailable equipment

- Insufficient equipment capacity

- Insufficient kitchen space

- Insufficient number of employees

- Incompatibility with employee skills

- Unavailability of some ingredients

- Incompatibility with the property's quality standards

- Sanitation problems

Once the pool has been narrowed down to menu items that guests will probably want and the property can produce, the selection of items for the menu can begin.

Entrées. Entrées are usually selected first. You must determine what kinds of entrées to offer: beef, pork, fish, entrée salads, etc. When planning, you may feel that you should have something for everyone and, therefore, be tempted to provide a wide range of entrées. This approach can create many operating problems. For example, a wider variety of food and ingredients must be ordered, received, stored, issued, and prepared. More equipment and more personnel with the necessary skills must be available.

Production and service problems are more likely. The reverse—offering only a few entrées—reduces these problems. Many specialty or theme restaurants offer relatively few entrées. This minimizes many in-house production and serving problems.

As indicated earlier, menu planners must consider methods of preparation when selecting entrées. Production problems and service delays occur when all or most of the entrées are prepared the same way.

Some restaurants list sandwiches as entrée items on their menus. Sandwiches are the only entrées for some fast-food properties and delis. Sandwiches are usually not high-profit items, so restaurants that offer a lot of high-profit entrées usually try to downplay their sandwiches by listing them in smaller type separately from the entrées. Restaurants whose sandwiches are real money-makers and traffic-builders should give sandwiches a more prominent place on the menu.

Appetizers/Soups. Appetizers include fruit or tomato juice, cheese, fruit, and seafood items such as shrimp cocktail. Popular appetizers can include buffalo wings, mozzarella sticks, jalapeño poppers, and chips and salsa. Appetizers are supposed to enliven the appetite before dinner, so they are generally small in size and spicy or pleasantly biting or tart. The number and variety of appetizers on a menu is determined by the type of property and its guests. Fast-food properties typically do not have appetizers; elegant restaurants may devote a whole page of their dinner menus to appetizers.

Many restaurants offer a limited selection of soups. Sometimes a "soup du jour" is listed (du jour means "of the day"). If more than two or three soups are offered, they are usually listed separately on the menu rather than lumped in with the appetizers. The kinds of soups offered are determined by the type of property. Seafood restaurants usually offer soups like clam chowder and shrimp or lobster bisque, while Italian restaurants often have minestrone soup. Upscale restaurants may offer chilled soups such as vichyssoise.

Starch Items/Vegetables. The next items to be planned are usually the starch items and vegetables. Sometimes the starch item is a part of the entrée—sirloin tips in gravy served over rice, for example. At other times, the starch item is separate—a baked potato or a side dish of pasta. In many restaurants a vegetable is served with the entrée. Vegetables can also be offered as side dishes.

Again, the type of property and its guests determine the variety of starch items and vegetables that are offered. The starch items at many seafood restaurants are limited to baked potatoes or french fries. A restaurant that features fine dining may offer a wide variety of rice, pasta, and potato items; potatoes, for example, may be baked, fried, creamed, mashed, prepared au gratin, etc. Chinese restaurants offer a great variety of vegetables; fast-food properties, few or none.

Salads. The first decision a planner must make about salads is whether they will be strictly side dishes, or whether some salads will be offered as entrées. If they are offered, salad entrées such as chicken salad, shrimp salad, or chef's salad are usually listed on the lunch menu. Tossed salad, coleslaw, potato salad, fruit salad, and cottage cheese salad are typical side-dish salads.

Desserts. The next menu items planned are the desserts. Desserts are typically high-profit items, so much so that even fast-food restaurants such as McDonald's have added a limited number of desserts to their menus. On the other end of the spectrum, many upscale restaurants offer a wide array of elaborate desserts. Low-calorie desserts can be offered for the health-conscious.

Beverages. Non-alcoholic beverages are often listed at the end of the menu. Coffee, tea, milk, and a selection of carbonated beverages are typical. Upscale restaurants may feature a wide variety of coffee—Colombian, Turkish, espresso, cappuccino, spiced coffee, and so on—and a number of teas such as Earl Grey and jasmine.

If a property offers alcoholic beverages, a decision has to be made about how many beverages will be included. Should a few standard beers be offered, or should the property carry a wide variety, including local and regional beers? How many different wines should be offered? Should dessert wines and cordials be included on the wine list? How many different brands of liquor should be offered? For chain restaurants and franchise properties, selection decisions are usually made at corporate headquarters. Managers in independent properties must make their own decisions, based on guest preferences, the restaurant's image, beverage inventory costs, space, and other factors.

Menu Balance

Once all the menu items have been selected, the menu should be reviewed for business, aesthetic, and nutritional balance.

Business balance refers to the balance between food costs, menu prices, the popularity of items, and other financial and marketing considerations. In commercial properties, the menu must help the property make a profit and the menu should be reviewed with that goal in mind.

Aesthetic balance refers to the degree to which meals have been constructed with an eye to the colors, textures, and flavors of foods. Obviously, balance is more important in a table d'hôte menu than in an à la carte menu, since guests are offered entire meals on a table d'hôte menu, and they have more freedom to choose their own food combinations with an à la carte menu. But even with an à la carte menu, some foods are commonly sold together—an entrée with an accompanying starch item and vegetable, for example.

Color is a very important component of a meal's attractiveness. A plate of baked whitefish, steamed cauliflower, and mashed potatoes makes for a boring and unappetizing presentation. Two or three colors on a plate are more interesting than one.

A meal should be composed of foods that vary in texture. Most guests would not like a meal of soup, stew, creamed corn, mashed potatoes, and chocolate pudding.

In general, firm entrées should have tender or soft side dishes; soft entrées should have crisp or crunchy side dishes.

Putting compatible flavors together is a matter of experience as well as knowing traditional combinations. Ham and eggs, for example, go together better than shrimp and eggs. Imagine a meal of grape juice, sweet and sour pork, and cherry pie! Such a meal would have too many sweets and sours for most people.

Nutritional balance has historically been more important for institutional food service properties than for commercial properties. But, managers of commercial properties should make sure the components of a well-balanced meal are available from among the menu items they offer. Nutritional concerns are now important to many guests and must therefore be important to restaurant managers.

Apply Your Learning 12.3

Please write all answers on a separate sheet of paper.

1. Why is proper menu planning important?

2. What five components of a property have a direct impact on what kinds of menu items can be offered?

3. What are some possible sources for selecting menu items?

4. Once the menu item pool has been narrowed down to "items guests may like," why might some of the items be eliminated?

5. What are the categories of menu items?

12.4 Menu Design

AFTER STUDYING SECTION 12.4, YOU SHOULD KNOW HOW TO:

♦ Identify the copy elements needed in menus

♦ Explain truth-in-menu laws

♦ Summarize important layout elements

♦ Describe the elements of a good cover

♦ List common menu-design mistakes

After menu items have been selected, they must be organized into a menu that encourages guests to order. A well-designed menu complements a restaurant's overall theme, blends in with the interior decor, communicates with guests, and helps sell the property and its menu items (see Exhibit 1).

How a menu is designed depends on the type of property. The menu in an elegant hotel dining room is far different from the menu offered in a nursing home cafeteria. In spite of these differences, there are many design and merchandising techniques that are nearly the same for almost all food service properties.

Menus are so crucial to a property's success that the menu planners of many independent restaurants seek the help of advertising agencies or freelance artists and designers. The menu planner should tell the designer about the restaurant's guests, show the designer the restaurant's interior, explain the number and complexity of menu items, how often the menu will be changed, what the menu should achieve, and the budget for the project. The designer can provide many creative layout ideas and educate the planner as to production costs and options. The menu planner must be careful not to let the designer take over the project, however. The designer's natural inclination to make the menu a "work of art" should not outweigh the restaurateur's own judgment about what's best for the restaurant.

Copy

After the menu planner has selected the items that will appear on the menu, copy must be written. Many properties hire a professional copywriter to write menu copy.

Just as with all the other menu design elements, the appropriateness of menu copy depends on the property, its guests, and the meal period. Copy on children's menus should be entertaining; copy on lunch menus, brief and to the point. Copy on dinner menus can be more descriptive because guests are more likely to have the time and inclination to read menu copy and take time in selecting menu items.

Menu copy can be divided into three elements: headings, descriptive copy for menu items, and supplemental merchandising copy.

**Exhibit 1
Sample Theme Restaurant Menu**

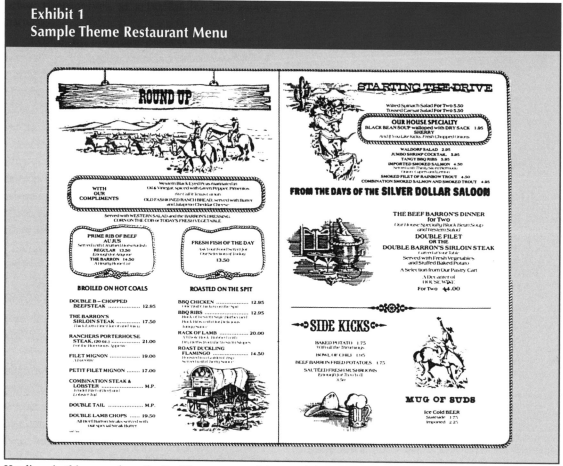

Headings in this menu from the Beef Barron are reminiscent of the Old West. Line drawings and the lariats circling important dishes reinforce the Western theme. (Courtesy of Hilton Hotels Corporation)

Headings. Headings include major heads, subheads, and names of menu items. Major heads usually identify courses: "Appetizers," "Soups," "Entrées," etc. Subheads under the main heading "Entrée" could be "Steak," "Seafood," and "Today's Specials."

Menu item names must be chosen with care. Some properties choose simple descriptive names for their menu items. Others choose more elaborate names. For most properties it's best to keep menu item names simple so that guests are not confused.

If menu item names are in a foreign language, a simple description of the item in English will help guests who do not know the language and it may increase sales of the item. On the other hand, if many of your guests do not speak English, pictures of the menu items may be helpful.

Descriptive Copy. Descriptive menu copy informs guests about menu items and helps increase sales. The menu item's main ingredient, important secondary ingredients, and

Exhibit 2
Ten Commandments of Menu Writing

1. **Extol the virtues, but avoid the puffery.** Descriptions should appeal to the guest's sense of taste, smell, feel, and sight, while extolling the virtues of the dish with words like *savory*, *mouth-watering*, and *succulent*. The descriptions should not create unrealistic expectations; customers are often skeptical of clichés like *excellent*, *classic*, and *the best*.

2. **Highlight the inspiration or origin of the meal.** Christening the dish with the name of a country adds to the allure of the dish, while the selections are backed up with well-supported explanations such as "seasoned with Indian spices, cilantro, tomato yogurt curry, and served with mango chutney."

3. **Mention the source or supplier of the ingredients.** When the source is symbolic of superior quality or identified with a local grower, it adds another dimension to the meal. Would you rather have pancakes with syrup or pancakes with *Vermont maple* syrup?

4. **Sell the sizzle: Describe the method of cooking.** Sizzle and adventure sell—the method of cooking conveys a visual image of the dish being prepared *(skillet-seared, blast-fried, slowly simmered)* and creates excitement, action, and vicarious involvement.

5. **Emphasize a positive welcoming message.** The guest's dining room experience can be made a little more personal with a short welcoming message from the manager or chef about the style of cooking or the restaurant's history.

6. **Say it in words we all understand.** Menus should be written in words that everyone understands—a guest shouldn't need a translator. If necessary, provide English translations or pronunciations alongside the native names.

7. **Highlight the appealing seasonings, flavors, aromas, and textures.** Dramatize the menu by describing the flavors and nuances of a dish. Sauces, for example, just don't *accompany*—they *embellish, adorn,* and *invigorate;* vegetables are *garden fresh, vine-ripened,* and *sun-drenched;* and spicy dishes are *pungent, incendiary,* and *volcanic.*

8. **Avoid topical references and trendy slang.** References to current movies, celebrities, political leaders, or sports heroes can often leave customers scratching their heads when those memories recede. For this reason, those references should be well thought out.

9. **Shine a spotlight on your "signature" dishes.** Draw attention to dishes that keep bringing guests back—enclose them in a box, preface them with stars, or place them at the top of the page. Adding the chef's name (Lulu's Sizzlin' Fajitas) also makes a statement.

10. **Keep it short, simple, and sweet.** This does not contradict any of the other commandments. It simply implies that the words should be fresh, well-chosen, full of flavor, and satisfying to both the customer and the chef. Long passages or winding descriptions are apt to go unread.

Adapted from *"A Guide to Good Menu Writing,"* Writing Market-Driven Menus, (Alexandria, VA: Club Managers Association of America, 1996), pp. 3–7.

method of preparation are often included in descriptive copy. The description should not be a recipe, though.

Flowery language, too many superlatives, and long sentences can turn guests off. Claims should be believable and made in short, easy-to-read sentences. A few well-chosen words are better than a long-winded paragraph. Exhibit 2 lists "ten commandments" for menu writing.

Many variables determine when to use descriptive copy. Most entrées are high-profit items and they usually get the most copy. Specialties of the house deserve extra copy, since they help define a property's character and appeal. Fancy appetizers and desserts, entrée-type salads, and wines are examples of other menu items that need descriptive copy. If an item's name is not very descriptive, more copy may be needed to explain the item. There should be no description when the item—"Low-Fat Milk," for example—is self-explanatory.

Truth-in-menu laws. One of the reasons that descriptive copy should not oversell a menu item is that it leads to disappointed guests. Another reason is that overselling can involve exaggerated claims that may be in violation of truth-in-menu laws. Some areas to be careful about include:

- *Grading.* If it is stated on the menu that a steak is USDA prime, then the steak served must be of that grade. Or if the copy says sirloin tips, then an inferior cut of meat cannot be substituted. Some foods are graded by size, and any size claims must be in line with official standards. If the menu says jumbo shrimp, for example, the item served must be jumbo shrimp, not extra large or large.

- *"Freshness" claims.* If the menu says an item is "fresh," then it cannot be canned, frozen, or "fresh-frozen."

- *Geographical origin.* You cannot make false claims about the geographical origin of a product. Cheese from Wisconsin cannot be sold as "imported Swiss cheese"; you cannot indicate "Gulf shrimp" when the product is actually Pacific Ocean shrimp.

- *Preparation.* The copy must be accurate in regard to menu item preparation. Senior citizens, dieters, and other health-conscious guests are especially concerned about how menu items are prepared. If the menu says the item is baked, it cannot be fried instead.

- *Dietary or nutrition claims.* Do not make dietary or nutrition claims that are insupportable by scientific data.

Supplemental Merchandising Copy. Supplemental merchandising copy is copy on the menu that is devoted to subjects other than the menu items. Supplemental merchandising copy includes basic information: address, telephone number, days and hours of operation, meals served, reservations and payment policies, etc. But supplemental merchandising copy can also be entertaining: a history of the restaurant, a statement about management's commitment to guest service, or even poetry. Many food service properties have a special feature, service, history, character, or locale that can make for interesting copy if handled well. Such copy can enhance a property's image and help make it stand out from competitors.

How much supplemental merchandising copy is used depends on the menu space that's available and management's ideas about whether more copy or something else—more artwork, for example—is the way to encourage sales.

Layout

Once menu copy has been written, the menu must be organized into a layout—a rough sketch of how the finished menu will look. Coming up with a layout includes listing menu items in the right sequence, placing the menu items' names and descriptive copy (if any) on the page(s), determining the menu's format, choosing the right typeface and the right paper, and integrating artwork into the menu.

Sequence. A meal has a beginning, middle, and an end, and menu items should be placed on the menu to follow this order: appetizers and soups listed first, entrées next, and desserts last. How other menu items are placed—side orders, salads, sandwiches, beverages, and so on—will depend on the property and the meal period. Salads may be listed with the entrées at lunch and with the appetizers at dinner. Alcoholic beverages are not listed at all on breakfast menus but may be listed first on dinner menus.

What order the various appetizers, entrées, etc., are placed in is usually determined by popularity and profitability. Those items that are most popular or are most profitable are typically listed first so guests can find them easily. The least popular or profitable items are usually listed last. Of course, this is not an unbreakable rule. There are many other ways to draw attention to a menu item besides putting it at the head of a list. Some designers may choose to draw a box around a high-profit item, place it in the center of a page, position eye-catching artwork next to it, or otherwise set it apart.

Placement. Once menu items have been placed in a tentative order, designers can draw a rough sketch of the menu, with boxes or a series of horizontal lines to represent the approximate space the descriptive copy for each menu item will take up. Room must also be set aside for supplemental merchandising copy.

Some designers may already know what kinds of artwork—drawings, borders, photos, etc.—they want to include on the menu. If so, space should be allowed for these elements as well. Designers should be careful, however, not to make the menu too crowded. Most designers favor a generous use of white space—blank areas not covered by words or artwork.

If a property uses a clip-on regularly, then blank space should be provided for it on the regular menu because many guests won't lift up a clip-on to see what is printed underneath.

Format. Once a rough sketch of the menu is completed, planners can get an idea of what format will be most appropriate.

"Format" refers to a menu's size, shape, and general makeup. There are many menu formats to choose from (see Exhibit 3). There is no one "correct" format; decision makers at each property must decide what's right for them. There are a few general guidelines to keep in mind, however. A menu that is too large may dominate a small table or cause guests to knock over glasses when they pick it up—it may even catch fire if there is a candle centerpiece! Menus that are too small are hard to read and are often overcrowded. Menus with too many pages may confuse guests.

Some adjustments may have to be made when working out the size and format of the menu. If there are too many menu items for the format chosen, the restaurateur has many options, including:

- dropping some menu items
- trimming back some of the descriptive copy
- dropping some of the supplemental merchandising copy
- going to a format that provides more space

If there are not enough menu items to fill up the space, options include:

- adding more menu items
- using the extra room for artwork or white space
- going to a different format

Typeface. At this point, the typeface—the style of the menu's printed letters—should be chosen. Some properties that want to project an informal and relaxed image use

Exhibit 3
Menu Formats

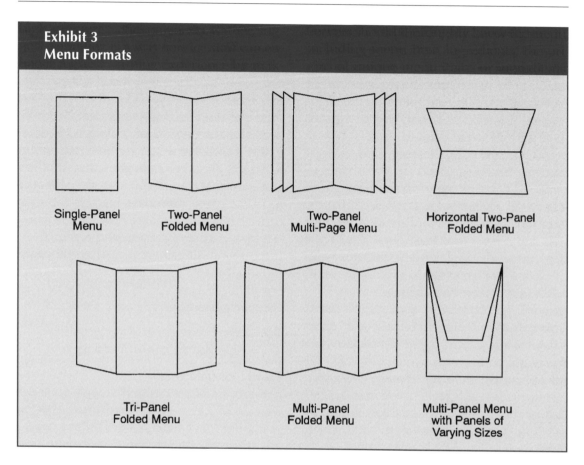

Single-Panel
Menu

Two-Panel
Folded Menu

Two-Panel
Multi-Page Menu

Horizontal Two-Panel
Folded Menu

Tri-Panel
Folded Menu

Multi-Panel
Folded Menu

Multi-Panel Menu
with Panels of
Varying Sizes

hand-lettered menus. Most menus, however, are printed. How well guests can read the menu is determined to a large extent by the typeface used.

- Since type comes in various sizes, a good general rule is to never set menu copy in type that is smaller than 12-point.

- Lines of type should not be set too close together; that is, there should be a comfortable amount of space between the lines.

- In general, type should be a dark color printed on light-colored paper for easy reading. Wise menu designers take into account the fact that lighting in restaurant dining rooms is usually much dimmer than in office work areas where menus are designed.

- Menu planners should remember that it is easier to read a combination of uppercase and lowercase letters rather than all capitals. Headings, menu item names, and copy that needs special emphasis should be the only copy in all uppercase letters.

- Each typeface has its own personality. Some type has a dark and heavy appearance on the page; other typefaces have an open and light feeling. Although the typeface chosen should reflect the property's personality, the bottom line is that the typeface must communicate. If a strange, hard-to-read typeface is chosen, guests will react negatively and sales may suffer.

After the typeface is chosen and type-set, a page proof of the menu should be made to see how the type looks. A page proof is a copy of the page as it will look when printed. At this point more adjustments may have to be made. If the menu appears too crowded, for example, the designer may choose to enlarge the menu, use a different typeface, or stay with the same typeface but go to a smaller point size. After the designer decides what changes to make, a new page proof should be checked to make sure the changes solved the problems.

Artwork. As mentioned earlier, artwork includes drawings, photographs, decorative patterns, and borders that are used to attract interest, highlight menu copy, or re-inforce the property's image. If artwork will be included on the menu, the artwork should fit in with the interior design or over-all decorative scheme of the restaurant. Artwork should not be so plentiful or com-plicated that the guest is overwhelmed or the menu is difficult to read. A cluttered, confusing menu is not inviting to guests and makes ordering difficult.

A freelance artist, or artists at the de-sign house or advertising agency in charge of designing the menu, can create original art for the menu. An inexpensive alterna-tive is to acquire CD-Roms or books that include graphics and illustrations in the public domain that can be copied by print-ers. A restaurant with an Early American theme may find an inexpensive source of art for its menu in old prints, woodcuts, or engravings.

The more artwork involved, the harder (and costlier) it is to put the menu together. The cost of reproducing artwork goes up if you want the artwork to appear in a differ-ent color than other menu elements. One way to make artwork more cost-effective is to use it elsewhere—on postcards, newslet-ters, guest checks, napkins, posters, and matchbooks.

Paper. A menu is something that is touched and held. The kind of paper the menu is printed on communicates something about the property to guests. An upscale property's menu may be printed on expen-sive textured paper. A deli may use a single sheet of ordinary typing paper for its menu.

There are many different kinds of pa-per. The texture of paper can vary from coarse to silky smooth. Paper varies in how shiny or reflective it is. Too much reflection causes glare and makes reading the menu difficult. Paper also differs in strength, opac-ity (the amount of transparency), and ink receptivity. And, of course, paper comes in every color imaginable—menus do not have to be printed on white paper.

Many interesting things can be done with the paper the menu is printed on. A menu's pages can be foil-stamped (a thin foil film applied onto the paper), embossed (an image can be stamped on the paper), laminated (sealed in thin sheets of plastic to protect them from stains and tears), or folded and die-cut for interesting designs. As mentioned earlier, children's menus often come in unusual shapes and may even include pop-up art.

The right paper for the menu depends in part on how often the menu will be used. If the menu is only used for one day and thrown away, it can be printed on inexpensive paper. However, if, as in most cases, the menu must last for a while, a water-resistant paper should be chosen that can stand up to rough usage.

The entire menu doesn't have to be printed on the same kind of paper. The cover can be a heavier, coated paper stock while the inside pages can be lighter and more inexpensive.

Cover

A well-designed cover communicates the image, style, cuisine, and even the price range of the property. It helps set the mood and creates expectations of the dining experience to come.

The name of the restaurant is all the copy the cover needs. Some menus also include basic information on the cover, such as the property's address, phone number, and hours of operation, but as a rule covers should not appear cluttered. Basic information may be better placed on the back cover. The back cover may be the place for other supplemental merchandising copy—the history of the restaurant, banquet information, take-out service information, and so on.

For most restaurants, cover stock should be heavy, durable, and grease-resistant (or laminated). The cover's design must be suitable to your property. If the restaurant looks like an English pub, the cover should match this decor; a steakhouse's cover may have images of the Old West.

The colors on the cover should either blend in or contrast pleasantly with the color scheme of the restaurant. Colors must be chosen with care, because colors produce many conscious and subconscious effects. Colors can make people feel happy, sad, cold, hot, and so on. Pastel colors suggest a warm, soothing atmosphere; deep purples and reds suggest richness and opulence.

Ethnic menus often have colors appropriate to the culture the food comes from. Bright reds, yellows, and oranges against a sand-colored paper suggest Mexico; black and red suggest Japanese or Chinese food; the colors of the Italian flag—red, white, and green—are often used on menus in Italian restaurants.

Color may also be used on the interior pages. Color can be used in the background, as trim, or in artwork to create a mood or draw the guest's eye to specific items.

Color gives the menu variety, but cost increases as colors are added. The more colors you print on the cover (and in the interior), the more expensive the menu will be. Using one color—usually black—is the least expensive; four-color printing gives you all the colors in the spectrum and is the most expensive.

Common Menu-Design Mistakes

Common menu-design mistakes include the following:

- *Menu is too small.* Crowded menus are usually not very appealing and do not do as good a selling job because they're harder to read.

- *Type is too small.* Not every guest has 20/20 vision, and lighting in some dining rooms is quite dim. Guests can't order what they can't read.

- *No descriptive copy.* Sometimes the name of the menu item is not enough to go on or does not do a good job of sparking guest interest. Good descriptive copy increases sales.

- *Every item treated the same.* A menu designer should use positioning, boxes, color, decorative borders, larger type, or some other device to call attention to the most profitable or best-selling items. If every menu item gets a low-key treatment, or if every item is in bold capital letters surrounded by exclamation points, the items you want to sell the most do not stand out from the rest.

- *Some of the property's food and beverages are not listed.* Some properties do not list all of the wines or specialty drinks they offer, or they have a line like "Selected Desserts" rather than a complete listing of the desserts they sell. How can guests order items that are not on the menu?

- *Clip-on problems.* Properties that regularly use a clip-on should allow blank space for it on the menu so the clip-on does not hide important menu items. The clip-on itself should match the design and quality of the menu. A disorganized clip-on poorly printed on cheap paper can destroy the effect of a well-designed and expensive menu.

- *Basic information about the property and its policies is not included.* It's surprising how many restaurants do not include their address, phone number, hours of operation, payment policies, etc., on the menu.

- *Blank pages.* A blank menu page is a page that does nothing to sell the restaurant or its menu items. The back cover is the page that is left blank on many menus. Unless a blank back cover adds to the restaurant's image, there's nothing wrong with putting additional menu items or supplemental merchandising copy there. For example, a seafood restaurant can devote its back cover to listing the types of fish it serves and their unique flavor and texture characteristics.

Apply Your Learning 12.4

Please write all answers on a separate sheet of paper.

1. What are the elements of layout that should be considered when designing menus?
2. What are the copy elements needed for menus?
3. What are some of the areas to be careful in regarding truth-in-menu laws?

For statements 4–8, write whether the answer is True or False.

4. The name of the restaurant is all the copy the menu cover needs.
5. Deep purple and red colors on a menu cover suggest a warm, soothing atmosphere.
6. Blank menu pages are an important part of a menu.

12.5 Menu Pricing

AFTER STUDYING SECTION 12.5, YOU SHOULD KNOW HOW TO:

♦ List subjective pricing methods

♦ Calculate prices using simple pricing methods

♦ Calculate prices using the contribution margin pricing method

♦ Calculate prices using the simple prime costs pricing method

An important part of menu planning is to determine at what price menu items will be sold. A variety of approaches are taken at each establishment, based on the individual menu items. The price must take into account the property's profit and the value that guests expect from the entire dining experience (including service, cleanliness, and ambience). Pricing approaches examined in this section are:

• Subjective pricing methods

• Simple mark-up pricing methods

• Contribution margin pricing methods

• Simple prime cost pricing methods

For the sake of illustration, we will follow the pricing decisions made by four fictitious managers: Sabrina, Felix, Amber, and Valentine. All of them are preparing a new menu for the family dining outlet at their mid-price hotel.

Subjective Pricing Methods

Sabrina uses **subjective pricing methods**. She believes that intuition and special knowledge about guests' ability to pay are the most important considerations. She uses the following pricing methods to determine what prices should be. All of them are based on her assumptions or guesses about what prices should be.

The Reasonable Price Method. This method uses a price that the food service manager thinks will represent a value to the guest. So when Sabrina was trying to determine prices for the appetizers on the menu, she asked herself, "If I were a guest, what price would I pay for this item?" Sabrina's best guess becomes the product's selling price.

The Highest Price Method. Using this plan, Sabrina sets the highest prices that she thinks guests are willing to pay.

The Loss Leader Method. With this plan, an unusually low price is set for an item (or items). Sabrina uses this method to set a price for the restaurant's specialty coffee drinks. She assumes that guests will be attracted to the property to purchase the low-priced item(s) and that they will then select other items while they are there. However, purchases of these other items is necessary for the restaurant to make the profit the hotel expects it to produce. This pricing method is sometimes used as an "early bird" or senior citizen discount to attract specific segments of the market.

The Intuitive Price Method. The manager takes a guess about the selling price. The intuitive price method differs from the reasonable price method in that there is less effort to determine what represents value from the guest's perspective.

Using these methods, Sabrina will have to draw upon her interaction with guests, experience in food service, and her own good judgment. It is likely she will have to change menu prices several times as she tracks which prices are successful in meeting the restaurant's goals.

Simple Mark-Up Pricing Methods

Some pricing methods consider a mark-up from cost of goods sold (for example, food costs for menu items). The mark-up is designed to cover all costs and to yield the desired profit. The desired profit is typically set by the property management to meet budget revenue projections.

Felix has budgeted for his restaurant to return a profit of $500,000 this year. In order to meet this profit, he reviews the volume of business that is forecast for the upcoming year. He then determines the food cost percentage he needs to achieve. (Food cost is the actual cost of producing food items. Food cost percentage is the percent of total food sales that the food cost represents. So if the restaurant sells $1,000 of food during the day and spent $450 to make the food, it's food cost percentage would be 45 percent). Felix decides that he needs to have a 40 percent food cost to meet his budget goals.

There are several simple mark-up pricing methods that Felix could use to set menu prices:

- Ingredients mark-up pricing
- Prime ingredient mark-up pricing
- Mark-up with accompaniment costs

Ingredients Mark-Up Method. The **ingredients mark-up pricing method** attempts to consider all product costs: food costs when pricing food items, and beverage costs when pricing beverages. The three steps to ingredients mark-up are as follows:

1. Determine the ingredients' costs.
2. Determine the multiplier to use in marking up the ingredients' costs.

$$\text{Multiplier} = \frac{1}{\text{Desired Food Cost Percentage}}$$

3. Establish a base selling price by multiplying the ingredients' costs by the multiplier to calculate a final selling price.

$$\text{Base Selling Price} = \text{Ingredients' Cost} \times \text{Multiplier}$$

A **base selling price** is not necessarily the final selling price. Rather, a base selling price is considered a starting point from which other factors must be assessed and the price adjusted accordingly.

The multiplier determined in step 2 is generally based on the desired food (or beverage) cost percentage (which might be established by in-house assessment procedures or from budget development). For example, Felix's desired food cost percentage is 40 percent, therefore, the multiplier would be 2.5, determined as follows:

$$\text{Multiplier} = \frac{1}{.40}$$
$$(2.5)$$

Assume a seafood platter has a standard food cost of $5.32. If a 40 percent food cost is desired, the price of the seafood platter is determined as follows:

Base Selling Price	=	Ingredients' Cost	×	Multiplier
$13.30		$5.32		2.5

If this price appears reasonable based on the market for seafood platters, then the item is sold for about $13.30.

Prime Ingredient Mark-Up Method. The **prime ingredient mark-up pricing method** differs from the ingredients mark-up method in that only the cost of the prime ingredient is marked up. Using the same seafood platter example (where lobster is the prime ingredient), assume the prime ingredient cost is $2.65. If a multiplier of 5.02 is used, the seafood platter is priced at $13.30. The price is calculated as follows:

Base Selling Price	=	Ingredients' Cost	×	Multiplier
$13.30		$2.65		5.02

If the cost of this lobster increases to $2.75, the new price would be $13.81 ($2.75 x 5.02).

The prime ingredient approach assumes that the costs of all ingredients change in proportion to the prime ingredient. That is, when the price of lobster increases 10 percent, it is assumed that all the other ingredients on the seafood platter increase 10 percent too.

Mark-Up with Accompaniment Costs. Using the **mark-up with accompaniment costs pricing method**, Felix would determine ingredient costs based only on entrée items and then add a standard accompaniment (or "plate") cost before multiplying by a mark-up multiplier. The **plate cost** is an average cost for all non-entrée and other relatively inexpensive items, including salad, vegetables, bread, butter, and non-alcoholic beverages. For example:

Entrée Costs	$ 3.15
Plate Cost	+ $ 1.25
Estimated Food Cost	$ 4.40
Mark-Up Multiplier	× 3.30
Base Selling Price	$ 14.52

Note that the plate cost is added to the entrée cost before the mark-up multiplier is used. An advantage of this method is its simplicity. Careful calculations for only the expensive entrée are necessary; time can be saved by combining all other food costs into an estimated plate cost. A disadvantage may be that plate costs are not truly representative of non-entrée food costs.

Contribution Margin Pricing Method

Our third manager, Amber, has decided to use the contribution margin pricing method. *Contribution margin* refers to the amount left after a menu item's food cost is subtracted from its selling price. It is the amount that the sale of a menu item "contributes" to pay for all non-food costs. Exhibit 1 lists the two steps Amber can use, with a **contribution margin pricing method**, to set base selling prices.

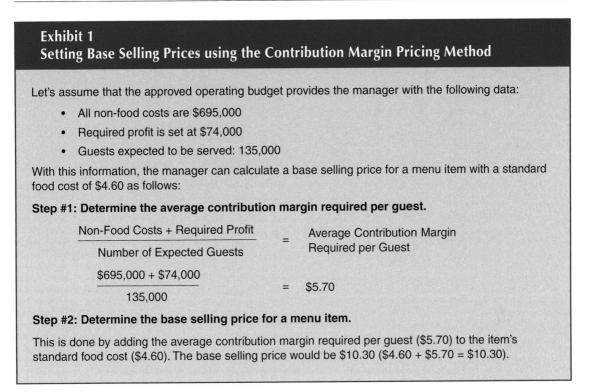

Exhibit 1
Setting Base Selling Prices using the Contribution Margin Pricing Method

Let's assume that the approved operating budget provides the manager with the following data:

- All non-food costs are $695,000
- Required profit is set at $74,000
- Guests expected to be served: 135,000

With this information, the manager can calculate a base selling price for a menu item with a standard food cost of $4.60 as follows:

Step #1: Determine the average contribution margin required per guest.

$$\frac{\text{Non-Food Costs + Required Profit}}{\text{Number of Expected Guests}} = \begin{array}{l}\text{Average Contribution Margin}\\\text{Required per Guest}\end{array}$$

$$\frac{\$695,000 + \$74,000}{135,000} = \$5.70$$

Step #2: Determine the base selling price for a menu item.

This is done by adding the average contribution margin required per guest ($5.70) to the item's standard food cost ($4.60). The base selling price would be $10.30 ($4.60 + $5.70 = $10.30).

Advantages of this method are its ease and practicality when reasonably accurate information is available from the operating budget. It is also practical when the costs associated with serving each guest are basically the same. A potential disadvantage of this method is that it assumes that each guest should pay the same share of the property's non-food costs and profit requirements.

Simple Prime Costs Pricing Method

Valentine decides that simply accounting for the costs of ingredients and food costs won't give a true picture of the costs his restaurant incurs. So he decides to use the prime costs pricing method. The term **prime costs** refers to the most significant costs in a food service property: product (food and beverage) and labor. A **simple prime costs pricing method** involves assessing the labor costs for the food service property and factoring these costs into the pricing equation. Exhibit 2 lists the three steps to simple prime costs pricing. Under this method, restaurants that have higher service costs will have higher menu prices.

Advantages of this method are its focus on both food and labor costs and the fact that it is easy to use. An obvious disadvantage is the need to assign an equal labor cost to each menu item, even though actual labor costs for menu items may vary greatly.

The **specific prime costs pricing method** attempts to overcome this problem by developing base selling prices that cover the specific menu item's fair share of labor

Exhibit 2
Calculations for Simple Prime Costs Pricing

Let's assume the food service manager has obtained the following data:

- Menu Item Food Cost: 3.75
- Labor Costs: $210,000
- Number of Expected Guests: 75,000
- Desired Prime Costs Percentage: 62%

The food cost is the standard cost derived by costing the item's standard recipe. Labor costs and estimated guests are obtained from the approved operating budget. The desired prime costs percentage combines projected food and labor cost percentages, also from the operating budget.

Step #1: Determine the labor cost per guest.

$$\text{Labor Cost per Guest} = \frac{\text{Labor Costs}}{\text{Number of Expected Guests}}$$

$$\$2.80 = \frac{\$210,000}{75,000}$$

Step #2: Determine the prime costs per guest.

Labor Cost per Guest	+	Menu Item's Food Cost	=	Prime Costs per Guest
$2.80	+	$3.75	=	$6.55

Step #3: Determine the menu item's base selling price.

$$\text{Base Selling Price} = \frac{\text{Prime Costs per Guest}}{\text{Desired Prime Costs Percentage}}$$

$$\$10.56 = \frac{\$6.55}{.62}$$

The food service manager would then adjust this base selling price in relation to other factors, such as the property's target markets and the competition.

costs. With this method, managers assign higher mark-ups to menu items requiring extensive preparation (and therefore having higher labor costs); conversely, items not requiring extensive preparation have lower labor costs that can be reflected in a lower mark-up.

Apply Your Learning 12.5

1. What are the four subjective pricing methods?

2. What are the three simple pricing methods mentioned in this chapter?

3. What is a base selling price?

4. The plate cost is an average cost for all non-entrée items, including salad, vegetables, bread, butter, and non-alcoholic beverages. In which of the following pricing methods is this important?

    a. prime ingredient mark-up
    b. contribution margin
    c. simple prime costs
    d. mark-up with accompaniment costs

5. Christine is the manager at the LaBella Restaurant. In order to draw more people into the restaurant, she sets the price of their specialty appetizer unusually low, hoping that once there the guests will order other, more expensive items. Which of the following subjective pricing methods is Christine using?

    a. reasonable price
    b. highest price
    c. loss leader
    d. intuitive price

Quick Hits

Chapter 12

SECTION 12.1—MENU STYLES AND SCHEDULES

- The menu dictates much about how your property will be organized and managed, the extent to which it will meet its goals, and even how the building itself should be designed and constructed.

- For guests, the menu lists available foods, communicates the property's image, and contributes to the overall dining experience.

- For production employees, the menu dictates what foods must be prepared.

- For managers, the menu is the chief in-house marketing and sales tool. It has an impact on almost every aspect of a food service property.

- The three types of menu pricing styles are table d'hôte, à la carte, and combination table d'hôte/à la carte. A table d'hôte menu offers a complete meal for one price. With an à la carte menu, food and beverage items are listed and priced separately.

- Menus can be categorized by how often they are used. Some properties have a **fixed menu**—a single menu that is used daily. Other properties use a **cycle menu**—one that changes every day for a certain period of days, then the cycle is repeated.

SECTION 12.2—MENU TYPES

- Three basic types of menus are breakfast, lunch, and dinner menus. Specialty menus appeal to a specific guest group or meet a specific marketing need.

- Breakfast menus typically offer fruits, juices, eggs, cereals, pancakes, waffles, and breakfast meats like bacon and sausage. The watchwords for breakfast menu items are "simple," "fast," and "inexpensive."

- Since lunch guests are usually in a hurry, lunch menus must feature menu items that are relatively easy and quick to make, such as sandwiches, soups, and salads. Lunch menu items are usually lighter and less elaborate than dinner menu items.

- Dinner is the main meal of the day for most people. Steaks, roasts, chicken, seafood, and pasta dishes like lasagna and linguine are typical dinner entrées. Wines, cocktails, and exotic desserts are more likely to be on a dinner menu than on a lunch menu.

- Common specialty menus include children's, senior citizens', alcoholic beverage, dessert, room service, take-out, banquet, California, and ethnic.

SECTION 12.3—MENU PLANNING

- When the menu has been properly planned, work will flow more smoothly, guests will be served more effectively, and profits will be greater.

- Planning a menu is a complex undertaking that requires a knowledge of the entire property.

- The quality of all the decisions about the menu depends on knowing your guests well. Guest preferences are learned by interviewing guests; reading surveys, comment cards, and trade journals; and studying production and sales records.

- The type of property helps determine what kinds of menu items are appropriate. At least five components of a property have a direct impact on what kinds of menu items can be offered: theme or cuisine; equipment; personnel; quality standards; and budget.

- Menu planners create a pool of possible menu items from many sources, including old menus, books, trade magazines, and cookbooks for the home market.

- The menu items listed on a menu can be categorized as appetizers, salads, entrées, starch items, vegetables, desserts, and beverages.

- Once all the menu items have been selected for the menu, the menu should be reviewed for business, aesthetic, and nutritional balance.

- **Business balance** refers to the balance between food costs, menu prices, the popularity of items, and other financial and marketing considerations.

- **Aesthetic balance** refers to the degree to which meals have been constructed with an eye to the colors, textures, and flavors of foods.

- **Nutritional balance** refers to the fact that managers should make sure the components of a well-balanced meal are available from among the menu items they offer.

SECTION 12.4—MENU DESIGN

- A well-designed menu complements a restaurant's overall theme, blends in with the interior decor, communicates with guests, and helps sell the property and its menu items.

- Menu copy can be divided into three elements: headings, descriptive copy for menu items, and supplemental merchandising copy.

- Descriptive copy should not oversell a menu item; exaggerated claims may be in violation of truth-in-menu laws.

- Creating a menu layout includes listing menu items in the right sequence, placing the menu items' names and descriptive copy on the page, determining the menu's format, choosing the right typeface and the right paper, and integrating artwork into the menu.

- *Sequence* refers to how menu items should be placed on the menu. They should follow this order: appetizers and soups listed first, entrées next, and desserts last.

- *Format* refers to a menu's size, shape, and general makeup. There is no one "correct" format.

- If artwork will be included, it should fit in with the interior design or overall decorative scheme of the restaurant.

- A well-designed cover communicates the image, style, cuisine, and even the price range of the property. It helps set the mood and creates expectations of the dining experience to come.

- Common menu-design mistakes include the following: menu is too small, type is too small, no descriptive copy, every item treated the same, some of the property's food and beverages are not listed, clip-on problems, basic information about the property and its policies is not included, and blank pages.

SECTION 12.5—MENU PRICING

- The most important considerations when using **subjective pricing methods** are intuition and special knowledge about guests' ability to pay. These pricing methods include the reasonable price method, the highest price method, the loss leader method, and the intuitive price method.

- The **reasonable price method** uses a price that the food service manager thinks will represent a value to the guest ("If I were a guest, what price would I pay for this item?").

- The **highest price method** sets the highest prices that a manager thinks guests are willing to pay.

- The **loss leader method** sets an unusually low price for an item (or items), assuming that guests will be attracted to the property and that they will then select other items while they are there.

- Using the **intuitive price method**, managers take a guess about the selling price, drawing upon their interaction with guests, experiences in food service, and their own good judgment.

- **Simple mark-up pricing methods** consider a mark-up from cost of goods sold. The mark-up is designed to cover all costs and to yield the desired profit. These methods include ingredients mark-up pricing, prime-ingredient mark-up pricing, and mark-up with accompaniment costs.

- The **ingredients mark-up pricing method** attempts to consider all product costs: food costs when pricing food items, and beverage costs when pricing beverages.

- A **base selling price** is a starting point from which other factors must be assessed and the price adjusted accordingly.

- The **prime ingredient mark-up pricing method** differs from the ingredients mark-up method in that only the cost of the prime ingredient is marked up.

- Using the **mark-up with accompaniment costs pricing method**, managers determine ingredient costs based only on entrée items and then add a standard accompaniment (or "plate") cost before multiplying by a mark-up multiplier. The **plate cost** is an average cost for all non-entrée and other relatively inexpensive items, including salad, vegetables, bread, butter, and non-alcoholic beverages.

- The **contribution margin pricing method** refers to the amount left after a menu item's food cost is subtracted from its selling price. It is the amount that the sale of a menu item "contributes" to pay for all non-food costs.

- The term **prime costs** refers to the most significant costs in a food service property: product (food and beverage) and labor. A **simple prime costs pricing method** involves assessing the labor costs for the food service property and factoring these costs into the pricing equation. The **specific prime costs pricing method** assigns higher mark-ups to menu items requiring extensive preparation (and therefore having higher labor costs).

Profile

Dixie Eng
General Manager, Hilton Washington Embassy Row, Washington, DC

Dixie Eng knows a lot of juicy gossip about the stars who stayed at Washington, D.C. Bristol Hotel when she was concierge there. But the secrets of Tom Cruise, Cher, and Jack Lemmon are safe with her.

"One of the secrets of a good concierge is that we never tell," says Eng. "I had access to so much personal and juicy gossip, but a good hotelier protects the privacy of the guest."

Eng has been taking care of guests for 20 years, beginning her hospitality career in the guest services division of the Key Bridge Marriott, where she became known as "Miss Hospitality." With her flair for guest relations, she soon became a concierge, working for several Washington, DC, hotels and earning membership in the prestigious Les Clefs d'Or organization.

In 1984, Eng was asked to join the pre-opening team for the Bristol Hotel, which became known as the "Hollywood Hotel" for celebrities visiting Washington. During her six years at the Bristol, Eng held the positions of head concierge, rooms division manager, and sales manager.

From 1991 to 1996, Eng was general manager of the New Hampshire Suites Hotel, where her skills in marketing and sales increased the property's profits and earned her team the 1994 Paul Whetsell Exceeding Expectations Award. In 1996, she became general manager of The Latham Hotel.

Currently, Eng is general manager of the Hilton Washington Embassy Row, where she has served many years before as a concierge. She is active in many hotel industry organizations, including the Hotel Association of Washington, DC, which she has chaired since 1997, and the Network of Executive Women in Hospitality, which honored her with its 1999 Joyce L. Johnson Woman of Excellence Award.

Eng encourages young people to try hospitality, because they will learn valuable skills for whatever career they choose.

"Hospitality provides one with a great foundation in customer service. This is a great career to build your people skills, which are useful in all fields," she notes.

For Eng, no other job can compare to the "magic of making the positive difference in the guest experience.

"There is something electric, something magnetic about the hospitality field," she states. "Sometime in our career, all hospitality professionals say that we will try something else, but we always come back. I think that says it all."

Dining and Beverage Service

Sections

13.1 Dining Service Staff Positions

13.2 Dining Service Styles and Procedures

13.3 Providing Superior Service

13.4 Responsible Beverage Service

13.1 Dining Service Staff Positions

AFTER STUDYING SECTION 13.1, YOU SHOULD BE ABLE TO:

♦ List typical dining service staff positions

♦ Describe the work performed by servers

♦ Describe the work performed by buspersons

♦ Describe the work performed by hosts

♦ Describe the work performed by cashiers

♦ Describe the work performed by dining room managers

In a table-service restaurant, a guest's full enjoyment of the food and beverages depends in large part on the quality and style of service. Food service managers choose the service style and level of service that is appropriate for their types of food service operations and their guests. Different table-service styles require different types of service staff positions.

Standard titles for dining service staff positions do not exist. Which titles are used depends on the food service operation's type of service and degree of formality, as well as management's preferences.

Server

In many restaurants, servers perform the bulk of the food and beverage serving duties, assisted by buspersons. Depending on the food service operation, servers may greet and seat guests, take their food and beverage orders, bring the ordered items to the table, check back with guests to make sure everything is satisfactory, present the guest check for payment, take the check to a cashier, return change to the guest, thank the guest, and clear tables. Managers sometimes require servers to also help with such minor food preparation tasks as adding dressings to salads, portioning soups, and dishing up desserts.

Servers must also perform **sidework**—service-related but non-guest-contact tasks such as making coffee, refilling condiment containers, and restocking side stations with service supplies. Servers must work quickly yet carefully. They must be able to do several things during one trip through the dining area, such as carry food to one table, present a guest check to another, and remove used dishes from a third. Exhibit 1 is a typical job description for a server in an operation that uses plate service (plate service will be discussed later in the chapter).

Exhibit 1
Sample Position Description: Server

Position Title: Server

Reports to: Dining Room Manager

Tasks:

1. Greets guests and presents them with the menu; informs guests of specials and menu changes; makes suggestions and answers questions regarding food, beverages, and service.

2. Takes food and beverage orders from guests (by either writing them down or memorizing them) and relays orders to kitchen staff and the bartender as appropriate.

3. Ensures that all food and beverage items are prepared properly and on a timely basis; communicates with the host, buspersons, kitchen staff, and the bartender; and coordinates his or her assigned station to ensure guest satisfaction with the food and beverage products and service.

4. Serves courses from kitchen and service areas promptly, garnishes menu items prior to serving them, and properly presents them.

5. Observes guests to ensure their satisfaction with the food and service, to respond to any additional requests, and to determine when the meal has been completed.

6. Totals guest bills and accepts payments or refers guests to the cashier or host as appropriate.

7. Assists buspersons with stocking side stations, removing soiled dishes and flatware from tables at the conclusion of each course, transporting soiled items to the dishwashing area, and cleaning and resetting vacated tables.

Prerequisites:

Education: High school graduate or equivalent; must be able to speak, read, write, and understand the primary language(s) of the work location; must be able to speakand understand the primary language(s) of the guests who typically visit the restaurant; must be able to perform simple mathematical calculations.

Experience: Should have first-hand knowledge of the sequence of service and basic dining room procedures; experience as a busperson helpful; must be guest-sensitive and possess a sense of timing to serve different courses at the proper time.

Physical: Must be able to move quickly and stand for periods of up to four (4) hours; must have a good sense of balance and be able to lift and carry trays and bus tubs that frequently weigh up to 25 pounds.

Busperson

Buspersons perform a wide array of tasks designed to help servers provide better service to guests. The primary duty of a busperson is to clear tables and deliver soiled dishware, glassware, and flatware to the dishwashing room. It is also common for buspersons to perform some or all of the following tasks:

- Clean tables and chairs (including highchairs and booster chairs)

- Reset tables with fresh linens, clean serviceware, and glasses

- Pour water and refill coffee and tea cups

- Take bread and butter, chips, or popcorn to tables

- Serve food and beverages during busy periods

- Perform preopening duties such as setting tables, filling ice bins with ice, and moving tables

A busperson's closing responsibilities might include the following:

- Cleaning side stations and stocking and replenishing side station supplies

- Emptying and cleaning food preparation carts

- Cleaning the coffee urn and the bread warmer

- Returning soiled linens to the laundry

If a restaurant offers tableside food preparation, buspersons may restock the food carts used for this purpose.

Host

The person who first greets guests when they arrive may be called a "receptionist," "host," "greeter," "captain," or "dining room manager," depending on the extent of his or her responsibilities. (Some restaurants use the term "hostess" for a female host, but "host" is acceptable for both men and women.) If the food service operation also has a dining room manager, the host's responsibilities usually are limited to welcoming guests, confirming the number of guests in a party, leading guests to the appropriate section of the restaurant, and providing menus. (If the operation does not have a dining room manager, the host usu-

ally will perform many of the duties described in the "dining room manager" section coming up.) Hosts may ask guests if they have seating preferences before choosing tables for them. The host is usually responsible for thanking departing guests and inviting them to return.

Cashier

A cashier collects payments of guest checks from servers or guests. Cashiers must follow income control procedures at all times and must accurately account for all transactions, collections, and disbursements. Cashiers who have guest-contact duties should be friendly and courteous. A cashier's responsibilities may overlap with those of a host, particularly the responsibility for thanking departing guests.

Dining Room Manager

The manager in charge of dining room service has a wide variety of responsibilities and tasks that differ according to the type and size of the operation. For example, in small restaurants, the dining room manager may perform the responsibilities of host and manage the entire restaurant as well as the dining room. In large restaurants, dining room managers may have one or more hosts who report to them, and these managers in turn may report to a general manager or owner/manager who manages the restaurant as a whole—in which case the dining room manager's responsibilities are more narrowly defined and consist mainly of managing the dining room and its staff. (See Exhibit 2 for a sample job description for a dining room manager.)

Typically, dining room managers have had many years of training and experience

---

Exhibit 2
Sample Position Description: Dining Room Manager

Position Title: Dining Room Manager

Reports to: General Manager

Tasks:

1. Oversees dining area; supervises food and beverage service staff in accordance with operating policies that he or she may help establish.

2. Maintains records of staff performance and operating costs; maintains payroll and bookkeeping records.

3. Works with food and beverage staff to ensure proper food presentation and proper food-handling procedures.

4. Checks function sheets against room setup and staff member scheduling; may help design, set up for, or service functions.

5. Schedules periodic food and beverage service staff meetings to ensure correct interpretation of policies and obtain feedback from staff members.

6. Trains service staff to deliver the various types of food service.

7. Handles guest complaints.

8. Assists in planning regular and special-event menus.

9. Establishes standards, such as the amount of linen to be used in dining areas, and sets labor cost goals.

10. Reviews financial transactions and ensures that expenditures stay within budget limitations; maintains a system of cost controls while managing service and purchasing items and services.

Prerequisites:

Education: College degree in restaurant or hotel field or equivalent experience; must be able to speak, read, write, and understand the primary language(s) of the work location.

Experience: Requires experience in various phases of guest service; must possess a general knowledge of food and beverage procedures and service; must understand and possess a strong sense of cost control.

Physical: Must have the ability to lift up to 25 pounds occasionally and up to 10 pounds frequently; requires good communication skills, both oral and written.

---

and have held several dining room positions before becoming managers. While some properties do not use the "manager" designation, they always employ one or more people who perform managerial tasks.

Before the dining room opens for guest service, the dining room manager inspects the entire room and checks side stations to see that they are adequately stocked. The manager may check the number and condition of menus or may assign this duty to the host. Dining room managers also look for safety problems such as loose tabletops and wobbly chairs.

Supervising dining service staff members is a major responsibility of the dining room manager. Dining room managers assign tables or dining room sections to servers and conduct preshift meetings to inform the staff about daily specials, menu changes, and other matters of interest. During the meal period, dining room managers make certain that service flows smoothly. They must know sanitation and safety procedures and ensure that staff members follow them. After the dining room closes, dining room managers supervise staff members as they set up the room for the next day.

Apply Your Learning 13.1

Please write all answers on a separate sheet of paper.

1. Name the most common dining service staff positions.

For statements 2–6, write whether the answer is True or False.

2. Managers sometimes require servers to help with minor food preparation.

3. It is common for buspersons to provide menus to guests.

4. The host's responsibilities are limited to welcoming guests.

5. A cashier's responsibilities may overlap with those of a host.

6. A dining room manager may perform the responsibilities of host.

13.2 Dining Service Styles and Procedures

AFTER STUDYING SECTION 13.2, YOU SHOULD BE ABLE TO:

♦ Summarize the basic procedures of plate service

♦ Describe how plate service affects dining room procedures

♦ Give tips for providing plate service

♦ Define cart service

♦ Summarize how cart service is offered in food service operations

♦ Define platter service

♦ Describe how platter service affects food production and service

♦ Explain how food service operations offer family-style service

♦ Describe buffet service

♦ Summarize popular buffet service layouts

There are many variations in the procedures and techniques food service operations use to serve food to guests, but most can be categorized under one of four main styles of table service:

• Plate service
• Cart service
• Platter service
• Family-style service

Some properties offer a combination of styles.

In addition to table-service styles, buffet service is being used by an increasing number of properties, often in combination with a table-service style. Some properties give guests a choice between eating at a buffet or selecting items from the menu. Others offer a special buffet only at certain times, such as on weekends or holidays (Mother's Day, Easter, or Thanksgiving, for example). In the United States, the Sunday buffet is very popular and can represent a significant percentage of business. Buffet service is also used for some banquets.

Plate Service

Plate service (also called American service) is the most common style of table service in the United States; most U.S. restaurants use variations of this style. Managers may combine plate service with some tableside food preparation or—in less formal establishments—with self-serve soup and salad bars.

Plate service follows these basic procedures:

1. Servers take guests' orders in the dining area.

2. Kitchen staff members produce food orders, portion them, and place them on plates in the kitchen.

3. Servers place the orders on trays, sometimes using plate covers to keep foods warm and facilitate stacking, and take them to the guests. They may use tray stands (also called tray jacks) to hold the trays while they place the orders in front of guests.

4. Buspersons assist servers and clear tables.

There are variations, however. In some restaurants, servers plate some menu items and add garnishes to the plates in the kitchen before taking orders to guests. In others, servers take trolleys of desserts out to guests and, after guests have made their selections, plate the desserts at tableside in front of the guests.

Before guests arrive, staff members usually set tables with all but the plates required for the entrée, so that bread and butter plates, water and wine glasses, napkins and flatware, and other items are already on the table when guests are first seated.

Servers generally serve several tables simultaneously. The actual number depends upon how much experience the server has, the distance from his or her side station to the food pickup area, the menu itself, and the number of guests that can be seated at each of the tables in the server's assigned section (generally, for example, it is easier to serve three tables that can each seat four guests than six tables that each seat two guests, even though both sections seat 12 guests).

Well-designed, well-stocked side stations for food servers are a must for plate service. Plate service requires that servers clear each course's emptied plates and used flatware before serving the next course (unless the guest prefers otherwise). For example, if a guest has soup or salad as a first course, the server should remove the dishes and soup spoons or salad forks before serving the entrée.

Do not scrape or stack plates in front of guests. Beverage glasses should not be cleared unless the guest is first asked or the glasses are completely empty. These procedures not only show consideration for guests but also reduce the need for a large inventory of tableware, because soiled tableware can be cleaned and put back into service more quickly. These procedures also minimize the chance that guests will take home as souvenirs such items as flatware and glassware that is imprinted with the operation's logo.

Guests who desire fast service are more likely to receive it with plate service than with some of the other table-service styles. Another advantage of plate service is that it does not require servers to have as much experience and training as staff members who provide cart or platter service. Finally, plate service has low equipment costs, since it does not require elaborate serving trays, carts, or other expensive service equipment. However, plate service does not offer the flair and elegance that cart and platter service offer. Except when menus state that different portion sizes are available, plate service also makes it difficult to modify portions to meet the specific needs of guests. Exhibit 1 offers some tips for providing plate service. Exhibits 2 and 3 focus on superior service dos and don'ts.

Cart Service

Cart service (also called French service) is popular internationally, but used less

Exhibit 1
Tips for Providing Plate Service

Greeting guests

Servers should acknowledge each guest with eye contact and a warm smile. Servers should use "Sir" and "Ma'am" when greeting guests; if they know the guests, they should use the guests' titles (Doctor, Mr., or Ms.) and their surnames.

Seating guests

When seating two guests at a table for four, the two additional place settings should be removed. This both reduces soiled tableware and provides guests with more room to enjoy the dining experience.

Dining areas usually have some tables that are not as desirable as others. Seats in high-traffic aisles, next to side stations, and close to the dishwashing and kitchen areas are examples. Servers or hosts should seat guests at these tables only after all others are full. They should also know which seats are best for privacy or for a good view of the surrounding grounds. If the best seats are occupied, servers or hosts should give guests the choice of sitting at a less desirable table or waiting until a better one becomes available.

Making introductions

If the server did not seat the guests, the server should give the guests a prompt and friendly greeting once they are seated. After this initial contact, servers should introduce themselves in a friendly manner, then proceed with attentive listening and helpful suggestions.

Presenting menus

Servers or hosts should present menus open, first to women, then to men, moving around the table clockwise. Daily specials should also be discussed at this time as briefly as possible without leaving out essential information. Service staff might use this opportunity to suggest menu items to guests.

Treating children appropriately

Servers should treat children as courteously as they treat adult guests. A smile and a promise to quickly bring a complimentary appetizer to the table go a long way toward beginning the dining experience well. If the property does not offer crackers, bread, or some other complimentary snack items for a party that has children, the server might ask the adults at the table whether it would be acceptable to serve the children first. If they welcome this idea, the server should try to expedite the production and service of the children's orders. Servers should also attempt to involve the children in the conversation. When children feel welcome and satisfied, so do their parents and other family members.

Checking quality

Because they perform the final quality control check of menu items before they are served, servers should be trained to recognize acceptable quality. Food quality can be judged by appearance; the appearance of foods should always match the pictures and descriptions of the items on the menu. The sizes and shapes of foods also contribute to their appearance. Broken, misshapen, or ragged vegetables, for example, can destroy the appearance of an entire plate of food.

The neatness of the food presentation also makes a statement about the property's standards. Food items should not be crowded on the plate or hanging over the edge. Liquid foods should not spill

(Continued)

Exhibit 1 *(continued)*
Tips for Providing Plate Service

or run over the edges of tableware. If two foods with sauces are to be served at the same time, one should be served in a side dish. If a menu item is served with a thin sauce, the sauce should be served in a side dish.

The textures and consistencies of food products are also important components of quality. Dried-out bakery products, broken bread sticks and crackers, wilted salads, lumpy gravies and puddings, and runny custards are examples of foods of poor quality. Some properties display photographs of standard food presentations in the pickup area of the kitchen so servers can easily compare their finished orders to the photos before taking the orders out to guests.

Product temperature contributes to the overall quality of food products as well. Hot foods should be served on heated tableware, cold foods on chilled tableware. When assembling orders, servers should gather room temperature products first, then chilled foods, then hot foods.

Knowing who gets what

When presenting and serving the guests' orders, servers should make sure they know who ordered what. Many guests are irritated when a server asks, for example, "Who gets the salmon?" After the food is served, servers should make such comments as "Your prime rib looks delicious," or "The spinach pizza has a wonderful aroma," in addition to asking "May I bring you anything else right now?"

Checking in

After giving guests a chance to taste their food, the server should go back to the table and check in. Instead of asking if everything is okay, servers should ask specific questions, such as "Is the entrée cooked exactly as you like it?" Servers should be empowered to remove unacceptable menu items and return them to the kitchen for a replacement or "repair" (for example, cooking a steak a little longer for a guest who ordered a "medium" steak and received a "rare" one). When an order is returned to the kitchen for replacement, the fresh order should always be brought back to the guest's table on a fresh plate.

Anticipating guest needs

Anticipating guest needs is a hallmark of superior service. Staff members can anticipate guest needs by offering something before it is requested and filling a water glass before it is empty. Removing used water glasses when guests have finished their entrées and providing fresh water glasses with ice water is a special touch. Servers should always check for the presence of proper eating utensils and other tableware as each course is served.

Handling the guest's payment

It is a good idea for servers to stay close to the guest's table once the check has been presented, to avoid unnecessary delays in processing the check and payment. If a guest pays with a credit card, the server should refer to the guest by name when the credit card charge is returned to the table.

Ending on a positive note

Ensuring that guests leave the restaurant on a positive note is one of the fundamentals of superior service. Guests should be thanked and invited to return. Guests also are likely to remember it if a staff member opens the door for them as they are leaving.

Exhibit 2
More Ways to Provide Superior Service

1. Serve soup hot at tableside to allow guests at the table to enjoy the aromas and to encourage guests at other tables to order soup.

2. When possible, encourage undecided guests to taste a food item or beverage before they order.

3. Offer and feature daily specials that appeal to loyal, regular guests.

4. Distinctively indicate which items are vegetarian on the menu.

5. Serve bakery products at tableside that are fresh out of the oven.

6. Clearly indicate by the color of the cup or coaster who is drinking regular or decaffeinated coffee at a table. That way, whoever provides refill service will know which cup to fill with what.

7. Warm desserts (as appropriate) prior to serving them to guests.

8. Briefly meet as a service team each day to review the menu, taste menu items, and review service standards and techniques.

9. Divide and plate in the kitchen those items that guests ordered to be shared.

10. When guests are asked to wait for excessive periods for a table, issue them personal electronic pagers.

11. Offer guests complimentary beverages if waiting periods are excessive.

12. Give guests something that they do not expect (e.g., a complimentary side dish, a cookie with their ice cream) to exceed expectations.

13. Offer cordless phones for use by those who need them in the dining room. (But be certain that this does not disturb other guests.)

14. When guests request the recipe for a signature menu item, give it to them on a preprinted card that has the operation's logo on it.

15. When servers are not serving, have them check tableware, ashtrays, water glasses and coffee cups, and other items on other servers' tables that might need attention.

16. Encourage staff members and reward them for learning guests' names and preferences.

17. Train staff members in telephone-answering skills.

18. Empower staff members to delete from guest bills the charges for food or beverage items that are unacceptable to guests.

19. Tailor menu suggestions to guests' unique needs.

20. Provide the kind of service that you enjoy receiving.

Source: Adapted from "55 Ways to Super Service," *Restaurants & Institutions*, November 15, 1993.

Exhibit 3
Unacceptable Service Practices

- Greeting guests with a single-word question, such as "Two?" or "Smoking?"

- Not acknowledging waiting guests.

- Seating guests at a table with a gratuity on it.

- Answering "I'll have to find out" in response to questions about the soup or specials of the day.

- "Auctioning off" food by saying such things as, "Who ordered this lasagna?"

- Talking to guests while holding dirty plates.

- Pouring coffee from a stained pot.

Source: Adapted from Gail Bellamy, David Farkas, and John Soeder, "Sensational Service," *Restaurant Hospitality*, July 1994.

frequently in the United States. Cart service is an elaborate service style in which menu items are prepared on a cart beside guest tables by specially trained staff members; menu items are cooked—sometimes flambéed—in front of the guests. In the United States, restaurants that use cart service are generally gourmet, high-check-average properties.

Cart service costs are high for several reasons. First, service staff need enough dining area space (with wide aisles) to move preparation carts through the dining area and prepare food alongside guest tables; this reduces the number of tables and seats in the dining area, which reduces the operation's gross sales potential. Cart service incurs higher equipment costs than other kinds of service because of the extensive amount of serving and preparation equipment required. Typically, serviceware for cart service is very elegant; ornate service pieces such as silver platters are often used. Operating costs are also higher; a large number of staff members are required to serve relatively few guests, and the table turnover rate is low. To generate enough income to cover labor and other costs, food and beverage prices in properties that use cart service must reflect those costs.

It is difficult to find professionally trained service staff who understand and can follow all of the procedures required for effective tableside food preparation; cart service requires highly skilled and experienced service staff who have been formally trained.

Cart service has many special rules of courtesy, etiquette, and tradition. The impact that cart service has on facility design, staffing, and guest satisfaction is profound. The use of cart service requires a configuration of the food preparation area that dif-

fers from the configurations other service styles require. Production personnel do not handle finished, plated foods; food preparation is finished at guest tables. The service staff required for cart service usually cannot be assigned to other tasks; they must be available to use their highly specialized skills whenever guests want them. Finally, the guests who desire and pay for cart service are unlikely to accept mistakes.

Platter Service

Platter service (also called Russian service) requires servers to deliver platters of fully cooked food to the dining room, present the platters to guests for approval, and then serve the food. This type of service is featured in many of the best international restaurants and hotels; some food service properties in the United States, particularly banquet operations, also use it.

The food is prepared (and sometimes precut) by food production staff in the kitchen. They arrange the food attractively on the service platters for food servers to deliver to the dining room. Generally, service staff members use a team approach; one server carries the entrée and a second carries the accompaniments. Servers line up in the kitchen and, at the appropriate time, parade into the dining area. After presenting (showing) the food to the guests, they place the platters on side stands to keep foods warm while they position a very hot, empty dinner plate in front of each guest. Holding the platter in the left hand, the server transfers the food to guest plates by artfully manipulating a fork and spoon held in the right hand. Service proceeds in this way around the table counterclockwise.

Platter service typically calls for servers to use their discretion in portioning food for guests; the platter must retain its attractiveness until the last guest is served, and the last guest served must receive an adequate portion. In many properties, the servers circle tables twice, serving each guest each time; any food remaining on the platter must be discarded. When guests order a wide variety of items, food servers may need to bring several different platters to the table concurrently, which can cause service problems. For this reason, some properties use platter service only at banquets where all guests receive the same menu items.

Platter service can be as elegant as cart service, but it is much more practical because it is faster and less expensive. Platter service can provide a special touch and still allow managers to control labor and product costs closely. Like cart service, platter service incorporates many traditions that mean superior service for guests; it also requires professionally trained—and highly skilled—staff members. Managers who are considering adopting platter service should recognize that they will have to make a sizeable investment in service platters and plate and bowl warmers.

Family-Style Service

Family-style service (also called English service) requires food to be placed on large platters or in large bowls that are delivered to the guests' tables by servers. Guests at each table then pass the food around their table and serve themselves.

Family-style service is relatively easy to implement, for service staff members do not need to be highly skilled. In fact, with family-style service, they generally put more effort into clearing tables than into presenting and serving the food. In effect, each of the disadvantages of cart service can be countered with the advantages of family-style service. Family-style service requires relatively little dining area space or special equipment (except serving bowls and platters); table turnover rates and service time can also be rapid, which makes it easy to serve foods at their proper temperatures. Additionally, properties need not charge exceptionally high prices for family-style service, since there are reduced equipment and labor costs. This service style is sometimes used for banquets.

One possible disadvantage of family-style service is that it is difficult to implement portion-control procedures. The last guests served may not receive as much of an item as they would like if the first guests served take too much. This problem can be reduced if the initial amount of food placed in the bowl or on the platter is generous.

The informal atmosphere of family-style service can be a major disadvantage if guests expect a more formal atmosphere or expect special attention from servers. If guests are seeking elegance or a great deal of contact with servers in their dining experience, they may not find family-style service acceptable.

Buffet Service

Buffets display food on counters or tables, and guests help themselves to as many and as much of the items as they wish to eat. Buffets can range from a simple offering of several food items to elaborate presentations that appeal to guests with sophisticated, gourmet tastes. Buffet service is sometimes used in combination with (rather than in place of) table service; for example, servers may serve drinks and desserts using plate service while allowing guests to serve themselves at a buffet for the main course.

Foods usually are placed on buffets in the following order: salads and other chilled meal accompaniments, hot vegetables, meats, poultry, fish, and other hot entrées. Some buffets feature "steamship" rounds of beef, large hams, and other roasts that servers or production staff carve as guests request a portion. Such items as crepes and omelets are sometimes cooked to order on a buffet line. Sauces, dressings, and relishes should be placed close to the menu items that they accompany. Desserts may be placed in a display area separate from the rest of the buffet to facilitate traffic flow.

There are many popular layouts for buffet service that can be used in place of the traditional straight-line setup (see Exhibit 4). Some organizations use a **scramble system** for their buffets. The term was first used to describe cafeterias in which guests could go to separate stations to be served, rather than waiting in a single line. For example, hot foods might be at one station, beverages at another, and desserts and salads at still others. Using this plan for buffets simply involves making each station a small buffet. While requiring more setup space than other buffet-service styles, the scramble system lessens bottlenecks because it doesn't force guests into a single line.

Buffet service requires a system to maintain cleanliness and order. Staff members must consistently keep buffet containers full, quickly attend to food spills on and around the buffet line, properly attend to guest tables in dining areas, and efficiently remove soiled serviceware from the room. Staff members should display only small batches of food to maintain proper temperatures and encourage frequent replenishing.

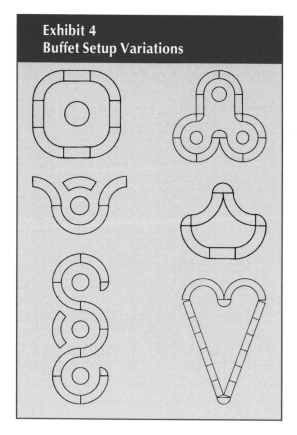

Exhibit 4
Buffet Setup Variations

Efforts to create an attractive buffet are often defeated if the buffet is left unattended during service. Spills, serving utensils that have been dropped into food products, almost-empty food containers, and unsightly, burned food left in hot chafing dishes can easily ruin a buffet's visual appeal.

The required serviceware must be constantly available during the buffet period. When flatware and plates are not available, guests have a right to complain. Guests also have a right to complain if they are given hot plates (just out of the dishwashing machine) for their chilled foods. These examples help illustrate why staff members must pay constant attention to buffet lines to ensure that they meet the quality standards expected by guests.

The fact that the work of servers is limited in buffets lowers labor costs. (Servers typically just remove soiled dishes, reset tables, provide beverage and sometimes dessert service, and perform related tasks.) Also, since food can be produced over a longer period of time and items do not need to be portioned, production labor costs may be reduced slightly. However, additional kitchen staff may be required to prepare such items as centerpieces and the large quantities and varieties of buffet food.

Apply Your Learning 13.2

Please write all answers on a separate sheet of paper.

For statements 1–5, match the following terms to their correct service style description.

Plate service

Cart service

Platter service

Family-style service

Buffet service

1. Food is displayed on counters or tables, and guests help themselves to as many and as much of the items as they wish to eat.

2. Also called Russian service, servers deliver fully cooked food to the dining room, present it to guests for approval, and then serve the food.

3. Food is placed on large platters or in large bowls that are delivered to the guests' tables by servers. Guests at each table then pass the food around their table and serve themselves.

4. Also called French service, this is an elaborate service style in which menu items are prepared beside guest tables by specially trained staff members; menu items are cooked in front of the guests.

5. Servers take guests' orders in the dining area; kitchen staff produce food orders, portion them, and place them on plates; and servers take the orders to the guests.

13.3 Providing Superior Service

AFTER STUDYING SECTION 13.3, YOU SHOULD BE ABLE TO:

♦ List information shared during preshift meetings

♦ Describe the components of suggestive selling

♦ Identify the importance of service guarantees

♦ Resolve guest complaints

♦ Describe the team approach to service

♦ Serve guests who have disabilities

- Service guarantees
- Resolving guest complaints
- The team approach to service
- Serving guests who have disabilities

Breaking the Bar

At the height of Prohibition, the folks in Frankenmuth, Michigan, managed to stay "wet," courtesy of two local hoteliers, Zehnder and Fischer, who secretly served homemade brew at their properties to friends and visitors.

At least, they did until July 30, 1930, when federal agents raided the hotels. The law did not let them off lightly: Zehnder was fined $4,000, and Fischer was fined $10,000 (the maximum penalty).

There was one sign of lenience, however. The judge offered to deduct $1,200 from their fines if the offenders allowed their beautiful oak bars to be smashed. The men agreed, and the bars became firewood on November 15, 1930. Yet, even with the deduction, Fischer ended up paying the largest fine handed down during all of Prohibition.

Once managers have decided which style or combination of styles their operation will use, they must provide their service staff with the skills, procedures, supplies, and equipment necessary to do their jobs properly and delight guests.

The section that follows discusses general strategies and procedures managers from many different food service properties might use to help their staffs provide excellent service to guests. This section will cover:

- Preshift meetings
- Suggestive selling

Preshift Meetings

Many food service properties use "line-up" or **preshift meetings** to facilitate staff communication and as an ongoing, daily method of training. Typically, a preshift meeting takes place just before the start of a shift and lasts 15 to 20 minutes. Pre-shift meetings should always begin on time and include all the appropriate staff members. Preshift meetings give dining room managers opportunities to gather information from the staff members as well as give information to them.

Managers should listen closely to the concerns and ideas staff members express during preshift meetings. For example, staff members might suggest a change that would improve service to guests. The way for managers to encourage such suggestions is to listen to them and adopt or at least try out the best of them.

Information given to service staff during a preshift meeting might include any of the following:

General Information

- Planned special events or promotions

- Events in the local community that could make the upcoming shift busier than usual

- Special arrangements for guests celebrating birthday parties, anniversaries, and other occasions

- Special arrangements for upcoming holidays

Product or Service Information

- Daily food and beverage specials (this may include taste tests)

- Strategies for or changes to food and beverage service

- Tips or in-depth instruction for handling equipment and supplies

- Readings of comment cards that guests have turned in

Sales Information

- Merchandising and upselling techniques

- Goals for food and beverage sales, either in general or for particular items

- Reports of ancillary income brought in by special-function business

Staff Information

- Introductions of new staff members

- Recognition of staff member achievements

Preshift meetings are ideal times for managers to emphasize teamwork and develop common goals with staff members. Preshift meetings should also give staff members an opportunity to ask questions and have them answered.

Suggestive Selling

Food and beverage properties have integrated the sales function into service position descriptions for so long that suggestive selling is viewed as a natural part of food and beverage service at many properties. Service staff often appreciate the opportunity to practice suggestive selling, because it is an area in which they are usually allowed to let their individual judgment and personal style shine. Staff members do not give in-depth sales presentations or use high-pressure tactics on guests. Rather, suggestive selling is a way service staff can enhance a guest's dining experience by making sure the guest orders all that he or she really wants. Food and beverage sales must always be based on the needs and expectations of the guests, not the operation. If servers understand what the operation offers and can communicate it to guests, they will be better able to match the requirements and expectations of guests with the operation's products and services.

There are three components to suggestive selling:

- Knowing your guests

- Knowing your products and services

- Matching guest needs and desires with your products and services

Know Your Guests. Being able to "read" guests and identify their requirements gives servers clues about what to sell. Guests who arrive as a family will often want quick service, including snacks or appetizers for the children and something to occupy them (activity books, games, or crayons and placemats to color) while they wait for orders to arrive. This gives servers the opportunity to sell appetizers appropriate for children. Guests who are primarily interested in conducting business over a meal have different requirements. Rapid, attentive, unobtrusive service will allow them to discuss their business without major interruptions. These guests may not be interested in hearing a long list of food and beverage alternatives, and servers should tone down their suggestive-selling efforts accordingly.

Know Your Products and Services. The second component of effective suggestive selling is a thorough knowledge of the products and services the operation provides.

Servers should thoroughly know the menu, including menu item ingredients, the origins of unique menu items or ingredients, the correct pronunciation of menu item names, menu item production methods and times, and how products taste and are presented (servers should know this for both regular and special menu items). Some organizations use flash cards with pictures when training servers, to enhance their retention of menu information. Some restaurant chains forbid new servers from serving guests until they can pass a test that measures their knowledge of the menu (and other subjects of importance to guests).

Servers should taste every item on the menu during their initial training. Specials of the day should be tasted each day during preshift meetings. Additional information that enhances a server's ability to sell includes a knowledge of the garnishes for each menu item, allowable substitutions, allowable portioning options (such as half portions or extra-large portions), and the plate presentation of each menu item. With a thorough knowledge of products, servers are better able to identify and describe items that truly match the needs of guests.

Match Guest Needs with Your Products and Services. The basic strategy of suggestive selling is to show guests how they can enhance their dining experience by ordering one of the server's suggestions. Some suggestive-selling techniques and strategies are listed in Exhibit 1. These should be adapted to the unique needs of the operation's guests.

Sometimes guests are unsure of what to order and may simply ask their server, "What's good here?" In such cases, servers should not answer, "Everything is good"; this approach will only frustrate guests. Rather, servers should take their cue to

Exhibit 1
Suggestive-Selling Techniques and Strategies

1. Evaluate the moods of guests and make recommendations based on your observations.

2. Very early in the ordering process, mention that the guest may want to save room for tonight's featured signature dessert.

3. Talk about menu items that the operation is famous for and take every opportunity to suggest these items to guests.

4. When describing menu items, mention brand-name ingredients that the chef uses; this creates an image of quality.

5. Recommend appetizers immediately after serving the first round of drinks.

6. Promote wine, either by the glass or in bottles, to enhance guest enjoyment and to increase server tips.

7. Instead of asking a question that can simply be answered "no," such as, "Would you like an appetizer?" ask a question that gives the guest a choice, such as, "Would you prefer our nachos or our fried mozzarella sticks as an appetizer tonight?"

8. Paint a creative picture of the food you are trying to sell, using descriptive images and stories. A brief history of how a dish became popular can add appeal. Also, by creating mental images through a unique story, servers can make menu items more memorable.

9. Present desserts on a tray or cart to enhance visual appeal. At no extra charge, offer extra dishware and flatware to guests who want to share their desserts with others.

10. Practice suggestive-selling techniques and strategies at every opportunity. The odds are that you will sell more.

make suggestions. Appealing descriptions of the operation's signature specialties are particularly appropriate when guests are undecided about what to order. Servers could also suggest dishes they themselves enjoy. However, they must never discourage a guest from ordering any item and must not let a guest know if they personally dislike the item he or she has ordered. It is the preferences of the guest, not those of the server, that must drive the process.

While servers should be enthusiastic when making recommendations to guests, they should never be pushy; servers should merely guide guests' decision making by highlighting options that fit guests'

needs and desires. Guests who know what they want may be irritated by a lot of suggestions from their server, so servers should learn to recognize when guests know what they want and tailor their service accordingly.

Service Guarantees

Borrowing from strategies in other, unrelated service businesses, some food service properties now offer **service guarantees**—unconditional commitments to complete guest satisfaction. With a service guarantee, guests who are not satisfied with their menu items or the service they received do not have to pay for their meals. Some properties have time-related service guarantees for time-sensitive meal periods such as breakfast and lunch; guests who do not receive their orders within 15 minutes of ordering are not charged, for example. Service guarantees work well when a food service operation and its management and staff are focused on the same desired outcome: satisfied guests.

Resolving Guest Complaints

Guests complain because their needs or expectations are not met. Few dissatisfied guests actually voice their complaints to service staff; most suffer in silence. Some guests will not complain directly, but will show by their actions that they are displeased. Some of the warning signs of guest dissatisfaction include asking a server to remove a beverage or menu item from the table soon after it is served, not eating or drinking the item or simply moving food around on their plate, covering the plate with their napkin, being rude for no apparent reason, or looking around for their server. It is critical for the server to investigate if he or she observes any of these behaviors, since the guest will leave dissatisfied if the server fails to turn the situation around.

The process of resolving guest complaints begins with an understanding of why guests complain. A sample list of reasons for guest complaints is presented in Exhibit 2. This list is not exhaustive, nor is it in any particular order; it's merely a sampling of the variety of reasons for which guests complain.

Fundamental to successfully resolving guest complaints is having the right attitude. With the right attitude, staff members can usually resolve complaints quickly. But if a staff member ignores a guest's dissatisfaction, retreats behind company policies, takes the complaint personally, blames the guest or other staff members, argues with or belittles the guest, makes the guest feel as if he or she was wrong to complain, or discusses the complaint so that other guests or servers can hear, the staff member will only further upset the guest. A fundamental rule staff members must remember is that "The guest is always right." While some properties have modified this rule to say "The guest may not always be right, but the guest is always the guest," the message is the same.

Guests want their complaints to be handled rapidly, fairly, and professionally. A complaint should never be ignored or allowed to fester. Rapid resolution of a complaint is in everyone's best interest: the guest wants someone to salvage his or her dining experience as soon as possible, and the operation wants to make sure the guest does not leave dissatisfied, because a dissatisfied guest will likely tell others about the problem and may never return.

Approaches to dealing with guest complaints should include four steps:

1. Calmly and patiently listen and empathize.

2. Apologize and commit yourself to solving the problem and satisfying the guest.

3. Identify a mutually acceptable solution.

4. Check back to determine if the complaint truly has been resolved.

Listen and Empathize. By calmly and patiently listening and empathizing, staff

---

Exhibit 2
Why Guests Complain

- Unfriendly staff or lack of a warm greeting
- Pushy servers
- Excuses by the server
- Lack of courtesy by servers
- Unhelpful attitudes of servers
- Overly friendly servers
- Inattentive service
- Inadequate response to guest complaints
- "Vanishing" servers who are unavailable to take care of needs
- Excessive waiting times
- High prices
- Unacceptable food quality or methods of preparation
- Unclean facilities, equipment, or servers

- Unacceptable noise levels
- Policies that are not guest friendly, such as charges for splitting or sharing items, automatic service charges, and a prohibition on substitutions
- Crowded parking lots, lobbies, or bathrooms
- Cramped dining area
- Unavailability of management
- Unequal treatment of guests, or "playing favorites"
- Unacceptable no-smoking sections—sections that are smoky or have a poor view or poor furniture
- Failure to thank guests for coming or to invite them to return

---

members can show courtesy and respect to complaining guests and prevent situations from spiraling out of control. Treating an agitated or angry guest with calmness and patience can be difficult, but it often quiets the guest, which is a necessary first step if the server is to learn about the reason for the complaint in detail.

Servers and other staff members should not make the mistake of becoming defensive. They should remember that it is impossible to please everyone all of the time and that different guests arrive with different ideals for their dining experience. When listening to complaints, staff members should avoid taking them personally; rather, they should concentrate on trying to understand the guest's perspective and the reason for the complaint. The best way to view complaining guests is as consultants to the operation; their complaints offer an

opportunity for the operation to identify weaknesses and areas for improvement.

Having empathy is being aware of and sensitive to the emotions of others. In short, empathy is knowing where someone is coming from—in this case, seeing the world through the guest's eyes. Empathetic responses include:

- "I think I know how you feel."
- "I understand what is upsetting you and I'm glad that you told me."
- "I can see why this is important to you and I want to resolve it right now."

When coupled with a sincere apology, an empathetic response will go a long way toward soothing a guest and beginning the process of resolving the complaint.

Apologize and Commit Yourself to Solving the Problem. Apologizing is not necessarily the same as accepting blame or passing the blame to another staff member—though when blame clearly belongs to the operation, the staff member should acknowledge that. A staff member can be sorry that an event occurred or that circumstances are what they are, even if the staff member had nothing to do with the event or the circumstances. An apology simply is an agreement that the guest's complaint or feelings have merit, and it helps to reduce the guest's feelings of frustration and anger. But a staff member should never assume that an apology by itself will satisfy a guest. After apologizing, the staff member should accept responsibility for the problem's resolution, regardless of who is at fault; the staff member must become the guest's advocate in fixing the problem.

Accepting responsibility means giving complete and undivided attention to resolving the complaint. This sense of urgency will communicate to the complaining guest that the problem is going to be taken care of—quickly.

Identify a Mutually Acceptable Solution. Once the staff member has listened to the complaint and apologized for the problem, the staff member and guest must identify a mutually acceptable solution. Some managers train staff members to simply ask the guest to suggest a way to resolve the complaint. Most guests respond reasonably. Other managers train staff members to offer guests alternatives or options. In any case, it is essential that the solution be mutually acceptable, one in which everyone wins. When a complaint is handled to the satisfaction of all involved, the complainer may be transformed into a loyal guest.

This brings us to some logistics for resolving guest complaints. If food items or

beverages are unacceptable, the staff member should immediately remove them and quickly offer to bring a replacement. If the new item is one that requires preparation or cooking, the staff member should immediately inform the person in charge of production of the need to quickly provide the item. If the staff member must continue serving other guests, he or she should tell the manager about the situation so the manager can go to the guest's table, apologize again, and explain to the guest what is being done to solve the problem. It may be necessary to void or alter the guest check if the guest does not desire a replacement.

What about complaints that have nothing to do with the food or beverages served? Some guests might complain that the restaurant is too cold, for example, or might complain about a smoker sitting at a nearby table. If a guest is too cold, a server might suggest a move to a table farther away from air-conditioning ducts or to a table next to a window (if it's sunny outside). In the case of a guest who complains about another guest's smoking, it is best to quietly move the guest who complains, not the guest who smokes.

Check Back and Follow Up. The final step in resolving a guest complaint is to check back to determine whether the complaint has truly been resolved. Depending on the situation, another apology might be in order, if for no other reason than to acknowledge the operation's failure to meet the guest's expectations on the first try. Some properties also follow up a day or so later with a letter or telephone call. This strongly demonstrates that the operation and its staff are genuinely committed to continuous quality improvement.

Additional intervention may be necessary with difficult guests—those who are grouchy, unruly, or just plain rude. When it becomes clear that the server cannot resolve a guest's complaint, the dining room manager should step in and try to handle the situation. This is particularly true when a difficult guest's behavior disturbs other guests or staff members.

The Team Approach to Service

The team approach to guest service helps all staff members view guest service as an activity to which everyone in the operation must be committed. It involves cross-training each staff member to perform a variety of service functions, including taking orders, using suggestive-selling techniques, delivering orders, resolving guest complaints, and busing and resetting tables. Team members may or may not retain traditional titles such as "server" and "busperson." For the team concept to reach its full potential, it takes motivated and enthusiastic staff members.

Server teams can have one of three structures: small teams, loose stations, or all-inclusive server teams. *Small teams* are responsible for one dining room area and are structured so that some team members focus on service in the dining room and others are responsible for delivering products from the kitchen and bar, clearing tables, and performing other general service tasks. In *loose stations*, servers are discouraged from thinking in terms of territories, a mind-set that is evident in statements like "It's not my station" (or "table" or "responsibility"). Instead, staff members are encouraged to focus on exceeding guests' expectations, regardless of the station or table location. The first-available-server system (guest orders are served as soon as they are ready by whichever server is

readily available) is an example of this kind of team approach. In an *all-inclusive server team*, not only do service staff and managers dress the same, but all perform guest service duties, respond to guest inquiries, and handle complaints.

Members of server teams usually have more authority than servers in traditional structures. This empowerment can lead to increased motivation and enthusiasm on the part of team members. If team service results in more team-member interaction and interaction with guests, communication will be enhanced both among team members and between team members and guests. Improved communication can result in an operation that is invigorated, attentive, and confident in providing guest service.

While those who oppose the team approach to service point out disadvantages that include extensive training, possible guest confusion, challenges with distributing tips, and possible over-service, in most circumstances—when correctly implemented with properly trained staff—team service is a dramatic leap forward in improving guest service.

Serving Guests Who Have Disabilities

Food service properties should be committed to giving the best possible service to everyone. In the case of guests with disabilities, this commitment is reinforced by the Americans with Disabilities Act (ADA), a law that gives people with disabilities the right to equal access to the goods and services enjoyed by the rest of the public.

Courtesy is the key to giving excellent service to all guests—including guests with disabilities. Staff members should offer to help, but should not insist on helping. Rather than assume they know what a disabled guest needs, staff members should ask the expert—the guest who has the disability. Staff members should be flexible about meeting the guest's needs; the guest can often help the staff member find a creative way to deal with an obstacle or some other problem.

Managers should inform all staff members about the operation's services for guests with disabilities. Knowledgeable staff members can help these guests feel welcome and wanted. Managers should train staff members to notify them of the presence and locations of guests with disabilities whenever an emergency arises.

Guests with disabilities have various needs that are related to their disabilities. What follow are some general guidelines only; as just mentioned, staff members should communicate with disabled guests in order to determine exactly how they want to be helped—if they want help at all.

Mobility Impairments. People with mobility impairments have difficulty walking or cannot walk; they may or may not use a wheelchair. If the guest is in a wheelchair, staff members should put themselves at eye level with the guest whenever they can. This puts the guest and the staff member on equal ground and helps the guest avoid neck or back strain. Staff members should not touch or lean on wheelchairs, and should only push a wheelchair if asked to do so. When pushing wheelchairs, staff members should push the chair at a normal pace, be careful around corners, and tilt the chair slightly back when going down ramps or over curbs.

Speech Impairments. Guests with speech impairments have difficulty speaking

clearly or easily. When speaking to a guest who has a speech impairment, staff members should be patient and ask the guest to repeat what they do not understand. It's okay if staff members don't understand, but they shouldn't pretend that they understand if they really don't. If necessary, staff members can ask the guest to show them what he or she is trying to say.

When talking with a guest who has a speech impairment, it's helpful for staff members to make eye contact with the guest and speak clearly and at a normal pace. Staff members do not have to talk loudly or slowly.

Visual Impairments. Guests with visual impairments are blind, have poor vision, or have certain eye diseases. When guests with visual impairments ask for directions, staff members should give the directions in specific and descriptive terms. If a staff member offers to lead the way and the offer is accepted, the staff member should offer his or her left elbow to the guest and let the guest follow close behind. As they move forward, the staff member should tell the guest about stairs, doorways, large plants, and other obstacles.

When giving change to visually impaired guests after they have paid their guest checks, staff members should identify each bill and coin separately. If braille menus and signs are not available, staff members should be trained in how to graciously read menus aloud to guests when asked. Lastly, if guests have guide dogs, staff members should help the dogs concentrate on their jobs by not petting them while they are working.

Hearing Impairments. Guests with hearing impairments cannot hear at all or cannot hear very well. When attempting to speak to a guest who has a hearing impairment, staff members might have to use visual signals or gestures to get the guest's attention. Staff members should let the guest decide how to communicate (through lip reading or writing things down, for example). If the guest has an interpreter, staff members should speak directly to the guest, not the interpreter. If the guest reads lips, staff members should speak at a moderate pace and use facial expressions that give visual clues about what they are saying. (However, staff members should not overly exaggerate their expressions.) Obviously, for lip reading to take place, there must be enough light for the guest to see faces and lips (this can be a problem in dimly lit dining rooms).

Mental Retardation. Guests who are mentally retarded might have any of a variety of mental disabilities. When serving adult guests who are mentally retarded, staff members must remember to treat them as adults, not children. Usually the best approach is to use simple, direct language and short sentences. Above all, staff members must be patient, take their time, and be positive and encouraging.

Apply Your Learning 13.3

Please write all answers on a separate sheet of paper.

1. What is the purpose of a preshift meeting?

2. What are the three components to suggestive selling?

3. What is a service guarantee?

4. What are the four steps to resolving guest complaints?

5. Explain the differences between the three structures of server teams.

13.4 Responsible Beverage Service

AFTER STUDYING SECTION 13.4, YOU SHOULD BE ABLE TO:

♦ Discuss types of liability laws

♦ Verify legal drinking age

♦ Monitor alcohol intake

♦ Cut off alcohol service

The careful service of alcoholic beverages is a responsibility of all who work in a food service operation. Alcohol is a factor in many of the driving fatalities in the United States every year. It also plays a contributing role in many fights, drowning accidents, and suicides. In states that have dram shop laws, servers, bartenders, and owners can be held liable if an intoxicated guest causes injury to another person.

There are proven techniques for serving alcoholic beverages responsibly. It is an obvious advantage that the public's awareness has increased when it comes to the responsible consumption of alcohol. Most guests understand that alcohol-service rules are not simply house rules, but apply at whatever operation they choose to visit.

Note: Most states require anyone serving or clearing alcohol to be at least a certain age. While you may not be able to serve or handle alcohol for many years, it is still important to understand the responsi-

bilities that come with alcohol service in the hospitality industry.

Liability Laws

Anyone who serves alcohol at an establishment can be sued for injuries or damages caused by illegal alcohol sales. That includes establishment owners, managers, servers, and bartenders.

The three basic types of laws which determine liability in alcohol sales cases include:

• Dram shop acts

• Common law

• Joint and several liability laws

In order to understand how these laws work, you must understand what is meant by the terms *first party, second party,* and *third party.*

• First party: The person buying the alcohol

• Second party: The person or establishment selling or serving the alcohol

• Third party: Someone outside the alcohol sales transaction

Most laws are designed to allow third parties to sue establishments for injuries and suffering caused by someone who is drunk.

Dram Shop Liability Acts

Dram shop acts are nothing new. They date back to the 1800s and were enacted to protect family members from habitual drunkards. Today, those acts extend the law to anyone who has been injured by an intoxicated person.

Dram Shop Acts. Dram shop acts vary from state to state, but in general, they provide consistent guidelines about who is responsible when third parties suffer because of an intoxicated person's actions.

Let's say something like this happens in an area where there is a dram shop act:

A man comes in a bar and drinks four Manhattans in an hour. Even though he is slurring his words and trips over a chair on the way to the jukebox, the establishment serves him two more Manhattans. When the man leaves the bar, he gets into his car and has a head-on collision with a van. He and the woman driving the van are both injured.

Under a dram shop act, the woman in the van can sue and probably win a case against the bar.

Common Law. Let's reconsider the example above of the intoxicated man who injured the woman in the van. Under common law, the woman could argue that the bar was negligent in serving the man, who was obviously drunk.

When an establishment is negligent, it means that its employees failed to do what any sensible person ought to have done under the same circumstances: stop service when the man showed signs of intoxication.

Joint and Several Liability Laws. What happens if something like this occurs:

A woman comes into a bar after work, has a beer, and leaves. Later that evening, after having more drinks in another bar, she gets into her car and has a head-on collision with a truck. The woman and the driver of the truck are both injured.

Under joint and several liability laws, the man in the truck could sue the first bar and its employees—even though the woman was not drunk when she left.

Verifying Legal Drinking Age

It is illegal to serve alcohol to minors. Since it can be difficult to tell whether someone is a minor, servers should always ask for identification when they are uncertain. Examples of a valid ID include a driver's license, a state-issued ID, an international driver's license, and a U.S. passport or military ID. When checking ID, servers should:

- Check the birth date on the ID. It should show that the person is of legal drinking age. (Servers should make sure the person looks to be the age indicated by the birth date.)

Exhibit 1
Alcohol Service and You

Servers have legal responsibilities when serving alcohol. What happens when establishments violate the laws regarding alcohol service?

- Owners, managers, servers, and bartenders can be sued if someone is injured because of irresponsible alcohol service.

- Owners, managers, servers, and bartenders can be arrested, fined, and sentenced to jail.

- Managers, servers, and bartenders can lose their jobs.

- Establishments can lose their liquor licenses.

When you understand your legal responsibilities in serving alcohol, you:

- Develop better judgment and confidence when serving alcohol.

- Enhance guest service and safely promote hospitality.

- Reduce injuries caused by intoxicated people.

- Increase community awareness and relations.

- Check the photo. Obviously, it should look like the person, but servers should keep in mind that the guest's weight or hairstyle may have changed. Many state IDs have a different-colored background for pictures of minors.

- Know how to spot fake IDs. They may have cuts, erasures, changes, different styles of type, or odd-sized seals. They may feel odd or be badly wrinkled or damaged.

- If a server suspects that an ID is false, he or she should ask for a second ID, or ask the guest to give his or her address, middle name, or height, and compare the guest's answer with the information on the ID.

- If a server still has doubts about an ID, he or she should refuse to serve alcohol to the guest, or should ask for assistance from a manager. Servers must remember that it is better to lose a guest than to lose a lawsuit or the operation's liquor license.

Exhibit 1 lists what can happen when establishments violate the laws regarding alcohol service.

Monitoring Alcohol Intake

Servers should keep track of the number of drinks guests have had; the size, type, and proof (alcohol content) of the drinks; and how quickly guests have consumed them. Managers should provide servers with a form they can use to easily tally drinks. Servers should know how much alcohol is in each drink they serve; alcohol content changes with the recipe, the glass size, and the amount of ice used. A 12-ounce beer, a 5-ounce glass of wine, a cocktail with 1.25 ounces of 80-proof liquor, and a cocktail with 1 ounce of 100-proof liquor all contain approximately the same amount of alcohol.

Servers should look for the following signs of intoxication as they monitor guests:

- *Unusual conduct.* Depending on a guest's personality, he or she may

Nonalcoholic Specialty Beverages

Specialty teas, mixed juices, alcohol-free cocktails, and coffee drinks are becoming increasingly popular as alternatives to alcoholic beverages.

Specialty Teas

Specialty teas include premium blended teas as well as teas flavored with botanicals and spices. Herbal teas are infusions of a variety of flowers, herbs, and spices; they are a popular alternative for guests wishing to limit their caffeine. In addition to these more traditional offerings, a number of coffee bars now offer specialty tea drinks—including *chai*, a spiced and sweetened milk-tea beverage that originated in India.

Mixed Juices

As an increasing number of people in the United States seek out healthier foods and beverages, juice bars have filled an important niche. Currently, more than 500 juice bars across the United States offer custom-blended juice cocktails made from freshly squeezed fruits and vegetables. Juice bars have given rise to "smoothie bars," which sell shakes made from blended fruits, juices, yogurt, and other ingredients. Some food service properties catering to health-conscious guests are adding an extensive variety of mixed juices to their beverage menus.

Alcohol-Free Cocktails

For guests who desire the look and taste of a traditional bar drink, but without the alcohol, food service properties may offer alcohol-free cocktails sometimes known as "virgin" cocktails or "mocktails" (for example, a Virgin Mary is a drink made of Bloody Mary mix without vodka). Proper ingredients and mixing techniques—as well as attention to presentation and garnishing—are critical to successfully merchandising these beverages.

Coffee Drinks

Specialty coffee drinks range from espresso to cappuccino to café latte. For servers to sell and serve specialty coffee successfully, they must know the specialty coffees' ingredients and how the coffees are made. Espresso, for example, usually is made with dark French-roast coffee beans and an espresso machine; the machine produces a "shot" of espresso by forcing hot water through finely ground coffee at high pressure. Servers should be able to answer guests' questions about any of their operation's specialty coffee drinks.

---

become outspoken, noisy or rowdy, overly friendly, withdrawn, sleepy, antisocial, or obnoxious. He or she may use foul language.

- *Impaired judgment.* Guests may become careless with their money, make foolish statements, or drink faster.

- *Slowed reaction time.* Guests may have glassy eyes, dilated pupils, or slurred speech.

- *Decreased coordination.* Guests may become clumsy, spill drinks, or lose their balance.

Some properties have adopted the so-called traffic light system for recognizing and rating a guest's level of intoxication. In this system, "green" means the guest is sober, "yellow" means the guest is becoming intoxicated, and "red" means the guest is intoxicated. Servers should adjust their service as a guest's status changes. For example, if a guest moves from "green" to "yellow," a server might suggest that the guest order an appetizer or a meal; the server should also wait for the guest to re-order an alcoholic beverage, rather than recommending additional drinks. Once the guest moves from "yellow" to "red," servers must be prepared to deal with the ensuing situation. Usually, that means stopping alcohol service altogether.

Cutting Off Alcohol Service

From time to time, beverage servers must face the prospect of telling a guest that he or she will not be served any more alcoholic beverages. Although this may initially seem daunting, the operation's managers—not to mention the law—will likely support such actions. In fact, when guests are at risk of becoming a danger to themselves or others, it may be the only responsible action to take.

Servers should keep these general guidelines in mind when denying or stopping alcohol service:

- If possible, ask a co-worker to accompany you when you refuse to serve alcohol to a guest. You may need the co-worker's help.

- Talk with the guest away from other guests.

- Calmly and firmly state your operation's policy: "I'm sorry, but I've served you all the alcohol that my manager will allow."

- Do not judge the guest, make accusations, or argue. Don't say, "You're drunk" or "You've had too much to drink."

- Repeat your operation's rules: "We care about your safety, and I can't serve you any more alcohol."

- Remove all alcohol from the guest's reach—even if it is his or her drink.

- When possible, offer the guest something to eat; food will absorb alcohol and help slow the rate of intoxication.

- Get a manager to help you if necessary or if this is the policy at your operation.

- Offer to phone for a taxi, if one is needed. Don't let an intoxicated guest drive away or even walk away—even if that means calling the police. It is better to risk making a guest angry than to risk lives.

- Make sure the guest has all of his or her personal belongings when he or she leaves.

- Fill out an incident report to describe the situation and record all actions taken; this will help protect the operation against lawsuits.

It is every staff member's responsibility to provide safe alcohol service. Managers and staff members should always be alert for situations that might bring harm to a guest or bystander.

Apply Your Learning 13.4

Please write all answers on a separate sheet of paper.

1. What are the three basic types of laws that determine liability in alcohol sales cases?

2. What are some examples of a valid ID?

For statements 3–8, write whether the answer is True or False.

3. The person or establishment selling or serving the alcohol is considered the first party.

4. If a server suspects that an ID is false, he or she should quiz the guest about information on the ID.

5. It is considered an invasion of privacy for servers to keep track of the number of drinks guests have had.

6. A 12-ounce beer and a 5-ounce glass of wine contain approximately the same amount of alcohol.

7. When it becomes time to cut off alcohol service to a guest, you should remove all alcohol from the guest's reach—even if it is his or her drink.

8. Servers and bartenders can be sued if someone is injured because of irresponsible alcohol service.

Quick Hits

Chapter 13

SECTION 13.1—DINING SERVICE STAFF POSITIONS

- Different table-service styles require different types of service staff positions. The most common positions include server, busperson, host, cashier, and dining room manager.

- Servers perform the bulk of the food and beverage serving duties. They may greet and seat guests, take their food and beverage orders, bring the ordered items to the table, check back with guests to make sure everything is satisfactory, present the guest check for payment, take the check to a cashier, return change to the guest, thank the guest, and clear tables.

- Buspersons perform a wide array of tasks designed to help servers provide better service to guests. The primary duty of a busperson is to clear tables and deliver soiled dishware, glassware, and flatware to the dishwashing room.

- Hosts first greet guests when they arrive. If the food service operation also has a dining room manager, the host's responsibilities usually are limited to welcoming guests, confirming the number of guests in a party, leading guests to the appropriate section of the restaurant, and providing menus.

- Cashiers collect payments of guest checks from servers or guests. They must follow income control procedures at all times and must accurately account for all transactions, collections, and disbursements.

- Dining room managers have a wide variety of responsibilities and tasks that differ according to the type and size of the operation. Their main responsibility is the supervision of dining service staff members.

SECTION 13.2—DINING SERVICE STYLES AND PROCEDURES

- Food service procedures and techniques can be generally categorized under one of four main styles of table service: plate service, cart service, platter service, and family-style service. Some properties offer a combination of styles.

- **Plate service** (also called American service) is the most common style of table service in the United States. It follows these basic procedures: servers take guests' orders; kitchen staff produce food orders, portion them, and place them on plates in the kitchen; servers place the orders on trays and take them to the guests; and buspersons assist servers and clear tables.

- **Cart service** (also called French service) is popular internationally, but used less frequently in the United States. It is an elaborate service style in which menu items are prepared on a cart beside guest tables by specially trained staff.

- **Platter service** (also called Russian service) requires servers to deliver platters of fully cooked food to the dining room, present the platters to guests for approval, and then serve the food. The food is prepared (and arranged attractively on platters) by food production staff in the kitchen for food servers to deliver to the dining room.

- **Family-style service** (also called English service) requires food to be placed on large platters or in large bowls that are delivered to the guests' tables by servers. Guests at each table then pass the food around their table and serve themselves.

- **Buffets** display food on counters or tables, and guests help themselves to as many and as much of the items as they wish to eat.

Section 13.3—Providing Superior Service

- Many food service properties use a "line-up" or **preshift meeting** to facilitate staff communication and as an ongoing, daily method of training. Typically, it takes place just before the start of a shift and lasts 15 to 20 minutes and should give staff members an opportunity to ask questions and have them answered.

- Information given to service staff during a preshift meeting includes general information (planned promotions, special arrangements), product or service information (daily specials, reading of comment cards), sales information (upselling techniques, food and beverage sales goals), and staff information (introduction of new staff, recognition of staff achievements).

- Suggest selling is a way service staff can enhance a guest's dining experience by making sure the guest orders all that he or she really wants. There are three components: knowing your guests, knowing your products and services, and matching guest needs and desires with your products and services.

- **Service guarantees** are unconditional commitments to complete guest satisfaction; guests who are not satisfied with their menu items or the service they received do not have to pay for their meals.

- Guests complain because their needs or expectations are not met. Approaches to dealing with guest complaints should include four steps: calmly and patiently listen and empathize, apologize and commit yourself to solving the problem and satisfying the guest, identify a mutually acceptable solution, and check back to determine if the complaint truly has been resolved.

- The team approach to guest service involves cross-training each staff member to perform a variety of service functions, including taking orders, using suggestive-selling techniques, delivering orders, resolving guest complaints, and busing and resetting tables.

- Courtesy is the key to giving excellent service to all guests—including guests with disabilities. Staff members should offer to help, but should not insist on helping.

Section 13.4—Responsible Beverage Service

- The careful service of alcoholic beverages is a responsibility of all who work in a food service operation. There are proven techniques for serving alcoholic beverages responsibly.

- Anyone who serves alcohol at an establishment can be sued for injuries or damages caused by illegal alcohol sales. That includes establishment owners, managers, servers, and bartenders.

- The three basic types of laws determine liability in alcohol sales cases are dram shop acts, common law, and joint and several liability laws.

- **Dram shop acts** vary from state to state, but in general, they provide consistent guidelines about who is responsible when third parties suffer because of an intoxicated person's actions.

- It is illegal to serve alcohol to minors. Since it can be difficult to tell whether someone is a minor, servers should always ask for identification when they are uncertain. Examples of a valid ID include a driver's license, a state-issued ID, an international driver's license, and a U.S. passport or military ID.

- When checking ID, servers should check the birth date and the photo on the ID. They should also know how to spot fake IDs. If a server suspects that an ID is false, he or she should ask for a second ID, or ask the guest to confirm information listed on the ID.

- Servers should keep track of the number of drinks guests have had; the size, type, and proof (alcohol content) of the drinks; and how quickly guests have consumed them.

- Servers should look for the following signs of intoxication as they monitor guests: unusual conduct, impaired judgment, slowed reaction time, and decreased coordination.

- Some properties have adopted the "traffic light" system for recognizing and rating a guest's level of intoxication: "green" means the guest is sober, "yellow" means the guest is becoming intoxicated, and "red" means the guest is intoxicated. Servers should adjust their service as a guest's status changes.

- From time to time, beverage servers must face the prospect of telling a guest that he or she will not be served any more alcoholic beverages. Although this may initially seem daunting, the operation's managers—not to mention the law—will likely support such actions.

Profile

Amy Isom
Vice President of Development and Operations
Carlson Vacation Ownership

Amy Isom, 33, has come a long way in the hospitality business-an industry she may not have discovered if the engineering school at Cornell had not been located right beside the hotel school. She was majoring in aeronautical engineering to fulfill her childhood dream to be an astronaut, but was having second thoughts. From her classroom window, she could see students in the hotel school.

"I remember thinking, "Those guys have a lot more fun.' They work hard, but it's a different kind of school, a close-knit group of people," she says. Isom wanted a career that allowed flexibility to have a family, and she loved to travel and to meet new people. Hospitality seemed like the right choice, so Isom changed majors.

Isom eventually secured a financial analyst position within Marriott Ownership Resorts, Inc. She spent a few years working in the timeshare industry before moving to join Radisson Hotels Worldwide.

When Radisson began studying the vacation ownership industry, questions were often directed to Isom as she was one of the few people at Carlson (Radisson's parent company) who had worked in the timeshare industry. Soon, she was asked to work on the plan to segment vacation ownership products along Carlson's multi-tier brands. She also worked on the acquisition of minority ownership in Interval International, an exchange network of 1,800 resorts in 70 countries.

Isom is currently vice president of development and operations for Carlson Vacation Ownership She works at increasing the number of qualified developers in each of the brands. She also ensures that all vacation ownership resorts are operated to the brands' highest standards.

A big part of Isom's job is forming personal relationships, which is the part she likes best. "I'm traveling to areas to talk to developers, make presentations about what it is we do, and explain the value for them to work with us."

Casual/Theme Restaurants

Sections

14.1 Marketing Perspective

14.2 Getting Ready for Service

14.3 Delivering Service

14.1 Marketing Perspective

AFTER STUDYING SECTION 14.1, YOU SHOULD KNOW HOW TO:

♦ Describe casual/theme restaurants

♦ Summarize the characteristics of casual/theme markets

♦ Explain the importance of guest feedback

♦ Identify some of the menu considerations for casual/theme restaurants

♦ Summarize how value can be a part of promotions

♦ Describe the role of design and decor

Casual/theme restaurants are classified as full-service; that is, they offer table service and a variety of menu items. There are many types of **casual/theme restaurants**, most of which have moderate to moderately high guest-check averages. Their common denominators are informal dining environments (although there are differing degrees of informality) and the availability of alcoholic beverages in most cases (although there are some family-oriented casual/theme restaurants that do not serve alcohol). Themes range from homey to exotic. There are themes that seem to scream fun, fantasy, great food, and special drinks; themes that subtly promote enticing entrées and pre-

mium wines; themes designed to recall the pleasures of old-fashioned home cooking; and even themes that replicate a rain forest, complete with healthy choices on the menu and rainstorms every 20 minutes.

Many restaurants in the casual/theme segment are more than just places to eat and drink. They offer escape, fun, and convenience; the pleasure of not having to cook dinner and clean up the kitchen; a chance to be with friends; freedom from telephones, faxes, and e-mails after a hectic day at the office; a chance for a couple to have a meal and conversation without children in attendance; a place to celebrate a birthday or anniversary; a chance to meet new people; a chance to catch up on the news in the sports world; and more.

Casual/Theme Markets

There are casual/theme restaurants for virtually every market imaginable. There are restaurants that appeal to the twentysomethings, the thirtysomethings, and senior citizens. There are ethnic restaurants, restaurants that feature certain foods or certain food preparation methods, and restaurants that appeal to sports fans, theater-goers, video game buffs, romantics, health and fitness enthusiasts, and people who just enjoy good food in a comfortable setting.

It would be impractical to attempt to describe every casual/theme market—there are local markets, visitor markets, single markets, family markets, and more. What follows are key characteristics of some of the major markets—Generation X, baby-boomers, influentials, and the affluent—and examples of what attracts them. (Keep in mind that there are many market overlaps; for example, an influential might also be a baby-boomer and an affluent.)

Generation X. Generation X (also known as the "twentysomethings") is made up of smart, value-conscious consumers. They respond to restaurant concepts promoting excitement, entertainment, and group interaction.

Baby-boomers. Baby-boomers, those born sometime between 1946 and 1964, make up roughly one-third of the U.S. population. Baby-boomers have busy lifestyles and are likely to have dual-career families and hold white-collar positions as managers or professionals.

Baby-boomers respond well to target marketing. Compared to Generation X, they are easier to accommodate and satisfy. Baby-boomers are more likely to choose moderately priced restaurants over quick-service (fast-food) restaurants.

Influentials. "Influentials" are leaders—people whose opinions on a variety of subjects are valued. If a restaurant can impress an influential by exceeding his or her expectations, the resulting positive word-of-mouth referrals could make the difference between profit or loss. By exceeding the expectations of influentials, a restaurant can connect with a large social network.

One of the most popular leisure activities of influentials is dining out, particularly on weekends. Influentials prefer full-service restaurants and report that they dine out often because it is fun. Influentials with children dine out to combine entertainment

with family time. They value service and have little tolerance for poor service. Influentials also are more likely to enjoy food in moderation and practice a healthy lifestyle than the general public.

Influentials who are subcategorized as "intellectually curious" are lured by restaurants offering a combination of education and entertainment to create intrigue, excitement, and positive memories. To attract the intellectually curious market, some restaurants feature teaching chefs who offer cooking tips and classes. Other restaurants offer theme dinners during which guests can learn about the history of the unique menu items they are eating and how the ingredients were grown and prepared. If a special wine is part of the dinner, sometimes suppliers will co-sponsor the dinner and provide speakers who are knowledgeable about wines.

The affluent. The affluent market is composed of U.S. adults who earn $100,000 to $250,000 a year. The affluent can afford to sample and enjoy the best that money can buy.

In general, the affluent seek out exceptional service, and the quality of service is a big factor in whether they decide to return to a given restaurant. They like to be pampered and at the same time feel they are getting value for the dollars they spend. Fresh foods, locally grown, are favorites of this market.

Guest Feedback

Casual/theme restaurants are constantly evolving to keep pace with the needs and expectations of guests. For that reason, managers and staff members of these restaurants must continually evaluate their products and services. To do so, they need to find out what their guests need and expect and then use that information. Guest feedback is only helpful if it is used properly.

Managers and staff members should seek guest comments on an ongoing basis. Guest comment cards, questionnaires, guest interviews, and other means can be used to determine guest needs and expectations and whether they are being met. One restaurant offers a free magazine subscription to those who complete and return its mailed questionnaire. Another restaurant phones guests two or three days after a private party to solicit feedback. One successful restaurant chain asks guests to complete "insight cards" and mail them back. When guests include positive comments on the cards, postcards are mailed to them, thanking them for their time. When negative comments are included, personal letters are sent that specifically address the comments and explain how the restaurant is going to deal with the problems raised.

Some restaurants use a **shopper's service** (also known as a "mystery shopper" service) to evaluate how guests' needs and expectations are being met. Shopper's services provide reports completed by anonymous "guests" (shoppers) who evaluate a restaurant's service from the guest's perspective.

Menu Considerations

Menus at casual/theme restaurants have evolved with the changing tastes of guests. Chicken, seafood, and salad entrées have become more popular. Based on the demand for healthier menu alternatives, vegetarian entrées are expected to continue improving in sales. Almost across the board, regardless of check average, beef entrées are being ordered less frequently by guests.

A major menu trend in casual/theme restaurants is the promotion of signature menu items. A **signature menu item** is one that guests perceive as special and closely associated with the restaurant promoting it. Outback Steakhouse's Bloomin' Onion appetizer is an example of a signature menu item. Signature menu items not only make the restaurant unique in the guests' minds, they also can help build repeat business and strong guest loyalty.

Premium menu items, as a category, are growing in popularity. Examples include premium baked products (freshly baked specialty breads, rolls, muffins, croissants), premium coffees (cappuccino, espresso, latte), innovative salsas and sauces with high-quality entrées, and seasonal or signature beers.

In keeping with the rising interest in local and regional cuisines, more "down-home" comfort foods—such American favorites as meatloaf, chicken-fried steak, and a variety of baked fruit cobblers—are being added to some casual/theme menus.

Many casual/theme restaurants are creating and featuring new sauces and condiments—particularly those restaurants featuring ethnic and regional cuisines. Examples include such entrée accompaniments as sweet-and-sour variations of teriyaki sauces, cranberry and cherry chutneys, Chardonnay artichoke salsa, and raspberry salsa—to name just a few.

Value

"Value" is the watchword for today's guests. The search for value is being led by increasingly sophisticated guests. Having experienced many dining-out occasions and a variety of dining concepts, guests are better educated in terms of what they want in food and beverage service. When they get what they expect and want relative to the price they pay, they perceive value.

Casual/theme restaurants need to emphasize and reinforce the value they offer. Value can be part of any number of promotions, including:

- Daily specials
- Gift certificates
- Seasonal specials and local or regional food tastings
- Senior-citizen discounts, often offered as part of early-bird dinner prices
- Complimentary samples of featured menu items
- Frequent-diner programs

The list can go on and on, as long as the promotions match what current and potential guests want and expect.

Several independent restaurants and table-service restaurant chains are promoting high-quality prepared foods to go. These restaurants are providing value by blending convenience and high quality for people on the go. Many people in the United States want high-quality elaborate foods at home, but they cannot or will not take the time to prepare them. In addition to traditional items such as chicken Kiev, lasagna, and chicken Marsala, unique items such as four-grain salads, veal entrées, and holiday specialties are being featured. The prepared-foods-to-go and home-replacement-meals concepts are driven largely by value. Restaurant-quality meals can be consumed at home where there are no service charges and consumers can dine as casually as they want. (See www.waiter.com or www.food.com for examples of how some restaurants are using the Web to market to

guests who want to purchase prepared foods to go.)

Some people view brunch as a value option. Brunch today in casual/theme restaurants often differs from the unlimited buffets that were popular in the recent past, featuring instead an à la carte menu that includes at least a few light items. Some interesting brunch items are omelets made with herbs, cheeses, beans, chili peppers, and vegetables; pancakes and waffles topped with apples, bananas, kiwis, mangos, nectarines, peaches, or raspberries; French toast made from brioche, French bread, multigrain bread, raisin bread, or sourdough bread and flavored with almond extract, vanilla, or liqueurs; skillet eggs scrambled with a variety of cheeses and vegetables; and crepes filled with meat (chicken, lobster, or shrimp) or sweet fruit fillings. These unique brunch items add value by exceeding guests' expectations.

Hotel Examples of Value. Most hotel restaurants are included in the casual/theme segment because hotel food service has undergone a dramatic change in the past few years, becoming guest-driven rather than chef-driven and changing from formal, upscale dining rooms (often offering French cuisine) to more casual, informal dining areas that are priced to reflect increased value.

Some hotel food operations have re-engineered their kitchens and dining areas around *sous vide*—a low-temperature food preservation method in which foods are packaged in plastic bags or pouches that are then vacuum-sealed, cooked, chilled, and refrigerated until they are reheated in hot water for service. *Sous vide* offers restaurateurs a means of providing value to guests because this technique allows restaurants to offer a greater number of high-quality hot

Exhibit 1
Examples of Hotel/Restaurant Alliances

Hotel Organization	Restaurant Organization
Best Western International	Pizza Hut
Budgetel Inns, Inc.	Applebee's Neighborhood Grill & Bar
	Bob Evans Restaurants
Cendant Hotel Division	Country Kitchen
	Pizza Hut
	TGI Friday's
Choice Hotels International	Metromedia Steakhouses Company
	Oh*la*la Coffee Company
	Pizza Hut
Country Inns	Country Kitchen
Embassy Suites	Pizza Hut
	Lettuce Entertain You Enterprises
Holiday Inn Crowne Plaza	McGuffey's Restaurants
La Quinta Inns	Denny's Restaurants
Loews Vanderbilt Plaza	Sfuzzi
Marriott Hotels & Resorts	Pizza Hut
Omni Ambassador East Hotel	Lettuce Entertain You Enterprises
Sholodge, Inc.	Shoney's Restaurants

Source: Adapted from "Linking Together," *Hotel & Motel Management* (May 9, 1994); Rajan Chaudhry, "Casual Dining Checks In," *Restaurants & Institutions* (November 1, 1993); and James Scarpa, "Hotel Market Segment Report," *Restaurant Business* (January 20, 1993).

foods while employing fewer production staff members (which helps keep costs down). *Sous vide* also has applications for a hotel's banquet and catering departments.

Some hotels have alliances with restaurant companies—that is, business agreements that allow the restaurant companies to operate restaurants in the hotels (see Exhibit 1). Many of these alliances provide value for hotel guests by offering them a familiar place to eat and drink.

The Dining Environment, Supplies, and Equipment

Design and decor play a major role in shaping a casual/theme restaurant's ambiance—which is a fusion of design, decor, image, and service and is one of the most important factors in many guests' restaurant selection.

Some casual/theme restaurant designs call for display kitchens and bakeries, some for furnishings reminiscent of neighborhood restaurants. Some casual/theme restaurants feature a nautical decor with a seafood theme; some, music of the '60s with a diner theme; and others, original artwork displayed with a gallery theme. Some restaurants spotlight sports memorabilia for an athletic theme, fresh pasta and garlic for an Italian theme, rustic furnishings for a steakhouse theme, and tropical live and robotic animals for a rain forest theme.

Some casual/theme restaurants have gone so far as to offer virtual reality dining. Virtual reality is computer technology that can provide pseudo, lifelike experiences. A restaurant in Los Angeles, for example, blends decor and electronic simulations of submarine travel with a menu that features upscale soups and sub sandwiches.

The supplies and equipment that dining-area staff members need in order to fulfill their responsibilities are not the same in every casual/theme operation. There are differences based on markets, restaurant image and size, level of service, check average, location, and other factors. For example, some restaurants have service bars where servers can pick up their beverage orders; in others, servers may be required to go to the bar or lounge area. Tablecloths, cloth napkins, and full tableware service may be used in some of the more upscale theme restaurants, and servers may even need to learn special napkin-folding techniques.

Apply Your Learning 14.1

Please write all answers on a separate sheet of paper.

1. Name the four selected major markets mentioned in this section, and give some characteristics of each.

2. What is a signature menu item?

3. Why do hotels have alliances with restaurant companies?

4. How can the restaurant's theme affect its design and decor?

14.2 Getting Ready for Service

AFTER STUDYING SECTION 14.2, YOU SHOULD KNOW HOW TO:

♦ Describe how managers set quality standards

♦ Summarize the training issues managers face

♦ Identify how the table-turn rate affects service

Casual/theme independent restaurants and restaurant chains develop their own service methods and procedures. Generally speaking, casual/theme restaurants use plate-service techniques with a casual approach based on their guests' desired levels of comfort. These service methods and procedures must be followed consistently once they are developed. For instance, if the house rule is to have the ends of flatware handles an inch away from the table edge, staff members should set all of the tables in the restaurant this way. Similarly, whether the menu is already on the table when guests are seated or the host or server hands menus to guests after they are seated depends more on the rules of the house than on rules of etiquette.

Another consideration in getting ready for service is quality standards. Based on guest requirements, a casual/theme restaurant's management team defines the quality standards that service staff members must meet as they get ready for service,

actually serve guests, and perform a wide range of duties, including operating equipment, using income control procedures, placing and picking up food orders, and interacting with bar staff. Guests evaluate many factors other than food and beverages while in the dining room; therefore, managers and staff members must pay close attention to all details to ensure cleanliness and the compatibility of atmosphere and service with the quality of the products offered.

The restaurant's manager is ultimately responsible for all these details and for ensuring that the restaurant's standard operating procedures incorporate a concern for quality guest-driven service.

Training

Training for casual/theme restaurant service should focus on menu knowledge and sales skills as well as courtesy, consistency, efficiency, and teamwork.

Providing menu information to guests is one of the most important services servers perform. In order to sell menu items, servers must know the menu and the house policies and rules about what they can and cannot do (allowing substitutions, for example). In order to do their jobs properly, servers must:

• Be thoroughly familiar with the menu.

• Know how to pronounce the name of each menu item.

- Know the daily specials and the restaurant's signature items along with their prices.

- Know how every item is prepared, including ingredients. (Some guests must avoid certain ingredients because of food allergies or other health considerations.)

- Know how to describe every item properly. Truth-in-menu laws in many states prohibit misrepresenting menu items and ingredients. For example, servers should not try to pass margarine off as butter or describe frozen foods as fresh.

- Know portion sizes and what side dishes or garnishes are included.

At times, guests will ask servers to describe how an unfamiliar item tastes. Some restaurants provide tasting sessions for service staff so that servers can describe how an item tastes; the chef or a cook can attend these meetings to provide information about the item.

Once servers know the menu, they will be able to use selling techniques that can increase not only guest satisfaction but also the guest check, to the benefit of both the servers and the restaurant. (Since tips are usually based on the check total, a larger total generally means a larger tip.) Suggestive selling involves encouraging guests to order such extras as appetizers, cocktails, wine, desserts, and after-dinner drinks. **Upselling** means suggesting more expensive (and often better-quality) items than those that the guest first mentions. Servers are often trained in suggestive selling and upselling on an ongoing basis to help the

restaurant build revenue and promote guest satisfaction. Exhibit 1 gives additional selling tips.

Server training also addresses timing and its effect on the **table-turn rate**—the average amount of time that a table is occupied. If a dining area seats 150 guests and staff members serve 300 guests during a specific shift, the table-turn rate is 2 (300 guests divided by 150 seats equals 2). In other words, each chair accommodated an average of two guests during the shift. Servers like to maximize table turns to enhance their tips (more people served in the same amount of time usually means more tips). Likewise, managers like the table-turn rate to be as high as possible for financial reasons. But as rates increase, it is important to ensure that the quality of service guests receive does not decrease. All other factors being equal, a high table-turn rate has a tendency to reduce levels of service. It is a balancing act to maximize both table turns and guest satisfaction. The timing of both production and service affects table turns. It is essential to time the entire dining experience so that guests do not feel rushed, yet the financial needs of the organization (dictated by table turns, in part) are met.

Servers in casual/theme restaurants provide personalized service. Some restaurants use computers to record information about regular guests, including favorite food and beverages, preferred table in the dining area, and preferred server. During preshift lineup meetings, this information is reviewed when these repeat guests have made a reservation. This personalized service helps the restaurant exceed guest expectations.

Exhibit 1
Tips for Effective Selling

Suggestive selling and upselling require tact and good judgment. If guests know exactly what they want, don't try to change their minds. However, you shouldn't hesitate to suggest additional items that will improve guests' meals. And learn to pick up on when guests want suggestions.

Suggestive selling might make you nervous. If so, it's probably because selling reminds you of a pushy salesperson you've known. Using suggestive selling and upselling techniques, however, is not being pushy. These techniques are part of providing good service.

The key to effective selling is knowing the menu. You should know all of the menu items your restaurant sells. When you are completely familiar with the menu and how each item is prepared, you can suggest dishes confidently and professionally.

Here are some tips for effective suggestive selling and upselling:

- Develop a "selling attitude."

- Be enthusiastic. It's easier to sell something you're excited about.

- Make food sound appetizing. Use words like "fresh," "popular," and "generous" when describing menu items.

- Ask questions. Find out if guests are really hungry or just want something light; whether they like chicken or beef; or if they feel like having something hot or cold.

- Suggest specific menu items. Don't simply ask: "Would you like soup with your meal?" Instead, point out: "A cold bowl of gazpacho would go nicely with your salad on a hot day like this."

- Suggest your favorites. Try as many menu items as you can, and tell guests you've tried them: "You'll like the chicken Kiev. It's one of my favorites here." But be honest—don't say that something is your favorite when it isn't.

- Offer a choice: "Would you like a slice of our famous cheesecake or our homemade pecan pie for dessert?"

- Suggest the unusual. People dine out to get away from the routine fare they have at home. And most people don't know what they want to order when they arrive.

- Suggest foods and beverages that naturally go together—soups and sandwiches, bacon and eggs, steak and baked potatoes, coffee and dessert.

- Compliment guests' choices. Make guests feel good about their choices even if they don't order what you suggest.

Remember to always ask for the sale. After you suggest and describe an item, ask if the guest would like it. A good way to do this is to describe several items and ask which the guest would prefer: "For dessert, we have our famous chocolate silk pie or our popular carrot cake. Which would you prefer?"

Source: Adapted from the "Restaurant Server Guide" in the *Hospitality Skills Training Series* (East Lansing, Mich.: Educational Institute of the American Hotel & Motel Association, 1995).

Apply Your Learning 14.2

Please write all answers on a separate sheet of paper.

1. What are some things servers must do to do their jobs properly?

2. Encouraging guests to order such extras as appetizers, cocktails, wine, desserts, and after-dinner drinks is an example of _____.

3. Suggesting more expensive (and often better-quality) items than those that the guest first mentions is an example of _____.

4. "Would you prefer a prime cut of beef?" is an example of _____.

5. "Can I offer you one of our specialty cocktails before dinner?" is an example of _____.

14.3 Delivering Service

AFTER STUDYING SECTION 14.3, YOU SHOULD KNOW HOW TO:

♦ Take reservations

♦ Manage waiting guests

♦ Greet and seat guests

♦ Present the menu and take beverage orders

♦ Place beverage orders

♦ Serve beverages

♦ Take food orders

♦ Place and pick up orders in the kitchen

♦ Serve the orders

♦ Present the guest check

♦ Serve guests with special needs

The delivery of guest-driven service requires service staff members who are people-oriented and able to focus on helping guests enjoy their dining experience. Guests can recognize whether servers truly enjoy their work and whether their smiles are genuine. Guest expectations, almost without exception, include friendly, prompt, courteous service.

Some procedures that food and beverage servers might use from the time guests are seated until they depart from the dining area are explained in the following sections. Many casual/theme restaurants use some or all of these procedures, but there are many others as well.

Taking Reservations

Many restaurants take reservations to allow guests the chance to reserve seating at a specific time. A reservation system increases the manager's ability to pinpoint slow and busy times and plan for them. In addition, such a system can increase business, since many guests desire a formal commitment

Funny Foods

Lest anyone think food is boring, Nancy Murphy has a collection of foodstuffs on display in her kitchen. She started her collection with a bag of anti-flatulent beans from Death Valley, Nevada, and grew to include Scorned Woman hot sauce, Alien ale, roadkill helper, armadillo droppings (dark pralines), Humbugs peppermint candy, cosmic cabbage, and cowboy caviar.

and guarantee about their dining arrangements and will visit only those restaurants that accept reservations. The use of reservations is a convenience and service to guests as well as a tool that helps staff members recognize guests by name, guarantee speed and quality of service, and promote production efficiency.

There are two basic types of reservation systems. One system offers seating at specific intervals during the meal period, such as seatings at 6:00 P.M. and 8:00 P.M. only. When this **interval reservations** system is used, at least 30 minutes must be allowed between serving periods to clean up, reset tables, and otherwise get ready for the next seating. Potential disadvantages to interval seating include crowd control problems when a large number of guests must be seated or allowed to leave the dining area at the same time, and food production problems when a large number of meals must be served simultaneously.

A second and more common type of reservation system is **staggered reservations**. This system staggers seating during the entire meal period; that is, reservations can be made for any time that tables are available (in other words, not yet reserved) during the meal period.

In order for a reservation system to work, the manager must be able to estimate the length of time it will take for guests to dine. For instance, because experienced managers know that large groups usually take longer to dine than small groups, they factor this into the reservation plan. The restaurant's environment and service style as well as the type of meal served are factors the manager considers as well.

Reservation commitments affect production. For example, if three eight-top tables (a table that seats eight persons) are seated at the same time, there may be a rush of work in the kitchen 20 to 30 minutes later when servers place 24 entrée orders at approximately the same time. Reservation-takers may need to suggest staggered arrival times for large groups so that neither the large groups nor other guests in the dining area are inconvenienced.

Because of the need to gather information efficiently and courteously, only staff members trained and authorized to accept reservations should do so. Typically, reservation information is entered in a reservation book or computer software program, and specific tables are reserved by indicating directly on a seating chart or into the computer the time of the reservation and the number of guests in the party.

Reservation-takers should obtain the following information from callers:

- The correct spelling of the name the reservation will be under

- The date and time of the reservation

- The number in the party

- Whether a smoking or non-smoking section is preferred

- Whether the guests want a table or a booth

- Special instructions

- The guest's phone number (or room number if the restaurant is in a hotel)

Some computerized reservation programs enable managers to keep very specific reservation information—such as the number of tables available, the number of guests to be seated, and the service staff needed—close at hand for several days in a row. Other computer programs provide detailed information only on the current dining period. Many programs indicate whether a specific table is in use, is being cleared and reset, or is ready to "sell." Such programs may also indicate, on a by-table basis, when tables are likely to be available. These aids are particularly helpful in large restaurants with several floors of dining space, or in other situations in which the manager or some other staff member would have to make several trips to the dining area to ensure that a table was ready for seating.

Handling Reservation Problems. What should be done when a guest with a reservation comes early or late, brings more or fewer guests than the reservation indicated, or does not wish to sit at the table that has been set aside for the group? Or what happens when a party arrives on time but the table isn't ready because the previous party is staying longer than the manager anticipated? Stated policies and procedures help staff members know what to do when these and similar problems associated with reservations come up. Common sense is also important. As problems arise, affected guests must be told the truth and offered appropriate alternatives; in other words, management must be prepared to find creative solutions so that guests are not frustrated.

Some restaurants offer an amenity, such as a drink or an appetizer, to guests inconvenienced by having to wait for their reserved table. This strategy may work well in some cases; in others, such as when guests have severe time limitations, it may not be adequate compensation for the inconvenience. Explaining to late-arriving guests that their table was held for 15 minutes past the reservation time but could be held no longer may be a good tactic if accompanied by management's promise to work the party into the dining area as soon as possible.

Managing Waiting Guests

Guests without reservations should be served on a first-come-first-served basis. When there is a waiting line, it is important that someone—the manager, receptionist, greeter, or another staff member—be at the door at all times to take the names of arriving guests and to call parties as tables become available. Names should be recorded on a waiting list. They should be printed very clearly along with the number of guests in the party. In some restaurants, the time of arrival is also noted.

As tables become available, guests should be paged. Some managers have the policy of paging a guest twice, two minutes apart. If, after two pages, the guest does not respond, the name is removed from the list and the next party of appropriate size is called. Some restaurants give waiting guests pocket electronic pagers to reduce noise and confusion.

Typically, the names of large groups are highlighted or listed separately so that they will not be overlooked. Generally, parties are called in the order in which they appear on the list, unless they include people who have disabilities, elderly persons, or families with small children requiring more immediate attention.

Policies about accepting tips from guests who want to reduce their waiting time should be developed and carefully followed. Generally speaking, staff members should never accept a gratuity before they render service; a tip before service is really a bribe. Guests typically do not like to wait for extended periods, and questions such as "We came in first—why were we not seated first?" are likely to arise if late-arriving guests without reservations tip the person greeting guests and are seated ahead of those who have been waiting.

Guests must be given the best estimate of the length of waiting time when their names are placed on the waiting list. Staff members should tell the truth. If guests must wait for a long period of time, they should be informed of this so that they can decide whether they want to wait or go elsewhere. After guests are told about the waiting time, they can be referred to the lounge or other areas where their wait may be more enjoyable. If guests choose not to wait, they should be thanked for coming and invited to return on another occasion.

Greeting and Seating Guests

The person who greets and seats guests is often the first representative of the restaurant to come in face-to-face contact with guests, so he or she needs to make a good impression. (If guests should seat themselves, a sign indicating this should be located where they will easily see it.)

Guests should be greeted by name if possible. If the restaurant takes reservations, the person who is greeting and seating guests should know and refer to guests by name and pronounce the name correctly. He or she might also identify regular guests: "Good evening, Mr. John, it's nice to see you again," or, "We have your usual table ready for you, Ms. Grace. Right this way." If the guest's name is known, it should be relayed to the server assigned to the table so that he or she can use the guest's name during the meal.

In contrast, some guests do not want their names announced, in which case their wishes should be respected. Well-known guests such as politicians, entertainers, and sports celebrities may well select restaurants in part because of their discretion when serving VIPs.

Staff members should be polite and use common sense at all times. For example, when they do not know the guest's name, they may address the guest as "Sir" or "Ma'am." If guests request a special table, they should get it if at all possible, and, of course, the table should be ready (clean tabletop, complete place settings, chairs free of crumbs) before they are taken to it.

While a guest's request for a certain table should be honored whenever possible, the manager often needs to balance server stations. For example, if a table of the appropriate size is available in several stations, a large party usually is given to the server with the least number of guests. However, managers in some restaurants feel that they should use a rotation plan so that each server has the opportunity to receive a fair share of tip income. Some restaurants do not use server stations; if seven food servers are on duty, each server gets every seventh party regardless of where the manager seats the group. This plan is used in some very famous, well-established restaurants with obvious success. Typically, however, a seating chart should be used to help even out server workloads, but it should be kept flexible to accommodate guests' requests.

In some casual/theme restaurants, the staff member who seats guests may also remove extra place settings, present menus, fill water glasses, and perform other preliminary tasks before the server arrives. If it is the policy of the restaurant, this service staff member also tells guests the name of their server. Some restaurants require the person who seats guests to check back with them after a few minutes to ensure that the server assigned to the table has welcomed them.

Presenting the Menu and Taking Beverage Orders

If guests do not already have menus or if menus are not already on the table, the server presents them as he or she welcomes the guests. Making guests feel welcome is an important task for the server. Servers should smile and be tactful and friendly. In many restaurants, servers identify themselves by name even if they are wearing name tags.

In some casual/theme restaurants, food servers bring glasses of water on their first trip to the table, present the menu, then ask the guests if they would like to order drinks. They may also tell the guests about daily specials at this point, or they may wait until after drinks are served. This is an ideal time for servers to use suggestive selling or upselling skills. To avoid offending those who cannot or do not drink alcoholic beverages, servers should suggest nonalcoholic drinks as well as alcoholic ones.

When taking beverage orders, servers should number guest checks so that they will know who ordered what, and note exact specifications from each guest—choice of garnish, whether the drink should be served with ice (on the rocks) or without ice (up or neat), and the specific call or premium brand if one is requested.

Placing Beverage Orders

Whether the beverage order is coffee, soft drinks, cocktails, or wine, orders are often filled at a bar or beverage station. Procedures for obtaining drinks at the bar are frequently similar to procedures for ordering food in the kitchen. Servers write the beverage orders on the guest check, often using the back of it. Many systems require beverage servers to enter the order into a precheck register before giving the guest check to the bartender for drink preparation. An intermediate step may require the bartender to mark the guest check after preparing the drinks so that he or she will know if a server has failed to enter orders for second and third rounds into the precheck register. In some restaurants, servers place and pick up beverage orders at a service bar; in other restaurants, servers go to the lounge or public bar area to get drink orders.

Serving Beverages

Drinks should be carried on a cocktail tray, which the server should rest in one hand while serving with the other; the tray should never rest on the table (to avoid jostling guests, and in case the bottom of the tray is dirty). Drinks are typically served from the right. Guests will need adequate time to enjoy their drinks and study their menus, so they should not be rushed.

Taking Food Orders

Unless one person orders for the party, it is traditional to begin with a woman and take orders clockwise. Servers should write the guest check in such a way that they will know "who gets what" when they serve the food or beverages. Many guests are annoyed if servers need to ask about the guests' selections at the time of service. Whenever possible, servers stand to the guest's left when taking orders. As servers take the orders, they should be certain to ask all necessary questions:

- What type of salad dressing would you like?

- How would you like your steak cooked?

- What vegetable do you prefer?

- Would you like coffee now or later?

Servers should use upselling and suggestive selling techniques and answer questions about the menu as they arise.

Placing and Picking Up Orders in the Kitchen

Procedures for placing orders vary greatly among casual/theme restaurants. Some use a precheck register. In others, servers simply call out orders. In still others, servers present guest checks to production personnel or use remote printing devices. It is important for servers to know and comply with the ordering systems established by management. Teamwork is critical to effective and efficient service.

Servers should follow procedures consistently in picking up orders. Before taking the food to the table, servers should check the written orders against the food and beverages on the serving tray to ensure that the order is correct. They should take the time to look at each plate and glass from the guest's perspective. Is the garnish attractive? Are there unsightly food spills on the rim of the plate that should be attended to? Does the food look tasty?

Servers must know how to carry a loaded tray. For safety's sake, the heaviest dishes and dishes containing liquids should be loaded toward the center of the tray. When trays are being loaded, hot dishes should be placed next to hot dishes, cold dishes next to cold dishes. When the tray is loaded properly, the server should bend from the knees, keeping his or her back straight and lifting the tray with the palm of the hand to shoulder height, using the other hand for balance. Experienced servers situate the heaviest side of the tray close to their bodies and make certain no items are likely to tip and spill.

There must be an established traffic pattern for service staff to follow. A server should announce "coming through" or "behind you" to alert others when he or she is going through a swinging door or is behind another staff member. When swinging doors are involved, they should be clearly marked "In" and "Out."

Serving the Orders

The restaurant's standard procedures determine how servers present food to guests. Typically, servers place their trays on food service stands, remove plate covers (if applicable), and then serve the guests. In some restaurants, service rules dictate that guests are served all food items from the left and beverages from the right. In others, guests are served everything from the right. In still others, especially those that have booths, the rule is "Serve with the least inconvenience to the guests."

Usually, children are served first, then women, then men. Entrée plates should be placed so that the main item is closest to the guest; for example, if a plate has a steak, some rice, and a vegetable on it, the plate is placed so the steak is closest to the guest. Any side dishes are usually placed to the left of the entrée plate.

Servers should check back with guests soon after delivering their orders. They should ask "Is everything to your satisfaction?" or a similar question and should ask if there is anything else the guests would like at this time. (Guests are more likely to appreciate this opportunity to comment if they are not in the process of taking a bite of food when asked these questions.)

When several courses are served, the dishes from one course should be cleared before the next course arrives; dishes are usually removed from the right. (This principle also applies to the service of drinks; if possible, the empty glassware should be removed—usually from the right—before the next round is served.) This method provides guests with more tabletop room, does not make them feel uncomfortable about eating too much, and puts dishes and glassware back into service more quickly.

Presenting the Guest Check

Timing the delivery of the guest check is important. Some guests may be in a hurry; others may linger over their meals. Whatever type of payment collection system is used, the check should be totaled and ready when the guest desires it. Servers should accurately complete each guest check and double-check the figures. If guest-check totals must be hand-tallied, servers will find that a calculator with a printing tape is very helpful.

There are two typical signals to guests that help them know how to pay the bill. Generally, if the guest check is presented on a plate or tray or in a folder, the server will collect the guest's payment and see that the guest gets proper change (or will handle the credit card transaction or charge the bill to the guest's room). Presenting the check without a plate or tray generally means that guests will pay at a cashier's stand. Many restaurants also clarify payment procedures for guests by printing them on the bill ("Please pay the cashier" or "Please pay the server"). Clarification from the server is also helpful ("I can take your payment for you when you're ready" or "You may pay the cashier when you're ready"). In all cases, servers should remember to thank the guests.

When presenting the check to a group, the server may already know who will pay the bill. A signal from the guest, an earlier conversation, or a specific request when the reservation was booked may have made this apparent. Servers undecided about who is responsible for the bill's payment often place the check in the center of the table.

The use of separate checks is also relatively common. While they create extra work for servers, many guests prefer them, and every restaurant should consider using them. Wise servers ask at the beginning of the meal whether the guests prefer individual checks.

When servers are responsible for taking guest payments, they should settle guest checks promptly and return the proper change, thanking the guest as they do so. If payment is by check or credit card, servers should follow the restaurant's procedures. Servers should not claim their tips until guests leave.

It goes without saying that the guests' last contact with the restaurant should be as pleasant as the first. The manager or some other representative of the restaurant should be on hand to say goodbye and cordially thank guests—by name, if their names are known—as they leave. Remembering and using a guest's name is a hallmark of personalized service.

Serving Special Guests

Although in one sense all guests are "special" and should be treated that way, servers sometimes find themselves serving guests who require out-of-the-ordinary attention. For example, staff members in family restaurants are trained to focus special efforts on children—one category of "special guests." What follows are other categories and considerations.

Guests with Special Diet Needs. Servers should know which menu items do not contain sodium and which items are available for vegetarians. Servers should know menu item ingredients in case guests have questions concerning food allergies. Servers should be able to suggest low-calorie menu items to those guests who request such information. People with special health concerns may need to speak to the manager or chef to ensure that their concerns are properly addressed.

Senior Citizens. Some older guests like light meals and tend to eat more slowly than other guests. They may prefer foods that are soft and bland rather than chewy and spicy. Some are on a limited budget. Servers should know which items senior guests might enjoy and, if asked, recommend them.

International Guests. Non-English-speaking guests should be spoken to slowly, not loudly. Servers should ask them if they have any special food preferences. Servers should try to put themselves in the guests' place and ask themselves, "How would I like to be treated if I were a visitor in another country?" Menus with pictures help communicate the identities of items.

Guests with Disabilities. Guests who have visual impairments should be welcomed in a normal tone of voice and asked whether they would like assistance, if they are not accompanied by guide dogs. (If a guest is accompanied by a guide dog, no one should attempt to feed, pet, or otherwise interact with the dog while it is "working.") If a guest who has a visual impairment desires assistance, the host should offer his or her arm and walk while informing the guest of steps, level changes, and crowded areas. Guests with visual impairments should be asked whether they prefer to receive a Braille menu (if one is available) or to have the menu read. The host or server should use the positions of numbers on a clock to describe locations of glassware, food on plates, and other tabletop items.

When welcoming guests who have hearing impairments, it is important to remember not to shout at them. Rather, since many can read lips, the server should face them directly and speak slowly and distinctly. Alternatively, the server can offer a pad of paper and a pen so the guest can write requests.

Guests in wheelchairs should be asked if they would like assistance. These guests should be seated at tables with sufficient space to comfortably accommodate the wheelchairs.

After Service

Controls help casual/theme restaurants achieve their goals and protect their assets. Guest feedback helps managers maintain and enhance guest service. Taking guest comments into consideration when planning fosters guest-driven service.

Ongoing procedures to keep dining areas sanitary and in good order are necessary to maintain the restaurant's public image. And, of equal importance, human resources policies and procedures must help managers select, train, schedule, and retain staff members who are enthusiastic about creating and delivering excellent service to guests.

The planning involved in providing good food and beverage service never ends; it is ongoing and must have as its goal the continuous improvement of the products and services the restaurant provides.

Apply Your Learning 14.3

Please write all answers on a separate sheet of paper.

1. What are the two basic types of reservations systems? How do they differ?

2. What information should be obtained when taking a reservation?

For statements 3–6, write whether the statement is True or False.

3. If a guest gives you a tip to reduce his waiting time, you should seat him right away.

4. When delivering drinks to a guest table, you should rest the tray on the table so you don't drop any drinks.

5. If the guest check is presented on a tray or in a folder, the server typically will collect the guest's payment.

6. Non-English-speaking guests should be spoken to slowly and loudly.

Quick Hits

SECTION 14.1—MARKETING PERSPECTIVE

- There are many types of **casual/theme restaurants**. Their common denominators are informal dining environments (although there are differing degrees of informality) and the availability of alcoholic beverages in most cases.

- There are casual/theme restaurants for virtually every market imaginable. Some of the major markets include Generation X, baby-boomers, influentials, and the affluent.

- Managers and staff members should seek guest comments on an ongoing basis. Guest comment cards, questionnaires, guest interviews, and other means can be used to determine guest needs and expectations and whether they are being met.

- Some restaurants use a **shopper's service** (also known as a "mystery shopper" service) to evaluate how guests' needs and expectations are being met. Shopper's services provide reports completed by anonymous "guests" (shoppers) who evaluate a restaurant's service from the guest's perspective.

- **Signature menu items**, or items that guests perceive as special and closely associated with the restaurant promoting it, not only make the restaurant unique in the guests' minds, but can also help build repeat business and strong guest loyalty.

- Casual/theme restaurants need to emphasize and reinforce the value they offer. These promotions can include daily specials, gift certificates, seasonal specials, senior-citizen discounts, complimentary samples of featured menu items, and frequent-diner programs.

- Some hotels have alliances with restaurant companies—that is, business agreements that allow the restaurant companies to operate restaurants in the hotels. Many of these alliances provide value for hotel guests by offering them a familiar place to eat and drink.

- Design and decor play a major role in shaping a casual/theme restaurant's ambiance—which is a fusion of design, decor, image, and service and is one of the most important factors in many guests' restaurant selection.

SECTION 14.2—GETTING READY FOR SERVICE

- Service methods and procedures must be followed consistently.

- Training for casual/theme restaurant service should focus on menu knowledge and sales skills as well as courtesy, consistency, efficiency, and teamwork.

- Providing menu information to guests is one of the most important services servers perform. In order to sell menu items, servers must know the menu and the house policies and rules about what they can and cannot do.

- Because guests will ask servers to describe how an unfamiliar item tastes, some restaurants provide tasting sessions for service staff; these sessions can boost the staff's sales skills.

- Suggestive selling involves encouraging guests to order such extras as appetizers, cocktails, wine, desserts, and after-dinner drinks.

- **Upselling** means suggesting more expensive (and often better-quality) items than those that the guest first mentions.

- **Table-turn rate** is the average amount of time that a table is occupied. It has a direct bearing on the quality of guest service.

SECTION 14.3—DELIVERING SERVICE

- Specific procedures for each casual/theme restaurant must be developed and all service staff members should be trained to use them consistently. Categories include: taking reservations, managing waiting guests, greeting and seating guests, presenting the menu and taking beverage orders, placing and serving beverage orders, taking food orders, placing and picking up orders in the kitchen, serving the orders, presenting the guest check, and serving guests with special needs.

- Many restaurants take reservations to allow guests the chance to reserve seating at a specific time. The two basic types of reservations systems are **interval reservations** (which offers seating at specific intervals), and **staggered reservations** (which staggers seating during the entire meal period).

- Reservation-takers should obtain the following information from callers: the correct spelling of the name the reservation will be under, the date and time of the reservation, the number in the party, whether a smoking or non-smoking section is preferred, whether the guests want a table or a booth, special instructions, and the guest's phone number (or room number if the restaurant is in a hotel).

- When greeting and seating guests, guests should be greeted by name if possible.

- Beverages should be carried on a cocktail tray, which the server should rest in one hand while serving with the other; the tray should never rest on the table.

- Teamwork is critical to effective and efficient service. Servers should follow procedures consistently in picking up and delivering orders.

- There are two typical signals to guests that help them know how to pay the bill. Generally, if the guest check is presented on a plate or tray or in a folder, the server will collect the guest's payment and see that the guest gets proper change (or will handle the credit card transaction or charge the bill to the guest's room). Presenting the check without a plate or tray generally means that guests will pay at a cashier's stand.

- Guests with special needs include guests with special diet needs, senior citizens, international guests, and guests with disabilities.

Profile

Chef Richard "Pete" Bowden
CEC, Executive Chef, Country Club of Fairfax

As soon as Chef Richard "Pete" Bowden first walked into a professional kitchen at age 14, he knew what it was he wanted to do. He wanted to be a chef.

Chef Bowden, a certified executive chef and winner of numerous awards, including the 1995 Chef of the Year Award from the Nation's Capital Chef's Association, started as a busboy for a private country club in the Tidewater, Virginia area. He then moved up to dishwasher, chef's helper, and assistant cook. Along the way, Chef Lonnie Johnson took notice of his drive and determination.

"I used to ask him if I could look at his cookbooks. On my lunch break I would look through the cookbooks and read recipes," Chef Bowden says. "I had a really early, fast start. I was pushed really, really hard to achieve and I can proudly say that I never let my employer down. I worked very hard, sometimes on my day off to try new recipes, trying to make the chef proud of me."

His executive chef went a step further and convinced the general manager to send Bowden to the Culinary Institute of America after his apprenticeship to continue his education. Bowden says the recognition he is most proud of is that of becoming a Certified Executive Chef (CEC) and his involvement in his local Chapter of the American Culinary Federation, Nation's Capitol Chefs Association.

"Educate yourself. That's the key. Connect with people that have experience doing the job you would like to do someday, you learn a lot from experience," Chef Bowden says. "Be a good instructor. We have to take courses to train ourselves before we can train other people. If you have an open mind, you'll continue to learn and continue to teach others as well. Always remember that you're a student of the art."

Now an executive chef at the Country Club of Fairfax, Chef Bowden often oversees large, elaborate banquets, a casual dining room, formal dining room, and golf outings. He is committed to delivering an outstanding product to every diner. One way he accomplishes this in a banquet setting is by purchasing the freshest ingredients, careful preparation, and plating food as each course is being served, staying perhaps 50 plates ahead of the servers. He says he has never liked pre-plating in advance of a banquet, "The appearance of your food is not very good when you do that, especially the appearance of your sauces."

"It's important that high school students really focus on a career. You should find something that you really, really like to do, something you will have fun doing. Don't look at the amount of money you can make, but something that you would like to do for a lifetime. You achieve a lot more if you do something you enjoy."

might not require an attendance estimate on the signing date. Some operations contact the client approximately two weeks before the event to get an update on the expected number of guests. If the event is large or requires special purchases, the operation will make this inquiry a month or more in advance of the function; operations may also contact the client for attendance updates more and more frequently as the date of the function approaches. In some cases (such as with conventions, which have optional attendance), ticket sales fluctuate so much from the original proposal that the group may need a larger or smaller room than was originally booked. On a date that is a certain number of days or weeks before the event and is specified in the contract (two days before the event for small-scale events is typical), the client must state the final number of attendees that are expected. This number is the **guarantee**.

A food service operation may apply a variance percentage to guarantees. For example, if the client guarantees an attendance of 240 guests, the operation might allow a 5 percent variance; since 5 percent of 240 is 12, the client would have to pay for at least 228 guests and at most 252, and the operation would prepare portions and set places for a maximum of 252 guests. Of course, if the menu is unusual or difficult to prepare, or if the estimated attendance is large, the variance percentage may be smaller. The larger the estimated attendance, the smaller the percentage of guests over the guarantee for which the operation should prepare. If an operation uses a 5 percent variance for an estimated attendance of 240, for example, it might prepare for only 3 percent over the guarantee for groups of 350 or more.

Unless the food service operation receives satisfactory credit references from the client, the contract often requires the client to pay a specific portion—as much as 100 percent—of the estimated cost of the function at least two weeks in advance of the event's date; clients usually pay any remaining balance within 30 days after the event. Food service operations generally reserve the right to cancel an event if the client has not established proper credit or made the required advance payment.

Typically, the following services are included in room rental rates:

1. Setup labor for normal meetings (tables, chairs, tablecloths, ice water, and ashtrays)

2. Movement of large furniture in the room to other locations

3. Removal of carpets

4. Public address system and microphones

5. Easels, chart boards, movie screens, tables for projectors, and extension cords

The following services are often *not* included in room rental rates but are charged separately:

1. Electrical layouts, plumbing, or other services for exhibits

2. Movie projectors, computers for PowerPoint presentations, VCRs, microphones, slide projectors, overhead projectors, and tape recorders (these items may be available from the operation for an additional charge, or the operation might obtain them from an outside supplier and charge the client a fee that reflects a markup for the operation)

3. Table decorations

4. A dance floor

5. Service staff, including audiovisual, electrical, or other technicians

Once the contract is signed, the salesperson must generate a function sheet to inform the rest of the banquet and catering staff about the event.

Function Sheets

A **function sheet** lists all of the details that apply to the function—everything anyone at the food service operation might need to know about the function to prepare for it and provide service during it (see Exhibit 3 for a sample function sheet). The salesperson who books the event completes the function sheet, then makes as many copies of it as necessary to distribute to the banquet/catering office, the manager who will schedule staff for the event, the beverage department (which schedules staff and orders the necessary products), the accounting department (which prepares the billing), the convention service or floor manager (if the beverage and catering operation is part of a large hotel; the convention service or floor manager is the person who arranges function room setups), the kitchen storeroom, the kitchen banquet staff, the kitchen's pantry area, the kitchen commissary, and the kitchen's bakeshop. Operations with computers may use software programs that make it easier to generate function sheets.

Apply Your Learning 15.1

Please write all answers on a separate sheet of paper.

1. What are the three documents that play a primary role in booking and planning banquet and catering events?

2. Managers and salespeople use the _____ to determine if a certain room is available for a particular function.

   a. guarantee
   b. function book
   c. contract
   d. function sheet

3. Every detail that the salesperson and client have discussed and agreed upon should be covered in the:

   a. guarantee.
   b. function book.
   c. contract.
   d. function sheet.

Exhibit 3
Sample Function Sheet

NOGA HILTON GENÈVE

BANQUETING DEPARTEMENT

Address		Date:
		Master N°:
		Telex:
		Telephone:
Name of the client:		Reservation N°:
INFORMATION BOARD		Client:

Time	Type of Function	Rooms	N° Pers. guaranted	CONFERENCE SET UP	Fr.
				Room rental	
				Table set up	
				School / Cinema Style.	
				Minerals	
				Writing pads / pencils	
				Flip chart.	
				Head table . . . . pers.	
				Stage.	
MENU:			Fr.	Speaker desk	
				Welcome desk	

LUNCH / DINNER
- Table set up . . . .
- Host table. . . . . pers. . . . .
- Candlesticks. . . . .
- Table numbers . . . .
- Stage. . . . .
- Dance floor. . . . .

ORCHESTRA by hotel. . . . .
by client . . . .
Police authorization by hotel . . . . h. . . . .
by client . . . . h. . . . .

TECHNICAL EQUIPMENT
- Video. . . . .
- Screen. . . . .
- Overhead projector . . . .
- Film / Slide Projector . . . .
- Large / small control center . . . .
- Telephone. . . . .
- Microphone . . . .
- Technician from . . . . to . . . .

COFFEE BREAK	Fr.	LUNCH / DINNER	Fr.	MENUS	
. . . .		Minerals		Simple print by our self	
. . . .		Wines		Double print by our self	
Croissant. . . . . Cake.				Print by client	
				Title:	
BAR / APERITIF					
Chips, peanuts, olives				**FLORAL DECORATIONS**	
International bar.				Round and long terrine	
Simple bar (without whisky, gin,				Arrangement	
wodka)				Green plant.	
		Liquors		By the client	
		Cigars		**WARDROBE ROOM**	
		Drinks		Stander.	
				. . . . personne(s)	

NH 6206　　**IMPORTANT: SIGNATURE AND CONDITIONS ON THE REVERSE SIDE OF THIS PAGE**

Courtesy of Noga Hilton Genève, Geneva, Switzerland

4. Everything anyone at the food service operation might need to know to prepare for a function would be listed in the:

    a. guarantee.
    b. function book.
    c. contract.
    d. function sheet.

5. Which of the following items or services are typically included in room rental rates?

    a. removal of carpets
    b. dance floors
    c. audiovisual technician
    d. VCRs

15.2 Getting Ready for Service

AFTER STUDYING SECTION 15.2, YOU SHOULD KNOW HOW TO:

♦ Set up a function room

♦ Schedule staff members

♦ Identify the special training needs of banquet staff

♦ Prepare, plate, and store food

Getting ready for service for banquets and catered events includes setting up the function room(s); scheduling staff members; and preparing, plating, and storing banquet food.

Setting Up Function Rooms

The design and decor of function rooms, like the food and beverages that are served in them, can take many forms. A simple coffee break may be served in an undecorated, themeless room, while an elaborate reception featuring foods from around the world may be served in a function room that has complex decorations to fit the theme. The type of function room chosen and how it is decorated are largely dictated by the needs and expectations of the client.

Frequently, managers come up with creative layouts for function rooms to help setup crews carry out instructions on the function sheet. Some clients have strong preferences about the layout of function rooms, and those might be expressed in unusual or creative layouts as well. Managers should carefully plan the location of such room elements as bars, food buffet stations, ice carvings, garden and tree decorations, and stages for speakers or entertainers. The location of these elements affects the guests' experiences in the room. The need for staff members to pay close attention to the details listed on the function sheet and illustrated on the layout is just as important for small events as it is for large, elaborate events.

Adequate space for display tables, guest tables, and other room elements (for example, stages and lecterns) is an important setup consideration for banquets and catered events. Crowded, hot rooms make for an unpleasant dining experience. Adequate space also allows for more efficient movement of inventory and people.

The client is usually responsible for reviewing any seating charts that the event may require. However, the manager can assist the client with that task and indicate the staff's preferences regarding seating arrangements.

Procedures for setting up function rooms vary according to the needs of the client and his or her group. The following is a partial list of activities and items that might be involved in setting up a function room:

1. Placing runways, carpets, and pianos

2. Placing dinner tables, meeting tables, and head tables

3. Placing chairs, sofas, and other seats

4. Placing bars, buffets, and cake tables

5. Placing the registration, gift, and display tables

6. Placing the video/movie screen, projector table, projector, and extension cords

7. Placing chalkboards, easels, and any other display equipment

8. Placing microphones, lecterns, and flags

9. Placing linens, ashtrays, sugar bowls, salt and pepper shakers, and other tabletop items

10. Placing cakes, candle holders, fountains, flowers, and decorations

11. Placing table numbers on each table, if necessary

Because guests at banquets and catered events must be served quickly, service stations should be set up to allow for maximum staff efficiency. Equipment requirements vary with the type of function and the menu, but function-room service stations may have the following:

- Microwave ovens
- Flatware
- Glassware
- Water, coffee, and tea
- Cream, sugar, and stirrers
- Placemats and napery
- Candles, flowers, or other table decorations

- Matches or lighters
- First aid kits
- Salt, pepper, and other condiments

Prior to opening the function room's doors and allowing guests to enter, the manager overseeing service for the event must ensure that the room setup is complete. Whenever practical, the manager should meet with the client immediately before the event to inquire about the latest guest count or any last-minute changes to the plan for the event. The manager should walk through the function room (or assign someone else to do so) to make a safety check. No cords should be positioned where someone could trip on them; supports for platform panels, acoustical shells, table leaves, and risers should all be secure; chairs and tables should not wobble, and all their legs should be sturdy; and doorways and hallways (especially fire exits) should not be obstructed.

The manager in charge usually holds a brief meeting with all service staff (and sometimes kitchen staff) to review details and give final updates just before the event begins.

Scheduling Staff Members

Managers must schedule the proper number of staff members and types of staff positions for each banquet or catered event. Based on the number of special functions scheduled each day, the banquet/catering director or manager must schedule staff members to set up and break down function rooms, as well as schedule service staff to perform all of the guest-contact service and related tasks involved in the events themselves.

The number of servers and other personnel that are scheduled for an event varies from operation to operation and from event to event. Among top private clubs, for example, the ratio may be one server for every 10 to 15 guests. A greater than usual number of servers and other personnel will also be needed for an event if a client asks for special services. **Synchronized service**, for example, requires the entire service staff to enter the function room through one set of doors to serve each course. In unison and using precise movements, servers place the courses in front of guests. Often wine service is also synchronized. This style of banquet service requires a great deal of training, rehearsal, skill, and additional staff.

Training. Training staff members to be banquet servers requires that trainers have a fundamental knowledge of all service styles and skills that might be used at events that the operation hosts. Rehearsals in which service actions are repeated a number of times are often the best way to help servers internalize service styles and skills. Special styles of service as well as the details of the "script" (the function sheet) should be reviewed during practice sessions.

Banquet and catering service personnel also must be trained to realize that, as guest-contact staff members, they give guests first and last impressions of the operation. Some guests at banquet and catered events may have unique service needs. For example, international groups may have unique cultural customs. Chinese business banquets end promptly after the host rises and gives a toast. Even interpretations of facial expressions and hand gestures differ from culture to culture. Staff members who will serve guests at international functions should be trained to be sensitive to the guests' customs.

In China, for example, someone named "Liang Cheng-wu" should be addressed as "Mr. Liang"; "Cheng-wu" is a compound of the man's first and middle names and it would be socially incorrect to use it. Some international clients may present a small gift to the banquet or catering manager, who should be prepared to give a modest gift in return.

Preparing, Plating, and Storing Food

The chef is an integral member of the planning team. When the input of the chef and other food production staff members is used to develop menus for banquets and catered events, few, if any, production problems should arise when the staff prepares these menus.

Some banquet and catering operations that handle events with large numbers of guests use an automated assembly line to portion meals. More commonly, however, operations use a manual plating process. Exhibit 1 shows one arrangement of people, equipment, and supplies that can be used to plate and set up one kind of meal. As illustrated in Exhibit 1, one person carves and places roast beef slices on plates, then passes (slides) the plates along the table to a second staff member, who portions the green beans amandine. A third staff member portions the potatoes au gratin and slides the plates across the table to a fourth staff member, who places sauce on the meat. A fifth staff member puts covers on the plates and loads the plates onto a mobile cart. Using this system, five staff members can plate food for 300 people in approximately 45 minutes. (If the client wants the meal to be served in less time, a second plating line

---

Exhibit 1
Possible Setup for Plating Banquet and Catered-Event Meals

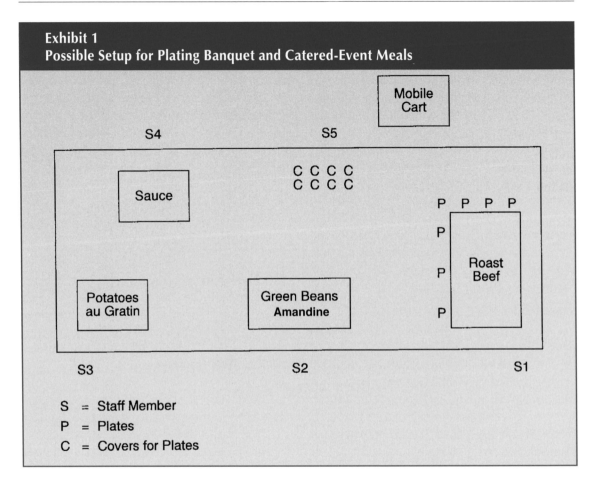

S = Staff Member
P = Plates
C = Covers for Plates

---

could be set up.) If the client had requested a plate garnish, the process would have required another staff member to provide it.

In banquet and catering service, time and temperature control for food is critical. It is virtually impossible to prepare hundreds of individual plates as service progresses. Therefore, foods are usually preplated for large banquets or catered events and then stored hot or cold in holding cabinets. Refrigerated mobile storage units must maintain internal product temperatures of 41°F (5°C) or less; mobile hot storage cabinets must maintain a minimum internal product temperature of 140°F (60°C). This keeps held food out of the temperature danger zone (TDZ). (Because the TDZ may be defined slightly differently in various areas of the country, managers should check with local and state health authorities to make sure they are in compliance with all food safety codes.)

For holding cold products, ice is usually an acceptable means of maintaining chilled temperatures. However, food must not be directly exposed to ice or melted water; instead, it must be held in bowls or containers embedded in the ice.

Hot food can be kept hot in a number of ways. Chafing dishes powered by electricity or canned heat are usually used to hold hot foods on a buffet table. Large roasts, hams, and turkeys that are to be carved in the function room should be displayed under infrared heat lamps. Sneeze guards or other equipment to prevent contamination of displayed food may be required by local or regional health regulations.

Outdoor service presents unique holding challenges. Food must be protected from dust and other contaminates, so staff members may need to use special coverings for food and beverage products to protect them between production and service. Outdoor food preparation involves other holding problems as well (such as maintaining foods at proper temperatures). It is a good idea to check with state or local authorities for laws governing the outdoor cooking and serving of food before planning such functions.

Apply Your Learning 15.2

Please write all answers on a separate sheet of paper.

1. Name some typical equipment or supplies found in function-room service stations.

For statements 2–5, write whether the answer is True or False.

2. Managers should meet with the client immediately before the event to inquire about the latest guest count.

3. Synchronized service requires the entire service staff to enter the function room through one set of doors to serve each course.

4. The automated assembly line style of portioning meals is most common in today's banquet and catering operations.

5. The temperature danger zone, or TDZ, is the temperature at which the food is in danger of burning.

15.3 Delivering Service

AFTER STUDYING SECTION 15.3, YOU SHOULD KNOW HOW TO:

♦ List challenges that managers and staff members face during banquets

♦ Explain beverage payment plans for banquets and catered events

♦ List examples of protocol issues

Because of all the planning and other preparatory work that goes into every banquet or catered event, you might think that a banquet or catering manager would only need to supervise staff members from a distance during the event itself. In reality, last-minute issues and challenges often occupy the manager throughout an event. Because challenges arise, the manager in charge should either be present at the event or easy to reach, both by staff members and the client. The following are examples of challenges that managers and staff members may face just before or during an event:

• Supply shortages

• Staff members who phone in sick or become ill during the event

• The arrival of an unexpectedly large number of extra guests

• Equipment malfunctions

• Guests who need assistance to operate equipment

• Conflicts between staff members

• Large or dangerous spills

• Injuries, choking, and other medical emergencies

• Angry guests

• Inebriated guests

• Speakers or entertainers who show up late or not at all

• Power failures

• Fire alarms

• Natural disasters

Wise managers have contingency plans in place for the most common challenges.

Beverage Service

Managers must carefully plan procedures for providing beverage service to guests at banquets and catered events. Just as lounges and bars must do, banquet and catering operations must observe liquor laws. Age limits and legal hours for beverage service are among the most important beverage laws that affect banquet and catering operations. In some localities, laws may require clients to obtain permits to serve alcoholic beverages to private groups in function rooms during certain hours. If this is the case, banquet/catering managers or salespeople must make this known to clients and tell them how to obtain the special approvals or permits. In addition, managers may need to curtail the service of alcoholic beverages on election days in some states.

The banquet and catering operation is responsible for preventing underage drinking in its function rooms; the operation's managers cannot delegate this responsibility to clients. Because of this, it is wise for a banquet or catering manager to closely monitor beverage service when underage guests attend an event.

Many operations use one or a combination of the following popular beverage plans to provide beverage service at banquets or catered events.

Cash Bar. At a **cash bar**, guests pay cash to the bartender or purchase tickets from a cashier to pay for drinks prepared by the bartender. With a ticket system, the cashier may be issued numbered tickets of various colors, which represent different drink prices. Guests pay the cashier for the drinks they want and are given tickets of the appropriate colors that they can present to the bartender. The banquet/catering manager or salesperson generally specifies the drink prices in the contract; the prices can be the same as or different from normal selling prices. Frequently, managers or salespeople will reduce beverage prices from the normal lounge rates in order to attract group business.

Host Bar: Charge by the Drink. A **host bar** that charges the host by the drink uses a system to keep track of the number of each type of drink served (through tickets turned over to the bartender by guests, transactions recorded by a point-of-sale system, or marks on a tally sheet). Guests do not pay anything. Managers will frequently reduce the prices of the drinks from the normal charges.

Host Bar: Charge by the Bottle. This plan involves charging for beverages consumed on the basis of the number of bottles used or opened. The difference between the number of bottles of each type of liquor, beer, or wine in the beginning inventory and ending inventory at the function room's portable bar represents the number of bottles used. An agreed-upon price for each bottle opened is assessed to the host (who is, in effect, purchasing the beverages that remain in open bottles but were not consumed by guests).

Host Bar: Charge by the Hour. This pricing plan charges hosts a fixed beverage fee per person per hour. This plan involves estimating the number of drinks guests will consume each hour. While estimates are not easy to make that will apply to all groups (health- or weight-conscious groups will probably consume less than fraternities, for example), a rule of thumb used by some banquet and catering managers is three drinks per person during the first hour, two the second, and one-and-a-half the third. Managers who want to price drinks for special events on a per-person, per-hour basis can use this formula to estimate the number of drinks each person will consume during the event. They must then multiply the number of drinks per person by an established drink charge to arrive at the hourly drink charge per person. As managers use the hourly charge system, they should maintain their own statistics on consumption; these statistics can assist them in more accurately setting hourly charges for future events.

Wine Service. When banquets or catered events involve wine service, service staff may circulate with bottles of several wines (red and white, dry and semi-dry) so that they can offer guests a choice. Of course, these staff members must be trained to serve wine properly. Other operations set up a portable bar in a nearby area so that bartenders can prepare glasses of wine (and other drinks) as needed.

Portable beverage service equipment makes the tasks of providing beverages at banquets and catered events much easier. Most portable equipment is on wheels; it can be stored in remote areas and wheeled to the point of use as needed.

Protocol for Special Banquets and Catered Events

Every banquet or catered event is special to the guests who attend it, and banquet and catering staff members must always be courteous and exercise common sense to make the guests' experiences as enjoyable as possible. However, there are some "special" banquets and catered events in which staff members must also understand **protocol**— the formal rules of etiquette used for ceremonies of state, military functions, and other special events.

There are rules that dictate the proper way to do things when very special guests are served. Managers and service personnel who will come in direct contact with special guests must understand and be able to practice protocol. The following examples illustrate the types of issues that can come up.

At formal events, the seat of honor at the head table is to the right of the host. The second seat of honor is to the left of the host. If another seat of honor is required, it is the second seat on the right of the host. The rest of the seats at the head table should be allo-

cated according to the rank or prominence of the guests. These guests should be assigned seats by alternating from the right to the left of the host out from the center of the head table.

Flag display is also important in protocol. In the United States, for example, at a cocktail party, a standing gathering, or an event with theater seating for which flags must be positioned before the guests arrive, the U.S. flag is placed on the left side of the front of the room, as viewed from the dining area. If a five-place arched flag stand is used, the U.S. flag takes the center (highest) position. Other flags are placed to the left and right of the U.S. flag in order of importance: the second most important flag is placed in the hole immediately to the left of the U.S. flag, from the audience's perspective; the third most important flag goes immediately to the right of the U.S. flag; and the next most important flag goes in the hole furthest to the left, leaving the hole furthest to the right for the least important flag.

When flags are used behind a podium, the national colors are placed on the physical right of the speaker as he or she addresses the audience. When displayed behind the speaker's platform without a pole, the flag must be flat against its display surface and must have its longest dimension parallel to the floor, directly behind and slightly above the podium.

Staff members should never use the flag of any country as a table cover, drape, rosette, or any other type of decoration. To decorate with bunting that has the national colors of the United States (red, white, and blue), staff members should place the color blue uppermost, then white, and finally red as the lowest of the three colors.

Apply Your Learning 15.3

Please write all answers on a separate sheet of paper.

1. What are some challenges that managers and staff members may face just before or during an event?

2. What beverage plans are available for providing beverage service at banquets or catered events?

For statements 3–6, write whether the answer is True or False.

3. Banquet and catering operations must observe the same liquor laws as bars and lounges.

4. When charging by the bottle for a host bar, the host must pay for any bottles which were opened, regardless of the amount served from the bottle.

5. Protocol is the set of formal etiquette rules used when serving beverages from a portable beverage cart.

6. An example of a decorative and creative table covering would be the guest of honor's national flag.

15.4 *After Service*

AFTER STUDYING SECTION 15.4, YOU SHOULD KNOW HOW TO:

♦ Describe the types of controls that banquet managers must practice

♦ Explain how guest comments can be collected and used

♦ Use feedback during banquet planning

After the completion of food and beverage service at an event, the manager in charge must perform several after-service tasks. One such task is supervising staff members to ensure that they complete their clean-up and breakdown duties properly. Exhibit 1 is a checklist for many of these required tasks. Staff members must clean up the function room(s) and break down temporary structures (such as a dance floor or stage). Managers must evaluate how well the operation handled the banquet or catered event. The experience gained from each event can help with the planning of other events.

During the cleanup and breakdown of the function room(s), control efforts must occur to ensure that both the client and the operation attain the goals established for the event. Guest comments must also be sought to provide guest input into continuous quality improvement.

Controls

Managers must establish systems of control for the food and beverages served in banquets and catered events.

Food Controls. Payments may or may not be collected from clients at the time of the banquet or catered event; the contract for each event specifies the payment terms that

Bear Facts

The legends surrounding the teddy bear seem to agree on only one fact—that President Teddy Roosevelt was involved. One of the legends involves the famous Hotel Colorado, a property that opened in 1893 near the hot springs. The hotel's most famous guest (among many celebrities and historical figures) was President Theodore Roosevelt who stayed in the hotel while bear hunting in 1905. The Hotel Colorado claims that the first teddy bear originated there either when the president's daughter named one of the bear pelts "Teddy" or when several maids stitched a small bear together out of scraps of cloth.

Other famous guests? It is reported that Al Capone convinced a bellman to deliver a case of gin to him during prohibition. In return, he tipped the bellman enough to pay for his college tuition.

Exhibit 1
Checklist for Post-Event Managerial Duties

Banquet/Catered Event

☐ Clear all tables of china, glass, flatware, and ashtrays.

☐ Remove all linens.

☐ Straighten legs on all tables.

☐ Rearrange all chairs around tables neatly.

☐ Store salt and pepper shakers, sugar bowls, ashtrays, water pitchers, and other tabletop items.

☐ Clear all remaining carts and lock them.

☐ Remove candles and any melted wax from candelabras and return to storage.

☐ Pour several pitchers of water into garbage cans in kitchen to prevent possible fire hazard.

☐ Check out with supervisor on duty.

Banquet/Catered Event Supervisor

☐ Supervise the banquet/catered event service staff.

☐ Turn off public address system.

☐ Collect microphones and cords and return to proper storage area(s).

☐ Collect projectors and other audiovisual equipment and return to storage.

☐ Search area for valuable items left behind.

☐ Check cloakroom and restroom areas.

☐ Secure any items found and turn them in to the Lost and Found the following day.

☐ Inspect for fire hazards.

☐ Turn off lights.

☐ Lock all doors. (If a group is moving out, remain until the move is completed).

☐ Leave written information regarding any maintenance problems or items helpful to the supervisor who will open the room the next day.

☐ Leave written information on the manager's desk regarding any guest complaints or serious staff-member relations problems.

☐ Lock, secure, and turn off lights and air conditioning units in all other function rooms.

the operation and the client agreed upon. However, when the banquet actually occurs, the operation must count the number of guests served to determine if payment is due for guests served in excess of the original estimate.

How do managers determine how many guests were served? If a buffet is planned in which no one can go back for seconds and therefore guests only use one plate, managers can take a plate count. The number of plates on the buffet line at the beginning of service plus any plates that were put on the line during service minus the number of plates on the buffet line at the end of service equals the number of guests served.

At buffets where guests go through the line more than once or at table service events, the manager must personally count the number of guests served. Typically, the manager takes a count that he or she confirms through separate counts taken by other supervisors in charge of specific function room areas or through counts of meals served by individual food servers. Another way to take a count is to count the number of empty seats and subtract that number from the total number of chairs set up; this gives the manager the number of guests served. In some operations, the guests receive tickets from their host that they turn in either as they enter the function room or after they are seated.

At stand-up receptions, a representative of the operation might be stationed at the entrance of the reception area to count guests as they arrive. To avoid re-counting guests who leave and return, a ticket system could be used; the count of guests served would then be based on the number of tickets turned in.

At coffee breaks and similar functions, the price charged to the client usually is based on the volume of products used to set up the event, such as gallons of coffee or dozens of pastries. If, however, a coffee break's price is determined by the number of people served, a manager should count the number of guests seated in the meeting immediately before the start of coffee service.

The responsibility for determining the number of guests served, no matter what type of service or counting method is used, rests with the manager in charge of the event. Having more than one count performed is a good way to ensure accuracy. It is often a good idea to involve the client in the process of counting guests or supplies, too. Managers try to avoid disagreements over counts, and when the client monitors or is otherwise involved in determining the count, he or she is less likely to dispute it later.

Beverage Controls. Managers can simplify the control procedures for beverages, since fewer kinds of alcoholic beverages are generally available at banquets and catered events than there are in dining rooms or restaurants. For example, if only two types of wine (house and call) are available, management can easily reconcile the amount of alcohol sold with the amount of income collected.

The amount of alcoholic beverages issued to a portable bar (both initially and during service) can be recorded on a form similar to the one in Exhibit 2. (Managers should remember to count partial bottles as whole bottles in the "Net Use" column on the far right if the payment plan is "charge by the bottle.") By conducting a beginning and an ending inventory, the amount of each product actually used can be determined. In a by-the-drink payment plan, the amount of income that the servers should have generated from a particular product can be determined by converting the figure in the farthest right column of Exhibit 2—"Net Use"—into standard portion sizes and then converting that into the number of drinks sold.

Guest Comments

After major functions, the client usually meets with the operation's managers to give

Exhibit 2
Portable Bar Setup Sheet

Function Order Number *1007-F* Number of People *25*

Name *Anne Helmstead* Date *5/2/XX*

Room *Blue* Time *5:00-6:00 P.M.*

Number of Bottles or Drinks

Name of Item	Size	Setup	Add'l.	Add'l.	Add'l.	Total	Returns			
							Full	Empty	Partial	Net Use
House Scotch	liter	*5*	*3*	*1*	*1*	*10*	*1*	*8*	*.5*	*8.5*
House Bourbon	liter	*3*	*1*			*4*	*1*	*3*	*0*	*3.0*
Call Scotch	liter									

feedback and to settle accounts as much as possible. After small functions, the review process may be more modest: the manager in charge may give the client an evaluation sheet and ask him or her to fill it out and return it. A telephone call to the client a day or two after the event provides the manager with an opportunity to thank the client and ask for additional feedback. This reinforces for the client the operation's commitment to guest service. It also helps communicate to clients that their future business is desired.

Using Feedback in Planning

Planning is a critical activity for banquets and catered events, and feedback about past events can help managers plan future events. Regardless of whether an operation holds a review meeting with the client after an event, managers should hold such a meeting with all staff members who were involved in providing service during the event. These meetings are particularly helpful when mistakes that guests noticed occurred. Such mistakes may happen again if managers do not take the time to review them and discuss possible solutions. Managers and staff should relay to each other any comments from guests or the client. This exchange should lead to action plans to correct problems that were mentioned most often by guests. Continuous quality improvement is the key to the development of a profitable and guest-pleasing banquet and catering operation.

Apply Your Learning 15.4

Please write all answers on a separate sheet of paper.

1. What are the two types of controls managers must establish systems for?

2. What are some ways managers can calculate the number of guests served?

For statements 3–6, write whether the answer is True or False.

3. It is a bad idea to get clients involved in the process of counting guests as they are likely to "under count" the actual number of guests.

4. Control procedures for cash bars are simplified since fewer kinds of alcohol are generally available.

5. A telephone call to a client a few days after the event reinforces the operation's commitment to guest service.

6. Feedback about past events is helpful for managers when planning future events.

Quick Hits

Chapter 15

15.1—BOOKING AND PLANNING EVENTS

- Three documents play a primary role in booking and planning banquet and catering events: the function book, sometimes called the daily function room diary; the contract or letter of agreement; and the function sheet, which is sometimes called a banquet event order (BEO).

- Managers and salespeople use the function book to determine if a certain room is available for a particular function at a particular time. It is used to reserve a room after an event is sold so that no one else will commit the room for another function covering the same time period. It also lists all of the operation's function space available for sale, and has a daily time log for each space to facilitate the recording of sold blocks of time.

- After the salesperson and client have agreed on terms, the salesperson should draw up a **contract** or **letter of agreement**. Every detail that the two parties have discussed and agreed upon should be covered in the contract, including the exact products and services that will be provided to the client's group, including the food, beverages, labor, and other direct costs incurred to produce and serve the items.

- A **guarantee** is the final number of attendees the client is expecting. A food

service operation may apply a variance percentage to guarantees.

- A **function sheet** lists all of the details that apply to the function—everything anyone at the food service operation might need to know about the function to prepare for it and provide service during it.

15.2—GETTING READY FOR SERVICE

- Getting ready for service for banquets and catered events includes setting up the function room(s); scheduling staff members; and preparing, plating, and storing banquet food.

- The design and decor of function rooms can take many forms. Managers should carefully plan the location of such room elements as bars, food buffet stations, ice carvings, garden and tree decorations, and stages for speakers or entertainers. The location of these elements affects the guests' experiences in the room.

- Managers usually hold a brief meeting with all service staff to review details and give final updates just before the event begins.

- Managers must schedule the proper number of staff members and types of staff positions for each banquet or catered event.

- The manual plating technique is commonly used to portion meals in banquet and catering operations that handle events with large numbers of guests. In this system, each staff member plates and portions one element of the meal and then passes it on to the next staff member.

- The temperature danger zone (TDZ) is the temperature at which food storage becomes unsafe.

15.3—DELIVERING SERVICE

- Wise managers have contingency plans in place for the most common challenges to delivering quality service.

- Banquet and catering operations must observe liquor laws just as lounges and bars do. Age limits and legal hours for beverage service are among the most important beverage laws that affect banquet and catering operations.

- Many operations use a **cash bar** or **host bar** or a combination of the two to provide beverage service at banquets or catered events.

- Portable beverage service equipment makes the tasks of providing beverages at banquets and catered events much easier.

- Some "special" banquets and catered events require that staff members understand **protocol**—the formal rules of etiquette used for ceremonies of state, military functions, and other special events.

15.4—AFTER SERVICE

- Managers must establish systems of control for the food and beverages served in banquets and catered events.

- Managers determine how many guests were served by a variety of methods, including taking a plate count, using a ticket system, counting the empty seats, and counting actual guests.

- The responsibility for determining the number of guests served, no matter what type of service or counting method is used, rests with the manager in charge of the event. Having more than one count performed is a good way to ensure accuracy.

- After major functions, the client usually meets with the operation's managers to give feedback and to settle accounts as much as possible. After smaller functions, an evaluation sheet may be filled out.

- Planning is a critical activity for banquets and catered events, and feedback about past events can help managers plan future events. Managers should also hold a meeting with all staff members who were involved in providing service during the event.

Profile

David A. Stout

Vice President of Operations, Grand Hotel, Mackinac Island, Michigan

David Stout didn't fall in love with the hospitality industry as much as he fell in love with a hotel. During a summer's break from Ohio State University, he went to the Grand Hotel at Mackinac Island to work at the pool. That began a lifelong love affair with the hotel and the island.

The 114-year-old Grand Hotel offered many alluring charms to tempt Stout away from Ohio State. The largest summer hotel in the country, the Grand Hotel is a Victorian luxury hotel made with Michigan white pine and sporting a 660-foot porch. Each room has its own unique décor. It is located on Mackinac Island—where no motorized vehclies are allowed and horse-drawn carriages are still a common sight.

The next summer, Stout decided he wanted to get inside the doors, so he left Ohio State for good, took a job as a bellman and ended up staying the whole season—and the rest of his career. "I stuck with it and enjoyed the heck out of it."

Stout chose wisely, for the Grand Hotel has a tradition of promoting from within—indeed, the family that now owns it first became associated with the hotel when their uncle, Stewart Woodfall, began working at the hotel as a desk clerk in 1917.

Stout encourages students to find a property they like. "I've seen a lot of people come in as hourly workers and end up as managers, regardless of the property. The hotel industry recognizes and rewards good workers."

Stout himself moved up from bellman to bell captain, director of services, and assistant manager of the hotel. In 1986 he moved into sales at another property on Mackinac Island and then to properties in Grand Rapids, Michigan. While he said he learned a lot about all areas of the hotel, he soon realized that it was Mackinac Island and the Grand Hotel that he was in love with.

"I came back in 1990; they'll have a hard time getting rid of me now." Now the vice president of operations, Stout enjoys working directly with guests. "I help keep a 114-year-old building operating, and you can't do that unless you have happy guests that keep coming back."

Stout is quick to credit the family owners of the Grand Hotel with making it such a fine hotel and workplace, "It's a great family to work for. There is no better person to learn from than Mr. Musser (the current owner)."

"It is absolutely wonderful to find something you can truly love and make a very good living at it, which is what happened to me," Stout said. "Hopefully, I can talk my son into going into the business."

Room Service

Sections

16.1 Getting Ready for Room Service

16.2 Delivering Room Service

16.3 After Room Service

16.1 Getting Ready for Room Service

AFTER STUDYING SECTION 16.1, YOU SHOULD KNOW HOW TO:

♦ List the key elements of well-managed room service

♦ Determine what information room service staff needs to know

♦ Describe the staffing requirements of a room service department

♦ Identify the major duties of room service staff

♦ Forecast room service demand and schedule staff

♦ Prepare for a service shift

Many lodging properties provide their guests with the opportunity to order and enjoy food and beverages in the privacy of their own guestrooms or suites. Some guests enjoy **room service** as a way of adding a special touch to a special occasion. Others see it as a status symbol, and still others appreciate it simply for its convenience.

In this chapter we will look at room service issues, including markets, marketing, menus, and room service variations and alternatives. We will then discuss the room service cycle: getting ready for service, delivering service, and attending to various responsibilities after the service has been delivered.

Room Service Issues

Many people, when they see a room service menu for the first time, are surprised at the relatively high prices. Even more surprising is the fact that few room service operations make a significant profit. Why, then, is room service offered? One simple reason is that guests at many properties want it. In a guest survey by *Lodging Hospitality*, room service breakfast was found to be the number one guestroom amenity for which respondents were willing to pay extra, out of a list that included video movies, Internet access, an in-room microwave oven, and in-room coffee. Professional hospitality managers have guest satisfaction as their goal. These managers know that when room service is well managed, it can give their property a competitive edge, enhance guest satisfaction, and enhance the property's public image.

From the perspective of guests, the key elements of well-managed room service include the following:

• Prompt and courteous responses when guests call to place orders

• Correctly filled orders

• Efficient and quick delivery of orders to guestrooms

• Tact and courtesy from staff members who deliver and serve orders

- Staff members who strictly adhere to rules of safety when using equipment that involves liquid fuels or open flames

- Hot and cold foods and beverages that are at the correct temperatures when they are served

- The prompt removal of trays and other equipment when guests have finished their meals or snacks

Room service needs to meet the needs of guests, but it also must be designed with the property's human and material resources in mind. A new room service program might require: new facilities to be built, new equipment purchased, and additional staff members hired. Some properties add a surcharge to room service menu items to cover some or all of these costs, although the industry trend is toward pricing room service menus at the same levels as dining room menus. For example, Wyndham Hotels and Resorts has eliminated room service surcharges and views room service as if it were simply another restaurant in the hotel.

Twenty-four–hour room service is much easier when one or more of the hotel's restaurants are also open around the clock; room service generally costs much more than it brings in if a separate production facility must be maintained for it. For this reason, room service at some lodging properties ends whenever the restaurant closes for the night. Some properties use separate production facilities for room service and transfer the production responsibilities from the room service kitchen to a restaurant or coffee shop kitchen only during slow times.

Increasingly, because of the growing number of alliances between hotel companies and chain or independent restaurants, hotel food and beverage departments that have not traditionally offered room service have added it but they have their partners provide it. For example, a Holiday Inn hotel with a TGI Friday's restaurant may provide its room service via the restaurant.

Some hotels do a large volume of **hospitality suite** business, offering food and beverage service for small group meetings, corporate meetings, organizations entertaining guests during conventions, and other occasions. These properties are able to increase the productivity of their room service operations by placing the responsibility for hospitality suites with room service rather than with the banquet or catering department. Room service then provides all food and beverage service in any hotel room, including suites, for any number of guests. Since food and beverage sales in hospitality suites usually produce a profit, they can help offset losses accrued from offering traditional room service.

Getting Ready for Room Service

Getting ready for room service includes attending to staffing requirements as well as gathering the inventory and equipment necessary to provide excellent room service. Room service managers must give careful thought to staffing. A limited-service property may have 10 or fewer room service staff members, while full-service properties may have large room service departments. The inventory and equipment required for room service ranges from simple trays for delivering continental breakfasts, to the carts, candles, special tablecloths and napkins, and other items involved in serving an elaborate candlelight dinner.

**Exhibit 1
Sample Task List: Room Service Attendant**

1. Perform beginning-of-shift duties.
2. Preset room service trays and carts.
3. Process express breakfast orders.
4. Deliver VIP amenities.
5. Use point-of-sale (POS) equipment.
6. Take and record room service orders.
7. Handle special room service requests.
8. Place the room service order.
9. Perform pantry prep for room service orders.
10. Prepare coffee.
11. Prepare hot tea.
12. Prepare hot chocolate.
13. Prepare iced tea.
14. Set up bottled wine or champagne for service.
15. Assemble the beverage order and food condiments.
16. Pick up the room service order.
17. Deliver the room service order.
18. Serve the room service order.
19. Serve coffee or hot tea.
20. Check guest IDs.
21. Open and serve wine or champagne.
22. Present and settle the guest check.
23. Retrieve trays and carts.
24. Close out the guest check.
25. Follow up with guests.
26. Respond to dissatisfied guests.
27. Clear and reset trays and carts.
28. Handle soiled room service linens.
29. Set up portable bars in suites or guestrooms.
30. Set up and serve small group dinners and receptions.
31. Set up and serve small buffet banquets.
32. Set up and serve coffee breaks.
33. Maintain room service sidestations.
34. Pick up and restock room service supplies.
35. Perform closing shift duties.
36. Make the shift deposit and collect due-backs.
37. Use the room service logbook.

Staffing Requirements

Managers of a new room service department or a department that is reorganizing need to decide how to allocate their staff members.

Managers first create a task list for each position (see Exhibit 1 for a sample task list for the room service attendant position). The tasks on task lists are arranged roughly in the order in which they should be performed. Tasks are not described in depth; detailed descriptions of how to do the tasks appear in separate job breakdowns for each task on the list. A job breakdown supplies all the information and instructions a staff member needs to perform the task being described. Finally, managers should construct a training schedule to plan their training.

While titles and duties vary from property to property, most of the duties listed under the position descriptions that follow must be performed at every property that offers room service.

Room Service Manager. The room service manager has a large number of management responsibilities, ranging from planning and executing the department's operation to enforcing its rules. He or she is responsible for organizing the room service staff and often selects, orients, trains, and schedules staff members. Handling problems with food and beverage orders and delivery, controlling costs, and ensuring that staff members collect all sales income due the operation are additional duties.

The room service manager must handle complaints from guests, staff members, and others; ensure that room service equipment is properly maintained; and order equipment and supplies. Room service is labor-intensive, so supervisory duties form a significant part of the room service manager's work.

Assistant Room Service Manager. In large properties that have an assistant room service manager, this individual performs some of the tasks that would otherwise be the responsibility of the room service manager. Frequently, the assistant room service manager supervises staff members, undertakes many of the daily or routine decision-making tasks associated with special functions, solves operational problems, and completes departmental records and reports.

Room Service Captain. During a specific shift, the room service captain is in charge of the department's order-takers, room service attendants, and buspersons. Captains help the assistant room service manager ensure that staff members follow all operating procedures and maintain performance standards. They also issue guest checks, ensure that room service supply areas are

adequately stocked, and personally supervise functions in hospitality suites. When VIPs order room service, the captains themselves may prepare and deliver the orders to these guests.

Room service captains may also expedite room service when special problems arise—such as an unexpectedly busy period, when they may reschedule or reassign room service attendants. Captains may make inspection rounds to ensure that buspersons remove room service equipment and dishes promptly from guestrooms and hallway floors. The captain may also check incoming orders to ensure that order-takers are taking them in a timely fashion and that room service attendants are delivering them quickly. Captains also may serve as checkers to confirm that outgoing orders are correct. Properties with heavy room service demand (such as resorts) may assign a captain to a room service area or pantry on each floor. Overall, captains help ensure that the room service operation runs smoothly.

Room Service Order-Taker. The room service order-taker or room service operator is a critical guest-contact position. As guests place room service orders, the order-taker must record their orders on the guest checks according to hotel procedures, see that the orders get to food production areas, and, in many properties, enter the check into a precheck register or another data machine. A room service order-taker may also serve as a food checker to confirm that orders that are about to be removed from the production area match the items listed on their corresponding guest checks.

The order-taker's role during initial contacts with guests is much like that of a food or beverage server with dining room guests; that is why suggestive selling and knowing the menu are among this staff member's responsibilities. The order-taker is really a salesperson rather than someone who simply takes orders.

Room Service Attendants. Room service attendants accept orders from production areas, ensure that all items listed on the guest check are on the food tray or cart, permit the order-taker or captain to double-check the order if procedures require it, deliver orders to designated guestrooms, and serve guests in their guestrooms. They may also perform station setup and breakdown tasks in the room service area and do the work of buspersons during busy shifts. Procedures for delivering room service orders will be discussed in more detail later in the chapter.

It is absolutely essential for room service attendants to be thoroughly familiar with the property's layout and the location of each guestroom and suite.

Buspersons. Buspersons may help set up room service stations in food production areas, assemble items for an order, deliver small orders, pick up room service equipment and dishes from guestrooms and hallways, take used serviceware to dishwashing areas, clean room service tables and trays, and perform miscellaneous tasks that increase the efficiency of room service attendants. Buspersons may help set up hospitality suites by placing tablecloths on tables and delivering serviceware and food and beverage supplies to the suites.

Forecasting and Staff Member Scheduling

Room service managers must plan carefully when scheduling staff members. Unfortunately, it is difficult to assess all of the factors that affect room service demand. Some of these factors include:

- occupancy levels (experienced room service managers can estimate from the house count the approximate number of guests who will desire room service)

- the number of guests who are traveling on an expense account

- the number of convention and business groups in-house (front desk and catering department staff can help room service managers forecast how many people will require room service based on the estimated attendance of organized meal functions)

- the number of guests whose room rates include a continental breakfast, a fruit basket, or similar in-room amenities

Some lodging properties transfer service staff back and forth between dining areas and the room service department as volume fluctuates in these areas. When this system is used, all service staff members must be well trained in all of the service procedures that apply to each area. Room service business that is arranged in advance (such as cocktails and appetizers in hospitality suites or small group dining in guestrooms) is not as difficult to staff. The schedule planner will need to study the applicable **function sheets** that provide detailed information about room service staff needs in those areas.

Preparations for Service Shifts

In well-run room service departments, room service attendants have completed preparation work during slow times or prior to the beginning of a service shift so they have only a minimum number of these tasks to

Exhibit 2
Checklist of Room Service Equipment and Supplies

Items	Amount Required			
	Day/Shift Weekday (A.M.)	Day/Shift Weekend (A.M.)	Day/Shift Weekday (P.M.)	Day/Shift Weekend (P.M.)
Service Trays				
Tables				
Tablecloths				
Cloth Napkins				
Paper Napkins				
Bread Baskets				
Placemats				
Coffee Cups				
Saucers				
Juice Glasses				

perform during peak business hours. Preset carts and trays are generally stored in out-of-the-way aisle areas where room service attendants can conveniently obtain them. To ensure that attendants have an adequate number of items at the beginning of their shifts, some managers use a checklist similar to the one in Exhibit 2.

Apply Your Learning 16.1

Please write all answers on a separate sheet of paper.

1. From the perspective of guests, what are the key elements of well-managed room service?

For statements 2–4, write whether the answer is True or False.

2. Tasks are described in full detail on the task list.

3. The room service captain is in charge of the department's order-takers and room service attendants.

4. Room service attendants should set room service carts immediately before the food is ready to be delivered.

16.2 Delivering Room Service

AFTER STUDYING SECTION 16.2, YOU SHOULD KNOW HOW TO:

♦ Take room service orders

♦ Route room service orders

♦ Prepare room service orders

♦ Deliver room service orders

♦ Identify clean-up and follow-up duties

♦ Provide special amenities

Taking the Order

Order-takers should follow the specific procedures developed by their lodging property as they take orders from guests. Order-takers should answer all telephone calls promptly and offer an apology if the phone rings for a long period of time. Many properties require the telephone to be answered promptly within three rings.

The order-taker should identify him- or herself and indicate that the caller has reached room service. The order-taker should use a cheerful voice to convey a spirit of hospitality.

Caller identification systems that identify guests' names for order-takers enable them to provide personalized service. Most guests are impressed when an order-taker uses their names when the guests haven't identified themselves yet. Some computerized systems create guest lists that can be printed at the front desk and taken to the room service department; other systems display the guest's name and room number when the phone rings. Order-takers should ask for the guest's name and guestroom number immediately if they are not already available.

Order-takers in automated room service operations can input orders at point-of-sale (POS) systems. They typically use the same type of POS system used by catering or other food and beverage departments at the property.

Order-takers should include all details about the order on the guest check or in the POS system, such as how the guests wish their eggs to be prepared or what type of salad dressings they prefer. Guests may make special requests about how a menu item should be prepared, such as without oil, salt, or sugar. They may also request a different type of side dish. Good communication systems allow special requests to be accurately and completely transmitted from the order-taker to production staff members.

The order should be repeated to the guest to confirm its accuracy. Order-takers should also give callers an estimate of the delivery time, particularly during rush periods, when several orders may be in line for preparation and delivery. Some guests may be in a hurry and will not want to wait for a room service order. If it later becomes clear that it will be impossible to deliver room service orders within the originally estimated time, the order-taker should call the guests and let them know when to expect delivery.

Order-takers can sell by suggestion. The same procedures that servers use in the dining room apply here. Suggestive selling gives guests the opportunity to order something extra. This helps guests enjoy the best that the property has to offer, helps the property receive higher revenues, and helps room service staff earn more tips. Everyone wins. Guests may forget to order beverages, appetizers, or desserts if order-takers do not specifically ask about these kinds of items. Informing guests about specials, describing item preparation and presentation, suggesting high contribution-margin items, and asking open-ended questions (as opposed to closed-ended questions, to which guests can answer yes or no) or forced-choice questions such as, "Which of our two excellent desserts would you like, Mr. Marshall?" are all techniques that can increase room service sales. Good order-takers learn to gauge how well callers know what they want. Suggestive-selling techniques should not be used on guests who seem to know exactly what they want, since they might become annoyed. When the order-taking process is completed, order-takers should always thank the guest.

Some properties use a voice mail or tape-recorded message system for room service; the guest phones the room service number and places the order without talking to a staff member. Other properties use this system only during very slow periods when an order-taker is not on duty. The impersonal service and the possibility of confusion about the guest's exact needs are two potential disadvantages to this system.

Telephone Technique. All staff should receive training on the rules of telephone etiquette. Whoever answers the phone should stop talking with others before picking up the receiver. Because guests should not have to hear unnecessary noise and background conversations, and to help ensure accurate order-taking, nearby staff members should not converse among themselves while another staff member is speaking to a guest on the phone.

Putting callers on hold the right way is a part of good telephone etiquette. When two phone calls are coming in or when a phone call comes in while the order-taker is on the line with another guest, the order-taker should put guests on hold using the following procedures:

- Ask Caller #1 if you may put him or her on hold to answer another line.

- Ask Caller #2 to please hold while you complete another order.

- Return to Caller #1, apologize for the delay, and finish taking the first order.

- Return to Caller #2, apologize for the delay, and take the order.

- If you think Caller #2 will be on hold for too long, or if a third call is received, apologize to Caller #2 and offer to call back for the order. Take the guests' orders as soon as possible.

- Anytime you must interrupt the conversation, explain the reason to the guest.

Exhibit 1 summarizes telephone etiquette guidelines and order-taking procedures for room service personnel.

Exhibit 1
Telephone Etiquette and Order-Taking Procedures

1. Answer the telephone promptly—within three rings when possible.

2. Identify yourself and your department with a friendly greeting. For example, a property may specify that from 7:00 A.M. to noon an order-taker named Carla should say, "Room Service, Carla speaking, good morning"; from noon to 6:00 P.M., "Room Service, Carla speaking, good afternoon"; from 6:00 P.M. to 9:00 P.M., "Room Service, Carla speaking, good evening"; and from 9:00 P.M. to closing, "Room Service, Carla speaking, may I help you?"

3. Politely ask for the guest's name and room number (if the room service department doesn't use a caller identification system or receive guest lists from the front desk).

4. Use the caller's name whenever possible, being certain that it is pronounced correctly. Ask the caller how to pronounce his or her name, if necessary.

5. Use a cheerful voice throughout the conversation.

6. Obtain a complete order by asking the guest about appetizers, entrées, desserts, beverages, and special preparation instructions.

7. Use suggestive selling to encourage guests to order something extra and help them make sure that they remember all they want to order. If it is clear that the guest knows exactly what he or she wants, make fewer suggestions or none at all.

8. To help eliminate errors, repeat the order the guest has placed.

9. State the approximate time that the guest can expect the order to be delivered. State a range of time, depending on the amount of business that room service is currently handling. If the guest has ordered items that require extra preparation time or that are usually prepared at tableside, inform the guest about this to confirm that the order will be ready when the guest wants it.

10. Thank the guest for calling. Allow the guest to hang up the phone first.

Routing the Order

After the order-taker receives a guest's order, he or she must route it to the appropriate food or beverage production area. There are several methods of doing so:

1. The order-taker may carry the guest check to the production area by hand. This system may work well when a separate room service kitchen and service bar are located close to the order-taker's telephone stand or when the order-taker is a cashier or receptionist in the dining room.

2. The order-taker may give the guest check to a room service attendant, who then takes it to the production area.

3. The order-taker may use a precheck register or POS system with a remote printer. With this equipment, the order-taker automatically transmits the order to production staff members as he or she enters the information into the precheck register or POS system. This technology can dramatically expedite the order-taker's job and speed service.

Order-takers using a manual system must then enter information from the guest

Exhibit 2
Room Service Control Form

Food & Beverage Department
Room Service Control

❶ Day_____ Date_____ Cashier_____ Shift_____

LOCATION ❷

Guest Name	Server	Order taken ❺	A.M./P.M.
Check No. ❸	Amount $ ❹	Tray out	A.M./P.M. ❻
Room No.	No. Served ( ) paid ( ) charge ❽	Tray in	A.M./P.M. ❼
Guest Name	Server	Order taken	A.M./P.M.
Check No.	Amount $	Tray out	A.M./P.M.
Room No.	No. Served ( ) paid ( ) charge	Tray in	A.M./P.M.
Guest Name	Server	Order taken	A.M./P.M.

❶ Complete the heading at the beginning of the shift.

❷ Write the guest's name and room number. This information should be checked with the front desk to verify:
   • The guests are registered
   • The correct room number
   • The guest's credit standing

❸ Write the guest check number and obtain the server's signature. This signals a change of responsibility from the order taker to the server for the proper use of guest check.

❹ Write the dollar amount of the order and the number of guests served.

❺ Record the time the order was taken.

❻ Record the time the tray is taken out for delivery.

❼ Record the time of day the tray is returned to the kitchen.

❽ Record the form of payment (cash or charge).

NOTE: Charged tips should be recorded on a tip tally form.

check onto a **room service order form.** Properties use this form to record information about each order, such as the room number, the guest's name, and the time the order was placed. The order-taker must also make an entry on the **room service control form** (see Exhibit 2), which keeps track of all guest checks. It indicates the person responsible for delivering the order, the time required to prepare the order, and the total amount of cash and charge sales generated by room service. A POS system can automatically generate reports covering the information recorded on both of these forms, since the system can maintain all of the information related to each order.

Preparing the Order

Room service attendants should be aware of the orders being prepared by production staff so they can do any additional setup work. For example, attendants may prepare or portion salads and desserts while production staff prepare other parts of the order. If necessary, attendants should cover these salads and desserts with plastic wrap or store them in protective containers to help maintain quality. Room service attendants could also obtain beverages, typically from a service bar located close to the room service area. Attendants must give the bartender a copy of the room service order indicating the beverages they need.

In properties with a central beverage storeroom, a manager issues full bottles of alcoholic and other beverages from the central storeroom to the room service beverage storage area. The manager can use a standard issue requisition and then transfer the costs of issued beverages to the room service department. If guests request full bottles from room service, room service attendants at some hotels may obtain bottles from the room service beverage storeroom. Room service managers must always have controls in place to keep track of beverage inventory, supply accounting information, and protect inventory from theft or quality deterioration.

When food orders are ready, the room service attendants pick them up, cover them with lids or some other insulated material, and present them to the order-taker, food checker, or another designated staff member for inspection. At some properties, room service attendants put caps or covers on cups to prevent spills. The entire cart or serving tray should be covered with a washable cloth or disposable clear plastic cover. The food and beverages are now ready for one final inspection and then rapid delivery to the guest.

Why is each order checked so thoroughly before it is delivered? A frequent guest complaint is that condiments or other items are missing from room service orders. Because guestrooms can be a long way from the kitchen, an error found by a guest takes more time to correct and creates more problems than it would if the error had been discovered in or near the kitchen by a staff member.

During the final inspection, room service attendants should look for the following:

- Does the order match the guest check? Is anything missing? Has everything been prepared as the guest requested?

- Are all of the appropriate condiments, sauces, side dishes, flatware, and beverages where they should be?

- Does the food look appetizing? If you were the guest, would you be pleased with the presentation of the order?

- Does the attendant have all the equipment (tray stands, special tables, serving utensils, matches or a lighter, heating or cooling devices) needed to serve this order?

Delivering the Order

It is imperative that room service attendants deliver orders as quickly as possible. Time and temperature are the most important elements in room service delivery, because as product holding times increase, so does the likelihood of contamination and loss of quality. The fastest route to the guestroom should be used; attendants and other room service staff members must know the layout of the property extremely well. Hot food should still be hot, and cold food should still be cold when it gets to the guest. Some properties offer **split service,** which means that room service attendants deliver courses separately. Split service helps maintain food quality and safety; each course can be portioned and served when it is ready, eliminating short-term holding in the kitchen. The disadvantage of split service is that it takes more staff to deliver courses separately and therefore is more costly.

Some lodging properties use **dumbwaiters** (small service elevators) to expedite order delivery. Using dumbwaiters to move products between floors may work well when continental breakfasts (coffee, juice, and rolls) are offered to all guests or when standard breakfasts are offered to VIPs and guests in guestroom suites. Some properties designate one or more freight or passenger elevators for room service use during busy periods. **Flying kitchens—** well-equipped elevators that enable service staff to prepare a limited number of menu items as they move between floors—are sometimes installed. A room service attendant could be assigned to one or more floors during peak business periods; after the carts are transported to each floor, the assigned attendant could deliver the orders.

Room service managers develop procedures for delivering room service orders. For example, all room service staff members should know that when entering or exiting elevators with a room service cart, the cart should be pulled rather than pushed. Why? Pulling gives the staff member more control over the cart and there is less chance

that a guest or another staff member will bump into it. Other procedures might include delivering orders approximately in the sequence in which they were received, using a uniform greeting and method of alerting guests that their orders have arrived (for example, a light knock followed by the statement "Room Service with your order"), greeting the guest warmly, and verifying the guest's name and room number when the guest opens the door. At some lodging properties, room service attendants ask guests for permission to enter their guestrooms, then ask them where they prefer their orders to be placed—on a table, left on the cart, or elsewhere. Hot foods should be left in warmers for the guest's self-service unless he or she indicates otherwise. If the order requires tableside preparation, attendants may be required to tell guests how long the order will take to prepare and to ask if they may begin the preparation.

Normally, room service attendants ask guests to sign a copy of the guest check to verify that they received the order. It is a good idea to give the guest the guest check and a pen before setting up the order. This will eliminate an awkward time lag while the guest reviews and signs the check. Usually, the guest's signature is sufficient; however, cash payments are required in certain circumstances, such as when the guest has no guest folio set up with the front desk.

The room service attendant should use discretion in the guest's room. It is critical to respect the guest's privacy and not disturb any of the guest's personal items. If it is absolutely necessary to move items to serve the order, the attendant should politely ask the guest for permission to do so. The attendant should offer to pour beverages for the guest. When serving food on the room service cart, the attendant should check the supporting braces of the cart extensions to be certain that they are secure and will not collapse. If the room service cart has a heating element, it should be extinguished by the attendant according to the property's procedures. Guests should be cautioned about handling plates that are hot.

Before leaving, room service attendants should offer additional assistance to the guest and remind the guest about cart or tray pickup procedures. Attendants may give the guest a number to dial for additional service or to request tray pickup; this information might also be provided on a courtesy card left on the tray or cart. The attendant should always thank the guest and wish him or her an enjoyable meal.

Clean-Up and Follow-Up

Properties should have a system in place for removing used room service trays and carts quickly. On their way back to the room service area after delivering an order, room service attendants should pick up any carts or trays left in hotel corridors.

If time permits, order-takers or other room service staff members should phone guests after their orders are delivered to ask them how they are enjoying the meal and to offer additional assistance. Many guests appreciate this extra service.

Providing Special Services and Amenities

Room service attendants may also be responsible for delivering fruit baskets, cheese trays, and other special amenities for guests; therefore, management should develop standard procedures for preparing, arranging, and delivering these items. In addition, if special amenities require cloth napkins, flatware, or plates, the attendants must ensure that those supplies accompany the orders. A form like the one shown in Exhibit 3 can be used whenever a hotel executive or a friend, relative, or business associate orders a special room service amenity for a guest. Often, these amenities are a good source of revenue for the room service department.

Frequently, a welcome card accompanies special room service amenities, and the room service attendant is often responsible for ensuring that it is in place. Managers design or write welcome cards simply to welcome a guest and to wish him or her a pleasant stay. This special touch can be instrumental in gaining the favor of a VIP.

Guests frequently order bar setups through room service. Typical items in a bar setup are alcoholic beverages, cocktail napkins, stir sticks, glasses, a pitcher of water, a bucket of ice, and appropriate garnishes. In addition to alcoholic beverages, the guest requesting a bar setup may order mixers such as tonic water, club soda, or bottled water. Depending on the guestroom's location, attendants may bring ice to the guestroom from the room service area or from an ice machine that is close to the guestroom.

Some properties offer executive coffee service. Guests who are staying on special VIP floors, specific guests identified by management, guests paying the full rate for expensive rooms, and others may receive this extra room service amenity. This complimentary morning coffee service may consist of juice, pastries, hot beverages, and a morning newspaper. Special order forms for executive coffee service typically supply the information that room service staff members need to provide this amenity.

Exhibit 3
Order Form for Special Room Service Amenities

Special Room Service Order

NR: __1555__

For Mr./Mrs.: _____   Room: _____

Delivery Date: _____   Cost Code: _____

From: ☐ _____   ☐ _____
      ☐ _____   ☐ _____
      ☐ _____

☐ $XX.XX   **Large deluxe fruit tray with one bottle of wine**
           (Selection of fruits and chocolate, presented on a
           silver tray including one bottle of wine white or red)

☐ $XX.XX   **Large deluxe fruit tray**
           (Selections of fruit and chocolate, presented on a silver tray)

☐ $XX.XX   **Small fruit mirror with cheese and $1/2$ bottle of wine**
           (Selection of fruit, cheese, and chocolate presented on a
           small mirror with $1/2$ bottle of wine)

☐ $XX.XX   **Small fruit mirror with cheese and chocolate**
           (Selection of fruit, cheese, and chocolate presented on a
           small mirror)

☐ $XX.XX   **Fruit arrangement in a wicker basket**
           (Assorted fruits in a basket)

☐ $XX.XX   **Presentation of chocolate cups with 2 small liquor bottles**
           (Presented on a blue plate with chocolate cups and flowers)

☐ $_____ Champagne Domestic _____ Import _____

Name: _____   Total Cost: $_____

Apply Your Learning 16.2

Please write all answers on a separate sheet of paper.

1. What is a forced-choice question? Give an example.

2. What are the three methods of routing a room service order to the appropriate food or beverage production area?

3. What things should room attendants look for during the final inspection before delivering the food?

16.3 After Room Service

AFTER STUDYING SECTION 16.3, YOU SHOULD KNOW HOW TO:

♦ Describe income control procedures

♦ Explain how to gather guest comments

♦ List typical guest complaints about room service

♦ Describe the use of feedback in planning

After room service has been delivered, issues important to managers include income control procedures, guest comments, and funneling feedback about room service into planning activities.

Income Control Procedures

While many of the income control procedures used in the room service department mirror those used in public dining areas, some are unique to room service operations.

Control procedures to collect payment for all orders served through room service begin at the time order-takers enter orders into a POS system. Charged sale information is electronically transferred to the guest folio at the front desk.

Most guests wish to have their room service charges billed to their guestroom accounts. Sometimes, however, charges are not possible. For example, a guest may have paid for the room in advance with cash, or guests may have reached or exceeded their lines of credit. The front office should regularly report guests who are on a cash basis to the room service department so that order-takers can note the need for cash payments on the guest checks of these guests. In addition, order-takers should inform these guests that the room service attendant will require cash when he or she delivers their orders. Some properties provide room service attendants with a credit card imprinter and appropriate supplies in anticipation of guests who wish to use their credit cards. Policies and procedures regarding the acceptance of credit cards and checks must comply with those developed by the lodging property for use in other property areas.

Guest Comments

Guest complaints about room service span a wide range of topics (see Exhibit 1). High prices are the main reason that guests do not use room service. Guests may resist tipping staff members because of perceived high menu charges; some hotels add an automatic gratuity percentage to room service charges for that reason. In general, business travelers are not as price conscious as pleasure travelers, most likely because their room service charges are often paid by their companies.

Exhibit 1
Why Guests Do Not Use Room Service

Reason	Percentage
High Prices	33
Slow Service	12
Don't Like Eating Alone	12
Food Not Hot/Cold	11
Limited Hours	9
Inadequate Menu	8
Insufficient Variety	7
Other	6
Mixed-Up Orders	1
Rude Staff	1

Source: Carlo Wolff, "Roomservice Blues," *Lodging Hospitality*, December 1992, pp. 55–56.

Some guests focus on the quality of the food and beverages served or the quality of the service rather than price. Guests dislike slow service. They often expect their meals to arrive no more than 20 minutes after they order. Some properties' room service order-takers cannot speak the native language well, so communicating with guests can be difficult. Guests who use room service often complain that the items that were delivered were not what they ordered, were delivered at improper temperatures, or were presented poorly. Many guests complain about dirty dishes left in hotel hallways from room service deliveries.

Guests sometimes complain that there is not enough variety on room service menus. Today's guests often expect a selection of fresh fruits and the option to design their own meals to suit their preferences or dietary restrictions. Clearly, guest expectations of room service today are high, and it is worthwhile for room service managers to familiarize themselves with the expectations of their property's target markets.

Managers may obtain guest comments by asking them in person or recording comments that guests made to service staff. They may also ask guests to complete comment forms that cover all areas of their hotel stay. Room service should be included on this form as a way to obtain additional feedback for planning.

Another strategy for obtaining detailed, timely guest feedback is to have the room service manager regularly phone a sampling of guests who have used room service. Specific details about menus, staff member service styles, and the overall room service experience can be obtained if the right questions are asked. As an incentive, managers could offer a slight reduction in the hotel's guestroom rate to guests who provide this valuable feedback.

Using Feedback in Planning

Information obtained during and after room service can be a valuable source of feedback for room service planners. Room service menus must continue to evolve based on the needs and expectations of guests. Guests today are generally in search of higher quality menu items, served in smaller quantities, at affordable prices. These three criteria translate to value for guests.

In a guest-driven room service operation, the needs and expectations of guests come first. Room service staff must be trained to embrace the philosophy that when they deliver a room service order, they are really bringing the dining room to the guest's room. By respecting the guest's privacy and providing prompt and attentive service, room service staff members can delight guests. Positive room service experiences can help give guests a good impression of the property, enhance the property's reputation, and increase revenues for all of the property's revenue centers.

Apply Your Learning 16.3

Please write all answers on a separate sheet of paper.

1. Control procedures to collect payment for all orders served through room service begin when the:

    a. order-takers enter orders in the POS system.
    b. room service attendant delivers the orders.
    c. guest signs the room service check.
    d. room service charge is posted to the guest folio.

2. When can room service charges *not* be billed to a guestroom?

3. What is the main reason that guests do not use room service?

4. What are some ways for room service managers to obtain guest feedback?

Quick Hits

Chapter 16

SECTION 16.1—GETTING READY FOR ROOM SERVICE

- The key elements of well-managed room service include: prompt and courteous responses when guests place orders, accurate orders, efficient delivery to guestrooms, tact and courtesy from staff members, staff members who safely use equipment that involves liquid fuels or open flames, the prompt removal of trays and other equipment when guests have finished.

- Some hotels do a large volume of **hospitality suite** business, offering food and beverage service for small group meetings, corporate meetings, organizations entertaining guests during conventions, and other occasions.

- The room service manager is responsible for planning and executing the department's operation, as well as selecting, orienting, training, and scheduling staff members.

- An assistant room service manager supervises staff members, undertakes many of the daily or routine decision-making tasks associated with special functions, solves operational problems, and completes departmental records and reports.

- The room service captain is in charge of the department's order-takers, room service attendants, and buspersons. The captain helps the assistant room service manager ensure that staff members follow all operating procedures and maintain performance standards.

- A room service order-taker records orders on the guest checks according to hotel procedures, sees that the orders get to food production areas, and, in many properties, enters the check into a precheck register or another data machine.

- Room service attendants accept orders from production areas, ensure that all items listed on the guest check are on the food tray or cart, permit the order-taker or captain to double-check the order if procedures require it, deliver orders to designated guestrooms, and serve guests in their guestrooms.

- Buspersons may help set up room service stations in food production areas, assemble items for an order, deliver small orders, retrieve equipment and dishes from guestrooms and hallways, take used serviceware to dishwashing areas, clean room service tables and trays, and perform miscellaneous tasks that increase the efficiency of room service attendants.

- Staff scheduling decisions will vary based on occupancy levels, the number of guests who are traveling on an expense account, the number of convention and business groups in-house, and the number of guests whose room rates include in-room breakfast amenities.

Section 16.2—Delivering Room Service

- When taking guest orders, order-takers should use suggestive selling to offer the guest an opportunity to order something extra. This can be done using open-ended questions or forced-choice questions.

- Order-takers usually route guest orders to the appropriate food or beverage production area through a POS system.

- During final inspection, room service attendants should check: Does the order match the guest check? Is anything missing? Has everything been prepared as the guest requested? Are all of the appropriate condiments, sauces, side dishes, flatware, and beverages where they should be? Does the food look appetizing? If you were the guest, would you be pleased with the presentation of the order? Does the attendant have all the equipment needed to serve this order?

- **Split service, dumbwaiters,** and **flying kitchens** are sometimes used to help expedite order delivery.

- Attendants may be responsible for delivering fruit baskets or cheese trays, and preparing and presenting other special amenities or services.

Section 16.3—After Room Service

- Control procedures to collect payment for room service orders begin when order-takers write orders on guest checks or enter orders into a POS system.

- High prices are the main reason that guests do not use room service.

- Managers may obtain guest comments by asking them in person or recording comments that guests made to service staff. They may also ask guests to complete comment forms that cover all areas of their hotel stay.

- Information obtained during and after room service can be a valuable source of feedback for room service planners.

account file—a file that holds information needed for serving a client's basic business needs. The file is started at the time of initial contact with a prospective client.

accountability—when people in authority must accept responsibility for their decisions and be able to justify their actions to those above them in the chain of command.

active voice—when the subject of the sentence does the acting. These sentences are tighter and more powerful, enlivening every sentence. (For example, *George hired four more room attendants.*)

aesthetic balance—the degree to which meals have been constructed with an eye to a pleasing variety of colors, textures, and flavors of foods.

airline-related guests—airplane crews and passengers who need accommodation because they are bumped from a flight or stranded due to mechanical or weather problems. Airlines negotiate rates with hotels, and rooms are usually booked in blocks at rock-bottom prices.

appointment calls—calls used to briefly introduce a prospective client to the features and services offered by the property and ask for a face-to-face meeting.

authority—the formal power granted by an organization to a management position. Authority is placed in a *position*, not in the individual who holds it.

autocratic managers—stress immediate, short-term results over concerns about people; they

expect to be obeyed without question and make decisions without staff input.

base selling price—the menu pricing starting point from which other factors must be assessed and the price adjusted accordingly; it is not necessarily the final selling price.

behavior-based interviewing—interviewing technique intended to determine how a candidate has responded under specific circumstances in the past, used by employers who believe that the best predictor of your future behavior is your past behavior.

bottom-up method—an upgrading/upselling method used when a guest has already made a reservation or has requested a low-priced room. During the registration process, the agent can suggest extra amenities or a higher-priced room. The higher rate must appear to be an attempt to enhance the guest's stay at only a small increase over charges anticipated by the guest.

brainstorm—group problem solving that involves the spontaneous contribution of ideas from all members of the group.

buffet—a service style which displays food on counters or tables, and guests help themselves to as many and as much of the items as they wish to eat.

bureaucratic managers—make decisions by enforcing rules, regulations, policies, and procedures that are already in place; concerns for results and for people take a back seat to doing things the way they have always been done—they resist change.

business balance—technique used in menu planning where the balance between food costs, menu prices, the popularity of items, and other financial and marketing considerations are reviewed.

call report—a sales record form generated during a cold call on a prospective client.

cart service—an elaborate service style in which menu items are prepared on a cart beside guest tables by specially trained staff. (Also called French service.)

cash bar—a beverage setup at a special function where each guest pays for each drink as it is ordered.

casual/theme restaurants—full-service restaurants distinguished by their combination of decor, atmosphere, and menu, all of which relate to a particular theme.

centralized organization—an organization in which most decision-making authority is at top management levels.

chain of command—the structure of authority where each higher level carries more responsibility and greater authority than the levels below them.

changed-use—any surface where one stops working on one type of food and begins working on another.

clarifying questions—open-ended or specific questions that make the speaker's message clearer.

cleaning—removes visible soil. Proper cleaning can prevent many food safety problems. See *sanitizing*.

code of conduct—ground rules for behavior on the team. It may include guidelines for team meetings, expectations about the quality and type of group interaction, and indications of expected attendance, level of participation, and preparedness expected of each team member.

competition analysis—part of the marketing audit that helps properties evaluate their competition. This enables a property to anticipate their competitors' actions and capitalize on their weaknesses by utilizing its own strengths.

contaminants—harmful substances or microbes which can enter through air, packaging material, equipment, spoilage, improper handling procedures, or contact with humans. Contaminants often cannot be seen, tasted, or smelled.

continuous-improvement teams—A team devoted to finding better ways of doing work. It is an important part of an organization's quality effort.

contract—when booking events, the letter of agreement which lists every detail that the two parties have discussed and agreed upon. Also known as a *letter of agreement*.

contract theory—a category of wrongful discharge whereby an employee might claim that a personnel manual, for instance, created an employment contract and that she was dismissed in violation of this "contract."

contribution margin pricing method—menu pricing which refers to the amount left after a menu item's food cost is subtracted from its selling price. It is the amount that the sale of a menu item "contributes" to pay for all non-food costs.

convention and association groups—delegates who stay in hotels where a negotiated package price covers rooms, meals, and functions; they usually share rooms and stay three to four days.

corporate groups—business travelers whose rooms are booked or blocked by their company or a travel agency; they usually stay for two to four days.

cost-plus pricing—an approach to setting prices whereby the hotel determines its actual costs, then adds on a reasonable percentage to arrive at the final retail price.

cross-contamination—occurs when one food contaminates another; it can be easily prevented by properly cleaning and sanitizing surfaces that touch food.

cross-functional teams—teams with members from several different departments or work areas within an organization.

cross-selling—using media in one area of the property to promote a different area of the property. (For example, matchbooks in the lounge may advertise the property's fine dining establishment.)

customer-based pricing—an approach to setting prices whereby companies determine what customers want and are willing to pay— and then figure out a way to deliver it.

cycle menu—a menu that changes every day for a certain period of days, then the cycle repeats.

decentralized organization—decision-making authority is distributed throughout the company.

democratic managers—tend to focus more on a participative process than on short-term, immediate results; they share decision-making and problem solving responsibilities with their staff and are open to new ideas.

devil's horns effect—a phenomenon whereby managers see everything someone does as negative, and often interpret that person's messages negatively; the opposite of *halo effect*.

dismissal for just cause—a discharge policy which assures dismissed employees that they

will receive fair and equal treatment and progressive discipline, if discipline is necessary.

diversity—the presence in the workplace of people who differ in gender, culture, race, ethnicity, and other attributes.

downward communication—communication with those employees and staff members whom you supervise.

dram shop acts—legislation that provides consistent guidelines about who is responsible when third parties suffer because of an intoxicated person's actions. Although these acts vary from state to state, bartenders, servers, and owners can often be held jointly liable if they unlawfully sell alcoholic beverages to a minor or an intoxicated person who then causes injury to others.

dumbwaiters—small service elevators used to expedite room service order delivery between floors.

empathy—the ability to see circumstances from the other's viewpoint. Empathy shows the speaker that you are a willing and understanding listener who can personally relate to his or her experiences and feelings.

employment at will—a discharge policy which allows an employer to terminate employees without notice, at any time, for any reason. Conversely, it allows an employee to terminate his or her employment without notice, at any time, for any reason.

empowerment—the practice of enhancing guest service and increasing profits for an organization by passing decision-making responsibility, authority, and accountability to every level within the organization.

essential functions—job tasks that are fundamental to a position. For example, cooking skills would be considered fundamental for a cook—but the ability to hear orders called by servers to a cook might not be considered fundamental.

FACTS—an acronym for the five areas you should consider when evaluating a job offer: fit, advancement, compensation, training, and site.

fair share—the number of room nights the specific property would sell if demand were distributed based on the number of rooms in each property in the local marketplace.

family-style service—a service style which requires food to be placed on large platters or in large bowls that are delivered to the guests' tables by servers; guests at each table pass the food around and serve themselves. (Also called English service.)

fixed menu—a single menu that is used daily.

flying kitchens—well-equipped elevators that enable service staff to prepare a limited number of menu items as they move between floors.

food warning sign—any threat to food safety that you can see, such as soiled kitchenware, broken dishes, or food spills.

food-contact surfaces—any surfaces that touch food.

food-grade container—a container specially designed to store food.

forced-choice questions—a sales closing technique which creates a choice between positive alternatives and limits the sales prospect to the answers presented by the salesperson. (For example, "Shall I book your tour group for Friday night or Saturday morning?")

forming—the first stage of team development, which begins when individuals become members of a group. This stage is characterized by tension, anxiety, and suspicion about a new situation.

four *P*s of marketing—product, place, price, and promotion. These four basic marketing responsibilities are used to make marketing decisions.

full block—the style in which most business letters are written. Paragraphs are separated by a single line space and are set flush with the left margin.

function book—a document that shows the occupancies and vacancies of function and banquet rooms; it is indispensable for effectively planning events.

function room reservation form—the form used in a manual system to reserve a function room.

function sheet—lists all of the details that apply to the banquet function, including everything anyone at the food service operation might need to know about the function to prepare for it and provide service during it. For the room service department, the forms provide detailed information about room service staff needs for scheduled business.

government and military travelers—a lodging market segment that is reimbursed on fixed per diem allowances.

groupthink—a phenomenon whereby groups in the norming stage, feeling the pressure to conform, might sacrifice valuable differences of opinion for the sake of team unity.

guarantee—prior to a function, the figure given by the client to the property for the final number of attendees/persons to be served.

guest mix—the variety, or mixture, of guests who stay at a hotel. (For example, a hotel's guest mix may consist of 60 percent individual business travelers, 20 percent conventioneers, and 20 percent leisure travelers.) The guest mix depends on a hotel's location, size, facilities, and operating philosophy.

guestroom control book—a document that lists the number of guestrooms allotted to each group and indicates whether the allotment is firm or tentative. It also specifies the maximum number of guestrooms the sales office may sell to groups on a given day. Also known as a hotel diary.

halo effect—a phenomenon whereby managers see everything someone does as positive, and often interpret that person's messages positively; the opposite of *devil's horns effect.*

hidden agendas—a barrier to effective interpersonal communication that can affect both senders and receivers. Senders with hidden agendas are seen as deceptive; receivers with hidden agendas interpret everything in relation to their own agendas.

hospitality suite—food and beverage service for small group meetings, corporate meetings, organizations entertaining guests during conventions, and other occasions, which are typically held in hotel suites.

host bar—a beverage setup at a special function where drinks are prepaid by a sponsor (host). The price, agreed on ahead of time, may be per bottle, per drink, or per person. Also known as an open bar or hosted bar.

individual business travelers—a lodging market segment that usually stays one or two nights and accounts for 60 percent of the hotel industry's business.

ingredient mark-up pricing method—menu pricing which attempts to consider all product costs (food costs when pricing food items and beverage costs when pricing beverages).

integrated marketing communications—a model used by many firms to organize marketing activities. It ensures that messages sent to employees, customers, the media, and others are consistent and that they are developed to achieve the overall mission of the organization.

interval reservations—a reservation system that offers seating at specific intervals; at least 30 minutes must be allowed between serving periods to clean up, reset tables, and otherwise get ready for the next seating.

inverted pyramid—style of writing used by reporters when writing hard-news stories, in which they put the most important information at the beginning and leave less-important details for the final paragraphs.

job preview—before getting hired, the practice of shadowing a manager for a day or two, during which you will actually work in a location for a short period. This allows a more complete opportunity for you and the employer to get to know each other.

lateral communication—communication with one's peers.

learned helplessness—a phenomenon whereby employees become unwilling or unable to provide guest-pleasing service because "it's not my job."

leisure travelers—a lodging market segment that often travels with their families on sightseeing trips, or on trips to visit friends or relatives. They typically spend only one night at the same hotel.

letter of agreement—the contract which lists every detail of a booked event that the two parties have discussed and agreed upon. Also known as a *contract.*

long-term stay/relocation guests—individuals or families moving to an area and requiring lodging until permanent housing can be found.

loss leaders—items that are sold at prices so low that they are not profitable in themselves, but which attract customers who may buy other items that *are* profitable.

market position—the perception of a property by its guests or potential guests.

market segmentation—the process of identifying or defining smaller market segments within the larger marketplace; these smaller markets generally have similar product and service preferences.

market share—determined by dividing the number of property room nights sold by the total market room nights sold.

marketing audit—the research step in the planning process for a marketing plan which evaluates the factors relating to sales potential. It gathers, records, and analyzes information about your property (property analysis), your competition (competition analysis), and the marketplace (situation or marketplace analysis).

marketing mix—the way the four *P*s of marketing are combined to meet the objectives of each business.

marketing plan—a business plan that combines sales, advertising, promotions, and public relations strategies into a structured plan

that can be communicated throughout an organization.

marketing—the promotion of a product or service which includes research, product development, advertising, publicity, and sales promotions, as well as the means to monitor the marketing program's effectiveness through such things as surveys or guest comment cards.

marketplace analysis—part of the situation analysis that identifies environmental problems that can affect business, including changes in demographics; positive and negative events in the community, region, state, and nation; the cost and availability of energy; government regulations; and travel costs.

mark-up with accompaniment costs pricing method—menu pricing in which managers determine ingredient costs based only on entrée items and then add a standard accompaniment (or "plate") cost before multiplying by a mark-up multiplier.

master card—a document that contains a summary of everything needed for an effective sales effort: the organization's name, the names and titles of key executives, addresses, phone numbers, month or months in which the group meets, the size of the group, where the group has met in the past, the group's decision maker, and other pertinent data that can help win that account's business and hold onto it.

microbes—bacteria, viruses, and parasites that are all around us but are too small to see. In small numbers, microbes are generally harmless; in large numbers they cause illness or even death.

mirroring—repeating some of a speaker's key words exactly, which shows the speaker just how a key word or phrase sounds to someone else. It also indicates that you are interested in the speaker's words and want to understand them.

mission statement—a brief statement explaining why the team exists and how it contributes to the overall goals of a department or organization. Creating a mission statement is one of the first tasks facing a newly formed team.

moment of truth—any episode in which the customer comes into contact with any aspect of the organization and gets an impression of the quality of its service.

networking—developing informal and personal connections with friends, acquaintances, colleagues, associates, teachers, counselors, and others, in order to identify potential job opportunities.

norming—the third stage of team development, when team members learn to cooperate and support each other. This stage is characterized by effective communication patterns and tolerance of other members' diverse perspectives.

nutritional balance—review technique used in menu planning that makes sure the components of a well-balanced meal are available.

occupancy and activity analysis—part of the situation analysis that analyzes the property's past, present, and potential operating statistics. It is used to track sales history patterns over a three- to five-year period.

open-ended questions—require more than a simple yes-or-no answer. Use these questions when you want to begin a discussion, find out the speaker's ideas, examine a touchy subject, or avoid influencing the reply.

outline—a list of significant points to make when you present information.

paraphrasing—using your own words to re-state what you think the speaker means and feels.

passive voice—when the subject appears at the end of the sentence, *receiving* the action instead of *doing* the action. These sentences sound dull. (For example: *The decision was made by George to hire four more room attendants.*) See *active voice.*

performing—the fourth stage of team development, when the team functions at its highest level of productivity. This stage is characterized by a shift from individual to group concerns as members know they can learn from one another.

plate cost—an average cost for all non-entrée and other relatively inexpensive items including salad, vegetables, bread, butter, and non-alcoholic beverages.

plate service—a type of table service where servers take orders, kitchen staff produces orders, servers place orders on trays and deliver them to guests, and buspersons assist servers and clear tables. (Also called American service.)

platter service—a service style which requires servers to deliver platters of fully cooked food to the dining room, present the platters to the guests for approval, and then serve the food. (Also called Russian service.)

portfolio—a collection of samples that showcases your interests, talents, contributions, and studies, and shows off your finest efforts for others to see. Your portfolio is used as a marketing tool to sell yourself to potential employers.

positioning statement—a statement that effectively communicates the property's advantages to its selected target markets. It should be targeted to market segments of sufficient size and should answer questions about customer perceptions.

positioning—the process of designing a property's market position.

power—the ability to influence others' behavior.

preshift meetings—informal meetings that facilitate staff communication and function as an ongoing, daily method of training. They give dining room managers opportunities to gather information from the staff members, as well as give information to them.

prime costs—the most significant costs in a food service property: product (food and beverage) and labor.

prime ingredient mark-up pricing method—menu pricing in which only the cost of the prime ingredient is marked up.

production employees—food service employees concerned primarily with food production; they usually have little contact with guests. Typical production personnel can include chefs, cooks, assistant cooks, stewards, storeroom and receiving employees, and bakers.

projecting—a barrier to effective interpersonal communication whereby you project your own attitudes, assumptions, or beliefs into messages, which can often lead to misunderstandings.

promotional calls—calls made by salespeople, telemarketers, or top management to introduce special promotions.

property analysis—part of the marketing audit that includes a written, unbiased self-appraisal used to assess the strengths and weaknesses of a property.

prospecting calls—outgoing calls made to gather information and learn the names of decision makers. Many of these calls end up as qualifying calls.

protocol—the formal rules of etiquette used for ceremonies of state, military functions, and other special events.

public policy theory—a category of wrongful discharge whereby an employee might claim that he was dismissed either for refusing to break the law or for insisting on obeying the law.

public relations calls—calls made to generate goodwill and create a positive impression.

qualifying calls—outgoing calls which determine whether prospects need and can afford the products and services offered by the property. These are not sales calls, but are used to find out if an individual or company warrants an in-person sales call.

rate-category-alternatives method—an easy and effective upgrading/upselling method used to sell middle-rate rooms to guests who might otherwise choose a lower rate. The agent or reservationist provides the guest with a choice of three or more rate-category alternatives and puts no pressure on the guest. In most cases, people will avoid the extremes and choose the middle rate.

reasonable accommodations—what employers must do to make the workplace accessible to people with disabilities, unless doing so imposes an undue hardship on the employer.

regional getaway guests—a lodging market segment made up primarily of nearby residents seeking a weekend getaway experience. Hotels promote special weekend packages designed to entice nearby residents to check in.

release date—the date when booked meeting rooms should be taken off hold. A hold period should not extend beyond the time when the space can be sold if the commitment is not firmed up.

revenue per available room (REVPAR)—an accurate way to determine how a property is doing against the competition. It is determined by dividing room revenue by the number of rooms available for sale.

revenue potential—the revenue that would be realized if all of the property's rooms were sold at full rack rates.

revenue realized—actual sales receipts of all the property's rooms.

room service—a service that allows guests to order and enjoy food in the privacy of their own guestrooms or suites; it can be viewed as a status symbol or just a matter of convenience.

room service control form—form used in manual systems which keeps track of all guest checks and indicates the person responsible for delivering the order, the time required to prepare the order, and the total amount of cash and charge sales generated by room service. A POS system can automatically generate reports covering this information.

room service order form—form used in manual systems to record information about each order, such as the room number, the guest's name, and the time the order was placed. A POS system can automatically generate reports covering this information.

sales—direct efforts to sell products and services by personal contact, telecommunication, and mailings.

sanitizing—a cleaning procedure that reduces the number of microbes to a safe level. Proper sanitizing can prevent many food safety problems. See *cleaning*.

scramble system—buffet-style layout in which guests can go to separate stations to be served, rather than wait in a single line. (For example, stations might include hot items, beverages, salads, and desserts.)

self-disclosure statements—comments that report experiences or feelings similar to the speaker's, helping the speaker to feel understood and less alone.

service calls—follow-up calls (after a sale or just to keep in touch) which are essential to maintaining and building business for the property.

service guarantees—unconditional commitments to complete guest satisfaction; guests who are not satisfied with their menu items or the service they received do not have to pay for their meals.

service personnel—food service employees concerned primarily with direct guest contact. Service personnel include dining room managers, hosts/captains/maître d's, food servers, buspersons, bartenders, beverage servers, and cashiers/checkers.

shopper's service—a "mystery shopper" service where anonymous guests evaluate a restaurant's service from the guest's perspective.

sidework—service-related but non-guest-contact tasks performed by servers, such as making coffee, refilling condiment containers, and restocking side stations with supplies.

signature menu item—the one menu item that guests perceive as special and closely associated with the restaurant promoting it; these items not only make the restaurant unique in the guests' minds, but can also help build repeat guest business and strong guest loyalty.

simple prime costs pricing method—menu pricing which involves assessing the labor costs for the food service property and factoring these costs into the pricing equation.

situation analysis—part of the marketing audit that researches the property's current position in the marketplace and reveals opportunities to promote the property. The two parts of this analysis are the marketplace analysis and the occupancy and activity analysis.

specific prime costs pricing method—menu pricing which assigns higher mark-ups to menu items requiring extensive preparation (and therefore having higher labor costs).

specific questions—questions that usually begin with *who, where, when, why, which,* and *how many,* which seek additional information about unclear statements.

split service—the practice of room service attendants delivering courses separately. Split service helps to maintain food quality and safety; each course can be portioned and served when it is ready, eliminating short-term holding in the kitchen.

staggered reservations—a reservation system than staggers seating during the entire meal period; reservations can be made for any time the tables are available.

storming—the second stage of team development, which is marked by conflict. This stage is characterized by frustration, anger, and disillusionment as members find that their initial expectations of the team are far different from the realities of trying to accomplish something together.

subjective pricing methods—menu pricing in which intuition and special knowledge about guests' ability to pay are considered.

suggestive selling—the practice of influencing a guest's purchase decisions by highlighting available choices and using sales phrases. (For example, "Which dessert would you like from our cart?")

summarizing statements—statements that condense parts of what the speaker said and stress important parts. They should be used when you want to focus attention on a certain topic, show that you agree on specific points, guide the speaker to another part of a subject, and help reach agreement on specific points. (For example, "As I understand it, your main idea is—")

synchronized service—a service style which requires the entire service staff to enter the function room through one set of doors to serve each course in unison using precise movements.

table-turn rate—the average amount of time that a table is occupied.

task-force teams—these teams are temporary groups that address new opportunities or problems.

team leader—the person who assists the team in reaching the goals that it sets for itself.

telemarketing—an effective sales tool that provides person-to-person contact, immediate feedback, and the flexibility of a variety of approaches without the costs of an in-person visit. It is characterized by systematic use of the telephone, often by a special staff of trained telemarketers, along with computers that provide instant access to information.

telephone sales blitz—an intensive sales event when callers contact a large number of new prospects, although the prime objective is usually to gather information, not sell.

temperature danger zone (TDZ)—the temperature range of 41°F (5°C) to 140°F (60°C), defined by the U.S. Food and Drug Administration as the range in which the most contaminant activity takes place and food spoilage can occur. TDZ may vary by locality; check state or regulatory agencies.

tickler file—a reminder system that provides effective means for following up on an account at a specific time. Also known as a tracer file, bring-up file, or follow-up file.

top-down method—an upgrading/upselling method used to encourage guests to reserve middle- or high-rate rooms. It begins with the employee recommending the guestroom sold at the highest rate. The guest accepts or rejects the recommendation. If the guest says no, the agent moves down to the next price level and discusses the merits of this accommodation—until the guest accepts a recommendation.

topic sentence—the main point that explains what the paragraph is about.

transforming—the fifth and last stage of team development, when the group is either preparing to disband or facing a major change in mission, membership, or environment. This stage is characterized by a regression to the unproductive team behaviors of the forming and storming stages of development—

enthusiasm is lost, conflicts may arise again, and members may depend on the team leader for motivation.

upselling—the practice of suggesting more expensive (and often better-quality) items than those the guest first mentioned.

upward communication—communication with one's boss or other higher-level managers.

yield management—a hotel pricing system used to track advanced bookings and then lower or raise prices accordingly to yield the maximum room revenue (average daily rate).

Index

À la carte menu, 301, 302
Account file, 182
Active listening
    Evaluating, 47
    Focusing, 46
    Interpreting, 46–47
    Responding, 47
Advertising, 199, 258
Affordable-funds budget, 167
Age discrimination, 21–23
    Age Discrimination in
        Employment Act, 22
Airline-related guests, 143
Alcohol service, 360–364
Alcohol service, checking IDs,
    361–362
    cutting off, 364
    liability laws, 360–361
    monitoring guest
        consumption, 362–364
    nonalcoholic alternatives,
        363
Ambassador Hotel, 201
Amenities, room service,
    435–436
American service, see plate
    service
Americans with Disabilities Act,
    23–25, 357
Appointment calls, 250–253
Assistant cooks, 282, 285
Assistant room service
    manager, 425
Automation, sales office,
    184–189
    yield management, 188–189

Banquet department, 194–212
    organization charts
        (exhibit), 195
    personnel, 194–197
Banquet director, 194–195
Banquet manager, 195–197
Banquet promotions, 199
Banquet sales, inquiries, 200–202
    letters, 200
    personal, 199–200
    telephone, 200
Banquets
    beverage service, 408–410
    booking and planning,
        396–400
    contracts, 397, 399–400
    controls, 412–414, 415
    food handling, 405–407
    function book, 396–397
    function room reservation
        form (exhibit), 398
    function sheets, 400, 401
    guest feedback, 414–415
    letters of agreement, 397,
        399–400
    menu, 308–309
    planning, 415
    post-event checklist
        (exhibit), 413
    scheduling staff, 404–405
    service protocol, 410
    setup, 403–404
    training, 405
Behavior-based interviews,
    98–101
Beverage controls, banquets,
    414, 415
Beverage manager, job
    description (exhibit), 284

Beverage service, banquets,
    408–410
Beverages, nonalcoholic
    specialty drinks, 363
Booking form (exhibit), 177
Bottom-up method, 226
Breakfast menus, 305
Budgeting, 167–168
    Affordable funds, 167
    Competitive parity, 167
    Percentage of sales, 167
    Zero-based, 167–168
Buffet service, 347–349
Business writing, 50–56
    active language, 51–52
    and plain English, 52–53
    checklist, 55
    inverted pyramid, 53
    letters, 54–56
    memos, 54–55
    tips, 51
    topic sentence, 53
Buspersons, 337–338, 426

California menu, 309
Career development, 84–117
    career fairs, 88–89
    corporate presentations, 89
    internships, 89
    interviewing, 97–104
    job offers, 105–110
    lifelong learning, 111–117
    networking, 91–94
    planning, 116–117
    research, 86–88
    resource materials, 88
    self-assessment, 84–89
    self-promotion, 91–96
Career fairs, 88–89
Career planning, 116–117

Career portfolios, *see* portfolios
Cart service, 342, 346
Cash bar, 409
Cashier, 338
Casual/theme restaurants
  alliances with hotels, 376
  design/decor, 377
  greeting and seating guests,
    385
  guest feedback 373–374
  markets, 372–373
  menu, 374
  order taking, 386–387
  placing and picking up
    orders, 387
  presenting the guest check,
    388
  reservations, 382–384
  serving orders, 387–388
  special guests, 388–389
  training, 378–380
  value, 374–376
Catering, off-premises, 206–207
Catering manager, 195–197
  job description (exhibit), 196
Centralized organizations, 9–12
Chefs, 282
Children's menus, 306, 307
Civil Rights Act of 1964, 21–23
Club food services, 275–276
Code of conduct, for teams,
  63, 65
Combination menu, 301–302
Communication
  common errors, 39
  downward, 35–36
  lateral, 36
  myths, 32–33
  self-test, 37
  telephone skills, 243–245
  upward, 35
Communication barriers, 36–39
  attitudes and emotions, 38
  evaluating the sender, 36
  hidden agendas, 38
  misinterpretation, 36
  personality conflicts, 39
  projection, 36
  stereotyping, 38
Communication process, 33–35
Competition analysis, 155–157
Competitive fact sheets, 156

Competitive rate analysis, 156
Competitive-parity budget, 167
Complaints, 222–223
  room service, 437–438
Conflict, and teams, 71–72
Contamination, prevention,
  289–293
Contribution margin menu
  pricing, 326–327
Control form, room service, 432
Convention and association
  groups, 142
Cooks, 282
Corporate groups, 142
Cover letters, 94–96
Covey, Stephen, 113–116
Creativity, 114–115
Cross-selling, 229
Customer-based pricing, 138
Cycle menu, 303–304

Decentralized organizations,
  9–12
Design, menu, 315–323
Design/decor, casual/theme
  restaurants, 377
Dining room manager, 285, 286,
  338–340
Dining service
  beverage service, 360–364
  buffet service, 347–349
  busperson, 337–338
  cart service, 342, 346
  cashier, 338
  dining room manager,
    338–340
  family-style service, 347
  guarantees, 353–354
  guest complaints, 354–357
  host, 338
  plate service, 341–342,
    343–344
  platter service, 346–347
  providing superior service,
    350–359
  server, 336, 337
  service styles, 341–349
  suggestive selling, 351–353
  team approach, 357

Dinner menus, 306
Direct mail, banquet sales, 199
Director of sales (exhibit), 133
Disabilities
  discrimination, 23–25
  guests with, 357–359, 389
Discrimination, 21–25
Diversity, 19–26
  benefits of, 19–20
Dram shop acts, 360–361

Eating and drinking places,
  271–272
Empathy, 115
Empowerment, 9–12
  and decentralization, 11
English service, *see* family-style
  service
Equal Employment
  Opportunity, 21–23
Equal Pay Act, 22
Equipment and supplies, room
  service, 427
Ethnic menus, 309
Evaluating, 47

FACTS, and job offers, 106–108
Fair share, 156–157
Family and Medical Leave Act,
  20
Family-style service, 347
FIFO (first in, first out), 291
Filing systems, sales, 180–182
Fixed menu, 302–303
Focusing, 46
Food and beverage division
  in hotel operations, 277–279
  managers, 281–282
  positions, 281–287
  production personnel,
    282, 285
  sanitation, 288–283
  service personnel, 285–287
  three-fold mission, 279
Food and beverage sales,
  233, 235

Food controls, banquets, 412–414
Food handling, banquets, 405–407
Food safety, 288–283
  banquets, 406–407
Food service industry
  business and industrial, 274–275
  categories (exhibit), 271
  clubs, 275–276
  composition/size, 270–271
  eating and drinking places, 271–272
  health care, 275
  hotel operations, 272
  leisure market, 273
  misconceptions, 278
  retail, 273–274
  school market, 275
  transportation market, 272–273
Food warning signs, 293
Forecasting, room service, 426
Formal banquets, 410
Forming (teams), 69–71
Four Ps of Marketing, 137–139
French service, see cart service
Front desk sales, 232–233, 234–235
Function book, 175–176, 396–397
Function room reservation form (exhibit), 398
Function sheets, 185–187, 400, 401
  room service, 426

Government and military travelers, 143
Group development, five stages of (exhibit), 70
Guest comments, banquets, 414–415
Guest complaints, resolving, 354–357
Guest feedback
  and planning, 438

casual/theme restaurants, 373–374
  room service, 437–438
Guest mix, 143
Guest relationships, 220–223
Guest service, 382–390
Guestroom control book, 176–179
  computerized, 187–188
Guests with disabilities, 357–359, 389

Handwashing, 290
Hiring, 219
Hospitality Partners (hotel management company), 15–16
Hospitality suites, 205
Host bars, 409
Hosts, 285–286, 338
Hotels, alliances with casual/ theme restaurants, 376

Immigration Reform and Control Act, 22
Incentive programs (sales), 236
Income control procedures, 437
Incoming calls, 256–258
  voice mail, 257
Individual business travelers, 141–142
Initiative, 113–114
Inquiries, 258
  e-mail, 201
  fax, 201
  in-person, 202
  telephone, 201–202
Internships, 89
Interpreting, 46–47
Interviews, 97–104
  cover letters, 94–96
  fundamentals (exhibit), 98
  illegal questions, 101, 102
  preparing, 97–101
  questioning the interviewer, 101–102, 103

sample questions, 99–100
second interviews, 103–104
thank-you letters, 102–103
Inverted pyramid (in business writing), 53

Job description
  beverage manager, 284
  catering director, 196
  restaurant manager, 283
Job offers, 105–110
Jobs
  advancement, 106–107
  choosing the best, 108–109
  compensation, 107
  evaluating, 106–108
  FACTS, 106–108
  fit, 106
  negotiating, 109–110
  site considerations, 108
  training, 107–108

Layout, menu, 318–322
Leadership, of teams, 63, 66–67
Learned helplessness, 10–11
Leisure travelers, 142
Letters, 54–56
Lifelong learning, 111–117
Listening, 46–49
  active listening, 46–47
  clarifying questions, 48–49
  mirroring, 47–48
  neutral words, 49
  paraphrasing, 48
  self-disclosure statements, 48
  summarizing, 48
  techniques, 47—49
Long-term stay/relocation guests, 142—143
Lost business report (exhibit), 178
Lunch menus, 305—306

Management
    and leadership, 7—8
    autocratic, 5
    bureaucratic, 5
    challenges, 7—8
    democratic, 5
    hurdles, 6—7
Management styles, 4—8
    traditional, 5—6
Managers
    authority and power, 11—12
    food and beverage,
        281—282
    responsibility, 12
Market segments, 141—143
Market share, 156
Marketing
    action plans, 166—167
    budgeting, 167—168
    definition, 126
    Four *Ps*, 137—139
    objectives, 165—166
Marketing and sales
    balancing, 126—127
    staff positions, 129—133
Marketing audit, 154—159
    competition analysis,
        155—157
    property analysis, 154—155
    resources list, 159
    situation analysis, 157–158
Marketing plan, 150–169
    and marketing team, 151
    cycle, 152
    monitoring and evaluating,
        168–169
    six steps of, 151–152
Markets, casual/theme
    restaurants, 372–373
Master account file,
    computerized, 184–185
Master card file (exhibit), 181
Meeting rooms,
    booking, 211–212
    furniture, 209–211

sales, 208–212
    setups, 209, 210
Meetings, managing, 212
Memos, 54–55
    checklist, 55
    sample format, 54
Menu
    à la carte, 301, 302
    balance, 313–314
    breakfast, 305
    casual/theme restaurants,
        374
    children's, 306, 307
    combination, 301–302
    cycle, 303–304
    design, 315–323
    dinner, 306
    ethnic, 309
    fixed, 302–303
    lunch, 305–306
    planning, 310–314
    pricing, 301–302, 324–328
    selecting items, 311–313
    specialty, 306–309
    table d'Hôte, 301
    types, 305–309
Menu design, 315–323
    common mistakes, 322–323
    copy, 315–318
    cover, 322
    formats (exhibit), 320
    layout, 318–322
    ten commandments of
        menu writing, 317
Menu pricing, 301–302, 324–328
    contribution margin
        method, 326–327
    simple mark-up method,
        325–326
    simple prime costs method,
        327–328
    subjective method, 324–325
Mission statement, for teams,
    63–65
Moments of truth, 14–16
Motivating, 219, 236

Negotiation, and job offers,
    109–110

Networking, 91–94
Norming (teams), 70, 72–73

Objections, overcoming,
    252, 253
Occupancy chart, 162
Old Faithful Inn, 242
Open-ended questions, 48
Order form, room service, 432
Order-takers, room service,
    425–426, 429–431

Percentage-of-sales budget, 167
Performing (teams), 70, 73–74
Place, 138
Plate service, 341–342, 343–344
Platter service, 346–347
Portfolios
    contents, 112
    creating, 111–113
    presentation guidelines, 114
Positioning, 162–163
Pregnancy Discrimination
    Act of 1978, 23
Presentation, telephone, 252
Presentations, 41–44
    controlling the
        environment, 44
    tips, 44
    visual aids, 43
Preshift meetings, 351
Price, 138–139
Priorities, setting, 115
Product, 137
Promotion, 139
Property analysis, 154–155
Prospecting calls, 247–249
Public speaking, 41–44
    tips (exhibit), 42
Pyramid of authority
    inverted, 17
    traditional, 17

Qualifying calls, 247–249
Quality service, 14–18

Rate-category-alternatives
    method, 226
Receptions, 205
Refreshment breaks, 204
Regional getaway guests, 143
Rejection, 105–106
Relationship selling, 220–223
Relationships, building, 220–221
Religious discrimination, 23
Reservations, 232, 382–384
    handling problems, 384
    interval, 383
    sales, 232
    staggered, 383
Responding, 47
Restaurant manager, job
    description (exhibit), 283
Restaurant server, tips for
    effective selling (exhibit),
    380
Revenue grid, 161
REVPAR, 157
Roles of individuals (teams)
    negative, 78
    positive, 77
Room service, 422–438
    attendants, 424, 426
    buspersons, 426
    captain, 425
    control form, 432
    delivery, 433–435
    equipment and supplies
        (exhibit), 427
    follow-up, 435
    guest comments, 437–438
    income control, 437
    management issues,
        422–423
    manager, 425
    menu, 308
    order checking, 433
    order form, 432

order preparation, 433
order taking, 429–431
order-takers, 425–426,
    429–431
POS systems, 431–433, 437
preparing for, 423
routing orders, 431–433
staff scheduling, 426
staffing, 424–426
Routing orders, room service,
    431–433
Russian service, *see* platter
    service

Sales blitz, 260–261
Sales call report (exhibit), 176
Sales calls, 253–254
    closing techniques, 254
Sales
    account file, 182
    automation, 184–189
    balancing with marketing,
        126–127
    booking form (exhibit), 177
    cross-selling, 229
    definition, 126
    departmental, 231–236
    filing systems, 180–182
    food and beverage, 233, 235
    front desk, 232–233, 234–235
    function book, 175–176
    general manager's role,
        218–219
    guestroom control book,
        176–179
    hiring, 219
    incentive programs, 236
    job description, 134–135
    lost business report
        (exhibit), 178
    master card file, 181–182
    meetings, 174–175
    motivating, 219
    organizational charts,
        130, 131
    records, 175–179
    reservations, 232
    sales call report (exhibit),
        176

service personnel, 235–236
suggestive selling, 227–229
switchboard, 231–232
tickler file, 182
training, 219
upgrading, 225–226
yield management, 188–189
Sanitation (food and beverage),
    288–293
Scheduling
    for banquets, 404–405
    room service, 426
Scramble system, 348
Scripts, telemarketing, 261–263
Self-assessment, 84–89
    interests and values, 86, 87
    self-rating tool, 85
    strengths, 84
    weaknesses, 84–85
Self-promotion/marketing,
    91–96
Selling, tips (exhibit), 380
Server, 336, 337
Service
    guarantees, 353–354
    superior dining service,
        350–359
Service personnel sales, 235–236
Service strategy, 15
Setups (meeting rooms),
    209, 210
*Seven Habits of Highly Effective
    People, The,* 113–116
Sex discrimination, 23
Sexual harassment, 25–26
Simple mark-up menu pricing,
    325–326
Simple prime costs menu
    pricing, 327–328
Situation analysis, 157–158
Special functions, 205
Special guest services, 435–436
Specific questions, 48–49
Split service, 434
Storming (teams), 70, 71–72
Subjective menu pricing,
    324–325
Suggestive selling, 227–229,
    351–353
    sample sales phrases
        (exhibit), 228
Switchboard sales, 231–232

Table d'Hôte menu, 301
Target markets
  positioning, 162–163
  selecting, 160–162
Task lists, room service, 424
TDZ, *see* temperature danger zone
Team development, five stages, 69–74
Team leaders, 63, 66–67
  self-evaluation form, 67
Teams
  and dining service, 357
  characteristics, 63
  code of conduct, 63, 65
  defining, 62–67
  development, 69–74
  forming, 69–71
  mission statement, 63–65
  norming, 70, 72–73
  performing, 70, 73–74
  roles of individuals, 76–79
  storming, 70, 71–72
  transforming, 70, 74
  "Triumphant Teams" exhibits, 62, 66, 71, 73, 79
  types, 63
Telemarketing, 260–263
Telephone
  communication basics, 243–245
  etiquette (exhibit), 244

listening skills, 245
Telephone calls
  appointment, 250–253
  etiquette, 430, 431
  incoming, 256–258
  promotional, 254
  prospecting, 247–249
  public relations, 255
  qualifying, 247–249
  sales, 253–254, 260
  service, 254–255
  voice mail, 257
Temperature danger zone (TDZ), 292, 406–407
Thank-you letters, 102–103
Theme restaurants, *see* casual/theme restaurants
Tickler file, 182
Tips, 384
Top-down method, 225–226
Topic sentences, 53
Tracer file, *see* tickler file
Traffic light system (alcohol service), 363–364
Training, 219, 221–223
  banquets, 405
  casual/theme restaurants, 378–380
Transforming (teams), 70, 74
"Triumphant Teams" (exhibits), 62, 66, 71, 73, 79
Tuckman, B.W., 69, 70

Upgrading, 225–226

bottom-up method, 226
rate-category-alternatives method, 226
top-down method, 225–226
Upselling, 379, *see also* upgrading

VIP guests, special services, 435–436
Visual aids, in presentations, 43
Voice mail (exhibit), 257

Wedding receptions, 205–206
Wine service, 409–410
Writing, menu copy, 315–318, *see also* business writing
Wrongful discharge, 23

Yield management, 188–189

Zero-based budget, 167–168